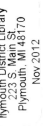

FRAMED

Framed

AMERICA'S

FIFTY-ONE CONSTITUTIONS

AND THE

CRISIS OF GOVERNANCE

SANFORD LEVINSON

OXFORD
UNIVERSITY PRESS

OXFORD
UNIVERSITY PRESS

Oxford University Press, Inc., publishes works that further
Oxford University's objective of excellence
in research, scholarship, and education.

Oxford   New York
Auckland   Cape Town   Dar es Salaam   Hong Kong   Karachi
Kuala Lumpur   Madrid   Melbourne   Mexico City   Nairobi
New Delhi   Shanghai   Taipei   Toronto

With offices in
Argentina   Austria   Brazil   Chile   Czech Republic   France   Greece
Guatemala   Hungary   Italy   Japan   Poland   Portugal   Singapore
South Korea   Switzerland   Thailand   Turkey   Ukraine   Vietnam

Published by Oxford University Press, Inc.
198 Madison Avenue, New York, NY 10016
www.oup.com

Oxford is a registered trademark of Oxford University Press

Library of Congress Cataloging-in-Publication Data
Levinson, Sanford, 1941-
Framed : America's 51 constitutions and the crisis of governance / Sanford Levinson.
p. cm.
Includes bibliographical references and index.
ISBN 978-0-19-989075-0 (hardback :alk. paper)
1. Constitutional law—United States—States.   2. Constitutional law—United States.
3. Federal government—United States.   4. Separation of powers—United States.
I. Title.
KF4530.L48 2010
342.7302—dc23
2012001177

1 3 5 7 9 8 6 4 2

Printed in the United States of America
on acid-free paper

For Jack Balkin and Mark Graber,
cherished friends and colleagues

CONTENTS

FRAMED

1

Introduction

I. CONNECTING THE DOTS

This book is the result of many years of reflection. But it—especially the
title—also is a response to contemporary American politics. The most basic
question that can one can ask about any political system is whether it is
capable of governing effectively, even if one recognizes that there will be
different criteria of "effectiveness." As the manuscript moved toward publication, the Minnesota state government was shut down for three weeks
because of the inability of its divided state government to reach agreement
on a budget.[1] In 2009, a similar budget crisis in California led to the nation's
largest state being unable to pay its public employees and other creditors for
several weeks; instead they were offered the equivalent of IOUs. In 2012, the
unwillingness of two Republicans in the California Assembly to support a
plea by Democratic Governor Jerry Brown to allow a public referendum
on retaining some taxes that were scheduled to expire led to what many
regarded as the decimation of the once-vaunted public education system
in that state.[2] (It takes two-thirds of the legislature to place an issue on the
ballot, and "only" a majority of the legislature was willing to place the issue
before the electorate.) In some ways even more dramatic, because it goes
to the heart of what one ordinarily thinks of as a basic attribute of government, is the possibility that the civil justice system in San Francisco will be
functionally shut down because of drastic cuts in the judiciary's budget.[3]

The U.S. government shut down briefly but notably in 1995, as the result
of seemingly irreconcilable differences between then Speaker of the House
Newt Gingrich and President Clinton. Another shutdown in December

2010 was averted only by an almost literally last-minute compromise between President Obama and Speaker of the House John Boehner. A shutdown almost occurred at the end of September 2011, and almost everyone expects similar episodes to recur prior to the 2012 election and, perhaps well afterward if, for example, President Obama is reelected and Republicans retain the majority in the House of Representatives and gain control of the Senate. But the major national political issue in the summer of 2011 was whether the United States would default on its debts because of congressional unwillingness to increase the national debt limit. Such default, it was widely (but not unanimously) agreed, would be calamitous for the American and—quite likely—the world economy.[4] This crisis, too, was averted at the last minute because of almost torturous compromises generated by a sufficiently bipartisan agreement that default would have unacceptable consequences.

This, however, did not prevent the decision by Standard & Poor's to downgrade American debt from AAA to AA status. Among the company's rationales for doing so was the following: "The downgrade reflects our view that the effectiveness, stability, and predictability of American policymaking and political institutions have weakened at a time of ongoing fiscal and economic challenges."[5]

The S&P analysis reflects the widespread view that the American political system has become profoundly dysfunctional. As the distinguished British writer Timothy Garton Ash wrote on August 3, 2011, "A couple of years back, it was still vaguely original to describe America's political system as dysfunctional. Now the word is on every commentator's lips."[6] Nor is this perception confined to elite commentators. One need only look at national polling data to realize the profound dissatisfaction that most Americans have with their government. Whether they are of the left, right, or center, they believe that there are unmet needs that our national and state institutions are failing to adequately confront, even if they disagree about what decisions should be made. A *New York Times* article on September 16, 2011, titled "Approval of Congress Matches Record Low,"[7] reported that only 12 percent of the American public indicated "approval" of Congress, a number reached earlier in August 2008. The week before a different poll had found a similar 12 percent approval rate while 87 percent disapproved, a full 75 percent difference.[8] Such numbers constitute a "bipartisan" rejection of what in a democratic system of government must surely be the most important single institution, the elected legislature. Analyzing responses to a somewhat broader question, the Gallup organization reported on September 26, 2011, that "Americans Express Historic Negativity Toward U.S. Government," noting that 81 percent of those polled were "dissatisfied" with the way the country is being governed.[9] Perhaps most shocking was an August 2011 Rasmussen poll finding that only 17 percent of those surveyed said that the present national government actually possesses the consent of the governed.[10]

The Gallup organization reports that trust in America's basic institutions is at historic lows. The most trusted governmental institution is the military; over three-quarters of the public has a "great deal" or "quite a lot" of confidence in our armed forces. At the other end of the spectrum is Congress, about which only a total of 12 percent are willing to express confidence. Four times as many respondents—a full 48 percent—described their confidence level as "very little or none." The presidency as an institution has the significant confidence of only slightly more than one-third of the public, 1 percent less than those with "very little or none." Even the U.S. Supreme Court must include the 41 percent who have "some" confidence to achieve a confidence level over 75 percent. If one adds those with "some" confidence, we find an overall 94 percent confidence level in the military.[11]

Would so few Americans have "approved of" or had confidence in the British Parliament or King George III had similar polls been taken in 1775?[12] Would three-quarters of all the colonists disapproved? It is impossible to answer these questions with any precision, but we do know that the numbers of Americans who strongly "disapproved" of those British institutions (including the British Redcoats) were sufficient to generate a violent secessionist movement within the British Empire that had monumental consequences.

No doubt it is hyperbolic to think that we are truly in an analogous situation today. But perhaps one should take seriously the comments of *Washington Post* columnist E. J. Dionne in his 2011 Fourth of July column on the Tea Party's rise in contemporary American politics. "Whether they intend it or not," writes Dionne, "their name suggests they believe that the current elected government in Washington is as illegitimate as was a distant, unelected monarchy... And it hints that methods outside the normal political channels are justified in confronting such oppression."[13] Consider the comments of Republican candidate Sharron Angle in her 2010 bid to represent Nevada in the U.S. Senate:

> Our Founding Fathers, they put that Second Amendment in there for a good reason, and that was for the people to protect themselves against a tyrannical government. In fact, Thomas Jefferson said it's good for a country to have a revolution every 20 years. I hope that's not where we're going, but you know, if this Congress keeps going the way it is, people are really looking toward those Second Amendment remedies [suggested by the "right to keep and bear arms"].[14]

Remarkable changes have occurred in polities across the world over the past generation with the development of mass social movements protesting the perceived failures of established political orders. Can we be absolutely certain that "American exceptionalism" inoculates our own political system against such political movements? (We did, after all, have our own exceptionally bloody secessionist movement between 1861 and 1865.)

Many Tea Partiers proclaim the virtues of local and state government, but one can wonder if Americans are really significantly more contented with their political institutions closer to home. Thus, the widely respected Field Poll in California found in September 2010 that approval of the California legislature was at a "record low,"[15] with only one in ten Californians expressing approval of the state legislature. A Marist poll conducted in New York following the November 2010 elections discovered that "71% say the way things are done in Albany need major changes, and another 11% believe government in Albany is broken and beyond repair."[16] It remains to be seen whether the governors elected in 2010 in both states, Jerry Brown and Andrew Cuomo, will be able to generate a greater degree of confidence from the residents in the overall structures of government, whether or not they earn high degrees of personal approval for their actions as governors. Even with the recent constitutional change that eliminates the need for a two-thirds vote to approve a budget, California has immense difficulty coming to basic budgetary decisions because of the continuing importance of the unrepealed two-thirds majority requirement for tax increases. The California that once seemed to be the beacon for America's bright future seems to have become more of a dystopia.

Public discontent is mirrored, and perhaps encouraged, by what can be found in mainstream journalistic commentary. *Newsweek,* for example, published a "viewpoint" essay in January 2010 titled "America the Ungovernable."[17] In 2009, the distinguished magazine *The Economist* labeled California "the ungovernable state," focusing on both its formal requirements for passing budget or tax legislation and on the crucial role played by a freewheeling process of popular initiative and referendum that, by definition, takes key decisions out of the hands of elected public officials.[18] Such referenda have amended the state constitution to both limit taxes and mandate expensive state policies,[19] a recipe for political breakdown.

A major premise of this book is that there is a connection between the perceived deficiencies of contemporary government and formal constitutions. This is especially true of the interplay between American national politics and the U.S. Constitution, but it is also true with regard to many state constitutions. To take the easiest case, almost no one believes that one can discuss California's problems without paying attention to the particularities of its state constitution, even if one acknowledges as well the importance of California's diverse political cultures, dramatically changing demographics, and the sheer size of its population.[20] Similarly, one can readily assign multiple causes to the present conditions in the United States and the consequent unhappiness and discontent of a large majority of its citizens. It may well be the case that these causes, in the language of modern political science, explain more of the "variance" between acceptable and unacceptable governance than do defects in constitutional structures.

But that does not render constitutions irrelevant unless they explain nothing at all, which is wildly implausible. And if this were true, then it logically follows that it is a mistake to credit the U.S. Constitution for what has gone well in American history, although doing so continues to be a common trope of American political analysts. All too typical are Thomas L. Friedman and Michael Mandelbaum, the authors of *That Used To Be Us: How American Fell behind in the World It Invented and How We Can Come Back,* who blithely assert that "for America's remarkable history, the Constitution deserves a large share of the credit."[21] Maybe yes, maybe no. But unless we believe that we have a perfect Constitution, one that generates only gains for the country and never imposes any losses, we should be prepared to pay equal attention to what may be the less-happy aspects of our constitutions, both national and state.

This book is very much about constitutional *structures*, and not, for example, about constitutional *rights*. A question hovering over it is the actual importance of such structures. Does it matter to the overall health of our political order that we have a presidential system of government, and not, like Great Britain or Canada, a parliamentary system in which the legislature is supreme? Is it truly significant in our presidential government that the president has the power to negate congressional handiwork simply by issuing a veto, which he may frequently exercise if Congress is controlled by the opposition party? How important is it that presidents can pardon even those who have not yet been convicted of felonies? Does it matter that Nebraska has only one legislative house, whereas its neighbors uniformly have two? Does the manner by which judges are selected—whether by election or appointment—or their tenure upon joining a court explain their actions upon taking the bench and therefore the quality of perceived justice (or injustice)?

One might think that these are simply rhetorical questions, but political scientists have been sharply divided for decades about the fundamental importance of constitutions, including their structural provisions. What is really important, many political scientists argue, is the underlying *political culture* of a given society, or its economic situation, its demography—is it ethnically and religiously divided or more homogeneous?—and the like. Adherents of this position, like Friedman and Mendelbaum, argue that if America is ungovernable, we should look beyond our formal institutional structures both for diagnosis and cure. We may "only" need to reform our educational institutions or be more attentive to the implications of immigration, leaving constitutional structures intact to solve our problems.

But the formalities can make a real difference. The distinguished political scientist David Mayhew has written that "the plain language of the Constitution may still be an unsurpassed guide to U.S. legislative behavior."[22] This sentence is worth deep reflection. It suggests that the basic institutional structures set out in the 1787 document help to determine the actual behavior—that is, the outcomes of most concern to members of the American political community—of legislators today and thus indirectly help to account for the levels of satisfaction or dissatisfaction felt by Americans assessing that behavior. Political scientists have become highly attentive to the "incentives" and "disincentives" created by particular political structures and how they help to shape the behavior of "rational" individuals seeking to gain their short- or long-term objectives.

There are, therefore, two basic ways to respond to the arguments of this book. One is to challenge the *empirical* assumptions, whether regarding a particular provision or the overall significance of any given American constitution, whether national or state. A second is to challenge the *normative* arguments that will also appear. We may agree, for example, on the empirical consequences of the U.S. Senate or the election of presidents by an electoral college but disagree profoundly on whether these consequences are desirable or undesirable.

Even if we believe that constitutions explain only relatively limited aspects of our lives together as members of various American communities, it may be the case that changing our constitutions, as difficult as it is, is easier than changing the other aspects of American society that undoubtedly play important roles in explaining both our triumphs and our tragedies. One might well, for example, emphasize the importance of the sheer size of the modern United States, in population or in territory, or its quite stunning cultural and religious diversity, or the implications of a global economy for retaining a traditionally strong manufacturing base. All these factors present their own challenges, including whether or not they are genuinely changeable. We can, though, at least in theory, imagine changing aspects of our constitutional realities.

Nothing in this book should be read to suggest that a "good constitution" is the cure to whatever ails a society or that a "bad constitution" is necessarily a harbinger of doom. It may be that other, non-constitutional factors are going so well that latent deficiencies in the Constitution don't matter. One might compare this situation to carrying in one's body a virus (or genetic defect) that remains dormant if one eats well, exercises, and gets ample sleep. But what if conditions arise where one doesn't (or can't)? At what point do latent diseases suddenly manifest themselves, causing serious, perhaps even fatal, damage to individual bodies—or the body politic? Do the survivors mutter to one another that the catastrophe could have been avoided by even relatively minor changes?

We regularly refer, with admiration, to the Framers of the U.S. Constitution. The very idea of a "frame" suggests a certain rigidity, whether one is thinking of a work of art or a constitution. It is fanciful, though, to believe that a frame that "worked" at one point in time will remain efficacious for all time. With art, we can talk simply about changed tastes; with constitutions we must address the extent to which a "framing document" fulfills the ends to which a society imagines itself devoted. Chapter 3 demonstrates that these ends are most likely to be set out in a *preamble* to the constitution, and that what follows the preamble are best viewed simply as proposed *means* to those ends. Frames may be necessary, but they can become problematic, even dangerous, if they remain unchanged in the light of new circumstances.

As will be seen throughout this book, state constitutions have often been transformed through amendment or, quite often, are replaced by a new constitution when they are deemed outmoded. Many analysts of California's situation take note of its state constitution—and, in some cases, the attendant need for a new constitutional convention to reform it. At the national level, however, critical analysts focus almost exclusively on the deficiencies of leadership or in the character of one's political adversaries, on an inchoate "political culture," or on the particular problems posed by campaign finance or partisan gerrymandering in the drawing of legislative districts. Again, all of these may well be worth discussing. But there is a refusal to "connect the dots" between the workings of our political system and the political structures that were adopted in 1787–1788—and left basically unamended ever since.

I return to Thomas Friedman because by any account he is one of the most influential columnists in the world today. He repeatedly decries "the failure of our political system to unite, even in a crisis, to produce the policy responses America needs to thrive in the 21st century."[23] His new book with Michael Mandelbaum is highly critical of our political system, calling it *"paralyzed"*[24] and "incapable or addressing [vital challenges] at the speed and scale we need."[25] The authors offer a vigorous critique of the "pathologies of the political system," including an "extreme polarization," particularly in Congress, generated at least in part by the corrupting role played by money in politics (and the need for an elected official to spend literally most of his or her time raising campaign contributions), and the rise of a hyperfragmented contemporary media.[26] California, which was formerly the instantiation of the "American dream," has now lost that status, perhaps most dramatically with the dramatic decline of its educational system. As they note, whereas California in 1980 was spending approximately 10 percent of its general revenue on higher education and 3 percent on prisons, "today nearly 11 percent goes to prisons and 8 percent to higher education."[27] They agree with *The Economist*'s 2009 diagnosis: "the state has become virtually ungovernable."[28]

Friedman and Mandelbaum deserve credit for recognizing the failures of our political system, but they seem oblivious to the possibility that the U.S. Constitution, like its California counterpart, helps to explain that failure. Their final chapter, which flamboyantly calls for "shock therapy" to help correct our political "pathologies" includes the dismaying assertion that the country does not "need fundamental changes to its system of government, a system that has served it well for more than two centuries and has proven equal to task of coping with a series of major challenges."[29] Friedman, a deserved winner of multiple Pulitzer Prizes, would surely be more acute if asked to analyze, say, Iraqi or Egyptian politics and the interplay between constitutional forms and political possibilities. But that theme is totally absent from his columns and his new book. Instead, his and Mandelbaum's "solution" to our political pathologies is to call for an independent third-party candidate for the presidency in 2012 who could shake up the American political system the way other losing insurgent candidates, including Teddy Roosevelt, George W. Wallace, and Ross Perot, did in 1912, 1968, and 1992.[30] They completely ignore the implications of the fact that we elect our presidents in a most peculiar manner, as dictated by the U.S. Constitution. I'm referring, of course, to the electoral college, which renders the popular vote irrelevant and generates campaign strategies aimed at a relatively few "battleground" states.[31] Their suggestion would make great sense in either France or the state of Georgia, both of which in their presidential or gubernatorial elections require runoffs between the two highest vote-getters (assuming neither garnered an initial majority). That, alas, is not the way we elect presidents in the United States, a basic bit of American civics ignored by these authors, and neither seems to recognize at all the degree to which the U.S. Constitution, like its California counterpart, helps to explain that failure or our current crisis of governance.

The conservative columnist David Brooks has written that the "British political system is basically functional while the American system is not." He notes that the "British political system gives the majority party much greater power than any party could hope to have in the U.S., but cultural norms make the political debate less moralistic and less absolutist." Thus, Brooks concludes, "We Americans have no right to feel smug or superior."[32] Two months later, in the heat of the debt limit debate, he lamented the unwillingness of the Republican Party to accept what were quite astounding compromises offered by President Obama because they would require relatively slight tax increases. He noted the role that anti-tax zealot Grover Norquist plays in the contemporary Republican Party. "He enforces rigid ultimatums that make governance, or even thinking, impossible." But Brooks goes on to mention other aspects of contemporary politics, including the rise of "talk-radio jocks" who "portray politics as a cataclysmic, Manichaean struggle. A series of compromises that steadily advance conservative aims would muddy their story lines and be death to their ratings." He also denounced "political celebrities, who are marvelously uninterested in actually producing results," and "permanent campaigners" who are devoted only to winning the next election and not to actually passing laws that might benefit the country.[33] It is easy enough for me to agree with Brooks's often insightful diagnoses even if I do not share his general politics. But Brooks has never chosen to write on the mechanics of the American constitutional order, preferring instead to focus on political culture or the dynamics of "leadership." He did not, for example, suggest that America take seriously what is desirable about British political institutions and think of changing our own accordingly.

More probing, though certainly no less depressing, is the complaint by longtime political analyst Bill Schneider that "hyperpartisanship is making American government dysfunctional."[34] Many other countries suffer less from this problem because "when a party has a strong majority and unified control of government, it implements its program, passes laws, and makes changes." But that is not the case in the United States. The "U.S. system of government was designed with checks and balances, separation of powers, and federal-state divisions. It was designed to make government as weak and as difficult as possible." In addition, there are "extra-constitutional rules, such as the filibuster, which has come to require a normal working majority of 60 votes in the Senate." Thus government in America, certainly at the national level, requires "the kind of consensus that usually comes out of a crisis, namely, an overwhelming sense of public urgency." But no such consensus is close to emerging regarding "the country's economic crisis, or the health care crisis, or the environmental crisis. Instead, each crisis has deepened the partisan divide and made government more dysfunctional." In some cases there is no agreement that there even is a crisis that must be confronted, and if there is such agreement, there are deep ideological divides on how best to address it. With his reference to the design of the U.S. government, Schneider at least suggests that we ask if we are well served by the eighteenth-century institutions within which our politics take place.

E. J. Dionne has written, "I've reached the point where I'd abolish the Senate if I could. It is more profoundly undemocratic than it was when the Founders created it and less genuinely deliberative."[35] *New Yorker* writer Hendrik Hertzberg (a former speechwriter for Jimmy Carter) has moved far closer to connecting the dots. Hertzberg wrote a laudatory review in 2002 of Robert Dahl's *How Democratic Is the U.S. Constitution?* agreeing with Dahl that the answer is "not nearly enough."[36] More recently, in January 2011, he wrote that

> the biggest obstacles to energetic, coherent action are systemic. Our ungainly eighteenth-century legislative mechanism, drowning in twenty-first-century campaign cash, is shot through with veto points. We have three separately elected "governments" (House, Senate, Presidency), all of which must agree for anything big to happen. Our two-year election cycle leaves little time for long-acting changes to ripen and be judged fairly. That basic structure has its pluses as well as its minuses, of course. Anyway, we're stuck with it.[37]

Hertzberg has also been a longtime critic of the electoral college and its vagaries.[38] Still, perhaps the most important sentence in the quotation above is the last one, for he is indirectly noting (as Dahl had emphasized) that the U.S. Constitution is functionally impossible to amend (this is the subject of Chapter 15). It therefore may appear fruitless to expend much energy on constitutional reform, even if one can intellectually connect the dots.

The most dramatic example of dot connecting among the punditry is probably Fareed Zakaria, who in March 2011 wrote a remarkable cover story for *Time* magazine titled "Are America's Best Days behind Us?"[39]

He lamented that "at the very moment that our political system has broken down, one hears only encomiums to it, the Constitution and the perfect Republic that it created. Now, as an immigrant, I love the special and, yes, exceptional nature of American democracy. I believe that the Constitution was one of the wonders of the world—in the 18th century. But today we face the reality of a system that has become creaky." *Creaky* is an odd word in this context, but Zakaria recognizes the problem caused by attempting to govern ourselves under a Constitution that can all too accurately be described as a relic of times long past.

A crucial question throughout this book, directed to readers in the second decade of the 21st century, is whether we continue to share the assumptions that underlay the U.S. Constitution in 1787. If not, why do we remain so devoted to a Constitution based on them? No one should believe that there are "perfect" constitutions waiting to be written. There are not. As Chapter 2 emphasizes, *all* constitutions necessarily involve tradeoffs and compromises. Nothing in this book should be taken to indicate otherwise. I may be quixotic in calling for rethinking, and perhaps changing, some basic features of our constitutions, both state and national. However, I do not view this as being utopian, which might suggest that there is a Platonic form of the one best constitution that we should identify and then adopt. To err is human, after all. But some errors and tradeoffs are worse than others; some compromises, indeed rotten rather than merely unfortunate. It may be, as James Madison argued with regard to equal representation in the U.S. Senate, that one must accept lesser evils. Yet evils they remain, and one should always be willing to ask how necessary it is to accept them and their consequences in our own contemporary world, so distant from the world in which these compromises were indeed explicable and, given exigencies of the moment, perhaps defensible. But times change.

This book is not intended to denigrate those who wrote our national or state constitutions. They were, with some exceptions, honorable persons genuinely trying to do the best they could. If I denigrate anyone in what follows, it is ourselves, for refusing to ask the probing questions the Framers were willing to ask about the adequacy of their own institutions. In the opening paragraph of *The Federalist*, Alexander Hamilton wrote that "it seems to have been reserved to the people of this country, by their conduct and example, to decide the important question, whether societies of men are really capable or not of establishing good government from reflection and choice."[40] The pride we take in our "founding" (and Founders) comes from a belief that such "reflection and choice" did indeed characterize the deliberations in Philadelphia and the ratification conventions thereafter. As Framers, they were not trying "to frame us" in the pejorative sense. (It would therefore have been a mistake to title this book "We Wuz Framed," which would analogize Madison and his associates to rogue police.) But Framers they were, generating a host of rigid structures with real consequences. One cannot believe that even the admirable deliberations that generated these structures were sufficient for all time. The Framers did not believe that, and neither should we.

As a matter of fact, there are some Americans who are, at least in their own way, connecting the dots. Among these are members of the so-called Tea Party, some of whom are vociferous proponents of at least two constitutional amendments. In June 2010, the Idaho Republican Party adopted a platform that advocates repeal of the Seventeenth Amendment, which provides that senators be popularly elected rather than appointed by their state legislatures.[41] Texas Governor and presidential candidate Rick Perry has also endorsed repeal.[42] An unsuccessful Utah Republican candidate for his party's Senate nomination explained his support of such a repeal: "We traded senators who represent rights of states for senators who represent the rights of special interest groups."[43] One may or may not accept the second half of his proposition, but it is hard to refute the argument that elected senators are less likely to care about the abstract "rights of states" and the prerogatives of state governments than senators appointed by state officials. To expect otherwise is to believe that voters happen to share that passion, an empirically dubious proposition.

Similarly, Randy Barnett, a noted law professor from Georgetown with a large following among Tea Party devotees, has proposed what he calls a Repeal Amendment that would give two-thirds of the state legislatures the right to invalidate any federal legislation.[44] I think that both proposals deserve emphatic rejection, but I have a grudging respect for their proponents, who at least realize that there is indeed a connection between political structures and the outcomes they support. The proper response to such proposals is not to denounce the very idea of constitutional change, an attitude best expressed in a well-known essay by former Stanford

Law School Dean Kathleen Sullivan dismissing all such suggestions as "constitutional amendmentitis"[45]—as if the very proposal of constitutional amendments constituted a disease. Instead of confronting proposed amendments on their merits, too many liberals have emulated Sullivan by condemning the very possibility of amendment. This comes dangerously close to suggesting that we have a basically "perfect Constitution" that should be worshipped rather than subjected to tough-minded analysis.

Moreover, a major theme of this book is that any consideration of American constitutionalism must pay ample attention to America's other fifty constitutions, those of the states. These constitutions are also the result of reflection and choice. Not only have they been far more frequently amended than their national counterpart, but many states have out-and-out replaced existing constitutions with new documents thought more conducive to facing the challenges of a new time. Even if one would not wish to emulate Georgia and Louisiana, which together have had almost two dozen constitutions, one might still believe that there is something to learn from the willingness of states to reflect on the adequacy of their existing constitutions and to do something about perceived deficiencies, in contrast to the all too rarely reflected-upon U.S. Constitution.

Americans should pay special heed to James Madison's ringing conclusion to *Federalist* 14:

> Is it not the glory of the people of America, that, whilst they have paid a decent regard to the opinions of former times and other nations, they have not suffered a blind veneration for antiquity, for custom, or for names, to overrule the suggestions of their own good sense, the knowledge of their own situation, and the lessons of their own experience?... Had no important step been taken by the leaders of the Revolution for which a precedent could not be discovered, no government established of which an exact model did not present itself, the people of the United States might, at this moment...must at best have been laboring under the weight of some of those forms which have crushed the liberties of the rest of mankind. Happily for America, happily, we trust, for the whole human race, they pursued a new and more noble course...They reared the fabrics of governments which have no model on the face of the globe. They formed the design of a great Confederacy, which *it is incumbent on their successors to improve and perpetuate*. (emphasis added)

We best honor the founding generation by forthrightly confronting the "lessons of experience" and accepting Madison's mandate to view the national Constitution and its state analogues as works in progress. We must therefore use our critical intelligence to "improve" them if they are to perpetuate themselves through time and, even more importantly, prove friends rather than enemies to achieving the great purposes most inspiringly set out in the Preamble to the national Constitution. This is especially important if we really are facing great challenges, even "emergencies," and if we have good reason to wonder whether our institutions are up to these challenges. We must connect the dots, even if that leads us to ask fundamentally critical questions about the Constitution we have been taught since childhood to venerate.

II. WHY IS THIS BOOK DIFFERENT FROM MOST OTHER BOOKS ABOUT THE CONSTITUTION?

Connecting the dots requires writing a book that is considerably different from almost all other books on American constitutionalism, and not only because it is more critical, both implicitly and explicitly, than the norm. Most such books, for example, focus almost obsessively on great interpretive debates attached to what Justice Robert Jackson once termed the "magnificent generalities" of the Due Process Clause of the Fourteenth Amendment.[46] Less upliftingly, he also refers to "the cryptic words of the Fourteenth Amendment."[47] Whether magnificent or cryptic, the words of the Fourteenth Amendment—and much else in the Constitution—are scarcely obvious in their meaning. It is not surprising, then, that many books have been written on the Fourteenth Amendment itself, let alone other parts of the Constitution that also beg for "interpretation." What unites many of those books, however bitterly they may differ, is the authors' claims that they have discerned the one true approach to constitutional interpretation. Whether one agrees or not, many of these books are certainly worth reading.[48] This book, however, focuses on other issues connected with the Constitution and is, I hope, worth reading for different reasons.

Because the history of American constitutionalism, especially at the national level, involves so much changing interpretation (along with the occasional formal amendment), books usually have a historical focus congruent with an emphasis on change. That, after all, is what history is about. One can lament changes or applaud them, but any understanding of the general powers of Congress over our 225-year history will necessarily involve an immersion in important changes that have structured this history. And, especially if the books are written by fellow members of the legal academy, they are likely to feature many cases decided by the U.S. Supreme Court. Again, for reasons to be explained more fully below, this is not such a book.

Finally, most people (and too many academics) believe that one understands all one needs to know about American constitutionalism by exclusive study of a single Constitution, the U.S. Constitution drafted in 1787 and ratified in 1787–1788. I do not. In order to understand why there are serious questions about the contemporary national government's capacity to govern, one does have to understand that particular constitution. As suggested above, however, if one is also interested in understanding the travails of many of our states, including the shutdown of the government of Minnesota or the chaotic government of California, the national Constitution will provide little help; knowledge of state constitutions is essential.

The inspiration for the title of this section is the opening of the Passover Seder, celebrating the Exodus from Egypt and the foundations of Jewish political identity. The youngest child chants the Four Questions, asking why Jews distinguish the Seder meal from all other dinners during the rest of the year. The Seder service is a self-conscious attempt to instill in youngsters the habit of not only connecting with the past but also of asking often critical questions about the answers given to the various questions. As Americans, we too are connected in complicated ways to those who forged new political identities, generated by an exodus from the traditions established as members of the British colonial empire and the forging (and "framing") of new understandings of political reality. We are most aware of the new *national* identity that was established and of the document, the U.S. Constitution, that signified it, not least by its opening invocation of "We the People." But there was also a spate of constitution-drafting within the states that had declared their independence from Great Britain in 1776. All of these developments required asking—and offering provisional answers to—profound questions about the nature of politics. Many of these questions continue to roil us today. They are not merely of theoretical interest, but arise within the context of fears about the very governability of contemporary America, whether at the national or state level.

So, the four questions underlying this book are as follows:

1. Most other books on constitutional law accept the Constitution as a given, while passionately debating exactly what certain passages of the document mean. So why does this book generally ignore such questions of constitutional "meaning" or constitutional "interpretation"?

2. Books on American constitutional law often (and properly) take an intensely *historical* approach insofar as their central goal is to understand the *changes* in constitutional understanding over time. So why is *stasis*, rather than *change*, the principal focus of this book?

3. Most American books on constitutional law focus exclusively on the federal Constitution. Why should we pay as much attention to the other fifty state constitutions that also make up "American constitutionalism"?

4. Finally, most books about American constitutionalism talk almost incessantly about the role of courts. Why does this book present only a relatively limited discussion of the role of courts (and judges) and almost no discussion of judicial opinions?

III. THE FOUR ANSWERS

A. Why does this book not focus on constitutional "meaning"?

There is a deceptively easy answer to this question. Debates about meaning generally arise only when there is a genuine controversy about how best to interpret a constitutional provision or practice. This does not mean that documents about which there is no controversy have no meaning. It is simply that if the meaning is clear to all the participants in a given conversation, the conversation shifts direction. The new discussion might well focus on the *wisdom* of the text in question, which is a very different question from its semantic meaning.

Consider two pieces of text from the U.S. Constitution. The first is the Inauguration Day Clause, which appears in the Twentieth Amendment. If you want to find out when an elected president takes office, this amendment tells you with great precision: "The terms of the President and Vice President shall end at noon on the 20th day of January...and the terms of their successors shall then begin." It would be odd if someone seriously asked, "What does the Constitution *mean* by January 20?" Take another example that applies directly to younger readers of this book, the "age qualification" clauses of the Constitution that disqualify even "natural born citizens" from serving in the House of Representatives, Senate, or the presidency until they turn twenty-five, thirty, or thirty-five, respectively. (A "naturalized citizen" may have to wait considerably longer to serve in Congress and will *never* be eligible to be president.) One can debate at length about the *wisdom* of these clauses, but there is no need to debate what they mean save in the most highly theoretical academic seminars that, for better or worse, have no genuine connection with "ordinary interpretation."

Contrast these examples with the Fourteenth Amendment, by which "all persons" are guaranteed "the equal protection of the laws" and the right not to be denied "due process of law." No one could seriously say that reading the text is sufficient to know what "equal protection" or "due process" means. That is, after all, why Justice Jackson could so easily describe the language as a "generality," whether magnificent or cryptic. Similarly, Robert Bork once described another notably cryptic passage of the Constitution, the Ninth Amendment, as an "inkblot." (Even the meaning of "persons" is less than self-evident, as revealed in contemporary debates about abortion or the protection to be accorded those "artificial persons" called corporations.)

Anyone who believes that the Equal Protection Clause requires only the application of a singular concept of equality should confront a fine book tellingly titled *Equalities*,[49] which identifies no fewer than 108 logically defensible theories of equality (and the text of the Constitution provides no practical help in determining which one of these is the best meaning). So perhaps we can place the Inauguration Day Clause at one end of a spectrum of constitutional clarity and the Equal Protection Clause at the other. The Inauguration Day Clause is scarcely "magnificent" (or even "cryptic"), and there is nothing "general" about it.

This book is far more concerned with analogues to the Inauguration Day Clause than to the Equal Protection Clause. Though their meaning is indisputable, there is nothing trivial about such clauses. In fact, they may better explain the failures of our political system and fears about governability than the "magnificent generalities" explain its successes. The two ends of the spectrum might be called the *Constitution of Settlement* as against the *Constitution of Conversation*. It is the very point of the former to foreclose conversations about meaning. Most other books on constitutional law deal only with the latter. This book is different because it focuses on the former.

What explains the existence of *both* these aspects within any given constitution? To answer this question, we should ask the most general of all possible questions: What do constitutions *do*? What is their point? Not surprisingly, there are a number of things that constitutions can be said to do. One extremely important function of a constitution is to *settle* basic political disputes by adopting decidedly nonabstract and noninspiring language that gives a clear and determinate answer to what otherwise might be disputed. However, this is certainly not *all* that constitutions do. They can also express the highest—and most abstract—aspirations of a society. This might be the function of our Preamble, the subject of Chapter 3. The Constitution also includes clauses (like the Equal Protection Clause) that serve as goads to sometimes endless—and often acrimonious—conversations. But if any given constitution generated *only* conversations, however interesting they might be, it would be an abject failure.

Some skeptics believe that it is a mistake to expect constitutions firmly to settle anything of great importance. Among the political realities, for example, is the necessity of compromise, the topic of Chapter 2. One common tactic of compromise is to "kick the can down the street."[50] One can do this either by adopting ambiguous language that is acceptable to both sides because it lacks clear meaning or by remaining resolutely silent about an issue that might be too volatile. (Think, in this regard, of secession.)

But Madison, in *Federalist 37*, expresses considerable skepticism about the possibilities of perfect clarity even in the best of circumstances. Even the "continued and combined labors of the most enlightened legislatures and jurists," he observed, have failed to provide the "delineat[ion]" we might hope for with regard to "different codes of laws and different tribunals of justice." Instead, "[a]ll new laws, though penned with the greatest technical skill, and passed on the fullest and most mature deliberation, are considered as more or less obscure and equivocal, until their meaning be liquidated and ascertained by a series of particular discussions and adjudications." We must be aware of the inherent limits of language. We are therefore faced with "unavoidable inaccuracy… according to the complexity and novelty of the objects defined." He concludes the paragraph with a truly stunning sentence: "When the Almighty himself condescends to address mankind in their own language, his meaning, luminous as it must be, is rendered dim and doubtful by the cloudy medium through which it is communicated." If the Almighty cannot be altogether clear, then why should we expect anything better from ordinary human beings? It would surely require the ultimate in delusions of grandeur. Madison does offer the possibility that disputes can be "liquidated" after sufficient conversation produces a consensus on meaning, though one wonders if such "liquidation" and settlement will ever occur with regard to the Fourteenth Amendment.

Perhaps, however, Madison was slightly exaggerating. One does not have to be a fundamentalist to believe that parts of the Bible have quite clear meanings. For example, while teaching at Harvard in 2009 I did not hold class on Monday, September 28, which was Yom Kippur, the Day of Atonement for even minimally observant Jews like myself. Why the 28th? Given that Harvard no longer schedules Saturday classes, why could the holiday not be observed on the previous Saturday, September 26th? Why put up with the frequent inconvenience to both me and my students caused by Jewish holidays falling on class days? Yom Kippur could be treated the way the United States treated Lincoln's and Washington's birthdays, combining them into a holiday called "Presidents Day," always celebrated, to public joy, on Mondays to create long weekends. The answer is easy: Leviticus 23:27 states that "the tenth day of this seventh month" of the Jewish calendar will forever after be the Day of Atonement. Beginning with a clear (perhaps too clear) text, practices have developed over what is now thousands of years, so that the date of Yom Kippur is as settled as, say, Inauguration Day. No doubt there are other examples as well. So perhaps we could even speak of the "Bible of Conversation"—the Ten Commandments or the parables of Jesus, for starters—and the "Bible of Settlement."

The Jewish calendar, like the Muslim or Chinese calendars, is a lunar one and is therefore different from the Christian calendar under which we generally operate, which is based on the earth's revolution around the sun. This could lead to some interesting tests of interpretation. The U.S. Constitution requires that the president be at least thirty-five. But it doesn't explicitly tell us under which calendar system, at least until one reads the very end of the Constitution declaring that it was signed in Philadelphia on September 17, "in the year of our Lord" 1787. But even if we use this as a conclusive determination that the Constitution is referring to the solar calendar, there is the fact that the Christian community was for several centuries divided as to how that calendar actually functioned. The traditional Julian calendar was succeeded by the reformed calendar introduced by Pope Gregory XIII in 1582 and adopted by most countries in the ensuing centuries. However, Protestant Great Britain (and therefore the American colonies) did not adopt the new calendar system until 1752, at which time it was necessary to correct the still-existing Julian calendar by eleven days. Thus Wednesday, September 2, 1752, was followed by Thursday, September 14, 1752. This meant also that George Washington's birthday suddenly shifted from February 11 to February 22. In any event, we treat the Gregorian form of the solar calendar as the "settled" way to measure age in the United States, so any claims based on alternative calendars would be rejected. This excursion into calendar systems illustrates the point that "settlement" often requires more than mere text; one must look to cultural assumptions underlying the bare-bones words in a document. Once one acknowledges the force of these underlying assumptions, though, conversation about "meaning" ceases with regard to texts of the Constitution of Settlement.

Many political scientists have emphasized that constitutions, if they are "to work," must ultimately be "self-enforcing," which means that members of the relevant community will voluntarily adhere to constitutional commands because such obedience is viewed as conducive to achieving mutually beneficial ends, including stability. What legal philosophers describe as "formal rules" are often conducive to achieving such stability.[51] Just imagine what would happen if there were genuine controversy as to when a newly elected president took office. Self-enforcement is no doubt easier if language appears to be "clear," at least within the operative assumptions of the relevant community. It can also be achieved, though, when most people agree that constitutional conversations will be brought to a close by the decision of a particular person or institution. In our system, that role is often assigned to (or eagerly embraced by) the U.S. Supreme Court. As already suggested, though, this book is far less interested in the roles played by such "ultimate decisionmakers," not least because their decisions are often vigorously contested, as is the case with the Supreme Court. Most of the self-enforcing provisions appear to be sufficiently obvious in their meaning that they require no adjudication at all; anyone disregarding the clear meaning would be engaging at the same instance in radical disobedience, perhaps even revolution.

So, return again to the Inauguration Day Clause as a paradigmatic example of "settlement." We know what day a president takes office (or is allowed to continue in office after a completed first term) simply by reading the Twentieth Amendment. A quick search on the Internet allows us to determine that the president elected in 2204—assuming the United States still exists and the Constitution has not been amended—will be inaugurated on Sunday, January 20, 2205, though it is possible that the inauguration celebrations will be delayed until Monday if a monstrous blizzard shuts down Washington (or if the United States has become so Christian in its public culture that it is thought unsuitable to have public celebrations on Sunday). But no one should believe that such a delay will have the slightest legal effect, for the presidency will have changed hands at noon the day before. That's just what the Constitution says!

Everyone should be aware that the Twentieth Amendment came along fairly late in our constitutional history, in 1933. So when were presidents inaugurated before then? The answer is March 4. Does the text of the Constitution give us that answer? Not quite. But the reason that all presidents who took office after George Washington were inaugurated on March 4 *does* follow from text that establishes the presidential term as four years, and not one day more or less. The last Congress operating under the Articles of Confederation, which the new Constitution supplanted, determined that the new government would begin operating—with all officers presumably taking their oaths of office—on the "first Wednesday of March 1789," which was March 4. As it happened, the new government scarcely got up and running with maximum efficiency, and George Washington did not take his oath of office until April 29, 1789. But he did take his second oath of office on March 4, 1793, not least because the terms of office of all representatives and one-third of the Senate expired at noon on the 4th (given that the Constitution establishes a two-year term for members of the House and that the terms of one-third of the Senate expire at the same time). Even if one can argue about whether Washington's term really began on March 4, 1789, or only when he actually took the oath of office for the first time on April 29,[52] the Twelfth Amendment, added to the Constitution in 1803, in effect specified March 4 as Inauguration Day.[53] So it follows that any merely legislative change would automatically violate the Constitution by either shortening or lengthening the mandated four-year term. As a matter of fact, the Twentieth Amendment establishing January 20 as Inauguration Day operated to reduce Franklin Roosevelt's first term of office by roughly six weeks; his second term began on January 20, 1937, though he had initially been inaugurated, prior to the Twentieth Amendment, on March 4, 1933.

No doubt many readers view Inauguration Day as a minor aspect of the Constitution, perhaps because lawyers never argue about its meaning or threaten to bring litigation changing the time at which a newly elected president will take office. To be sure, many of the examples in the remainder of the book may grip the reader more. But it is a mistake to believe that there is no interesting conversation to be had about the Inauguration Day Clause. Indeed, this book is predicated on the proposition that almost *all* of the Constitution of Settlement is very much worth talking about by anyone interested in the practicalities of American government However, the nature of the discourse about the Constitution of Settlement is quite different from that generated by the Constitution of Conversation. The latter involves constitutional *meaning*; the former involves the *wisdom* of clear constitutional commands.

One might well believe that in the twenty-first century January 20 is as defective a day for inaugurating new presidents as the twentieth-century supporters of the Twentieth Amendment thought March 4 was. The outgoing incumbent continues to possess all the legal authority of the office, including the ability to issue pardons to persons convicted of violating federal law. But the incoming president, who has no legal authority, may possess a great deal of political authority, especially if he or she received a majority of the popular vote (in addition to the majority of electoral votes). Things get even more complicated if the incoming president was elected on what might be termed a "repudiationist" platform vis-à-vis the incumbent.

The most dramatic illustrations of this phenomenon under the old regime occurred when Thomas Jefferson replaced the defeated and widely unpopular John Adams (1800–1801), Abraham Lincoln took over from the slavery-supporting James Buchanan (1860–1861), and Franklin D. Roosevelt trounced Herbert Hoover during the Great Depression (1932–1933). In all cases, basically a full five months separated the election from the inauguration of the successor. In the post-Twentieth-Amendment world things have gotten better, but perhaps not enough to lull us into complacence. Most readers of this book personally experienced during the winter of 2008–2009 the phenomenon of a soundly repudiated (even by the candidate of his own party) incumbent sitting in office and a president-elect, elected while the United States suffered through the greatest economic crisis of the past seventy-five years, possessing not a scintilla of legal authority until January 20. Older readers may recall that Richard Nixon had to wait to succeed Lyndon Johnson in 1969; Jimmy Carter, to succeed Gerald Ford in 1977; and—perhaps most notably— Ronald Reagan, to replace Jimmy Carter in 1981.

At one level—that is, ascertaining constitutional *meaning*—it really doesn't matter whether one applauds Inauguration Day or considers it a reprehensible feature of the Constitution. It is simply there, a settled feature unless a further amendment gives us a different—and perhaps more desirable—system than the one we have now. But we can still vigorously debate whether the Constitution *should* be amended, which requires arguing about whether we are well served by this feature of the Constitution.

In such a debate, it might prove illuminating to look at the quite different decisions of a variety of foreign countries and the fifty American states with regard to inaugurating their political leaders. Most notable, perhaps, is the practice in Great Britain of the incumbent prime minister leaving 10 Downing Street the day after the election, promptly replaced by the victorious candidate. There is no notion of a "transition period" in that country because the premise of the British parliamentary system is that the out-of-power party always contains a "shadow cabinet," ready to take over at a moment's notice. No American state has adopted a parliamentary system; all emulate the national government by having a governor chosen independently of the legislature. Still, no state waits as long as the national government to install its new leader. In 2010, for example, both Alaska and Hawaii inaugurated their governors on December 6.[54] The new governors of New York and Michigan took their oaths of office on New Year's Day 2011, and a spate of governors, including California's, took office between January 3–6. The outliers are Alabama (January 17), Texas (January 18), and Maryland (January 19). Most states, however, appear to wish to limit the amount of time of de facto "caretaker governments," a term usually associated with parliamentary regimes and referring to an existing government in the interim between election and the new government's installation, which can take several months in a multiparty system.[55]

Even those who concede the practical relevance of inauguration clauses might be tempted to dismiss the importance of the various qualification clauses, whether the age requirements that prevent millions of American citizens, even natural-born citizens, from serving in national office for some years[56] or disqualify *any* naturalized citizens from ever aspiring to be president. But the Natural-Born Citizen Clause explained the inability of then—California Governor Arnold Schwarzenegger to run for the presidency in 2008, when he might have been a stronger opponent of Barack Obama than John McCain proved to be.[57] Not only does no state emulate the United States in barring naturalized citizens from serving as governors, but it is also almost certain that the Supreme Court would strike down any such attempt as a violation of the Equal Protection Clause. What prevents the national candidacy of someone like Schwarzenegger is the power of the raw text and the absence of a plausible argument that it has been amended by anything added to the Constitution since 1787. One might also believe that Bill Clinton would have run for reelection in 2000 and thereafter had the Twenty-second Amendment not clearly limited presidents to two terms. The meaning of these clauses is not open to practical doubt. Formalism rules, regardless of the practical consequences of denying Schwarzenegger or Clinton the right to run for the presidency.

Almost all of this book examines similar pieces of text that constitute our Constitution of Settlement: How many houses of Congress or state legislatures are there, with how many members, selected by what means?

What is the scope of presidential or gubernatorial vetoes, and how many legislators are necessary to override such vetoes? This book is an opportunity to converse and argue with its readers, but none of these arguments will really concern, at a pragmatic level, what the Constitution *means*. Instead, we talk about the *wisdom* of various constitutional provisions.

Return a final time to the Inauguration Day Clause and whether it is wise for the country to have to wait until January 20 to install new presidents. Quite obviously, any discussion in "real time" will inevitably have political overtones. Such political overtones will be even more present when we are discussing whether incumbent presidents should retain the power to veto legislation or whether it is defensible for Wyoming to have the same number of votes in the Senate as California. It would be foolish to ignore the political dimension of the topics considered throughout this book. Indeed, one of its purposes is to expose the connections between constitutional design and politics. But whether we have the capacity to think in terms of a longer time horizon than immediate political realities is crucial to determining the kinds of conversations we can have and the possibility of deciding to change aspects of our political systems in the future.

It may be tempting to discuss some of these issues only in the short run by focusing on the implications for particular presidents, such as George W. Bush, Barack Obama, or one of President Obama's opponents in 2012. That temptation should be resisted. For there is also the long-run aspect that involves confronting some basic questions in political philosophy and the practicalities of designing a government. To what degree do we want, into the indefinite future, a constitutional system that empowers majorities? Or should we instead prefer one that allows aggrieved and structurally well-located minorities to block majority-supported proposals? To what extent should the federal Constitution be redesigned to resemble the fifty state constitutions, which are significantly different in many dimensions? (Or, conversely, should state constitutions be rewritten to look more like their national counterpart?) Whatever your answers, you should imagine amending the Constitution in ways that would not take effect until a future date that will have political realities about which we are currently quite clueless, say, 2017 (or, should you be reading this book in 2015, until 2021 or 2025). Inevitable disagreements about various topics to be considered in this book need not divide us neatly into Democrats or Republicans, liberals or conservatives, or even Tea Partiers or their opponents. Such division would almost certainly occur if we focused only on current events and immediate changes, of which the beneficiaries would be obvious. But once one adopts even a moderately long-term perspective, discussions that necessarily have *political* dimensions need not inevitably turn into *partisan* conversations.

B. Why is this book relatively ahistorical, in contrast to a book about the meanings of disputed portions of the Constitution?

My own approach when teaching American constitutional disputation—which is another way of referring to the Constitution of Conversation—is extremely historical. It is vitally important for anyone interested in the powers of Congress or the actual protections accorded "the freedom of speech" to know that the relevant assigners of meaning, including the U.S. Supreme Court, have historically offered sharply different notions on these issues. The same is obviously true of any "conversational" provisions of state constitutions. Indeed, with regard to state constitutions, one might well note not only states' frequent amendment of even "hardwired" provisions but also that most states have replaced an existing constitution with a sometimes quite different brand new one.

But the fact that the Constitution of Conversation must be taught historically does not mean that the same is true of the Constitution of Settlement. Whether we think of our own individual lives or of entire societies, dramatic changes often take place against a background of unexamined (and settled) givens. Each reader may have changed in profound ways, but none has developed a third eye or, as yet, the ability to run the mile in three minutes.

But much great literature has been written on how what we accept as a given can change in an instant, and we are well advised to consider our own assumptions and whether they are so unchangeable as we may think. Some may well be, but others might be malleable if only we have the imagination and the will. Would our lives actually be better if we made efforts to change some of the givens, or are they so "hardwired" (like our innate awareness that we all, sooner or later, actually die) that efforts to change are simply delusional?

Because this book focuses on the Constitution of Settlement, there is much more emphasis on what is static in American political life than one what has changed. Indeed, I will be offering a "Narrative of Statis" far more than the conventional "Narrative of Change" that typifies most books on American constitutionalism. History is not entirely absent. Certain practices associated with the veto or the electoral college have changed over time. Still, the emphasis is on the degree to which the world we are living in today is still, fundamentally shaped, politically, by decisions made in 1787.

C. Why should we pay at least as much attention to the fifty American state constitutions as to the national Constitution, especially when discussing the structures within which American politics are conducted?

If one is trying to understand the realities of "American constitutionalism," it is essential to look beyond the U.S. Constitution to the many other constitutions that are part of the American political system. To identify a single constitution, however important it may be, with the entirety of American thinking about the constitutional enterprise is equivalent to offering a course on European art that turns out to focus exclusively on the art of the Italian Renaissance. There is much to be learned by looking intensively at that particular tradition, but there is also much that is missed if one ignores what was occurring over many centuries in other parts of that complex continent (not to mention within Italy itself). Similarly, one simply does not understand American constitutionalism if one knows only about the national Constitution. "[T]here has never been," Laura Scalia has written, "a singular constitutional tradition in the United States."[58] John Dinan has similarly written a splendid book, *The American State Constitutional Tradition*,[59] in which he demonstrates at length the existence of a distinctive American state constitutional tradition that not only complements but is often in significant tension with the norms underlying the national tradition. Both must be considered by anyone attempting to learn how Americans think of organizing themselves politically. In addition, one should also be attentive to the extent that state constitutions make their own contribution to the turmoil—and potential ungovernability—that characterizes many contemporary states.

"When Americans speak of 'constitutional law,'" James Gardner has written, "they invariably mean the U.S. Constitution and the substantial body of federal judicial decisions construing it."[60] This is a mistake, in every conceivable way. Almost all of the more than three hundred million residents of the United States[61] live under *two* constitutions: one for the United States, the other for the states they inhabit. (And Americans who split their time in two or more states, or even foreign countries, come under the jurisdiction of additional constitutions.) It is therefore quite appalling that a 1988 poll demonstrated that "52 percent of the respondents did not know that their state had its own constitution"[62] and that a report issued the following year by the Advisory Commission on Intergovernmental Relations concluded that even "lawyers tended to be unaware of their state constitutions."[63] This is far more disturbing than the often cited fact that far more Americans can name the Three Stooges than any member of the U.S. Supreme Court.

One might easily explain this disregard of state constitutions if state governments dealt with mere trivialities of no interest to ordinary people (or even if they raised no interesting "interpretive issues" of the kind that legal academics obsess over). But either assertion is preposterous. Daniel Rodriguez has noted that "the basic range of policies and policy choices made by state and local officials dwarf—indeed *always have dwarfed*—national political activity."[64] Even if one accepts the proposition that constitutional federalism—that is, a state autonomy free from national government control—is only relatively weakly protected by the national Constitution, there can be no doubt that many issues of great public importance are decided—or, *not* adequately confronted—within the states. State constitutions—again, think of California—are relevant to such decisions, whether one thinks of state-level constitutions of conversation or analogous constitutions of settlement that, by structuring state politics in certain ways, have significant consequences for the actual decisions that will be made.

Many have written in recent years about American provincialism regarding other countries, and there are occasional references throughout the book to what we might learn by looking at aspects of various constitutions around the world. But it is important to recognize a more important provincialism, which is the almost willful ignorance of what we might learn by looking at our own country and its extraordinarily rich constitutional experiences instead of remaining fixated on the singular U.S. Constitution. After all, there may be contemporary models of truly well-governed states; if so, it would be useful to try to understand if formal institutions might contribute to such a blessed state.

D. Why will the role of courts and judges be treated only in two chapters—and why will there be so little discussion of judicial opinions in the rest of the book?

Courts are especially important with regard to the Constitution of Conversation. There will *always* be litigation about "equal protection" or the meaning of "freedom of speech" because these are what political theorists call "essentially contested concepts." Equally important, there will always be people and groups interested in bringing such cases before courts in the hope that they can win victories perhaps unavailable through other institutions, such as legislatures or administrative agencies. And if we concentrate on those issues that are brought to the attention of courts, we will necessarily have to discuss what we believe the role of courts should be. Furthermore, we would also necessarily have to discuss the processes by which courts and other adjudicators assign concrete meanings to the contested concepts.

But if one takes seriously the notion of the Constitution of Settlement, then by definition there will be little litigation testing what has become settled. Even those who were upset at the delay of President Obama's inauguration until January 20 did not run off to the nearest courthouse in search of a determination that because this was so stupid it was therefore unconstitutional. Similarly, no one outraged at the equality of voting power between California and Wyoming in the Senate would file suit claiming that it violates the Constitution in addition to being indefensible under any attractive version of twenty-first century democratic theory.

Two chapters *do* address the role of courts and judges, but only because courts are significant institutions; concomitantly, a host of interesting questions arise with regard to designing judicial systems, including our own. Begin only with the fact that the U.S. Constitution is virtually unique in its establishment of a judiciary appointed and confirmed for life by highly active and self-interested politicians. Most readers probably live in states that elect judges, and very few live in a state or another country that grants its judges what might be called "true life" tenure, that is, tenure until death rather than a stipulated age like seventy or seventy-five. Again, this illustrates the importance that *comparative constitutional analysis* plays in this book. But, as already implied, there is certainly no reason from the perspective of the Constitution of Settlement to treat courts as more significant than legislatures or executives, so two chapters are more than sufficient.

The argument for putting courts "in their place," at least with regard to the Constitution of Settlement, also explains why cases are basically absent. If there is no litigation—because we are talking only about what is deemed to be settled—there are no opinions to read or discuss. It really is as simple as that!

IV. CONCLUSION: THE FOUR CHILDREN

Anyone who has ever attended a Seder knows of the parable of the "four children," described as "wise," "simple," "evil," and "the one who does not know even what to ask." For our purposes, perhaps the most important division is between the "wise" and "evil" children, for the difference is rooted in *identification*, not in cognitive knowledge. Signifying shared membership in the community of questioners (and answerers), the "wise child" asks, "What is the meaning of the events described in the Seder service to *us*?" The "evil child," on the other hand, asks, "What is the meaning of these events to *you*?" thereby indicating a profound lack of identification and membership.

I would certainly be gratified to have readers from abroad, who are simply curious about American politics—or, perhaps, are charged with designing a new constitution for their own polities and wondering if there are any valuable lessons, either positive or negative, to be learned from the broad American experience with constitutionalism. There is no reason at all to expect such readers to view themselves as part of the American political community, just as a reader from Massachusetts is unlikely to feel part of what is distinctive about the Oregon political community as instantiated in its constitution. That being said, I anticipate that most of my audience will be other Americans, almost all of whom are also citizens of one of the fifty states. But common citizenship is not enough to assure that we share a sense of community in the enterprise of achieving the magnificent goals set out in the Preamble to the U.S. Constitution. Some readers, even Americans, may be sufficiently alienated to ask only what the Preamble means to *others*. My hope is that you will be "wise" readers and citizens who are willing to see us as involved in a set of common projects—most dramatically at the national level but in our respective states as well—even if you have genuine worry about our capacities for effective self-government. Those most committed to enhancing that capacity might be especially likely to offer "loving criticism" of our various constitutions, including the one drafted in Philadelphia in 1787. We should not allow flaws and limitations inherent in the Constitution of Settlement to prevent us from aspiring to create the kind of country (or states) we desire for ourselves and our posterity.

2

Of Compromises and Constitutions

The Philadelphia Convention—like all other constitutional conclaves—teaches a variety of lessons about constitutional formation. One is that there is a basic decision involved between continuing with some existing set of "rules laid down" or choosing instead what one thinks best for the social order, even if the latter requires significant transformations from the status quo. This, to a great extent, involves a discussion of legal rules, such as those established by the Articles of Confederation, which are discussed extensively in Chapter 16. But there are other rules, including moral rules (or norms), that are inevitably a part of any discussion of what constitutions should say. But do these moral norms have absolute priority when designing constitutions? "Free constitutions," James Madison once wrote, "will rarely if ever be formed without reciprocal concessions."[1]

Do such concessions sometimes include waiving what one might consider, for very good reason, fundamental norms of justice? Ideally, we hope that the answer would be a resounding no. This answer would be offered by anyone influenced by John Rawls, the dominant American political philosopher since World War II. Rawls's *A Theory of Justice* (1971) used as its central conceit the notion of deriving basic norms of politics behind a "veil of ignorance" that limited one to having almost no knowledge of his or her own concrete social reality (including, for that matter, gender identity). Rawls argued that under such circumstances—especially if additional assumptions about risk aversion are held—rational decisionmakers would almost automatically choose (so long as they remained "rational") what all of us would readily accept as the basic norms of justice and "fairness." Since one would not know what one's identity (in terms of race, gender, religion, economic resources, etc.) would be when the veil was lifted, one would make sure that everyone was guaranteed certain basic rights and liberties. It is not my intention to offer any further analysis of the Rawlsian argument; many bookshelves could be filled with both critiques and defenses of Rawls's positions. Rather, there is simply no reason to believe that the U.S. Constitution, or any other constitution in the history of the world, was drafted under Rawlsian conditions of fundamental ignorance of one's own situation and the linked inability to predict whether one would be the beneficiary or loser under any particular proposed constitutional settlement. Constitutions are *always* drafted in what might be called "real time" by people who have a very strong knowledge of the groups with which they identify. Not surprisingly, they are primarily concerned with protecting the perceived interests of those groups. This is to say only that constitutions are the products of political struggle and invariably respond to what might be termed "facts on the ground." The desire to actually achieve a constitutional settlement thus may require a willingness to compromise one's basic convictions, including what may be described—especially by critics—as "selling out" the (legitimate) interests of one group in order to achieve the greater goal of establishing a constitutional order.

To be sure, I suggested in the last chapter that readers detach themselves from the immediate political moment by contemplating the powers they would wish (or at least be willing) to grant the (unknown and unpredictable) president who will be elected in 2016 (or 2020) and inaugurated in 2017 (or 2021). This invitation gestures to Rawls; by adopting a longer time horizon, we can tame some of the partisan passions almost necessarily present if we focus on known political leaders or groups. The question facing anyone grappling with issues of constitutional design is whether people can successfully lift their eyes from present actualities and take a longer-term perspective. Still, even if able to do that, one would inevitably be required to decide among conflicting values and therefore discern what kinds of compromise one would be willing to make.

I. CONCRETE STRUGGLES (AND COMPROMISES) IN PHILADELPHIA

The delegates who did come to Philadelphia were hardly agreed on many basic issues. Consider only the two central issues that generated the most famous and enduring "great compromises" that made the Constitution a political possibility: political representation and slavery.

A. The basis of representation

1. The Senate

Representation is obviously a major issue facing any constitutional designer. Any decisions reflect debatable resolutions to profound questions of political theory. But those decisions inevitably have real consequences for the various interests—each eager to maximize its own power—contending in the here and now over the shape of a new government. But for now we focus on the issue that admirers of the Convention call the Great Compromise: the resolution of the deep conflict between large and small states over representation in the Senate. By definition, proportional representation based on population favors large states; equal representation, small states. The Great Compromise was to have one house committed to each principle. The House of Representatives would rest on proportional representation, while the Senate would be organized around the equal representation of states. This meant that Delaware, which was the smallest state (population of about 59,000 in the 1790 census), would have the same number of senators as Virginia, the largest state (population of 691,000, if one included its slaves). Indeed, the delegates from Delaware had been instructed— apparently at the behest of John Dickinson, one of the delegates—by the legislature that picked them to walk out of the Convention if the principle of equal representation was not adopted. In the late eighteenth century, the population ratio of Virginia to Delaware was approximately 11.5:1; today, the comparable ratio is that of California to Wyoming, approximately 70:1.

Madison, a Virginian, was appalled by equal representation of states and was determined to reject the idea. But he was ultimately persuaded to accept it. The reason was not that he changed his mind about its merits in some abstract sense; rather, he accepted as credible the threat by Delaware and its allies to simply walk out of the Convention, torpedoing the whole project of constitutional revision. (Perhaps it was also relevant that the small states outnumbered the large ones and that the voting rule in Philadelphia was by state, not by individual delegates.) If one believed, as did Madison and many other delegates to the Philadelphia Convention, that the United States would not long survive under what they viewed as a thoroughly inadequate Articles of Confederation, failure to achieve a new constitution would doom the Union. Thus came about the Great Compromise, by which the Constitution became a genuine possibility and the Union was preserved.

2. The House of Representatives

But the Senate was not the only forum for compromises about representation. The House represents states on the basis of their population. This may seem a simple enough notion, until one addresses the all-important question: how, precisely, would the delegates define the population that to be "represented"? Recall the comparison offered above between Virginia's and Delaware's populations. As a matter of fact, Delaware was also a slave state, as were most states in 1787. A 1783 case decided in Massachusetts did suggest that slavery was no longer legitimate in that state, so perhaps we can say that the approximately 379,000 persons counted in the 1790 census from that state were all "free." New Hampshire, with its population of 96,540 in 1790, was also "free," inasmuch as slavery had seemingly been legally and morally delegitimated there as well. But slavery did not end in New York until 1827,[2] which means that the population recorded in at least the first four censuses included both free persons and slaves.

The central question was whether the basis of representation in the House would rest only on the free population or on the entire population instead. Note that this differs significantly from arguing that representation should be based either on the number of people entitled to vote or the actual voters. We are referring to the most elemental distinction between free (even if subordinated) persons, such as women and children on the one hand, and slaves on the other. The decision was to adopt the Three-Fifths Compromise, whereby the representation base was computed by adding the number of all free persons and three-fifths of the slaves. Thus, 100 free persons and 100 slaves would compute as a total of 160 persons. If the representation were based only on free persons, then there would be no "bonus" for slave states. Whatever one thinks of the three-fifths rule, it had nothing to do with slaveholders believing that their slaves were only three-fifths human. The slave states would have been utterly delighted to count each slave as a whole person, *so long as no right to vote was attached to that status*. It was the anti-slave states that insisted on slaves counting as only three-fifths of free persons, and that was indeed a compromise from their preferred outcome that slaves not count at all in computing the basis for representation. And, after all, why should they count? There was no plausible argument that those entitled to vote in a slave state would take the interests of slaves into account, though there were arguments made at the time about women being "virtually represented" by their husbands, fathers, or brothers. (One need not agree with such arguments with regard to the wives, children, or sisters. However, it was widely thought at the time to be a good argument, whereas no one made similar virtual representation arguments that required masters to identify with their slaves and thus take their interests into account.)

So the outcome in Philadelphia was that slave states got an enormous bonus with regard to the number of representatives they would be electing. And this bonus scarcely stopped at the entrance to the House of Representatives. Given that the president was elected via the electoral college, in which the vote allotted each state was the total of its number of representatives and its two senatorial votes, slave states also gained additional power to select our chief executive. This might help to explain why seven of the first nine presidents were slave owners—the two exceptions being the Massachusetts presidents, John Adams and his son John Quincy Adams, each of whom served only one unsuccessful term. John Adams, however, would have been reelected in 1800 had it not been for the slavery bonus that gave Thomas Jefferson the advantage. Moreover, John Quincy Adams was elected by the House of Representatives, given that none of the candidates received a majority of the electoral votes. (The House votes by state, with each state delegation having one vote, so Adams had to concern himself only with gaining a majority of the states in the House rather than a majority of the actual representatives.)

The three-fifths rule affects not only the House and the presidency; inasmuch as it is presidents who nominate members for the Supreme Court, it also helps to explain why the Supreme Court was consistently pro-slavery until 1861. So, the three-fifths rule takes us fully into the belly of the beast, in other words, the quite literally "compromised" nature of the original Constitution and the utter inapplicability of any "veil of ignorance" notion associated with Rawls's ideal political process.

B. Collaborating with slavery

Hard-wired structures versus parchment barriers

Thus, the second great compromise—and one may believe that it was more important to the nature of the American Union than the makeup of the Senate—involved slavery. Three important aspects of that compromise were found in the Constitution: (1) the fugitive slave clause, (2) the protection of the international slave trade until 1808, and (3) the three-fifths clause.

It's worth taking a few moments to distinguish among these three aspects of the Constitution. The first one, the fugitive slave clause by which states promised to return any slaves who had "unlawfully" escaped from a slave state, might be described, in the dismissive words used by James Madison in the forty-eighth *Federalist*, as a "parchment barrier." That is, the text of the Constitution did not include a mechanism of enforcement; nor, as is well known, did it even use the words *slave* or *slavery*. Slave states had to rely on the good faith of other states, some of which were already quite dubious about the legitimacy of slavery. Yet one had to believe that these latter states would readily comply with the implicit promise to return fugitive slaves (and not only indentured servants who decided to renege on their contractual commitment to work for a certain number of years before becoming a full-scale member of the free labor force).

To be sure, Congress passed the Fugitive Slave Law in 1793 that provided some teeth to the guarantee. However, there were no guarantees in 1787 that Congress would in fact pass such a law; nor is it absolutely clear—from a reading of the grant of powers to Congress in Article One, Section 8 of the Constitution—that such a law would necessarily be constitutional. (As a matter of fact, the Supreme Court, in an 1842 opinion by Justice Joseph Story of Massachusetts, *did* uphold the Fugitive Slave

Law as within Congress's power, largely on the grounds that any other conclusion would imperil the Union—as might well have been the case.) Moreover, there was the felt need in 1850 to pass a new Fugitive Slave Act, as part of the so-called Compromise of 1850, inasmuch as the mechanisms established in 1793 were scarcely thought sufficient to protect slaveowners as fully as they desired. Abraham Lincoln, for all of his resolute anti-slavery beliefs, defended the 1850 Act as part of carrying out the bargain with slaveowners living in states that recognized the legitimacy of slavery. The 1850 Act was generated by the fact that American politics in the 1840s and thereafter amply demonstrated that many of the residents of non-slave states—and state leaders responsive to these residents—were not at all eager to comply with their ostensible duties to return alleged fugitives.

The protection of the international slave trade for twenty years took a somewhat different form; it was presented as an absolute limitation on the powers that Congress had been assigned in Article I, Section 8. One might well think, for example, that Congress's power to regulate inter-state and international commerce easily reached to prohibition of the slave trade. Maybe yes, maybe no. The real point is that it didn't matter. The international slave trade was given an embedded status for two decades (at which time Congress in fact prohibited American participation in the international slave trade). But what if Congress had jumped the gun by passing a prohibitory law in, say, 1802? One might easily enough say that it would have been unconstitutional for Congress to do so, but who, precisely, would get to say? Perhaps the president, arguably under a constitutional duty to veto any such legislation, whatever his own beliefs about slavery. But one can also imagine that someone involved in the international slave trade would have run to the nearest court, claiming that Congress had no authority to stop the trade prior to 1808. This involves the question, among other things, of judicial review, which will be the subject of later discussion.

A gigantic leap of faith might not have been necessary in 1787 with regard to protection of the international slave trade at least until 1808, compared with the somewhat vaguer promises contained in the fugitive slave clause, but there was still no self-enforcing mechanism for the bar-gain struck in Philadelphia. One had to trust Congress not to pass a statute abolishing the trade, or trust the president to veto such a statute, or trust the judiciary to invalidate any such act that was, perhaps, passed over a presidential veto.

It was entirely different, though, with regard to the three-fifths clause. All one had to do was count the population in the constitutionally mandated census—an important part of the Constitution, incidentally—and then multiply the number of slaves by three-fifths to get the total population by which representation would be calculated. To return to a central theme of this book, it provides nothing about which to have a conversation as to constitutional meaning; there is only a settled rule, the violation of which—by, say, the concerted refusal of a majority of free state representatives to seat the "extra" representatives sent by slave states—would trigger a basic collapse of the polity and, perhaps, civil war.

III. REFLECTIONS ON COMPROMISE

It is worth taking some time to reflect on some of the broader problems presented by the notion of "compromise." Is a willingness to compromise necessarily a virtue, or does it sometimes raise the most troublesome of questions? One view was well expressed by Edmund Burke in 1775, in his great speech criticizing the policies of King George III and his ministers vis-à-vis the American colonies, which he gave just weeks before the outbreak of revolutionary violence at Concord and Lexington and more than a year before the American Declaration of Independence. "All government—indeed every human benefit and enjoyment, every virtue and every prudent act—is founded on compromise and barter."[3] Madison's emphasis on the necessity of "reciprocal concessions" in order to form "free constitutions" can be viewed as supportive of Burke's insight.

These eighteenth-century insights are certainly not absent from our present understanding of politics. A basic textbook written by the late political scientist Clinton Rossiter began: "No America without democracy, no democracy without politics, no parties without compromise and moderation."[4] More recently, an anguished 2011 article by former Representative Mickey Edwards decrying the partisanship of contemporary

American politics notes that the very absence of a "consensus" in our 300-million-person polity makes it even more necessary to recognize that *"compromise* is the key ingredient in legislative decisionmaking."[5]

Especially illuminating in this regard is a remarkable book, *Constitution by Consensus,* written in the aftermath of over two years of intense meetings and debates among a group of diverse Israelis about what form a written constitution for that country might take. The group was not so diverse as it might have been; it included no Israeli Arabs, for example. But it certainly drew from both the secular and sectarian Jewish communities, as well as from strong nationalists and more cosmopolitan liberals. The first section of the book is a group of essays titled "I Believe," in which the participants write quite candidly of their mixed feelings regarding their common enterprise. The chair of the group, Arye Carmon, refers to "compromise as an integral element" of resolving the "existential need in Israel now."[6] Not surprisingly, the word *compromise* reappears often in the various statements and in a final collective statement acknowledging that necessary "compromises and concessions will be painful" in order to achieve the goal.[7] There is, however, no guarantee that compromises—because they *are* painful—will in fact take place. There is only the expression of a strong belief that a failure to compromise may be fatal to the future of the Israeli project, however defined.

There was nothing at all inevitable about the secession of the American colonies from the British Empire. A willingness on the part of King George III and Lord North to compromise and barter, or to adopt more moderate policies, might have fundamentally transformed subsequent world history. The events of 1775–1783 exemplify what can happen when an obtuse officialdom refuses to compromise and instead stands on ostensible principle, in this case, the continued sovereign authority of the British Parliament over its colonies.

Similarly, one can view the events of 1787–1790 as equal exemplars of the importance (and presumptive goods) attached to a willingness to compromise. There simply would never have been a Constitution without the two especially important compromises involving slavery and the Senate. But the addition of the Bill of Rights itself can be viewed more as a compromise by supporters of the Constitution (like Madison) than as a reflection of any deep conviction that the addition of so many "parchment barriers"—likely to make little difference to the actual governance of the new political system—would truly enhance the Constitution. (As a matter of fact, the Bill of Rights was almost entirely irrelevant to the American constitutional order until well into the twentieth century.)

Moreover, consider an all-important 1790 dinner arranged by Thomas Jefferson, motivated, as he later wrote, by his belief "that reasonable men, consulting together coolly, could [not] fail, by some mutual sacrifices of opinion, to form a compromise which was to save the union."[8] The Compromise of 1790, as Stanford historian Jack Rakove labels it, accomplished this goal by trading Jefferson's support for national assumption of states' war debts—a windfall for financial speculators—in return for Hamilton's support for establishing the new nation's capital along the Potomac River in what would of course come to be called Washington, D.C.

One can fast-forward to the aftermath of the shellacking taken by Democrats in the 2010 midterm elections, when President Obama negotiated a compromise with Senate Republicans that, among other things, extended all the Bush-era tax cuts for two years. Castigated by many members of his own party, the president answered them at a news conference, noting that the United States is

> a big, diverse country and people have a lot of complicated positions[;] it means that in order to get stuff done, we're going to compromise...This country was founded on compromise. I couldn't go through the front door at this country's founding. And if we were really thinking about ideal positions, we wouldn't have a union.[9]

So is this a set of stories designed to vindicate Burke and underscore the necessity of compromise and, concomitantly, to scoff at those stiff-necked persons resistant to compromise? Is *everything* subject to compromise, or are there circumstances when one expects people to draw lines in the name of presumed absolutes? Should we understand President Obama to in effect praise those anti-slavery delegates who accepted the various compromises on slavery (which had the consequence of entrenching the oppression of his wife Michelle's ancestors) lest they risk the dissolution of the Union?

Return to Israel—one of the few countries in the modern without a formal written constitution—and consider the following statement made by a member of the Israeli Knesset in 1948 during the debate over whether the new country should adopt a written constitution:

> I would like to warn: the experience of drafting a constitution would necessarily entail a severe, vigorous uncompromising war of opinions. A war of spirit, which is defined by the gruesome concept of *Kulturkampf*...Is this a convenient time for a thorough and penetrating examination of our essence and purpose? It is clear that there is no room for any compromises, any concessions or mutual agreements, since no man can compromise and concede on issues upon which his belief and soul depend.[10]

A similar comment was offered by the Israeli minister of welfare: "The Jewish people are willing to resign themselves to many things," said Yitzhak Meir Levi, "but the moment the issue touches upon the foundations of their faith, they are unable to compromise. If you wish to foist upon us this type of life or a constitution that will be contrary to the laws of the Torah, we will not accept it!"[11] These turned out to be winning arguments, inasmuch as Israel did not in fact adopt a canonical written constitution. As Arye Carmon and his associates emphasize, Israel will get a constitution in the twenty-first century only if those like Levi agree to compromise in return for similarly anguished compromise from their secular opponents.

Perhaps Americans are tempted to view comments (or threats) like those above as simply an example of sectarian intransigence that we in this country were blessedly spared in our own halcyon days of 1787 and the drafting of our own Constitution. We *did* get a Constitution, purchased through two central compromises and a host of smaller ones. There was, one might argue, relatively little kicking the can down the road for decisions to be made later on. Instead, slavery *was* protected, and small states *did* get their disproportionate power in the Senate.

But consider now arguments made by another Israeli, the philosopher Avishai Margalit, in his recent book *On Compromise and Rotten Compromises*.[12] As the title suggests, he sharply distinguishes between acceptable compromises and those that should be condemned as "rotten" and therefore indefensible, except *perhaps* (and therefore perhaps not even then) in the most exceptional of conditions. He defines a "rotten political compromise" as one that agrees "to establish or maintain an inhuman regime, a regime of cruelty and humiliation, that is, a regime that does not treat humans as humans."[13]

It takes no great feat of imagination to think of slavery in this context and therefore to ask whether the U.S. Constitution was purchased through a truly rotten compromise, what abolitionist William Lloyd Garrison so memorably called "a covenant with death and an agreement with hell" that, indeed, led to further compromises to preserve the Union, such as the already-mentioned dreadful strengthening of the 1793 Fugitive Slave Act in the interests of slaveowners as part of the Compromise of 1850. (A distinguished historian refers to the collection of bills passed in 1850 as the *Armistice* of 1850, precisely because it responded to the already-existing tensions between North and South that exploded into full-fledged war roughly a decade later.[14]) Margalit quotes Garrison's statement that "with the North, the preservation of the Union is placed above all other things— above honor, justice, freedom, integrity of soul."[15] There is more than a trace of similarity between Garrison and Rabbi Levi quoted above, but does that automatically lead us to condemn one or the other?

Are there times to reject compromise in the name of higher values? Should one accord some validity to the dictum *Fiat justitia ruat caelum*, usually translated as "May justice be done though the heavens fall"? Or, on the contrary, should *everything* be subject to sacrifice in order to prevent such a dire outcome? Consider an exchange at the Virginia ratifying convention between George Mason, a leading opponent of ratification, and James Madison regarding the Constitution's guarantee of a twenty-year period protecting the international slave trade before Congress could regulate (and presumably ban) it. Mason was willing to accept the prospect of union without "the Southern States," by which he meant Georgia and South Carolina, which apparently would not accept a Constitution that did not protect the slave trade. As Pauline Maier writes in her magisterial history of the ratification debates, "Mason was ready to leave those states out of the Union unless they agreed to discontinue 'this disgraceful trade.'" What was Madison's response? "'Great as the evil is, a dismemberment of the Union would be worse.'"[16]

Two recent discussions of Henry Clay—known to American history buffs as "the Great Compromiser"—are illuminating. In the first, historian Andrew Cayton, reviewing two books on Clay,[17] noted that both authors appeared to view "compromise as an unqualified good...Good men (Clay) compromise; bad men ([John C.] Calhoun) don't." But, wrote Cayton, "that approach obscures the obvious fact that...sometimes people value a sense of justice above everything else. After all, had the Founders of the Republic pursued compromise in 1776, there might never have been a Union to save. Similarly, the price of compromise in 1850 was prolonged enslavement for millions." Indeed, if one privileges compromise above all, particularly when viewed as instrumentally necessary either to form the Union (as in 1787) or to save it (as in 1850), then what do we wish to say about Abraham Lincoln, who refused to compromise on the issue of extending slavery into the territories of the United States? Had he been willing to compromise, it would almost certainly have prevented the war that broke out in 1861 and cost the lives of a full 2 percent of the American population. Lincoln, of course, could not have known in advance the full costs of the war, but he certainly had reason to know that he was choosing war by what many viewed as his intransigence on the issue of allowing slaves in the territories. Cayton concludes his review by stating that "we remember Lincoln more than Clay, in short, not just because he saved the Union, but also because he insisted that a Union worth saving was a Union that stood for something more than itself."

At least as interesting as Cayton's review was the second discussion, in the maiden speech of Kentucky's Senator Rand Paul to his new colleagues—he was swept in by the "Tea Party" tidal wave in November 2010—in which he took the occasion to distance himself from his Kentucky predecessor Henry Clay. Paul noted that on arriving in Washington, "one of my new colleagues asked me with a touch of irony and a twinkle in his eye, 'Will you be a great compromiser?'"[18] To his credit, Paul took the question with consummate seriousness and devoted his first speech to answering it. He began by describing Clay's life story as, at best, sending a "mixed message," given that so many of his compromises involved slavery. He critically compared Clay with other great Americans of the time, including William Lloyd Garrison and Frederick Douglass. He also spoke at length about Cassius Clay, a cousin of Clay's who became an abolitionist.[19]

"Cassius Clay was a hero," said Paul, "but he was permanently estranged from Henry Clay. Henry Clay made no room for the true believers, for the abolitionists." And then Paul asks the key question: "Who are our heroes? Are we fascinated and enthralled by the Great Compromiser or his cousin Cassius Clay?"

Presumably, it occasions no surprise that Paul casts his own vote for Cassius against Henry. "As long as I sit at Henry Clay's desk, I will remember his lifelong desire to forge agreement, but I will also keep close to my heart the principled stand of his cousin, Cassius Clay, who refused to forsake the life of any human simply to find agreement." And perhaps it occasions no surprise that the *Washington Post* headlined a commentary on the speech, "Rand Paul, the Great Uncompromiser,"[20] in which Dana Milbank, quoting a number of historians, takes Paul to task for his seeming disrespect to Henry Clay. He notes, altogether accurately, that Abraham Lincoln was also a great admirer of Clay. Finally, Milbank plays the counterfactual history card, suggesting that Clay's compromises, including the Compromise of 1850, were eminently defensible: they in effect purchased the North additional time to prepare for the oncoming war. Had secession occurred in 1850, Milbank argues (again quoting some eminent historians) the Confederacy might well have been successful. Not only is there no way of knowing this for sure, but there is also a recent argument by Paul Finkelman, one of leading historians of slavery, that the North was even stronger than the South, relatively speaking, in 1850 than in 1860, so a civil war at that time might have led to an easier Union victory at less cost than 2 percent of the entire population of the United States.[21] At the very least, this illustrates the inevitable admixture of abstract principle and empirical consequences in making basic decisions about the legitimacy of compromise—and the selection of one's heroes.

So, for better or worse, one *must* ask if the heavens would have fallen had there been no Compromise of 1850 or even no Constitution at all in 1787 (or, perhaps, as George Mason suggested was possible, a Union that did not include South Carolina or Georgia?). If the Philadelphia Convention had failed, it is certainly likely that there would have been at least two, possibly three, separate countries taking form, distinguished, among other ways, by their stance toward chattel slavery. Was it worth entrenching slavery into the Constitution through, most importantly, the three-fifths clause, which gave slave states a huge bonus not only in the House of Representatives but also in the electoral college? More to the point, how do we calculate worth?

There are very good reasons to believe that our collective history would have been very different had the Convention not succeeded. As political scientist David Hendrickson has well argued, the Philadelphians were consumed by the fear that multiple countries in what we today think of as the United States would no more be able to remain at peace than the multiple countries sharing the European continent. Thus the overwhelming *necessity* for a peace pact, which—as we all know—almost inevitably requires compromises, often with extraordinarily unattractive enemies (or, more accurately, those one wishes to turn into former enemies.) Truly "imposed" peace settlements, like that at Versailles after World War I, rarely prove stable and indeed may provoke such a backlash on the part of the ostensibly victimized state that it ends up triggering yet another war. The so-called Reconstruction Amendments added (i.e., imposed on defeated white Southerners) in the immediate aftermath of the Civil War, particularly the Fifteenth Amendment prohibiting denial of the right to vote on grounds of race, had remarkably little effect on the law of race relations until almost a century later, not least because the Compromise of 1877 basically sacrificed the interests of beleaguered African Americans to those of Southern whites who were ever more welcomed back into the Union they had tried to leave.

As already noted, the compromise over slavery was not the only one deemed necessary to purchase acquiescence to the Constitution that was signed on September 17, 1787. There was also the decision to accept the extortionate demand of Delaware and other small states for equal voting power in the Senate. As a matter of fact, as Jack Rakove noted, Madison correctly viewed this as a "defeat, not [a] compromise"[22] for a very simple reason: American bicameralism, unlike many bicameral systems around the world, gives each house a death lock over any legislation passed by the other. We have a constitution filled with veto points, and among the most important of these is the ability of what Madison regarded as an indefensibly structured Senate to kill any and all legislation it finds unacceptable. A "compromise" might have allowed, say, the House, with the support of the president, to override a senatorial veto with an attainable supermajority, as is possible in some European bicameral systems. We pay the costs every day, even over two centuries later, for *both* of the great compromises that procured the 1787 Constitution.

Even if one finds the Senate as created by the Constitution loathsome—the best that Madison could do, as we shall explore at greater length later, was to describe equal voting power in the Senate as a "lesser evil" (to having no Constitution at all)—would one describe it as a "rotten compromise" similar in its moral offensiveness to slavery? Or would one consider that an example of rhetorical "wretched excess"? Politics, as both Burke and President Obama suggested, is indeed the art of accepting all sorts of "lesser evils," and one might well agree with Madison that equal voting power in the Senate was a price worth paying in 1787. This does not in the least suggest that we should not wish in our own time to have a better Constitution than the one we have, but that's a different topic.

Perhaps the correct analogy is the price paid in 1945 to gain assent to the creation of the United Nations, which involved not only the "great power" veto system in the Security Council but also the de facto granting of extra representation to the USSR by giving seats to Ukraine and Belarus. That the particularities of the veto system may make little sense two generations later—and, indeed, may do a great deal of damage to prospects for a stable world order—does little to demonstrate that it was a mistake in 1945. *Rather, the mistake is feeling ourselves indelibly wedded to such institutional structures long after their rationales have ceased to make much sense.*

One might argue that one of the differences between the two "great compromises" of 1787 was that those who made the compromise with regard to voting power in the Senate bore the costs. That is, states such as Virginia were the big losers in the decision to give equal voting power to Delaware and Rhode Island, just as the United States and the rest of the West paid a marginal cost by giving the Soviet Union extra representation in the General Assembly. Bargaining, by definition, involves a willingness to bear direct personal costs in order to attain a desired goal. Madison, as one of Virginia's delegates, ultimately decided that it was a cost worth paying by Virginians, as did the Virginia ratifying convention when it decided to grant its own assent to the Constitution. And Virginia was the big beneficiary of the Three-Fifths Compromise, which increased its power in the House and the electoral college (and therefore the White House and the Supreme Court appointed by presidents). But the parallel doesn't really work, for the obvious point is that those who paid the primary costs of the Great Compromise involving slavery, the slaves themselves, were in no plausible sense represented in Philadelphia or the beneficiaries of the successful founding of a new political order. Slavery *did* ultimately end, but only as the result of a catastrophic war, itself fundamentally caused by various aspects of the Constitution, and its carnage.

IV. STRUCTURING COMPROMISES

It is worth noting that some structures may be more conducive to encouraging compromise than others. We shall certainly have occasion to discuss this further when considering institutions like bicameralism or the presidential veto. But the question of how one assures a tilt toward compromise was very much at the center of organizing the Philadelphia Convention. A number of decisions made compromise easier than it might otherwise have been. Consider the remarkable fact, almost incomprehensible to anyone living today, that the vow of secrecy taken by all of the delegates was maintained through the entire Convention (and for many years afterward, for that matter). There were no leaks, period. This has led the political theorist Jon Elster, studying the procedures involved in the drafting of a number of national constitutions, to argue that, in many important respects, the opacity characteristic of the Philadelphians is far preferable to transparency, at least if one wishes to reach agreement. This is the case precisely because transparency, by definition, means that often-intense outsiders can monitor the deals on offer and do whatever they can to thwart them, even threatening retribution against their ostensible representatives, should they be viewed as compromising vital interests.[23] This is obviously an empirical assertion, and full consideration is beyond the scope of this book. It is certainly plausible, though; assume for argument's sake that it is correct.[24] Does this suggest that one should actively *prefer* compromise-producing structures, even if that means reduced transparency in the process by which agreements are produced? Carrie Menkel-Meadow has written that "the brilliance of our Framers... was not only in the substance of their constitutive documents, but in the processes they selected to create them,"[25] including, most obviously, secrecy. If Elster and Menkel-Meadow are correct in linking the success of the Convention, assuming that one in fact admires the outcome, to the almost complete opacity of its process, does this have any implications for the institutions actually designed in a constitutional convention? If opacity is thought conducive to gaining a constitution in the first place, then why would one not infer that it would be equally conducive to gaining more desirable legislation than a transparent political system?

If one believes that one explanation for the present polarization and gridlock in American politics is too much transparency, might one suggest greater secrecy and therefore reduced accountability (save perhaps for whatever accountability attaches to the final product of the compromise, e.g., the text of the Constitution itself, a medical care bill, or whatever)? To a significant extent, this turns democracy, which is often thought to require a great deal of transparency in order to gain an adequate sense of the public opinion on which most democratic theories rely, into a negative rather than a positive attribute of a political system. Precisely this is argued by former Obama budget director Peter Orszag in an article forthrightly titled "Too Much of a Good Thing: Why We Need Less Democracy": "Our current legislative gridlock is making it increasingly difficult for lawmakers to tackle the issues that our central our country's future," he writes. He calls for "jettison[ing] the Civics 101 fairy tale about pure representative democracy." Instead, we should "begin to build a new set of rules and institutions that would make legislative inertia less detrimental to our nation's long-term health." Orszag advocates, among other things, the increasing use of "more independent institutions," such as commissions of independent experts who are empowered to make binding decisions unless Congress affirmatively overrules them.[26] In fact, the accountability mechanisms that are generally thought to be the sine qua non of representative democracy may assure the near inability to make decisions at all about important issues of public policy—particularly if much of the relevant electorate is taken by the idea of an "uncompromising" champion of their interests doing battle against an often-demonized opposition. Transparency might have doomed the Philadelphian enterprise and therefore assured that the United States had no Constitution at all.

V. THE CENTRAL QUESTION: WAS THE
CONSTITUTION WORTH IT?

What *does* one think about the U.S. Constitution and the compromises that were almost certainly necessary to achieve it? Does the willingness to compromise bring honor to the Framers? Do we share Margalit's view that the entrenching of certain slaveowner interests was ultimately a morally indefensible "rotten settlement" because it required accepting chattel slavery? Recall his definition of "rotten compromise": "an agreement to establish or maintain an inhuman regime, a regime of cruelty and humiliation, that is, a regime that does not treat humans as humans." Can there be any doubt that this describes chattel slavery in America?

It is often argued, altogether accurately, that one cannot make an omelet without breaking some eggs. And, to revert to Burke, we properly honor those who make significant concessions, even regarding their most precious values at times, in order to achieve or preserve peace. Indeed, it is no coincidence that Margalit is a longtime critic of many Israeli policies vis-à-vis Palestinians and laments the uncompromising rigidity of many Israeli positions, just as he is critical of similar rigidity on the part of Palestinian leadership. Thus he describes the aim of his own book as "provid[ing] strong advocacy for compromises in general, and compromises for the sake of peace in particular."[27] But there are limits, and his notion of rotten compromise is just such a limit. Ultimately, better no peace than a rotten compromise that preserves the peace by the ruthless subjugation of others.

But was peace or war the dilemma facing the Philadelphians and those called upon to ratify the Constitution afterward? One might believe the answer was yes, for the strongest arguments for ratification in fact involved the various threats—today we would speak of national security—facing the young country from Great Britain, France, Spain, and many American Indian tribes, some of them former allies of Great Britain in the Revolutionary War. After all, a basic purpose of the new Constitution, enunciated in the Preamble, is to provide for the common defense.

Alexander Hamilton offered an especially broad exegesis of this basic constitutional end when he wrote in Federalist 26 that the "powers [relating to the common defense] ought to exist without limitation, *because it is impossible to foresee or define the extent and variety of national exigencies, or the correspondent extent and variety of the means which may be necessary to satisfy them.* The circumstances that endanger the safety of nations are infinite, and for this reason no constitutional shackles can wisely be imposed on the power to which the care of it is committed." To adopt a modern phrase, one might ask if it was rational to view the United States in 1787 as facing an "existential threat" to its very existence. If so, that carries implications not only for the assignment of powers to the new government—in other words, whatever is necessary to meet the threat—but also for the making of compromises requisite to getting a constitution in the first place. In this context, think of the alliances countries enter into when fighting a war, particularly a war that is viewed as involving existential threats. The United States notably allied with Stalin's Soviet Union in order to fight (and defeat) Nazi Germany. There are times, as recently argued by Harvard Law Professor Robert Mnookin, that one must indeed make "pacts with the devil," even if, obviously, one wants to minimize the occasions for doing so.

I conclude with the following three questions:

1. If one assumes that the consequences of not reaching agreement in Philadelphia or not ratifying the proposed Constitution would have been dissolution of the Union *and* bloody warfare, resulting from the two or three countries being carved out along the Atlantic coast, does that justify the compromise on slavery and the consequent costs imposed on the slaves themselves?[28] If one defends the compromise on such basically consequentialist grounds, what implications does that have for those charged with drafting constitutions in the twenty-first century? Think only of the process of drafting new constitutions in Iraq or Afghanistan. How much of, say, the rights of women or of those who don't share a particular vision of Islam would one be willing to sacrifice in order to gain (relative) peace and avoid civil war and possibly catastrophic bloodshed, not to mention the bleeding over of such wars into adjacent countries like Iran and Pakistan?

2. What if one confidently believes that the failure to achieve consensus would have resulted in three separate countries—call them New England, Mid-Atlantica, and Dixie—that would have grown to interact with one another in the same way that the United States has learned to deal with

Canada and Mexico, sometimes awkwardly, but only rarely by embarking on war? Is compromise with slavery justified under this latter scenario? Under this set of assumptions, is Margalit correct in saying that the great compromise involving slavery was and remains a rotten compromise that, however explainable, is not defensible?

3. Can we simply avoid wrestling with such questions by declaring that what was done in 1787 is irrelevant to our own world and its concerns? That was then and this is now, one might say. But on what basis does one decide that the past is or is not relevant? Is there a historical statute of limitations after which it is "unfair" to dredge up what happened "long ago"? If so, when does that occur and, all importantly, who gets to decide when we as a society "move forward" and "put the past behind us" rather than wrestle with what may be monumental past injustices whose consequences resonate even in our own world today?

3

What Is the Point of Preambles
(in Contrast to the Rest
of a Constitution)?

Why discuss preambles in a book that emphasizes Constitutions of Settlement? One might think that preambles are quintessential examples of Constitutions of Conversation. After all, they often use abstract, even grandiose, words articulating value commitments like "justice" and "liberty," to mention just two of the key words in the Preamble to the U.S. Constitution. The reason to consider preambles is twofold. First, they often help us to understand the *point* of the particular constitution's enterprise. Evaluating constitutions requires having some sense of what they are intended to do, and it is a feature of the clauses that are the central subject of this book that they rarely, if ever, announce their purposes. To return to my favorite example, the Inauguration Day Clause, we are not told *why* January 20 is the appropriate day, only that it is the day required by the Twentieth Amendment. But the best way to address the Constitution of Settlement is to ask how well it does (or does not) work to achieve the constitution's purposes, and preambles are the first place one should look to find out what the ostensible purposes are.

Secondly, it is an anomaly of American—and much other—constitutional discourse that the Constitution of Conversation rarely includes overt reference to preambles, for reasons that are explored below. So, if one aim of this book is to encourage long overdue conversation about ignored features of our constitutions, then preambles have their own claim to our attention.

Relatively few drafters of the hundreds of written constitutions that now exist have limited themselves only to setting out basic institutional structures or even to enumerating the rights that their new constitutions should guarantee. Most constitutions also include preambles. Some are short and easy to memorize, as is the case with the Preamble to the U.S. Constitution: "We the People of the United States, in Order to form a more perfect Union, establish Justice, insure domestic Tranquility, provide for the common defence, promote the general Welfare, and secure the Blessings of Liberty to ourselves and our Posterity, do ordain and establish this Constitution for the United States of America." Some are even shorter, such as the preamble to the Texas Constitution: "Humbly invoking the blessings of Almighty god, the people of the State of Texas, do ordain and establish this Constitution." And there is the Greek Constitution, which begins simply by invoking the Greek Orthodox Trinity. Others are considerably longer, as illustrated by the preamble to the Massachusetts Constitution of 1780, the oldest continuing constitution in the United States:

> The end of the institution, maintenance and administration of government, is to secure the existence of the body-politic; to protect it; and to furnish the individuals who compose it, with the power of enjoying, in safety and tranquillity, their natural rights, and the blessings of life: And whenever these great objects are not obtained, the people have a right to alter the government, and to take measures necessary for their safety, prosperity and happiness.

> The body-politic is formed by a voluntary association of individuals: It is a social compact, by which the whole people covenants with each citizen, and each citizen with the whole people, that all shall be governed by certain laws for the common good. It is the duty of the people, therefore, in framing a Constitution of Government, to provide for an equitable mode of making laws, as well as for an impartial interpretation, and a faithful execution of them; that every man may, at all times, find his security in them.

> We, therefore, the people of Massachusetts, acknowledging, with grateful hearts, the goodness of the Great Legislator of the Universe, in affording us, in the course of His providence, an opportunity, deliberately and peaceably, without fraud, violence or surprise, of entering into an original, explicit, and solemn compact with each other; and of forming a new Constitution of Civil Government, for ourselves and posterity; and devoutly imploring His direction in so interesting a design, DO agree upon, ordain and establish, the following

Declaration of Rights, and Frame of Government, as the CONSTITUTION of
the COMMONWEALTH of MASSACHUSETTS.[1]

A number of preambles of contemporary national constitutions—such
as those of Croatia, Pakistan, or Vietnam—are far, far longer. Asking why
reveals important lessons about the functions of preambles, which—unlike
the rest of the constitutional text—may have relatively little to do with
"law" in its ordinary sense.

So, just as we should ask why most nations and states think it is important to have *written* constitutions rather than to rely on customary conventions, we should also ask why so many drafters of constitutions believe
that it is essential to include preambles. What is *their* point? With regard
to written constitutions, it is easy enough to emphasize a functionalist
explanation of the benefits of having clear-cut rules for the gaining and
maintenance (and loss) of political power that constitute a Constitution of
Settlement. It is harder, though, to come up with a functionalist account
of preambles, and not only because they often feature glittering generalities (like "establishing justice"). They also generally do not serve as invita-
tions to *legal* conversations; moreover, if they were taken too seriously with
regard to non-legal conversations, they might well serve more as sources
of instability than of settlement. So we must explain why constitutional
drafters feel impelled to precede the identification of political officials and
their powers—or even the delineation of protected rights—with the kinds
of statements that are regularly found in preambles. Preambles presumably have a point but certainly not the same kind of point that would be
attributed to the main body of a written constitution.

I. THE LEGAL STATUS OF CONSTITUTIONAL
PREAMBLES

The easiest way to demonstrate the difference between preambles and the
main bodies of constitutions, at least in the United States, is by reference
to their very different legal statuses. The Preamble to the U.S. Constitution
is rarely cited—and even more rarely seriously discussed—by the Supreme
Court, which tends to set the terms of legal argument for most lawyers.

One of the earliest decisions of that Court, *Chisholm v. Georgia* (1793), in holding that Georgia was liable to being sued in a federal court by a resident of South Carolina, did include just such a discussion in the separate opinion of Justice James Wilson, one of the primary figures in both the Philadelphia Convention and the Pennsylvania ratifying convention. Wilson justified the decision from "the declared objects, and the general texture of the Constitution of the United States," including its commitment "to form a union more perfect, than, before that time, had been formed." Moreover, he noted, "Another declared object is 'to establish justice.' This points, in a particular manner, to the Judicial authority."[2]

Wilson was offering what is sometimes called a *purposive* reading of the Constitution. That is, the Constitution has a point, which is to achieve the purposes set down in the Preamble. Whenever possible, therefore, a judge should resolve any constitutional dispute by choosing that outcome that would lead to a "more perfect Union" or take us closer to "establish[ing] justice." Why, after all, would one ever choose an outcome that makes us "less perfect" or generates "injustice"?

One response is to note that such terms are what political theorists call *essentially contested concepts,* which means that there is endless debate about what terms like "justice" mean. Everyone agrees that justice is important, and almost everyone in the modern world applauds the notion of democracy. The problem is that there is not—and, according to some theorists, there never will be—agreement on what exactly constitutes these notions. After all, John Rawls's great book is titled *A Theory of Justice* rather than *The Theory of Justice,* as if to acknowledge that there has been at least a 2500-year-long debate about the meaning of justice, and it scarcely came to an end upon the publication of Rawls's contribution in 1971.

The Court's decision in *Chisholm* was met with a storm of protest from objecting states, which most certainly saw the decision as both unjust and dangerous to the Union. In fact, the very first amendment to the Constitution following the Bill of Rights—the Eleventh Amendment—was designed to overrule the offending decision in *Chisholm*. That might have been enough to discourage citation of the Preamble, but John Marshall notably adverted to it in what is perhaps the most important single decision in our constitutional canon (especially concerning the Constitution of Conversation), *McCulloch v. Maryland,* an 1819 case that upheld a capacious national power to establish national banks while at the same time limiting the right of the state to tax that bank. "The government proceeds directly from the people," Marshall reminds the reader; it is "'ordained and established' in the name of the people; and is declared to be ordained, 'in order to form a more perfect union, establish justice, ensure domestic tranquility, and secure the blessings of liberty to themselves and to their posterity.'"[3] Why does he bother to do this? Presumably, it is to bolster the view that it would be anomalous for the Court to construe a Constitution with such noble purposes in a crabbed manner that would make fulfillment of those purposes more difficult. Still, even the example of the person often described as "The Great Chief Justice," writing in a truly canonical case, was not enough to make the Preamble an ordinary part of the lawyer's argumentative arsenal. Far more important, and basically dispositive for practicing lawyers, was the Court's comment over a century ago: "Although th[e] preamble indicates the general purposes for which the people ordained and established the Constitution, it has never been regarded as the source of any substantive power conferred on the government of the United States, or on any of its departments."[4] Nor, just as importantly, has it been treated as a source of establishing the *limits* on governmental power.

One reason for such reticence was well stated by the nation's first attorney general, Edmund Randolph, in his 1791 memorandum to George Washington concerning the constitutionality of Congress's chartering the proposed Bank of the United States. Had Congress been granted power to do such a thing under the terms of Article I, Section 8 of the Constitution, which sets out the powers "herein granted" to Congress? Since the Constitution had been sold to some of its state-oriented detractors as establishing only a "limited government of assigned powers," many of the great debates early in our history concerned the extent to which the promise of a limited national government would be adhered to. Or would clever lawyers instead come up with arguments for the endless expansion of national power (and the concomitant diminution of state power)?

President Washington did not see the Constitution as obviously "settling" the question of whether Congress in fact had the power to charter a national bank. So he asked the three members of his cabinet—Thomas Jefferson (secretary of state), Alexander Hamilton (secretary of the treasury), and

Randolph—to write him memoranda stating their views on the question. Hamilton had been the Bank's active proponent, so it is not surprising that he believed it was thoroughly constitutional, given a capacious reading of the Necessary and Proper Clause at the conclusion of Article I, Section 8, defining *necessary* to basically mean "convenient" or "useful." Thomas Jefferson, on the other hand, advised Washington that Congress was restricted to passing legislation described quite specifically in the Constitution, unless failure to act would doom the entire constitutional fabric. No clauses allowed Congress to charter corporations, and the Bank, even if "useful," didn't meet the stringent conditions Jefferson established for "necessity."

Randolph agreed with Jefferson that the Bank was unconstitutional and that Washington should therefore exercise his constitutional power to veto the bill, since signing an unconstitutional bill would violate the oath of office. Noting that some proponents of the Bank relied on the Preamble, Randolph told Washington that "the Preamble if it be operative is a full constitution of itself; and the body of the Constitution is useless."[5] If, after all, it became sufficient to make direct appeals to "establishing justice" or "assuring domestic tranquility," then why bother either demonstrating that Congress had been assigned specific powers or—even more to the point— pay any heed to barriers to governments achieving such happy goals? Thus, he pronounced "the legitimate nature of preambles" to be "declarative only of the views of the convention, which they supposed would be best fulfilled by the powers delineated."

Randolph might have been correct that the authors of the Constitution believed that the purposes set out in the Preamble would in fact "be best fulfilled by the powers delineated." But it is an *empirical* question as to whether that is the case, and one might well believe, especially with the passage of time, that the "powers delineated"—or perhaps the explicit restraints on such powers—might prove inadequate. In that case, which should take priority, the achievement of those great purposes or adherence to the text? Consider in this context perhaps the most remarkable aspect of Marshall's opinion in *McCulloch*. Marshall emphasized that "we must never forget, that it is a *Constitution* we are expounding" and then went on to explain that the U.S. Constitution is "intended to endure for ages to come, and consequently, to be adapted to the various *crises* of human affairs." In effect, Marshall recognized that the United States Constitution *had* to be a living Constitution (a term that he did not use) if it was to achieve the most fundamental purpose of "endur[ing] for ages to come." In this belief, he was a faithful disciple of his despised adversary Thomas Jefferson, who wrote that just as "manners and opinions change with the change of circumstances, institutions must advance also, and keep pace with the times."[6] Such adaptation is surely an important part of our constitutional history. This is presumably what Oliver Wendell Holmes meant by emphasizing that "the life of the law" was experience, or what he called "the felt necessities of the time," rather than responses to the ostensible demands of cold "logic."[7] Yet even Marshall did not succeed—assuming that he wished to—in preserving the Preamble as part of the repertoire of standard American legal rhetoric.

There is nothing unusual about this. Although most constitutions around the world include preambles, few of them seem to invite legal arguments based directly on them. Probably the most notable exception is modern France, operating under the 1958 constitution establishing the Fifth Republic. In 1971, the French Constitutional Council, which can be analogized to the U.S. Supreme Court, invalidated a law passed by the French parliament based in part on the "fundamental principles" instantiated in the preamble.[8] So perhaps it is fair to place the U.S. Preamble at one end of a spectrum as barely "legalized," whereas the 1946 French preamble, given new life by the Constitutional Council, has become strongly generative for modern French constitutional law.[9] Still, even taking into account such examples, one might find it safe to say that only rarely is the motive force behind writing a preamble to provide material from which lawyers can directly draw their arguments.[10] So if preambles typically—and most certainly so within the United States—are not meant to supply the basis for standard-form legal arguments, what functions *do* they serve?

II. THE "NON-LEGAL" FUNCTIONS OF CONSTITUTIONAL PREAMBLES

A. Delineating the nation

For better or worse, one important clue regarding the importance of preambles is provided by the German legal philosopher Carl Schmitt, whose legal brilliance is certainly complicated by his support in the 1930s of the Nazi Party. For Schmitt, the existence of a political nation (which may or may not have been organized into a political state) precedes the adoption of a constitution and indeed gives life to it. It is the unified political will of a people (as in "We the People") that creates a constitution—at least in those political orders that purport to rest on popular sovereignty. And any constitution adopted by a national *volk* instantiates the particular perspectives of that discrete national entity, including, for Schmitt, the all-important differentiation of the world into friends and potential enemies. To define who is within a nation is, logically speaking, also to declare who is outside, with potentially ominous consequences.

Consider in this context the Preamble to the Swiss Confederation, which proclaims its "intent of ... maintaining and furthering the unity, strength and honor of the Swiss nation."[11] Even if the Swiss do not look askance at the unity, strength, and honor of other nations, these are clearly not the concerns of those gathered together under the auspices of the Swiss constitution. It may not be entirely coincidental that Switzerland has some of the most rigorous barriers to immigrants gaining citizenship of any country in the world. It is worth noting, incidentally, that—at least since the addition of the Fourteenth Amendment to the U.S. Constitution in 1868—no American state can adopt such a parochial conception of its purpose. Individual states, unlike the United States as a whole, have no control over who can join their community. If citizens or even aliens who are legal residents of the United States wish to move, say, from Massachusetts to Wyoming, there is nothing Wyoming can do to stop them. And, at least since several Supreme Court decisions in the 1970s, these new residents—if citizens of the United States—are also entitled to vote no later than two months after their arrival.

The South African Constitution may be remarkably universalistic and cosmopolitan in some of its language, including the emphasis expressed in the preamble on advancing universal "human rights and freedoms."[12] Still, no one reading the preamble would doubt that the constitution is aimed at residents of South Africa, even "citizens" of South Africa. Perhaps the best evidence of its non-universalism is the concluding phrase, in which God's blessings are invoked in the eleven official languages of South Africa (including—in addition to English and Afrikaans—isiZulu, isXhosa,

Sesotho, and Xitsonga). Whatever the multitude of languages, they are all "local." Arabic, for example, is *not* an official language, nor are any of the other languages identified with other parts of Africa, such as Swahili.

Returning to the American Preamble, we can ask about the precise referent of the phrase "We the People." After all, Article VII provided for constitutional ratification by the individual states, most certainly not by a national convention. There can be little doubt that most of the population had a greater sense of themselves as Virginians or New Hampshirites than as Americans. This is, after all, one of the reasons that the United States of America disintegrated in 1861 when West Point–trained Robert E. Lee, among many others, gave his identity as a Virginian priority over any national loyalties. So does the Preamble mean to evoke one national people—"the People of the United States of America"—or rather a group of peoples (plural) living in the various states of the Union?

The draft of the Preamble that was sent to the Committee of Detail in August 1787 spelled out the names of each of the thirteen states, including Rhode Island and Providence Plantations. However, the final draft, signed on September 17, 1787, omitted the names. One possible explanation for this is that it was a clever way of announcing that the states were being rendered next to irrelevant, at least as a source of basic identity, and that they would be supplanted by a single national American identity. It might have been far easier to do this if, as some had suggested, the name of the country had been changed to, say, Columbia. But the very term "United States" is fatally ambiguous, depending for its force on whether one inflects "united" or "states." Thus the other rationale offered for the final draft of the Preamble is that Article VII contemplated the possibility that one or more of the thirteen states would in fact refuse to ratify the new document, as was originally the case with regard to North Carolina and Rhode Island, and it would be embarrassing to include that state in the Preamble if it chose to remain out of the Union.

It is illuminating to consider in this context the preamble to the United Nations Charter of 1945, which begins:

WE THE PEOPLES OF THE UNITED NATIONS DETERMINED to
save succeeding generations from the scourge of war... and to reaffirm faith
in fundamental human rights, in the dignity and worth of the human person,

in the equal rights of men and women and of nations large and small, and to establish conditions under which justice and respect for the obligations arising from treaties and other sources of international law can be maintained…HAVE RESOLVED TO COMBINE OUR EFFORTS TO ACCOMPLISH THESE AIMS.[13]

Would anyone easily refer to a "world political community" that had effaced the reality of national identities? After all, what is the point of referring to "nations large and small" if they are to be rendered irrelevant by membership in de facto world government?

B. Are "the people" constituted by a given religious identity?

But let us look at a number of other preambles and discern what they might be telling us about the visions of their authors (and the social groups they represent). One might, for example, wish to ascertain the relevance of religion to the communities for which a constitution's framers purport to speak. Although the South African Constitution would not strike most observers as religiously sectarian, it does acknowledge the community's presumptive belief in a God who is capable of "blessing" South Africa's new venture in democratic constitutionalism. In this the South African Constitution is not alone.

Americans, for example, need only look to their north to find the opening words of the Canadian Charter of Rights and Freedoms: "Whereas Canada is founded upon the principles that recognize the supremacy of God and the rule of law."[14] Switzerland begins its preamble "In the Name of God Almighty!" And Germany's post–World War II Framers were "Conscious of their responsibility before God and Men."[15] One might well regard these invocations of "God" as relatively non-sectarian, unless one does not believe in any god. But one might be a religious believer who, however, presumes that the "God" invoked by Canada, Switzerland, or Germany is some version of a Christian (or, at best, Judeo-Christian) god that one might not in fact believe in. And, obviously, this is not simply a matter of integrating Islamic members of such communities. There are, after all, said to be over three-quarters of a million Hindus in Canada;

perhaps they could be forgiven for believing that the ostensible community that is organizing itself around the Charter of Rights, by referring only to "God" instead of multiple "gods," at worst excludes them or at best merely tolerates the alien presence of religious deviants.

One cannot take refuge in some vague invocation of the post–World War II "Judeo-Christianity" (or its contemporary variant "the Abrahamic communities") when reading some other preambles, even of those countries considered well within the West. The preamble of the Greek Constitution is simply: "In the name of the Holy and Consubstantial and Indivisible Trinity."[16] Probably the most remarkable of such constitutions, in what we usually call the West, is Ireland's, whose preamble begins by speaking "In the Name of the Most Holy Trinity, from Whom is all authority and to Whom, as our final end, all actions both of men and States must be referred," and immediately "acknowledg[es] all our obligations to our Divine Lord, Jesus Christ, Who sustained our fathers through centuries of trial."[17]

Can it possibly be the case that a predicate condition of membership within the "people of Eire" is "humbly acknowledging all our obligations to our Divine Lord, Jesus Christ"? What is the status, then, of those who acknowledge no such obligations? Many years ago, Dublin had a Jewish mayor, Robert Briscoe, who presumably acknowledged no such obligations. Any attempt by contemporary Ireland to deny citizenship to, say, immigrants who do not acknowledge such obligations might well run afoul of the European Convention of Human Rights. But then how do we really make sense of the existing preamble? Should the Irish be expected to change it to acknowledge the decidedly new reality of their membership in the contemporary European Union?

As one moves away from the West, one finds even more religiously assertive statements of identity. Perhaps the best non-Western analogue to Ireland's constitution is that of the Islamic Republic of Pakistan, whose preamble can also be described as a form of political theology. It begins by noting that "Almighty Allah alone" enjoys "sovereignty over the entire Universe," including, presumably, Pakistan itself.[18]

Needless to say, not all countries in the modern world, even (or especially) those with distinctly sectarian pasts, wish to embrace such a sectarian self-understanding as do Greece, Ireland, or Pakistan (among many other examples that might be given). Thus, the preambles of at least some constitutions written in recent years, especially in Europe, seem to wish to define the relevant political community—and its ostensible "unity"—in less religious terms. Especially interesting in this regard is Poland, not least because of its strong historic identification with Roman Catholicism, but also because its new constitutional self-understanding was developed during the reign of "the Polish Pope," John Paul II. The preamble, written as part of the 1997 constitution, speaks of "the Polish Nation," but it defines that nation as "all citizens of the Republic, Both those who believe in God as the source of truth, justice, good and beauty, As well as those not sharing such faith but respecting those universal values as arising from other sources." Similarly, there is recognition that "our culture [is] rooted in the Christian heritage of the Nation and in universal human values."[19] Given Poland's history, one can only rejoice that the sectarian lion is being invited to lie down in peace with the secular lamb, but there is certainly nothing "innocent" about the phraseology adopted by the Polish framers.

Huge controversies broke out, for example, with regard to the preamble to the draft treaty that would have established a constitution for Europe[20] and whether it would make any kind of bow to the Christian past of most of Europe, as the Catholic Church and several European governments (including Italy) demanded. The answer was no, partly because of the militant opposition of France, but also, one suspects, because one major issue before the European Union is the ultimate admission of Turkey, which, however described, is most certainly not Christian. One might be forgiven if one thinks of Turkey as Islamic, especially given the country's current government, but its constitution is in fact probably the most militantly secular constitution of any major country in the world today.[21] Its preamble defines loyal Turks as those committed to "the concept of nationalism outlined and the reforms and principles introduced by the founder of the Republic of Turkey, Atatürk, the immortal leader and the unrivaled hero." Among these values is "the principle of secularism": "there shall be no interference whatsoever of the sacred religious feelings in State affairs and politics."

So let us return to the Preamble to our own Constitution, which is clearly among the most secular of national preambles. The Preamble offers nothing to support the notion, for example, that we are a "Christian nation" in anything more than a sociological sense. The lack of any such theological pronouncement is indeed striking in its absence, and one might even go so far as to say that it "settles" that aspect of our national identity. Whatever it means to be part of the national "We the People," religious identity has nothing to do with it. Moreover, Article VI of the Constitution explicitly states that "no test oath," such as belief in the Trinity or presumably even belief in God, shall be required of any public official.

Before one accepts this reading of the Constitution—either joyfully or with regret—one should also consider the very last line of the Constitution: "Done in Convention by the Unanimous Consent of the States present the Seventeenth Day of September in the Year of *our* Lord one thousand seven hundred and Eighty seven and of the Independence of the United States of America the Twelfth." One might view this simply as the thoughtless English specification of the often-used *Anno Domini*. Although this sentence plays no part in standard legal argumentation, it may have importance for those who are interested literally in every word of constitutions regardless of their interest to ordinary lawyers. It should be clear that even at the time of the framing, when a synagogue had long been established in Newport, Rhode Island, there was not a unanimous belief in a common "Lord" who was born (more or less) 1787 years prior to the great events in Philadelphia. One can be confident that the use of any such language in a contemporary statute passed by Congress would properly be found to violate the Establishment Clause of the First Amendment. Still, there it is, in every copy of the Constitution.

There is one other clause of the Constitution worth noting, relating to the number of days the president has to decide whether or not to veto legislation sent him by Congress. It is, obviously, very important that this be settled. It would be decidedly awkward to allow the president a "reasonable time" to read and then to decide on the fate of a given bill. So, says Article I of the Constitution, "If any Bill shall not be returned by the President within ten Days (Sundays excepted) after it shall have been presented to him, the Same shall be a Law," at least if Congress is in session. It does not seem difficult to explain why Sundays are excepted, though one might ask if anyone designing a constitution for the America of the twenty-first century would include such a phrase.

But, as suggested earlier, we make a serious mistake, when delineating "American constitutionalism," to refer only to the U.S. Constitution and its Preamble. Perhaps its message is that the states and their assorted populations do not share a particular religious identity, at least if by "particular" one means the specific denominations within Protestantism.[22] Or one might even argue that the particular members of the political elite who were in Philadelphia were significantly less religious than were more ordinary Americans. George Washington, the President of the Convention, was notable for making no overt references to Jesus during the course of his political career, though he did proclaim the "utility" of religion as a social bond; importantly, he didn't seem to emphasize any particular religion. He was notable as well for reaching out to the Jewish community of Newport, Rhode Island, and assuring them of their rightful place in his America.

But can we infer similar views about American society or stances toward religion from a look at American state constitutions? When we look at them, we discover a remarkable pervasiveness of religious language. I have already quoted Texas's brief preamble: "Humbly invoking the blessings of Almighty god, the people of the State of Texas, do ordain and establish this Constitution." Texas may be exceptional in many ways, but this is not one of them. *All* the preambles to American state constitutions include religious evocations,[23] even if sometimes they are a bit muted, as was the case with the 1780 Massachusetts Constitution, drafted largely by John Adams:

> We, therefore, the people of Massachusetts, acknowledging, with grateful hearts, the goodness of the great Legislator of the universe, in affording us, in the course of His providence, an opportunity, deliberately and peaceably, without fraud, violence, or surprise, of entering into an original, explicit, and solemn compact with each other, and of forming a new constitution of civil government for ourselves and posterity; and devoutly imploring His direction in so interesting a design, DO agree upon, ordain, and establish the following declaration of rights and frame of government as the CONSTITUTION of the COMMONWEALTH of MASSACHUSETTS.[1]

If one proceeds alphabetically through the American state constitutions, one finds first the 1901 Alabama Constitution: "We the people of the State of Alabama, invoking the favor and guidance of Almighty God, do ordain and establish the following Constitution."[24] Finally, there is Wyoming's constitution of 1890: "We, the people of the State of Wyoming, grateful to God for our civil, political, and religious liberties ... establish this Constitution." One might see these as reflecting the cultures of particular regions and the particular times in which they were drafted. We have, though, already seen that even the 1780 Massachusetts Constitution, however "deist" its language might be, is considerably less secular than the U.S. Constitution written seven years later. And consider the New Jersey Constitution, drafted in 1948, which retained the language of its nineteenth-century predecessor: "We, the people of the State of New Jersey, grateful to Almighty God for the civil and religious liberty which He hath so long permitted us to enjoy, and looking to Him for a blessing upon our endeavors to secure and transmit the same unimpaired to succeeding generations, do ordain and establish this Constitution." Similarly, the 1972 Montana Constitution speaks of "We the people of Montana [who are] grateful to God for the quiet beauty of our state, the grandeur of our mountains, the vastness of our rolling plains." The most recent state constitution is that adopted by Rhode Island in 1986, whose preamble states that "We, the people of the State of Rhode Island and Providence Plantations, grateful to Almighty God for the civil and religious liberty which He hath so long permitted us to enjoy, and looking to Him for a blessing upon our endeavors to secure and to transmit the same, unimpaired, to succeeding generations, do ordain and establish this Constitution of government."

American Indian tribes have also contributed to the American constitutional fabric. The preamble to the 1928 Constitution and Bylaws of the Oglala Lakota (or Sioux) People defined the object of the constitution as "securing to ourselves, and our posterity the political and civil rights guaranteed to us by treaties and statutes of the United States," including the "encourage[ment] and promot[ion of] all movements and efforts leading to the good of the general welfare of our tribe, acknowledging Almighty God as the source of all power and Authority in Civil government, the Lord Jesus Christ as the ruler of Nations, and His revealed will as of supreme Authority."[25] This constitution did not endure, replaced in 1936 by the present amended constitution, which included a new preamble that recognized "God Almighty and His Divine Providence."[26] One should be aware that the Establishment Clause of the First Amendment, though it certainly applies to states, does not apply to Indian tribes. However, no one has suggested that the state preambles must be rewritten to conform with the prohibition on establishment of religion.

Justice William O. Douglas notably wrote in a controversial 1952 Supreme Court decision that Americans "are a religious people and our institutions presuppose a Supreme Being."[27] It is hard (though not impossible) to support this proposition from looking at the U.S. Constitution. If, however, one looks only at state constitutions or the Oglala Sioux constitution, one finds almost overwhelming support for Douglas's statement. Moreover, as Gordon Wood notes, both "Connecticut and Massachusetts continue[d] their tax-supported Congregational establishments" into at least the early nineteenth century. Indeed, "the Revolutionary constitutions of Maryland, South Carolina, and Georgia authorized their state legislatures to create in place of the Anglican church a kind of multiple establishment of a variety of religious groups, using tax money to support 'the Christian religion.'"[28] Most of the states imposed religious tests for public office. Maryland and Delaware were relatively liberal among this group in requiring only that one be Christian, though Delaware required a belief in the Trinity as well. New Hampshire, Connecticut, New Jersey, North Carolina, and Georgia specified that officeholders be Protestant; no Catholics need apply. Pennsylvania and South Carolina officials had to believe in one God and in heaven and hell. The outliers in this regard were Georgia, Virginia, New York, and Massachusetts.

So we have to determine the implications of this collection of facts about both the past and present of American state constitutionalism. Anyone familiar with contemporary American culture would be hard-pressed to deny the hold that the purported connection between "Americanness" and religiosity, even if religious "particularism" for millions has become something named the "Judeo-Christian tradition."[29] One can say with confidence both that the U.S. Supreme Court is completely unlikely to declare these various state preambles unconstitutional[30] and that it would be foolhardy in the extreme to throw one's energies into campaigns to amend any of these state preambles in order to make them as secular as the U.S. Constitution.

C. "National narratives" and civic tutelage

I have mentioned the Turkish preamble in the context of its full-throated embrace of a secular polity (whatever the realities of modern Turkey).

But that preamble raises many questions beyond those of religion and secularism. It is also suffused with Turkish nationalism. It appears to require, for example, that all who wish to be deemed "good Turks" must recognize Atatürk as their "immortal leader" and "unrivaled hero," in spite of the fact that any mulicultural society will almost by definition feature a multiplicity of "heroes," some of whom—like Robert E. Lee and Ulysses Grant or Abraham Lincoln and Jefferson Davis—may be out-and-out adversaries and unlikely to be objects of universal admiration. Like more concrete public monuments, preambles can be tutelary inasmuch as they attempt, with whatever degrees of empirical success, to shape the consciousness of the citizenry, including future generations who must be inculcated with norms of political correctness. Most often, future generations forget whom the monuments are intended to commemorate and, more importantly, why. Perhaps that is the fate of preambles as well, especially if they lose purchase as part of our ongoing constitutional conversation.

Few other preambles are so specific as is the Turkish one in its valorizing Kemal Atatürk. Many, though, reflect the desire of their authors to model a suitably inspiring history of the particular nation that, as Schmitt suggested, precedes and therefore is basically to be served by the new constitution. Exemplary in this regard is the constitution of Croatia, written in the aftermath of the dissolution of the multiethnic state of Yugoslavia in 1992, itself the prelude to a devastating civil war. The preamble presents an extended history lesson, presumably part of an effort to educate the surrounding community, though one assumes that it will also play a role in the future civic education of young Croatians. Again, it is very long, as one might expect of a document dedicated to outlining the "millenary identity of the Croatian nation and the continuity of its statehood" beginning in the seventh century and continuing to the present. Thus it concludes by referring to "the presented historical facts and universally accepted principles of the modern world, as well as the inalienabile and indivisible, non-transferable and non-exhaustible right of the Croatian nation to self-determination and state sovereignty, including its fully maintained right to secession and association, as basic provisions for peace and stability of the international order, the Republic of Croatia is established as the national state of the Croatian nation."[31] It does recognize membership of other "national minorities" within the state, including Serbs, Czechs, Slovaks, Italians, Hungarians,

Jews, Germans, Austrians, Ukrainians, and Ruthenians. Although they are guaranteed "equality with citizens of Croatian nationality," they should presumably always be aware that the primary purpose of the Croatian state is to vindicate the particular narrative of the Croatian people and to return them fully to the stage of world history. It would be reassuring to believe that the commitment to self-determination, a concept identified with President Woodrow Wilson, who made that one of the principal aims during World War I, can coexist easily with multinationalism and pluralism. Yet there is all too much evidence that this may not be the case, and one might be especially doubtful with regard to countries that present themselves in their preambles in the language of assertive nationalism.

Similarly tutelary is the preamble to the 1992 constitution of the Socialist Republic of Vietnam, which, after referring to the "millennia-old history" of "the Vietnamese people," goes on to offer a synopsis of developments "starting in 1930, under the leadership of the Communist Party of Vietnam formed and trained by President Ho Chi Minh."[32] Needless to say, this includes reference to the 1945 declaration of independence by the Democratic Republic of Vietnam and the military victories over France and the United States that "reunified the motherland, and brought to completion the people's national democratic revolution." Along the way constitutions were adopted in 1946, 1959, and 1980. A constant throughout, though, is the commitment, "in the light of Marxism-Leninism and Ho Chi Minh's thought, [to] carrying into effect the Programme of national construction in the period of transition to socialism."

Imagine what difference it might have made had the American Framers included as part of the Preamble the "long train of abuses" charged against King George III in the Declaration of Independence. That would have transformed the Preamble from a highly abstract statement of admirable goals to an attempt to educate future generations as to the particulars of the American past that generated independence and then the new Constitution. No such mistake is made by the drafters in Croatia or Vietnam. Still, one wonderful thing about the American Preamble is its brevity; it has literally been set to music. In contrast, one may find many of the contemporary preambles tedious to read unless one is a devotee of nineteenth-century organic nationalism or of vanguards that claim to speak in the name of the entire social order.

III. DO WE SHARE A COMMITMENT TO "FUNDAMENTAL VALUES"?

We come to the final and most important question posed by the phenomena of preambles. How accurate is the frequent positing by preambles of social or national unity on the part of the particular people ostensibly behind the constitution? There is a reason, after all, that Hanna Lerner titled her book on Israel, Ireland, and India *Making Constitutions in Deeply Divided Societies*, or that Sujit Choudhry similarly titled an excellent collection of edited essays *Constitutional Design for Divided Societies*.[33] Or consider a famous 1905 opinion written by Justice Oliver Wendell Holmes, which proclaimed that the U.S. Constitution *"is made for people of fundamentally differing views."*[34] Even if there is a consensus that certain terms form the basis of our conversation, they may indeed be "essentially contested" and therefore serve at least as much to divide as to unite us. So perhaps anyone who agrees with Holmes's perspective should agree that the writing of preambles is at least as much a testament to a yearning for homogeneity— whether of religion, ethnicity, or political ideology—as the reflection of a far more complicated, and often disconcerting, actuality. And, if one does not share the visions instantiated in a particular preamble—including the religious overtones of all the state preambles—is it fair to view them as exemplifying a power play in the struggle over defining (or "constituting") particular societies?

When teaching about "constitutional design," I ask students to imagine themselves as "certified constitutional designers" requested to consult with constitutional framers near and far. So, imagine your own response to clients who ask if they should write a preamble to a newly drafted constitution. What would be its point—and, therefore, what would you advise them?

4

How Does a "Republican Form of Government" Differ from "Democracy" (and to Which Should We Be Committed Today)?

1. PROLOGUE

As already noted, most of this book is about the *structures* set out in our national constitution and in various state constitutions, and how these structures constitute our political system in fundamental ways. They are seas within which we swim politically, and it is altogether too easy to emulate fish by accepting these structures as a given and failing to ask if there might be any alternatives. The answer, for fish, may be "no." But we are not fish, and our political system is only metaphorically oceanic.

All these structures rest on presuppositions. None can be described as literally "thoughtless." All were, at the time the constitutions were written, believed to serve some purpose, even if, as with the compromises discussed in Chapter 2, the purposes endorsed by some were condemned by others. At the national level, especially, we can often get a good sense of the initial presuppositions by turning to historical sources, including the debates at the Philadelphia convention itself or during the intense arguments over ratification afterward. The most famous such arguments, of course, are those set out in the eighty-five *Federalist Papers*, written by Madison, Hamilton, and John Jay. I draw on those debates and arguments throughout much of this book. In keeping with the emphasis on the Constitution of Settlement, my goal is to set out the assumptions that underlie the institutions we continue to live with today. Although I intend these chapters to be historically accurate, my ultimate purpose is to engage readers in a "conversation" about the extent to which we today—in 2011—share these assumptions. If we do not, as I think is often the case, then we must ask if we are as helpless as the fish in the ocean or whether we, unlike them, can seek to climb out of the water, perhaps encouraged by some of our fellow citizens whose state constitutions in effect offer challenging critiques of the presuppositions of 1787.

What characterizes *all* American governments, national, state, and local, is that they are attempts to vindicate the proposition set out in the Declaration of Independence, that legitimate government rests on the consent of the governed. It is not enough to assert that a particular government has such consent. Instead, there are multiple ways of attempting to establish the level of consent, most commonly, of course, through *elections*. Such elections bespeak our general commitment to *representative democracy*, whereby "we the people" choose those who will govern us in lieu of more direct self-governance.

Yet, as we shall see in this and the next chapter, what counts as an adequately "representative" democracy is scarcely self-evident; even more to the point, a number of states, while not rejecting the importance of representation, supplement it with options for more *direct democracy*. It turns out, for example, that citizens of the United States who are also citizens of California swim in quite different political seas, and one can ask which is preferable (under what circumstances and assumptions). Answering that question requires that we become fully aware of the difference between "republican" and "democratic" government and the need to decide for ourselves which better captures our own sense of a desirable contemporary polity.

2. ON A "REPUBLICAN FORM OF GOVERNMENT"

Those who framed the U.S. Constitution never intended to establish a "democracy." Most probably would have agreed with John Adams's observation in 1814 that "democracy never lasts long. It soon wastes, exhausts, and murders itself. There never was a democracy yet that did not commit suicide."[1] The authors of the U.S. Constitution instead aimed to create what Article IV obliquely calls a "REPUBLICAN FORM OF

GOVERNMENT" whose maintenance is "guaranteed" to every state in the Union. No such guarantee is specified with regard to the national government, though the entire Constitution was thought to instantiate what the framing generation believed to be that particular form of government. The burden of proof would fall very heavily on anyone to explain why states were "guaranteed" such a government while the national government was free to become "non-republican," whatever precisely that might mean.

The more basic problem is that the Constitution provides no canonical definition of what constitutes a republican form of government. It is very definitely *not* part of the Constitution of Settlement. As a matter of fact, like the Preamble, it is not part of the ordinary lawyer's Constitution of Conversation: the Supreme Court in 1849 ruled it a "non-justiciable" part of the text, which means that the Court will not decide cases premised only on the ostensible violation of the Republican Form of Government Clause.[2] As a practical matter, American lawyers and law professors have exhibited little interest in discussing republican government inasmuch as it is not litigated.[3] We should recognize, though, that many of the rationales behind institutional decisions that make up the Constitution of Settlement require placing them within the context of eighteenth-century discussions about republicanism. Even in the twenty-first century, anyone assessing American constitutions, particularly the national Constitution, must have an informed view about which, if any, of the eighteenth-century notions of republican government deserve to survive.

A belief that nothing in the 1787 Constitution violates the tenets of republican government requires recognizing that such a government can protect chattel slavery and deny most citizens the right to vote—women, to take the easiest example. One might say that a "republican" form of government must be something quite different from the monarchy overthrown by the Americans during the Revolution, which—like most monarchies—relied on inheritance as the basis of kingship. Even if the British Parliament willingly breached that principle in favor of replacing the discredited King James II (rightly suspected of being Catholic) with William of Orange or looking to the German House of Hanover to take the Crown in the eighteenth century, no one ever imagined that the monarch should be chosen in a popular election. But there are many ways to reject (and replace) a monarch. Moreover, many countries in the world today—including Great

Britain, Denmark, Sweden, Spain, and Norway—remain monarchies but at the same time would instantiate much of what is now understood to be meant by a "republican form of government." Still, the task facing the Framers was to give the notion of republican government concrete meaning, both in the design of our basic institutions in 1787 and then during the great debates afterward about the desirability of that institutional structure.

Madison's own hostility to democracy was set out clearly in *Federalist* 10: "Democracies have ever been spectacles of turbulence and contention; have ever been found incompatible with personal security, or the rights of property; and have, in general, been as short in their lives as they have been violent in their deaths." Gordon Wood emphasizes that the Constitution was generated as much by what various Framers viewed "as the excesses of American democracy" as specific deficiencies in the Articles of Confederation, which might have been cured without obliterating our first constitution and replacing it with a strikingly different political structure.[4] Indeed, Wood describes as "perhaps the most frustrating and disillusioning years" of James Madison's life the period between 1784 and 1787 during which he was a member of the Virginia legislature. Madison, according to Wood, "found out what democracy in America might mean…The Virginia legislators seemed so parochial, so illiberal, so small-minded, and most of them seemed to have only 'a particular interest to serve,'" in contrast to being motivated by more general "public interests." They were, in addition, devoid of a due "regard for public honor or honesty."[5]

Such attitudes scarcely disappeared with the establishment of the new political order, as illustrated by Adams's dour 1814 comment. His son John Quincy Adams similarly opined in an 1839 speech celebrating the fiftieth anniversary of Washington's inauguration that "the experience of all former ages had shown that of all human governments, democracy was the most unstable, fluctuating and short-lived."[6] There were certainly outliers far more supportive of democracy, most notably including Thomas Jefferson (who had nothing to do with the writing of the Constitution).[7] But the point is that Jefferson *was* an outlier, and his at times almost Jacobin view would have been rejected by almost everyone in Philadelphia and by most of the American elite afterward.

Many of the Framers were still heirs to an analysis going back to Aristotle, who was in this instance following Plato.[8] Aristotle identifies six forms

Table 4.1 *Aristotle's Six Forms of Government*

	ADMIRABLE	PERVERSE
One ruler	Kingship	Tyranny
Few rulers	Aristocracy	Oligarchy
Many rulers	Polity	Democracy

of government along the lines of what might informally be described as "admirable" or "perverse." What defines "perversity" is the subordination of the "public good" to one's own desires or interests. Although Adam Smith published *The Wealth of Nations* in 1776, just as Americans were declaring their own independence, this was not a generation that accepted the view that pursuit only of one's self-interested goals was adequate to achieving a decent society.[9] The French philosopher Bernard de Mandeville, in *The Fable of the Bees*, famously declared that those motivated exclusively by "private vice" could nonetheless produce—thanks to what Smith called the invisible hand—"public benefit," but few Philadelphians would have agreed.

Aristotle's distinctions were as shown in Table 4.1. For centuries, this typology structured political discourse. Then came Thomas Hobbes, whose *Leviathan* in 1651 is one of the truly transformational works in the history of political thought. A key argument occurs in a chapter tellingly titled "Of the Several Kinds of Commonwealth":

> The difference of Commonwealths consisteth in the difference of the sovereign, or the person representative of all.
>
> When the representative is one man, then is the Commonwealth a monarchy; when an assembly of all, then it is a democracy, or popular Commonwealth; when an assembly of a part only, then it is called an aristocracy. *Other names of government are but these same forms misliked.* They that are discontented under monarchy call it tyranny; and they that are displeased with aristocracy call it oligarchy: they which find themselves grieved under a democracy call it anarchy. (emphasis added)

Here Hobbes establishes a key divide in political theory and analysis, as fundamental in its own way as the impact on Western culture of Copernicus and his displacement of the earth's centrality in the cosmos. Hobbes basically dismisses the Aristotelian sextet, whose cogency depends on the ability to distinguish objectively between governments committed to the public good and those that are not, in favor of a far simpler trio of forms. These forms, too, are subject to "objective" analysis, but the basis is simply figuring out how many, or what portion of, the people actually play the role of "rulers." To assess them further—by describing a monarch as a tyrant, for example—is simply to say that the assessor "mislikes" the monarch in question. It is a mere statement of opinion rather than an objective judgment that can be evaluated as true or false.

The Constitution was drafted at a time when the older political philosophy represented by Aristotle and the "modern" approach of Hobbes (and John Locke) contended with one another. Though Madison and his compatriots were not Aristotelian in a thoroughgoing sense, Madison certainly believed in the existence of a "public interest" or "public good," which public officials were tasked to discern and then implement.[10] "Republicanism" in many ways was the equivalent of the Aristotelian term *polity*, and both are distinguished—for Madison and others of the time—from "democracy." No doubt the phrase "republican form of government" sounds antiquated in our more "democratic" age. But we should remain attentive to how the two concepts may differ in important ways and consider which we truly prefer even in our own time.

One might, for example, define democracy as the relatively unimpeded ability of political parties that gain the support of electoral majorities to work their will, even if constrained by certain substantive constitutional norms protecting a set of privileged rights. But then one should recognize that the five modern monarchies mentioned above are considerably more "democratic" than the modern United States with regard, for example, to the degree that their parliaments represent the majority of the population. (None has anything equivalent to the U.S. Senate.) Each of the fifty state constitutions within the United States also appears to be more democratic than the governmental system laid out in Philadelphia. But what, exactly, does one learn from this observation?

At the very least, any discussion of the Constitution necessarily requires that we wrestle with our own beliefs about republicanism *and* democracy. My previous book was titled *Our Undemocratic Constitution*, and it was not intended to be a compliment. It argued that the Constitution was indefensible with regard to what have become widely accepted criteria for identifying a political system as democratic. Think only of the maxim "one person, one vote" and then think of the U.S. Senate, which gives California and Wyoming the same representation even though the 2010 census indicates that California has almost 12 percent (37,250,000 people) of the entire population of the United States while Wyoming has less than one-fifth of 1 percent (approximately 565,000 people) of the nation's population. That is only the most glaring example; there are many, many others.

Critics of my work frequently remind me, kindly or otherwise, that the Constitution was never intended to be democratic—and a good thing, too! To be "too much" of a democrat is viewed as almost un-American. That was certainly the view held by many Federalists at the turn of the nineteenth century, particularly those who detested Thomas Jefferson as an almost satanic worshipper of the French Revolution and its embrace of Rousseauean democracy. The first three words of the Preamble may be "We the People," but one should not infer that "the People" should actually rule in any uncomplicated sense.

As Gordon Wood has written, "The Federalists of the 1790s...believed in popular sovereignty and republican government, but they did not believe that ordinary people had a direct role to play in ruling the society."[11] Nor did they embrace a politics by which those who were chosen to rule paid all that much attention to the specific wishes of the ostensible electorate. But this Federalist vision of the polity—however basic the views held by most members of the Philadelphia Convention in 1787—scarcely survived even a generation. The theme of Wood's magisterial history of the early republic is its defeat by the far more democratic vision attached to the name of Thomas Jefferson.

A principal purpose of this book is to understand why proponents of republicanism and de facto opponents of democracy advocated the actual institutional structures that were adopted in 1787 and remain significantly unchanged more than two centuries later. Readers are certainly invited to decide whether they want a more democratic Constitution or whether its many anti-democratic—does this mean "republican"?—features are just fine. In contemporary jargon, we can ask if they are "features" rather than "bugs." This debate about the comparative merits of republicanism and democracy has great consequences for our assessment of the current practices of the American system of government. But it also has implications for the way the United States currently presents itself to the world and ostensibly conducts its foreign policies.

Most presidents over the past century, after all, have embraced what might well be called "the democracy project." Woodrow Wilson justified American entrance into World War I in 1917 by reference to making the "world safe for democracy." We can do a fast-forward to perhaps the most Wilsonian chief executive since the former Princeton president, George W. Bush.[12] Both of the twenty-first-century American wars in Afghanistan and Iraq were justified, at least in part, by their ostensible contribution to creating more democratic systems in those two countries (unlike, say, the first Iraq War conducted by President George H. W. Bush, which was prosecuted in order to push Iraq out of Kuwait, not to remove Saddam Hussein from power).

The election of Barack Obama did not change this reality. On one of his first foreign trips following his inauguration, President Obama told a student questioner in Strasbourg, France, in April 2009, "We spend so much time talking about democracy—and obviously we should be promoting democracy everywhere we can."[13] This was treated, one might say, as a "self-evident truth." Similarly, in a major speech on the "Arab Spring," President Obama announced that "it will be the policy of the United States to promote reform across the region, and to support transitions to democracy."[14] One may wonder exactly what this means, given the status of democracy as what political theorists call an essentially contested concept. That is, there is no single widely shared notion of the term. The only thing that does seem to be agreed on, with some exceptions across the world, is that democracy is a "good thing."

But is it? Perhaps it would be just too confusing to most people if we retitled it "the republican form of government project." But we should acknowledge the possibility that there is indeed a difference between "democratic" and "republican" government, at least if we wish to understand the particular political vision captured in the 1787 Constitution of Settlement. We should determine what we wish to embrace in the twenty-first century, whatever might have been the case over two centuries ago. Otherwise, our rhetoric may confuse not only various foreigners, but even members of our own political community who falsely believe that

American constitutionalism coincides with any particularly robust notion of "democracy."

II. SELF-GOVERNANCE

One of the most important attributes of any modern constitution, at least outside of those few monarchies like that found in Saudi Arabia, is to establish a system that recognizes some degree of popular participation in government. Most countries today do accept one or another version of "liberal democracy," which means, at the very least, a commitment to *some* abstract notion of "self-governance." But the central questions are which *actual* selves do the governing and to what degree are they accountable to other members of the polity who do not occupy political office themselves (other than what some theorists might regard as the extraordinarily important office of "citizen"). As to the first question, are members of the polity given a *direct* role in making decisions that may be of fundamental importance to them, or is their role limited only to choosing those particular citizens who will make the actual decisions? If the answer is the latter, that brings us to the second question about the accountability of the actual decisionmakers.

Perhaps the ultimate question is the meaning of the vaunted term "popular sovereignty" suggested by the first three words of the Preamble to the U.S. Constitution. It may be that the national Constitution suggests different answers than the many state constitutions. As Laura Scalia has insisted, the "national constitution" was drafted by individuals deeply committed to the protection of "inalienable rights" and, concomitantly, suspicious about the dangers presented by too much popular participation in government. "State constitutions, on the other hand, have always tipped the scales in favor of popular sovereignty," which means far more popular control.[15]

Even if we focus only on the election of ultimate decision makers, we are still required to ask first if *everyone* gets to participate in the choice and, similarly, if *everyone* is eligible to be chosen. If we discover that there is no *universality* either of choosers or the potentially chosen, what explains the carveouts of the eligible and the ineligible? And what role do the Constitution or the constitutions of the various states play in determining the answers for the United States?

Representative government: Madison's argument in Federalist 10

If democracy is rule "by the people"—the *demos*—one might obviously think of designing institutions that include some genuinely active role for the people beyond simply picking those who will make the actual decisions. Numerous readers of this book will live in one of the many American states that includes the possibility of citizen initiative and referendum. We know what an aroused public can achieve with regard to such issues as tax policy, affirmative action, assisted suicide, or same-sex marriage. For example, in 2009, Maine voters exercised their constitutionally granted right to vote yea or nay on a bill passed by the state legislature and signed by the governor to legalize same-sex marriages. In Maine the joint decision of the legislature and governor did not constitute finality; instead, the Maine constitution allows the electorate to express their own views on the specifics of the legislation, and 53 percent of them voted to reject it. California voters had earlier voted for Proposition 8, which overruled a decision of the California supreme court that found same-sex marriage to be protected by that state's constitution.[16] Would we describe California and Maine—or countries like Switzerland, Ireland, Australia, and New Zealand, all of which have forms of national referenda—as more democratic than the national government of the United States? And if so, is this level of democracy *attractive*?

Perhaps the best way to explore the issues at stake is by a thorough exploration of the *Federalist* 10. Authored by James Madison, it became by the early twentieth century a canonical work of American political thought. How does Madison defend the particular form of representative government that he sees as the heart of the new system? To understand Madison's hostility toward any unfettered forms of democracy, one must begin with his extraordinarily influential theory of "faction."

1. Faction

The fear that drives Madison is that of faction, which he describes at the outset of his essay as "the mortal diseases under which popular governments have everywhere perished." Thus we see manifested what might be called Madisonian anxiety, rooted in his remarkable historical study of comparative government, which led him to the unhappy conclusion that prior "popular governments have *everywhere* perished." How will America escape this dreaded fate? He believes that the Constitution may offer potential cures for this "disease," but he is hardly confident. After all, he notes the widespread fears, based on observing the states in the immediate post-Revolutionary period—and undoubtedly reflecting on his own experience in the Virginia House of Delegates—"that our governments are too unstable, that the public good is disregarded in the conflicts of rival parties, and that measures are too often decided, not according to the rules of justice and the rights of the minor party, but by the superior force of an interested and overbearing majority."

Had there been even a modicum of confidence in the existing forms of government established by the Articles of Confederation, there would have been no constitutional convention in Philadelphia, and, even more certainly, it would not have been led by the unique figure of George Washington. Transformational change all too often requires the presence either of actual catastrophe—think of what occurred in Germany and Japan following World War II—or a belief that catastrophe may be looming if something is not done, *now*. Madison believed that the new country was in desperate straits because of a mixture of a completely inadequate national government and the political dysfunctionalities, whether trade wars or the simple inability to fund the new government, revealed in the behavior of the thirteen American states that had come together to form the new country.

If democracy is straightforward majority rule, then it is crucial to recognize that Madison is fearful of potential *misrule* by "an interested and overbearing majority" that is indifferent "to the rules of justice and the rights of the minor party." The central question is whether there is a way to design a constitution that will achieve its central goals without relying on the good faith of those in charge. Madison was famously skeptical about what he called "parchment barriers," including, for example, clauses promising to protect certain rights, whether those found in the Bill of Rights or the ostensible rights guaranteed to states in a federal system. Promises are easy to make and even easier to break when it seems "rational" to do so in order to achieve one's goals. History seems to support Madison's suspicions, as treaties are renounced and alliances reversed whenever convenient. So what will save the United States from the fate of other "popular" governments ravaged by the diseases associated with faction?

Understanding the disease requires that we have a clear understanding of the concept of a faction. Madison's definition is short, elegant, and problematic: "By a faction, I understand a number of citizens, whether amounting to a majority or a minority of the whole, who are united and actuated by some common impulse of passion, or of interest, adverse to the rights of other citizens, or to the permanent and aggregate interests of the community." It is as if Madison is emphasizing that democracy itself is no cure at all for the disease of faction, even if it presumably offers some measure of protection against *minority* factions. But this would be equivalent of buying insurance only against fire and ignoring the more likely risks of floods or earthquakes.

What is problematic is the possibility of achieving sufficient agreement on what count as "the rights of other citizens" and, even more so, "the permanent and aggregate interests of the community." How does one identify these interests, especially at a level of specificity that allows distinction between concrete policies on the grounds that one does and the other does not promote these interests? The Preamble's injunctions to "establish justice" or "secure the blessings of liberty" may inspire, but they provide almost no guidance. Which, if any, of the various medical care bills or proposals regarding American immigration policy considered by Congress in recent years qualified under these standards? Can we make sense of what political theorist Michael Sandel calls the "politics of the common good," or are we reduced to simply asking, with regard to any legislation, what's in it for us or our favorite group?

So how do we control the disease of faction, especially if we realize, as Madison does, that it cannot be eliminated? After all, as Madison writes, "the latent causes of faction are thus sown in the nature of man." Both human nature and political sociology assure the existence of factions. One cannot completely separate "reason" and "self-love." David Hume famously suggested that reason is the "slave" of the passions. And as contemporary behavioral economists have argued, people become passionately—perhaps irrationally—attached to their "endowments," including property.

What would later become labeled "class conflict" is central to Madison's vision of the political world (and therefore of the Constitution designed to manage that world). Madison tells us that "the most common and durable source of factions has been the various and unequal distribution of property. Those who hold and those who are without property have ever formed distinct interests in society." To be sure, property was not the only potential cause of factions. Madison mentions as well the "zeal for different opinions concerning religion" and the possibility that religious "zealots"—persons possessed with "zeal"—will attempt to gain control of political institutions for their own "partial" ends. Many of us could wince in recognition at Madison's description of a polity "divided…into parties, inflamed…with mutual animosity, and rendered…much more disposed to vex and oppress each other than to co-operate for their common good."

Indeed, Alexander Hamilton, in *Federalist* 1, lamented that "among the most formidable of the obstacles which the new Constitution will have to encounter" will be "the obvious interest of a certain class of men in every State to resist all changes which may hazard a diminution of the power, emolument, and consequence of the offices they hold under the State establishments." They will be joined by "the perverted ambition of another class of men, who will either hope to aggrandize themselves by the confusions of their country, or will flatter themselves with fairer prospects of elevation from the subdivision of the empire into several partial confederacies than from its union under one government." Hamilton admits that "ambition, avarice, personal animosity, party opposition, and many other motives not more laudable than these, are apt" to be present even among supporters of the new Constitution, though far more likely to explain opposition to the proffered document.

Interestingly enough, in *Federalist* 22, Hamilton denounces especially the ability of self-interested minorities to prevent the majority from ruling. The consequence of such power given to political minorities "is to embarrass the administration, to destroy the energy of the government, and to substitute the pleasure, caprice, or artifices of an insignificant, turbulent, or corrupt junto, to the regular deliberations and decisions of a respectable majority." If what Hamilton refers to as a "pertinacious minority" can in fact dominate the majority, it will be true by definition that "the majority, in order that something may be done, must conform to the views of the minority; and thus the sense of the smaller number will overrule that of the greater, and give a tone to the national proceedings. Hence, tedious delays;

continual negotiation and intrigue; contemptible compromises of the public good." Because it may prove impossible to gain the requisite number of votes that a supermajority system requires, "measures of government must be injuriously suspended, or fatally defeated. It is often, by the impracticality of obtaining the concurrence of the necessary number of votes, kept in a state of inaction. Its situation must always savor of weakness, sometimes border upon anarchy." In one sense, then, Hamilton appears to be a partisan of democracy, at least with regard to deciding who should prevail among the group, small or large, that actually participates in politics.

Still, like Madison, Hamilton has no great optimism about the capacities of most of his fellow citizens to rise above their selfish passions, whether the system is described as majoritarian or supermajoritarian. As Hamilton told his colleagues at the Philadelphia Convention on June 18, 1787, "All communities divide themselves into the few and the many. The first are the rich and wellborn, the other the mass of the people ... *The people are turbulent and changing; they seldom judge or determine right.* Give therefore to the first class a distinct, permanent share in the government" (emphasis added). The implicit argument is that this "first class" is more likely to "judge or determine right" than are the "mass" or the "many." Many of us even today might share Madison's and Hamilton's fears of truly popular government, even if relatively few Americans would explicitly speak in favor of government by "the rich and wellborn." But even today "populism" is at least as likely to be a term of denigration as of applause. So we should look more carefully at the argument that the Constitution does offer a valuable way of guarding ourselves against the dangers of faction.

Madison describes politics as necessarily involving the clash of basic interests. Whom can we trust to resolve these clashes? To embrace majority rule would mean that any majority could dominate vulnerable minorities. One example cited by many in Philadelphia was Rhode Island's passage of de facto redistributive "debtor relief" legislation that, by definition, limited the rights of creditors in favor of the far more numerous debtors. Such controversies about redistribution and its limits are not the only examples of ostensible "tyranny by the majority." As Madison tells us, "It is in vain to say that enlightened statesmen will be able to adjust these clashing interests, and render them all subservient to the public good." So how can we organize a system that will be at least relatively likely to make decisions in the public good?

2. The insufficiency of majority rule

Majority rule *does* provide an adequate response to minority factions. "Relief is supplied by the republican principle," Madison proclaims in *Federalist* 10, "which enables the majority to defeat its sinister views by regular vote." But it makes little sense to define "the republican principle" as equivalent to majority rule. After all, that provides no guard against majoritarian factions. Madison remains decidedly pessimistic: "If the impulse and the opportunity [to achieve one's factional goals] be suffered to coincide, we well know that neither moral nor religious motives can be relied on as an adequate control." Madison's anxiety runs deep. He has little faith that "moral or religious education" can adequately discipline temptations to pursue private interest or passion regardless of the public good. We are who we are, unlikely to be reshaped by institutions. Moreover, anticipating social psychologists who emphasize the degree to which we are influenced by those around us, Madison also notes that any such moral or religious restraints "lose their efficacy in proportion to the number combined together, that is, in proportion as their efficacy becomes needful."

All of us, unfortunately, can think of painful examples of this phenomenon, whether in this country or throughout the world, where apparently civilized and certainly well-educated individuals can be induced by circumstances to do truly awful things. So Madison leaves us with little optimism about controlling the disease of faction and therefore preserving a "republican form of government," at least if that means a government that will pay sufficient attention to those without the power to dominate.

At this point in his argument, he says that "it may be concluded that a pure democracy, by which I mean a society consisting of a small number of citizens, who assemble and administer the government in person, can admit of no cure for the mischiefs of faction." Presumably, he is referring to the form of democracy found in ancient Athens or, for that matter, the so-called town-meeting democracy found still today in some New England towns. "Such democracies have ever been spectacles of turbulence and contention; have ever been found incompatible with personal security or the rights of property; and have in general been as short in their lives as they have been violent in their deaths." We must find some other form of government if we are to avoid doom.

Then Madison relieves our anguish by announcing the good news: "A republic, by which I mean a government in which the scheme of representation takes place, opens a different prospect." It offers the cure against the ravages of "pure democracy." But what does this cure consist of? "The two great points of difference between a democracy and a republic are: first, the delegation of the government, in the latter, to a small number of citizens elected by the rest; secondly, the greater number of citizens, and greater sphere of country, over which the latter may be extended." Let us look at each of these in order and then ask whether Madison's arguments are truly persuasive.

III. GOVERNMENT BY REPRESENTATIVES

Assumptions about electoral virtue (or lack of same)

Madison obviously far prefers representative to what he calls "democratic" government, that is, the kind of direct democracy found in ancient Athens or, perhaps, even small New England townships.[17] We should pay very careful attention to his argument. Representative government, he says, will allow us

> to refine and enlarge the public views, by passing them through the medium of a chosen body of citizens, whose wisdom may best discern the true interest of their country, and whose patriotism and love of justice will be least likely to sacrifice it to temporary or partial considerations. Under such a regulation, *it may well happen that the public voice, pronounced by the representatives of the people, will be more consonant to the public good than if pronounced by the people themselves, convened for the purpose.* (emphasis added)

But why would one expect elected representatives to be more devoted to "the public good" than "the people themselves"? After all, Madison readily concedes that "men of factious tempers, of local prejudices, or of sinister designs, may, by intrigue, by corruption, or by other means" gain election to public office. What really seems central is his second argument relating to the size of the new country, for he suggests that such scoundrels will be far more easily isolated in a *national* legislature than would be the case in a smaller state one. But this still doesn't explain why we should think more highly of those elected to office than, say, a group of our ordinary fellow citizens who, as in ancient Athens, might be chosen by lot to fill political office and to deliberate on what the public good requires.

The extended republic

Madison's argument also rests in significant measure on the importance he assigns to the sheer size of the new American nation. He rejects the view, linked with Montesquieu and others, that one can hope for a republican form of government only in a small and basically homogeneous polity. If this were so, it would almost necessarily doom the success of the American experiment in republican government. Madison argues that a larger society will have more persons "fit" for public office than will a smaller one, just as one might expect that California contains more persons likely to discover a cure for cancer than does Wyoming or Alaska. Not only are larger units likely to have more people who are interested in discovering a cure for cancer in the first place, this larger number will also provide what may be an all-important *community* of people with shared interests—widely thought crucial to intellectual and technological breakthroughs. Sociologists refer to the *agglomeration* of people who correctly believe that their own flourishing requires being with a critical mass of people with similar interests.

Still, it is unclear that such numerical comparisons tell us anything at all about the relative likelihood of "fit" persons being *elected* to office. Madison seems to suggest that the electorate, composed of persons who are unfit to engage in actual political rule themselves and will tend to elect persons of insufficient political virtue to *state* offices, can nonetheless be counted on to choose those among them who are "fit" for *national* public office by possessing the requisite commitment to the "public good." Patrick Henry, the principal opponent of the Constitution at the Virginia ratifying convention, attacked what Pauline Maier has described as "the contempt for democratic state legislatures that ran through the private writings of Madison and other Federalists." The Constitution, said Henry, "presupposes that the chosen few who go to Congress will have more upright hearts, and more enlightened minds, than those who are members of the individual

Legislatures."[18] As Henry suggests, it is difficult to understand why the same voters will select such fundamentally different people for national and state office. Madison appears to believe that those casting votes are intelligent and morally acute enough to recognize what is in the public interest *and* have the psychological self-discipline to always (or frequently enough) vote for a candidate for national office who promises fidelity to the public interest even at the cost of voters' more selfish personal preferences.

An interesting experiment of sorts was run in the 2010 senatorial election in Alaska, where the official Republican party candidate, Joe Miller, campaigned on a platform of explicit refusal to seek any "earmarks" (special federal spending directed at Alaska), whereas his principal opponent, incumbent Republican Senator Lisa Murkowski, just as explicitly promised to emulate the late Republican Senator Ted Stevens by trying to bring home as much bacon to Alaska as humanly possible. Although defeated in the Republican primary, she became the first person in over a half century to be elected (or, in her case, re-elected) to the U.S. Senate by a write-in vote. There were, undoubtedly, many reasons to reject Miller (who received approximately 35 percent of the total vote), but one can well wonder if various Alaskan voters decided they wished a less "public-spirited" and more "Alaska-centered" senator.

The concluding paragraphs of this most famous of all *Federalist* essays declare that "the same advantage which a republic has over a democracy, in controlling the effects of faction, is enjoyed by a large over a small republic." One advantage "consist[s] in the substitution of representatives whose enlightened views and virtuous sentiments render them superior to local prejudices and schemes of injustice." Madison simply asserts that "it will not be denied that the representation of the Union will be most likely to possess these requisite endowments." Surely we should be suspicious of thundering assertions of what is "undeniable," at least when we are talking about matters other than hard science. And he returns as well to the advantages of size. "The extent of the Union gives it the most palpable advantage." Even if "factious leaders may kindle a flame within their particular States," they will be unable to spread a general conflagration through the other states.

A religious sect may degenerate into a political faction in a part of the Confederacy; but the variety of sects dispersed over the entire face of it must secure the national councils against any danger from that source. A rage for paper money, for an abolition of debts, for an equal division of property, or for any other improper or wicked project will be less apt to pervade the whole body of the Union than a particular member of it; in the same proportion as such a malady is more likely to taint a particular county or district than an entire State.

In the extent and proper structure of the Union, therefore, we behold a republican remedy for the diseases most incident to republican government. And according to the degree of pleasure and pride we feel in being republicans, ought to be our zeal in cherishing the spirit and supporting the character of Federalists.

Are you persuaded by Madison's argument? A negative answer returns us to the almost frightening pessimism with which he begins his essay about the unlikely survival of republican government given the reality of factions. So what do we say? Perhaps we respond that it is literally meaningless to discuss factions because we are modern skeptics who find all discussion of the "public good" to have no more intellectual substance than do ghosts or astrology. For such skeptics, the fact that millions of people might believe in poltergeists or astrology is irrelevant, and the same would be true regarding the fact that millions (including some famous philosophers) believe in the reality of the common good or justice. Or perhaps we agree that the public good can be identified, especially if we design suitable institutions encouraging deliberation about how to achieve it. In that case, factions might be far less likely than Madison believed. Or, if you have not been lulled into complacence by either of these arguments, maybe there are other ways of reining in the negative consequences of factions. But, unless you dismiss the entire intellectual structure underlying his notion of faction, Madison does seem to have identified a problem that anyone concerned with the health of this, or any other, political system must confront.

An important thread of eighteenth-century political thought held that republican government was possible only in relatively small and homogeneous societies. What is the basis for Madison's view that a republican form of government is truly likely *only* in an extended—that is, large—republic? The foundation of Madison's argument is empirical, not conceptual, and it lies basically in political sociology. Although Madison was a longtime friend and ally of Thomas Jefferson, he was extremely different from Jefferson in his political sociology. Jefferson admired local government. Madison did not. "The smaller the society," he asserts, "the fewer probably will be the distinct parties and interests composing it; the more frequently will a majority be found of the same party; and the smaller the number of individuals composing a majority, and the smaller the compass within which they are placed, the more easily will they concert and execute their plans of oppression."

Local control of government seems almost synonymous with tyranny of the majority for Madison. Gordon Wood notes that Madison has towns, cities, and counties named after him throughout the United States, not least because he was president during the War of 1812. What Wood doesn't say is that there is a certain irony in such naming, given Madison's relative disdain of the what he viewed as the actualities of local—including state—government. We will have occasion to return to some of these arguments when we look at the Constitution's protection of federalism, which is significant state autonomy. Why, after all, would one wish to protect federalism if one basically feared the kind of governance one would find in a small society? For Madison, bigger seems to be better: "Extend the sphere, and you take in a greater variety of parties and interests; you make it less probable that a majority of the whole will have a common motive to invade the rights of other citizens; or if such a common motive exists, it will be more difficult for all who feel it to discover their own strength, and to act in unison with each other." This may explain why Madison vigorously fought in Philadelphia for a provision empowering Congress to override all state legislation deemed counter to the national interest. He lost.

Does the evidence support Madison's optimism? In particular, he ignores the possibility that the country might need national political parties in order to "solve" some of the coordinating problems presented by the existence of so many factions. He does not consider that somewhat similar factions in a number of states could capture control of a major national party and therefore gain national power by electing presidents or a critical mass of representatives and senators. Perhaps it is marginally harder for them to do that than to capture a given state, but to the degree that Madison is optimistic at all, it seems necessary that he regard such capture as *highly* unlikely rather than only somewhat more difficult. And, if the national government has vast powers—which is certainly the case today—then the costs of such capture to the citizenry at large may be far greater than those attached to control of individual states, just as the benefits to the capturing faction give them a very high incentive to pay whatever costs may be involved in organizing and then winning power.

Constitutions set ostensible limits on what government can do, but as already noted, Madison was pessimistic about the utility of such "parchment barriers." Madison remains worth reading and wrestling with today because of his emphasis on the importance of *structures* in providing us the basis for a republican form of government. We must decide whether the structures he advocates do the job with regard to safeguarding a properly republican (or democratic) form of government. Madison may be far too optimistic that only "majority factions" generate serious problems for a republican form of government. If the political system adopted sets up a lot of "veto points," it is altogether possible that minority factions, even if they cannot pass their own programs, can prevent the passage of opponents' programs, including those that would in fact serve the "public good." Recall Hamilton's similar observation in *Federalist* 22: "If a pertinacious minority can control the opinion of a majority…the majority, in order that something may be done, must conform to the views of the minority; and thus the sense of the smaller number will overrule that of the greater, and give a tone to the national proceedings. Hence, tedious delays; continual negotiation and intrigue; *contemptible compromises* of the public good" (emphasis added). Madison, though, offers no real discussion of the possibility. He simply assumes that the only tyranny we need concern ourselves with is tyranny of the majority.

Let's assume for the moment that Madison was correct that it is harder to assemble a potentially tyrannical majority faction in an extended republic than in a small one. Does his argument apply to any and all extensions? After all, he was writing in an America that in 1790 had a total population of fewer than four million people (many of them barred from participation in politics, so that one might speak of a relevant political universe of at most a million people). Madison's America extended only to the east bank of the Mississippi River and from what is now Maine to the southern border of Georgia.

Madison had to contend not only with eminent political philosophers like Montesquieu and Hume, but more immediately with more homegrown opponents of the new Constitution. So consider a principal opponent of Constitutional ratification who wrote under the name Agrippa. He described it as "in itself an absurdity, and contrary to the whole experience of mankind" to imagine a republic in a country "on an average one thousand miles in length, and eight hundred in breadth, and containing six million [sic] of white inhabitants" and to imagine them "all reduced to the same standard of morals, of habits, and of laws."[19] Just imagine what Agrippa might had said about an ostensible republic that is now over 5,100 miles in breadth, from the tip of Maine to Hawaii in the mid-Pacific and—depending on one's views about Puerto Rico—to the mid-Caribbean as well, with a population according to the 2010 census of over 305 million people. Although 75 percent are white, several major states, including California and Texas, are now "majority minority" (if one does not count Hispanics as "white" or—in the Texas vernacular—"Anglos"). And, for what it's worth, only 51 percent of the population, according to the Central Intelligence Agency, are Protestant,[20] even if most of the remainder can still be defined as Christian. Given that the census does not ask about religion, it is difficult to know precisely how many Muslims there are within the United States; estimates range from 1.3 to 7 million.

It is worth asking if we share Madison's optimism about the possibility of an "extended republic" in the twenty-first century. Perhaps there *are* limits to the size and population (and, possibly, heterogeneity) of a republican government, even if they are considerably larger than those suggested by devotees of Montesquieu in the late eighteenth century. If we deny this and support what might be called infinite expansion, then Madisonian logic, paradoxically or not, would lead to endorsing world government (or at least North American or Western Hemisphere government).

World government is clearly not on the horizon, and no American politician seeking public office would dare suggest it. Instead, American political discourse still features regular invocations of the importance of federalism and "states' rights." So a final question is the implications of accepting Madison's general argument for the reality of contemporary American states. Many of them, regardless of the Constitution's "guarantee," could not be regarded as properly "republican" under Madison's criteria inasmuch as they permit—indeed almost seem to encourage—recourse to "direct democracy" as a substitute for the representative government that he thought essential.[21] These are not merely "abstract" or "theoretical" questions, given that the citizens of American states from Maine to California have engaged in direct democracy under their own state constitutions. To these realities, and some of the questions they raise, we now turn.

In the November 2011 state elections, for example, the Ohio and Maine electorates exercised their constitutionally authorized prerogative to overturn recently passed legislation (signed by the governors) that, respectively, limited the unionization rights of public employees and repealed the former ability of would-be voters to register to vote on Election Day itself (which works, among other things, to suppress voter turnout). One might speculate on the possible consequences if the US Constitution allowed disgruntled citizens, by gaining sufficient signatures on a petition, to trigger a national referendum on President Obama's signature Patient Protection and Affordable Care Act of 2010.

5

Elections and a Republican
Form of Government

I. HOW IMPORTANT IS THE BALLOT BOX? AND
WHO HAS ACCESS TO THE BALLOT?

Almost every definition of democracy includes elections and ballot boxes. But that only begins the conversation. Should *all* offices, or only some, be filled through an electoral mechanism? With regard to those that are selected by election, who has a right to be a candidate, and who can vote? How often should elections take place? How easy is it for the electorate to actually "vote the rascals out" should officeholders fail to be paragons of civic virtue? All of these clearly raise basic issues both of constitutional design and political theory. Various answers are given in America's fifty-one often quite different constitutions.

A. *The absence of "We the People" from national governance*

It is, for Madison, a huge plus that "We the People," once they establish the Constitution, play no real role in the actual making of decisions. Such decisionmaking would be left exclusively to the persons chosen to come to the nation's capital, originally New York, then Philadelphia, and finally Washington, DC in 1800. How are they to be selected? Later we shall discuss how we select presidents and vice presidents—the only executive branch officers[1] subject to any kind of election at all—indirectly though decidedly *not* by a majority of the national electorate. Similarly, no direct role was originally given to the public with regard to selecting senators. They were initially selected by the legislatures of their states. To be sure, throughout the nineteenth century, legislative selection was complemented by some forms of popular participation, and in 1913 the Seventeenth Amendment ended legislative selection in favor of popular election of senators. But, at least as a formal matter, the Framers envisioned no necessity for a single person who was *not* a member of a state legislature to play any role at all in selecting members of the "upper house." So now let us turn to what is sometimes called "the people's house," the House of Representatives, which was always envisioned as composed entirely of popularly elected officials. "When vacancies happen in the Representation from any State," Article I, Section 2, Clause 4 of the Constitution says, "the Executive Authority thereof shall issue Writs of Election to fill such Vacancies." Contrast this, for example, with the 2009–2010 Senate, which at one point included seven members appointed by their governors (as allowed by the Seventeenth Amendment) to succeed senators who had been elected president (Illinois) or vice president (Delaware), joined the president's cabinet (New York and Colorado), simply resigned (Florida), or died in office (Massachusetts and West Virginia).

The manner by which members of the House are elected is clearly set out in Article I, Section 2, Clause 1: "The House of Representatives shall be composed of Members chosen every second Year by the People of the several States, and the Electors in each State shall have the Qualifications requisite for Electors of the most numerous Branch of the State Legislature." We immediately learn that "the People of the several States" hardly means "everyone within the polity." The quoted language gives states the power to set out "Qualifications for Electors" (i.e., voters) who participate in choosing "the most numerous Branch of the State Legislature." This is an acknowledgment of the fact that twelve of the original states chose to adopt a bicameral (two-house) legislative system; in 1776, Pennsylvania had adopted a one-house legislature, though it chose the two-house option when writing a new constitution in 1790. Only Nebraska, since 1934, has chosen to make do with a unicameral legislature. What in bicameral states is usually called the "lower house" always has more members; in addition, during the early years of the American Republic, these "lower houses" were often elected by a greater pool of eligible voters than were the "upper houses," for which qualified voters might have to possess a given amount of property. So whoever could vote for, say, the New York Assembly was entitled to cast a vote in the election for the federal House of Representatives. But it should be clear that this didn't come close to universal suffrage.

We know of the general exclusion of non-whites and women. New Jersey did allow some women to vote until 1807, and, as Justice Curtis noted in his dissent in *Dred Scott*, "At the time of the ratification of the Articles of Confederation, all free native-born inhabitants of the States of New Hampshire, Massachusetts, New York, New Jersey, and North Carolina, though descended from African slaves, were not only citizens of those States, but such of them as had the other necessary qualifications possessed the franchise of electors, on equal terms with other citizens." North Carolina completely racialized the suffrage by depriving even free blacks of the right to vote under a new state constitution in 1835. Justice Curtis's allusion to "other necessary qualifications" acknowledges property requirements that were pervasive at the time the Constitution was adopted. New Hampshire, for example, amended its constitution in 1792 to exclude "paupers" from the suffrage, as did another thirteen states by the end of the nineteenth and beginning of the twentieth century. Other states at the time had affirmative property qualifications, that is, the requirement that one own sufficient property to participate in the polity.[2]

This requirement reflected the belief, going back to Aristotle, that those without independent economic resources were unlikely to have sufficient independence of judgment to warrant being part of the electorate. Dependent on others for their livelihoods, they would also likely fall under the political sway of their economic masters, who could often exact retribution for failure to follow their guidance, especially in the days before the rise of the secret ballot in the nineteenth century. ("Elections" for the generation that framed the Constitution were decidedly *public* events, where one gave public witness to one's political loyalties.) There were many other voting qualifications, particularly in many southern states following the end of Reconstruction. Literacy tests, for example, were widely used to bar African Americans from voting; the Fifteenth Amendment had made it illegal to bar voters because of their race, but not because of the inability to satisfy a local voting registrar that they were sufficiently literate.

Many of these voting rules, particularly involving property, changed in the states in the early nineteenth century as part of what has come to be called the "Jacksonian Revolution." In 1869, Wyoming, "the Equality State," became the first American territory to allow women's suffrage, which it maintained upon entry into the Union. The Constitution itself was amended—in the Fifteenth, Nineteenth, Twenty-fourth, and Twenty-sixth Amendments—to restrict the state's ability to deny the franchise on grounds of race, gender, ability to pay a poll tax, and being under twenty-one. But the very fact that constitutional amendments were deemed necessary confirms that the Constitution left this extremely important decision in the hands of states. Anyone familiar with contemporary elections knows how important state qualification rules continue to be, even if states have less latitude than two centuries ago. The most important contemporary example involves the exclusion of convicted felons from eligibility to vote. At least four million persons, who are disproportionately African American males, are excluded from the vote on this basis.[3] Some states impose a lifetime exclusion, others only a limited exclusion. But the point is that that decision is left in the hands of states.

Thus, quite different answers to the conundrum of achieving a republican form of government might be offered in various states. This is no small matter. Akhil Amar argues that military reconstruction in 1866 was justified under the Republican Form of Government Clause. He views Congress as correctly concluding that the former Confederate states, which conducted their elections under a "whites only" restriction—the Fifteenth Amendment was not added to the Constitution until 1870—and therefore disenfranchised large percentages of its population, were no longer "republican." Military intervention was thus necessary in order to provide the republican form of government that is "guaranteed" by Article IV. Amar's argument is clever, but one can still find it altogether problematic not only because it seemingly ignores the fact that African Americans were scarcely allowed to vote in the non-rebellious states but also because of the denial of the vote to women. It was not until the twentieth century that one could say with any confidence that even a majority of the U.S. population was legally entitled to vote. At the time of the Constitution and for more than a century thereafter, voting was restricted to a numerical minority of the population. While white boys could hope to vote if they simply lived until voting age, blacks and women could have no such expectations for decades.

This history suggests that the republican form of government test might well be treated as of the Constitution of Conversation; not only are there conflicting possible meanings, but the most widely accepted meanings change through time. The fact that what was perfectly acceptable in 1788 or even 1888 is certainly unacceptable today suggests that any scholarly analysis of "republican government" in American political life must necessarily be part of what I earlier called the "narrative of change." Even the most committed "originalists," proclaiming their commitment to returning to the pristine visions of the Framers, will not be heard to advocate denial of the vote to non-whites[4] or women or the insufficiently propertied. A broader notion of suffrage is, therefore, part of the "living Constitution."

II. THE FREQUENCY OF ELECTIONS

Rousseau famously argued in *The Social Contract* that the English were free only once every five years, when they exercised their sovereign capacity as a collective people to vote for Parliament. The rest of the time, he suggested, they were basically unfree, under the sway of their leaders "chosen" on election day. "Consent of the governed," one might say, must mean something more than the occasional ability to pick leaders and then, should they run for reelection, engage in a retrospective assessment of their adequacy.

Even if one rejects Rousseau's argument, which seems highly sympathetic to the mechanisms of direct democracy to be discussed later in this chapter, one may still ask about the frequency of elections. A common maxim, especially among opponents of the new Constitution, was that "oppression begins when annual elections end." (Legislative elections in Rhode Island took place every six months![5]) Thus it was no small matter that members of the House were elected for two-year terms. Even if we put to one side for the moment the fact that the pre-Seventeenth-Amendment Senate was appointed by state legislatures instead of being popularly elected, the term of office has remained six years. Presidents are guaranteed four years in office, so long as they avoid impeachment for having committed "high crimes and misdemeanors." And federal judges appear authorized to serve quite literally until they die, although this is almost uniformly rejected by the American states.

Does this represent "enough" access to the ballot, or might we wish, in the contemporary world, terms of different length? One can imagine arguments for both longer and shorter terms. Many people certainly believe that members of the House, who face a reelection campaign almost within eighteen months of taking their oath of office (in January) for a new term would behave "better" if they had four years in office. By the same token, maybe six years is too long for senators. And one finds, within the United States and across the world, varying terms of office for governors or chief executives in countries that have adopted "presidentialist" systems instead of parliamentary ones. The president of Mexico serves for six years, for example, while the French chief executive has a five-year term (down from seven years). By now, almost all American governors serve four-year terms, though New Hampshire and Vermont retain their original eighteenth-century practice of two-year terms.

III. ONE PERSON, ONE VOTE

Deciding to elect officials and how frequently to hold elections does not even begin to resolve crucial collateral issues presented when designing an election system. The original Constitution is almost completely silent on actual voting rules of the new country, save for the question of frequency. There would be elections, but it would be up to the states to decide how to run them. Many opponents of the Constitution were much concerned by the now-obscure Article I, Section 4: "The Times, Places and Manner of holding Elections for Senators and Representatives, shall be prescribed in each State by the Legislature thereof; but the Congress may at any time by Law make or alter such Regulations, except as to the Places of chusing Senators." Fears were expressed, for example, that devious national officials would require poor but honest yeomanry to trek to Boston or Philadelphia in order to vote.

No such interventions ever occurred. However, anyone trying to understand the U.S. House of Representatives should know of an 1842 statute of Congress requiring that each member of the House be elected in a *single-member* district. Some states, including Pennsylvania, had engaged in "at-large" election, which meant that a slender majority of voters, perhaps concentrated only in one part of a state, could elect *all* of the state's representatives. The move to geographically based single-member districts solves this particular problem, even if, as is often the case with reforms, it creates others, the most important of which is surely gerrymandering. This involves the conscious drawing of political boundary lines in order to help the party in control while disadvantaging its opposition in future elections.

There have been a number of constitutional amendments relating to voting eligibility; these are obviously important, but they scarcely go to the heart of what sorts of voting systems might prove most satisfactory in achieving various (and sometimes conflicting) goals attached to elections. One such goal, after all, is assuring participants that their votes (and opinions) might really matter; another is placing into office a group of officials who can organize themselves into an effective government. These two basic goals may not always be compatible, and fundamental choices must be made as to which goal should be preferred.

There *is* a major thread of decisions of the U.S. Supreme Court going back to 1963 that established the so-called one person, one vote norm.[6] The Court's decisions suggest that it violates basic tenets of American democracy for one person to have ascertainably greater voting power than another person. By definition, this was not regarded as a constitutional requirement prior to the 1960s, when it was thought perfectly acceptable to award an equal number of representatives to voting districts that might differ substantially in the number of voters.

In the half century since the Supreme Court entered what Justice Felix Frankfurter critically termed the "political thicket" of assessing political districting, the Court has provided almost no illumination on what the mantra "one person, one vote" actually means. In the seminal voting rights case *Reynolds v. Sims* (1964), which invalidated the legislative districting systems in operation in almost all of the states, Chief Justice Earl Warren wrote that the "right to vote freely for the candidate of one's choice is of the essence of a democratic society, and any restrictions on that right strike at the heart of representative government. And the right of suffrage can be denied by a debasement or dilution of the weight of a citizen's vote just as effectively as by wholly prohibiting the free exercise of the franchise." It is not enough for each person to have the right to vote and to have the vote counted. Rather, the relative *weight* of the vote is also important. It would clearly be unconstitutional if a state adopted a local version of John Stuart Mill's proposal for so-called plural voting by which those with more intelligence are given extra votes. Indeed, until after World War II, England in effect gave graduates of Oxford and Cambridge an extra vote inasmuch as a member of Parliament was explicitly elected from each of those schools. Oxbridge graduates got to vote in two elections, their home locality and their university, whereas everyone else could vote only in their locality.

One might well argue that if all it takes to elect a representative in District A is one thousand votes, while it requires two thousand votes to generate a majority in District B, then the voters in District A have twice the effective voting power as those in District B. Statistically, it is more likely that one might cast the "decisive vote" in a one-thousand-person electorate than a two-thousand-person one. In any event, this is what lies behind adoption of the one person, one vote mantra. "The concept of 'we the people' under the Constitution," wrote Warren, "visualizes no preferred class of voters but equality among those who meet the basic qualifications. The idea that every voter is equal to every other voter in his State, when he casts his ballot in favor of one of several competing candidates, underlies many of our decisions." Thus, according to the majority of the Court, "it is inconceivable that a state law to the effect that, in counting votes for legislators, the votes of citizens in one part of the State would be multiplied by two, five, or 10, while the votes of persons in another area would be counted only at face value, could be constitutionally sustainable. Of course, the effect of state legislative districting schemes which give the same number of representatives to unequal numbers of constituents is identical."

Warren defines representative government as "self-government through the medium of elected representatives of the people, and each and *every citizen has an inalienable right to full and effective participation* in the political processes of his State's legislative bodies. Most citizens can achieve this participation only as qualified voters through the election of legislators to represent them. *Full and effective participation* by all citizens in state government requires, therefore, that each citizen have an equally effective voice in the election of members of his state legislature" (emphasis added).

One might wonder whether "full and effective participation…in state [or national] government" is achieved simply by being able to vote in an election that will predictably send someone to Washington or Sacramento that the voter vehemently disagrees with from a district that was explicitly designed to make the election of a candidate from the voter's own party next to impossible. The Supreme Court has never addressed this obvious cause for skepticism other than to assert, entirely implausibly, in another case that it is simply the case that representatives in fact pay genuine attention to *all* of their constituents, not only the members of their own political party (or, in modern parlance, "base"). Such an assertion ignores the role that political parties play in modern politics, especially in an age when representatives seem increasingly worried by antagonistic challengers in party primaries challenges should they be perceived as too accommodating to the other political party.

A similar dismissal of the importance of political parties underlies Chief Justice Warren's declaration that "the basic principle of representative government remains, and must remain, unchanged—the weight of a citizen's vote cannot be made to depend on where he lives."Warren's dictum, if taken seriously, challenges the legitimacy of *any* political system that, like our own, selects *all* legislative officials from geographically defined areas. Even if the votes in all districts meet some criterion of equality, the probability of your being represented by someone you actually agree with is entirely a function of where you happen to live (and the distribution of political views of others who live in the same district). There is much that is inspiring and even noble about the language of *Reynolds v. Sims.* But regrettably, there is even more that serves primarily to confuse anyone who tries to flesh out the meaning of Warren's rhetoric. So what are some of the problems that the Court did not discuss in framing its approach to one person, one vote?

It does *not* mean that each congressional or state legislative district must contain an equal number of voters, whatever the emphasis placed on the premise that each voter should cast an "equally weighted" vote. The Court has ruled that each congressional district—the standards are a bit more relaxed for state legislative districts—must contain an equal number of *residents.* Perhaps this is what Chief Justice Warren means by constituents, but there is no necessary correlation between numbers of residents and voters. Bedroom suburbs may contain large numbers of children—all of them citizens—none of who can (or, for that matter, ought to be able to) vote. Or think of districts that contain significant numbers of prisoners, an ever-increasing number in the United States, which incarcerates a greater percentage of its population than any other country in the world today.[7] As a matter of fact, though, the population base for designing geographical districts includes not only non-voting children but also significant numbers of persons who, as non-citizens, are ineligible to vote (even though the Constitution does not formally bar states from offering non-citizens a ballot). Most numerous are resident aliens—legally in this country though not citizens of either the United States or the state in which they reside—but "illegal aliens" are also counted by the census as part of a state's population. Paradoxically or not, bastions of opposition to illegal immigrants may gain extra representation in the House because of them. There were, for example, roughly 1.7 million undocumented aliens in Texas at the time of the 2010 census. Given that each House district will have roughly 700,000 persons, Texas gained at least two districts that it would not have were these aliens excluded from the count by which states are assigned representatives.

In any event, it is quite possible that two given districts with equal populations will be quite different from one another with regard to the number of potential or actual voters. Perhaps this is irrelevant, because indeed the key term is *persons* instead of *voters*, but that ultimately makes hash of Warren's one person, one vote notion. The weight of your vote continues to be a function of geography if it is determined by whether you happen to live in a district composed overwhelmingly of adult retirees or in a bedroom suburb where half the population is too young to vote.

One might argue that representatives will faithfully represent all persons whether or not they can vote, but this rests on a highly debatable theory that representatives are indifferent to the power of constituents to reward or punish candidates at the polls. Most modern theories of representative democracy emphasize the degree to which representatives care about re-election, which means that they are likely to be highly attentive to potential voters, either in primaries or in the general election, and relatively indifferent to those who can neither help nor hurt their re-election prospects. Perhaps a truly "virtuous" representative would be unmoved by such considerations, but as Madison noted, reliance on such "enlightened statesmen" may be quite foolish.

What constitutes "majority rule"?

We have already been introduced to the notion of "essentially contested concepts," such as democracy. Not surprisingly, majority rule presents similar difficulties. Chief Justice Warren, in *Reynolds v. Sims*, had pronounced it a "logical" proposition that "in a society ostensibly grounded on representative government, it would seem reasonable that a majority of the people of a State could elect a majority of that State's legislators." But this condition is regularly violated in the United States because of the way that electoral districts are organized and voting rules established. With rare exception, most states in the United States follow the "first-past-the-post" system. The front-runner wins, even if he has received only 39 percent of the vote, as happened in the 2006 Texas gubernatorial election of Rick Perry. Democrats might have won control of the U.S. Senate in 2006 only because third-party candidates in Virginia and Montana took enough votes from Republican incumbents to allow Democrats to slip through with less than a majority of the overall vote (but more votes than the Republican incumbents received). This would not have happened, for example, in Georgia, which, as noted in Chapter 1, requires run-offs between the top-two candidates if the initial top vote-getter has not attained majority support. Most states, however, stick with first past the post. And, as we will see when we consider the electoral college, a candidate regularly wins the entire electoral vote of a given state without having to win a majority of the vote within the state. This was the case most prominently (and notoriously) with George W. Bush in Florida (and New Hampshire) in 2000. The issue received a great deal of attention in 2000 because Bush did not receive more votes nationwide than Al Gore, an outcome that the electoral college system of choosing presidents makes irrelevant. Far less attention was given to the fact that even in several states where he finished first, he (like many other presidential candidates in the past) did not have the support of a majority of the electorate.

There is nothing wrong with someone who receives less than a majority of the vote being elected a representative. This is almost by definition the result in a system of proportional representation that elects multiple representatives from the same geographical unit and adopts voting rules that allow numerical minorities without the voting clout ever to win a race in a single-member district to elect a favorite in a multimember district. The design of multi-member institutions, like legislatures, offers many possibilities for creativity if one's desire is to maximize the number of people who feel some sense of genuine linkage with their putative "representatives."

Even single-member offices, like the presidency or governorship, allows more room for imaginative design than one might normally think. John Allen Paulos—famous for his critiques of "innumeracy," that is, the widespread inability to understand basic mathematical concepts and their role in everyday reasoning—demonstrated in an entertaining article written in 1992 how a plausible argument could be made on behalf of the democratic bona fides of a victory by each and every one of the five candidates running in party primaries that year for the Democratic nomination in a given state, depending on what specific voting system was adopted. The first-past-the-post system will often produce a different winner than would a runoff between the two top candidates. But these are only two of numerous systems that have been devised (and used) over many years. Imagine, for example, an "approval voting" system where voters are entitled to indicate every candidate whose election they would "approve" of rather than selecting one from that set. The candidate approved by most of the voters would be selected, even if that particular person would not be the winner if voters indicated only their first choices. Even if this system minimizes the sense of elation felt by intense supporters of a losing candidate, it would presumably maximize the overall level of satisfaction inasmuch as the winner would, by definition, have been approved by more voters than anyone else. Or one could ask voters to rank their preferences, so that their second choice would spring to life if a particular voter's first choice failed to gain enough support to survive a de facto runoff. As an American election expert, commenting on the ability of Hamas to prevail in the 2006 elections in Gaza without having received a majority of the vote, noted, "Election systems always seem arcane until the day after the election. It is always difficult to get people interested in the details of the rules" until, in effect, it is too late.[8]

George Szpiro, a journalist–mathematician, has written a book tellingly titled *Numbers Rule: The Vexing Mathematics of Democracy, from Plato to the Present*, which offers a systematic examination of the strengths and weaknesses of various schemes that have operated at various times and places.[9] The obvious question is how one decides what the "best" theory of voting is, given that very different representatives will be produced depending on which method is chosen. And it is altogether likely that the preferred scheme will depend on *which* persons or party one desires to win. The power of the Rawlsian "veil of ignorance" as a design process is precisely that one does not know in advance who the specific beneficiaries of a given rule are. However, as already suggested, no constitution or election rules (often central bones of contention in constitutional negotiations) have been designed behind such a veil.

On the contrary, it is clear who the winners and losers (at least in the short run) will be under any given scheme. Some states, for example, have recently curtailed early voting, which allows voters to cast their ballots over a one- or two-week period prior to the standard election day.[10] The explanation for this, according to many, is that early voting favors Democrats over Republicans, and Republicans who gained control of state governments in the 2010 elections are eager to remove Democrats from the electorate. Turnout levels, which can in given contexts benefit a particular party or candidate, can be affected not only by whether or not early voting is allowed but also by holding elections on Tuesdays—as is currently legislatively required—instead of, for example, during a long weekend.

Gerrymandering

Does the "reasonable" requirement that a majority of the voters (who presumably are a controversial proxy for "the people") be able to elect "a majority of that State's legislators" (or, say, a majority of the state's delegation to the national House of Representatives) place any limits on the level of majoritarian "success"? As already noted, it is an 1842 act of Congress that mandates election of representatives through single-member districts; that legislation was sparked by the phenomenon of a statewide majority being able to gain *all* of the state's seats in the House, leaving what might be a substantial minority high and dry. At the very least, this reveals a deep tension between a simple (and simplistic) notion of majority rule and the common belief that too much majority rule can easily be described as tyranny of the majority. Anyone designing election systems, whether as part of a constitution or as a statutory scheme, must inevitably try to balance majority and minority interests.

The congressional act obviously doesn't forbid first-past-the-post systems, which by definition do *not* require that the winner demonstrate an ability to gain the support of the majority. Anyone committed to majority rule, though, might well prefer voting systems that generate someone who can plausibly claim to be the majority's choice, which is not the case with first past the post. We might also wonder if any given voting system should be "constitutionalized"—that is, inscribed in a constitution that is quite likely difficult to amend—or instead should be treated as subject to change by ordinary legislation. Proponents of "constitutionalization" might rationally fear that political "ins" will be unable to resist the temptation to revise an existing voting system in favor of one that will predictably entrench their own power. (One form of this fear is exemplified by gerrymandering.) But constitutionalization makes it very difficult—perhaps impossible, depending on the difficulties in the way of constitutional amendment—to change the election system when it is widely thought to be deficient.

This brings us back to the basic tension between a constitution as a means of *settling* basic questions or generating what may be endless, and often acrimonious, *conversations* about the meaning of disputable propositions, such as those set out in *Reynolds v. Sims*. It is interesting to contrast the Constitution's specificity with regard to the electoral college mechanism for electing presidents with its almost casual assignment to the states of responsibility for establishing the electoral process with regard to the House of Representatives. In a 1998 collection of essays in which various analysts were asked to identify the "stupidest" feature of the Constitution, Jeffrey Rosen picked its assignment of voting system selection to the various states. He argued strongly that there should be a single national system of voting. That, however, might come from a congressional statute, and a future Congress can always revise the legislation passed by a predecessor. The presumptive importance of constitutions is that they limit the possibility for such changes, since they require surmounting the hurdles placed in the way of constitutional amendment. But this could be a curse as well as a blessing, precisely because it makes it so difficult to correct a past error if the amendment process is distinctly skewed in favor of maintaining the status quo.

If majority rule presents its own endless difficulties, just consider Warren's invocation of the importance of "*effective* representation." This, presumably, requires far more than the simple (albeit surely important) ability to cast a vote and to have it counted. It even requires something more than each vote being theoretically equal to the vote of all other individuals: no one gets two votes while others get only one. (Nor are the problems solved even if the raw numbers of voters in different districts are equal.)

Instead, the reality of our political lives is that our votes have genuine impact only as part of groups, usually called political parties. Our individual vote is basically symbolic. Economists delight in demonstrating, by calculating the costs of waiting in lines and so on, that it is irrational for any given individual to vote where the electorate is large. It is only rarely rational, should one be motivated by a desire to actually determine who wins, to vote even as part as a small electorate. In union there is strength, however, and that union is usually expressed through membership in political parties and turning out to vote as a measure of the solidarity one feels with one's fellow party members.

It is this fundamental insight about the importance of political parties that is at the heart of political gerrymandering, named after Massachusetts Governor Elbridge Gerry and his early nineteenth-century redrawing of political districts to favor Republicans against Federalists. The point of gerrymandering, from then until now, is to identify likely groups of voters and then, by artful drawing of district lines, to achieve the maximum electoral return for those groups you identify with and, concomitantly, the minimum return for your opponents. The easiest way to do this is to "pack" a given district with 100 percent of your political opponents, which means that many votes are "wasted" inasmuch as only 51 percent of the vote is needed to elect a member of that political party. At the same time you can arrange a number of other districts where 60 to 65 percent of the voters are from your own party, while the remaining 35 to 40 percent are in the opposition. This usually means that you are very likely to win the district and your opponents are condemned to the status of a permanent minority, never being able to elect one of their own. Two eminent legal academics who write on voting coined the term "filler people" to refer to the hapless members of minority political parties whose sole function is to fill out the denominator with regard to meeting the ostensible equality standard established in *Reynolds*.[11] What makes them "filler people" is that there is no real likelihood that their votes will *ever* really matter in the general election. Significant challenges to the incumbents are more likely to take place in party primaries than in the general election. It therefore becomes a real question whether minorities in artfully gerrymandered districts should feel represented in any serious sense if the representative from their district has no interest at all in appealing to them for their vote. (Indeed, if the representative *does* reach out to the minority, there is more than a finite probability that disgruntled members of the majority would threaten to run a "purer" candidate in the party's primary, which becomes the *real* election with regard to who will represent the district.)

Our obsession with legislative line-drawing and gerrymandering derives from the fact that the United States is in a distinct minority of countries in the world that relies basically exclusively on *territorial* representation by a single representative. There are lots of other ways to elect representatives, including, for example, the approach chosen first in Germany and then by New Zealand, which elects half its representatives in single-member districts and the other half in a nationwide election by proportional representation. Moreover—and crucially—the final allocation of the second group of representatives is contingent on the relationship between the actual vote and the number of seats won in the geographically based elections. Thus, if because of geographical location of voters, a party winning only 50 percent of the national popular vote gained 55 percent of the geographically assigned seats, that party would receive only 45 percent of the other seats, so the total percentage of seats (50 percent) would mirror the actual votes received. In the United States, however, as James Glanz notes, clever gerrymandering by Georgia Democrats in 2000 led to a situation where Republicans, who won 1.8 million total votes, gained only seven of Georgia's congressional seats even as Democrats got six seats with only 1.1 million votes.[12] What's fair about that (unless one is a partisan Democrat)?

IV. SHOULD WE LOOK AT VOTING AS AN "INDIVIDUAL RIGHT" OR AS A PROBLEM IN STRUCTURAL DESIGN?

The Supreme Court, in *Reynolds,* strongly suggested that voting was an "individual right." This is one of the implications of carefully weighing the comparative impact of one person's vote. Political theorist Jonathan Still demonstrated in a brilliant article several decades ago that the one and only voting system that truly satisfies the quest for an individual right to an equally weighted vote, as described by the Supreme Court, is proportional representation, whereby the number of seats in a multimember body like a legislature is a function of the percentage of votes actually gained by that party in a nationwide poll.[13] (To rely exclusively on geographically based seats, as the United States does, is simply to guarantee that the "actual value" of one's vote will inevitably depend on where one lives.) So why isn't proportional representation the obvious choice with regard to designing a voting system? If Still is correct, the answer cannot be that any other system is better with regard to protecting the voting power of any given individual.

The answer is that proportional representation has a variety of well-known *structural consequences*, including the propensity to generate far more political parties than is the case with geographically based single-member district systems, which tend to generate only two major parties. More to the point is the widely shared view that by electing legislators who represent these additional parties and the sometimes single-issue preferences linked with them, it is considerably harder to form an effective government in the legislature itself. It is altogether possible that small single-issue parties would tend to produce more "uncompromising" legislators than a larger "big-tent" party. This, obviously, is a special difficulty with parliamentary systems, which rely on a prime minister to be head of government, but it could just as easily be a problem within the United States, given the centrality of Congress to passing legislation.

As we are seeing in the United States, it's hard enough to govern even in a presumptive two-party system. One might well think it would be impossible if the House of Representatives included no true majority party and instead consisted of a set of voting blocs whose members represented unusually intense particular constituencies even more resistant to any notion of compromise. So, as election theorists like Samuel Issacharoff and Richard Pildes have insisted, it is important to take a *structural* approach toward analyzing given voting schemes rather than fixate on some notion of an *individual* right independent of structural implications. One way of summarizing this point is that we need to be concerned not only with abstract *representation* of voters but also the creation of an effective *government.* There is an inevitable tension between these two valuable ends. One may have to sacrifice a certain level of representation, especially for relatively smaller blocs of voters, in order to create the possibility of a more effective government. Effectiveness, in such a case, may mean that government will pay little or no attention to the views of a small bloc of voters unable to actually elect anyone to the legislature.

V. IF VOTING SERVES THE "PUBLIC WELFARE," SHOULD EVERYONE BE NOT ONLY ENTITLED BUT EVEN *REQUIRED* TO VOTE?

Do we really care whether people vote? After all, if we view voting as simply one device among many by which egoistic maximizers of their own self-interest act in the world, we might legitimately be indifferent to whether any given individual votes. On the other hand, we might have a more communitarian, civic-republican conception of the voter, by which voting is a public duty of the engaged *citizen,* who asks not simply what is in his or her own self-interest but, far more importantly, what best serves the interest of the general community. Madison seems to suggest this is not only desirable but also possible. If it is a public duty, then is there an argument that it should be *required* in the same way that jury service or payment of taxes (or military service in a conscription system) is non-discretionary?

Norman Ornstein, a distinguished political scientist affiliated with the American Enterprise Institute, has for many years advocated that the United States emulate Australia (and several other countries) by making voting mandatory. In a *New York Times* op-ed titled "Vote—or Else," Orenstein bewailed the generally low turnout of the electorate, particularly in what are increasingly becoming all-important party primaries. "With participation rates of about 10 percent or less of the eligible electorate in many primaries to 35 percent or so in midterm general elections to 50 percent or 60 percent in presidential contests," Ornstein wrote, "the name of the game for parties is turnout—and the key to success is turning out one's ideological base. Whichever party does a better job getting its base to the polls reaps the rewards of majority status. And what's the best way to get your base to show up at the polls? Focus on divisive issues that underscore the differences between the parties."[14] Ornstein, like many political scientists, sees a direct connection between the mechanisms by which the relatively small universe of actual voters is selected (by voting registration mechanisms, including exclusions from eligibility) and then self-selected (by deciding whether or not to vote on election day) and the overall health of the body politic. The oft-commented-on polarization of American politics, he suggests, could be considerably diminished if everyone had to vote, instead of leaving choices up to those with the requisite passion to participate. The voting turnout in the unusually dramatic 2010 midterm congressional elections was well under 50 percent overall; particularly telling, though, was the low turnout of various subgroups, including young voters and members of racial and ethnic groups. Younger voters made up 18 percent of the total voters in 2008, but fell to only 11 percent in 2010.[15] Though political scientists differ about the composition of non-voters relative to voters, there is no reason to believe that those who vote constitute a "perfect sample" of the general electorate. Indeed, if one wishes elections by such samples, better to rely on scientific public opinion polls that can pick carefully selected national samples that mirror public opinion with a relatively small percentage of error.

One shouldn't overemphasize the importance of mandatory voting. Most countries do not require voting—even though most do have higher turnout rates because of far less restrictive voting registration policies than those found in the United States—and many of them have admirable political systems. That being said, is there something to Ornstein's view, and is it a defect of American state constitutions—they are, after all, ultimately in charge of the American electoral system—that none of them emulate Australia's insistence that voting is not only a right but also a duty of anyone who is truly a member of the polity?

VI. DOES THE RIGHT TO VOTE
NECESSARILY ENTAIL THE RIGHT
TO SERVE IN PUBLIC OFFICE?

The answer to this question should be obvious. Any reader who is a naturalized citizen can vote for presidential electors, but thanks to the Constitution's requirement of "natural-born citizenship"[16] can have no hope of becoming president him- or herself, in the absence of a constitutional amendment. Similarly, anyone under twenty-five or thirty has been allowed to vote since turning eighteen, but is ineligible to serve in the House or the Senate. One might regard these limitations as relatively trivial (similar to the "except Sunday" parenthesis in the veto clause), but they do underscore the point that there is a difference between voting and serving in office.

Are the age limitations self-evidently justifiable? One might well be wary of a twenty-five-year-old senator, but why shouldn't that decision be left up to the electorate rather than being forbidden through the ostensible Constitution of Settlement? Some principles certainly do need to be settled, and one can even concede that *some* specificity concerning age is desirable with regard to voting. But why shouldn't any and all voters be eligible for all offices, rather than drawing age-based lines among various offices? This appears to be the approach taken by both Ohio and Wisconsin, which allows anyone eligible to vote—that is, anyone over eighteen—to vie for any elected office.[17] Many states do have slightly stricter age-eligibility criteria; most, though, fall well short of those established in the U.S. Constitution, save that three states—Kentucky, New Hampshire, and Tennessee—do require their state senators to be thirty. If one accepts the legitimacy of age-based limitations, not least because it would be unworkable to say simply that candidates must be of a "reasonable age" or "sufficiently mature" to hold public office, is there any particular reason to believe that the Constitution picks the right ages for us today? Perhaps, given the complexities of modern life and the importance of various experiences, one would reject the practices of the states in favor of a requirement that representatives be at least thirty, senators thirty-five, and presidents no younger than forty. But how would one rationally demonstrate the virtues of any particular age?

One of the more peculiar features of both the Fifteenth and Nineteenth Amendments is that each refers only to voting. Does this mean that it would have been constitutional for a state to say that its public officials had to be white males, with African Americans and women only able to vote for their favorite white male? The lawyerly answer is certainly not. Such limitations would easily be dismissed as unconstitutional today, though—tellingly—on the basis of the Equal Protection Clause of the Fourteenth Amendment rather than the texts of the Fifteenth or Nineteenth Amendments.

However, consider in this context what I call in *Our Undemocratic Constitution* our "second-class citizenship" clauses. The most dramatic one prohibits a naturalized citizen from ever serving as president of the United States. Naturalized citizens are treated better with regard to the House and the Senate, but, thanks to the text of the Constitution of Settlement, after naturalization they must wait seven and nine years, respectively, to be eligible to serve. Ask yourself, though, how we would respond in the twenty-first century to a *state* constitution that tracked the national one by distinguishing between U.S. (and state) citizens on the basis of the *duration* of their citizenship. Full discussion would take us well into the realm of the Constitution of Conversation, particularly the Equal Protection Clause of the Fourteenth Amendment and the (il)legitimacy of such distinctions when adopted by state governments. But if one would support reading the Equal Protection Clause to prohibit *states* from using such criteria to establish eligibility for public office, then this suggests that such criteria survive at the *national* level only because of the forcefulness of the language in the text. It does appear to have "settled" the matter at least as a topic of specifically *legal* conversation. But we have already seen that there is no reason to associate the Constitution of Settlement with moral goodness or otherwise necessarily defensible propositions. All one can say is that, for whatever reason, including the political exigencies of the moment, a given policy was adopted and entrenched by being given constitutional status rather than being adopted in a statute that could simply be repealed at a future date if majority sentiment shifted. But, presumably, the meaning of the Constitution of Settlement with regard to eligibility for office is that it is irrelevant that a majority of the public might want someone foreign-born to be their president or a recently naturalized citizen to serve in the House or the Senate.

VII. MUST ELECTIONS BE ABOUT CHOOSING REPRESENTATIVES? THE CRITIQUE OF REPRESENTATIVE DEMOCRACY

A. Direct democracy[18]

Our discussion so far has presumed that we must have elections to select those who will hold office and therefore be empowered to make decisions in the name of the people, whether because a majority actually chose them or because we accept a system that simply gives us a defined "winner." But it is time at last to confront the challenge set down by many U.S. states—not to mention foreign countries like New Zealand, Switzerland, and Australia—all of which incorporate the possibility of direct democracy into their constitutional orders. All would be described as adherents of representative democracy, but they incorporate features of direct democracy as well by which "the people" are permitted to decide for themselves one or another vital issue—and not merely select those who are then given power to make such decisions. Their adherence to representative democracy is evidenced by the fact that they have elected parliaments or legislatures. If they were all-out direct-democracy buffs, there would be no such institutions, and all decisions would be made only after direct consultation with—and decision by—the citizenry. Instead, like most American states, these countries complement traditional representative democracy with options for direct participation by the electorate.

Why? Former Illinois Governor Edward Dunne, addressing the Illinois constitutional convention in 1920, offers one powerful answer: "The people have ascertained that at the State Capital in recent years a third house, not recognized by the laws or Constitution of the State, has exercised potent and malign influence in the matter of drafting legislation; the contaminating lobbies, financed by corporate influence, have infested legislative halls and the hotels where legislators live, and have influence the legislators by sinister arguments delivered in closets and bathrooms, behind closed doors."[19] Proponents of direct democracy were not, obviously, universally triumphant. Notice should be taken, though, that every American state except Delaware either allows or requires popular ratification of constitutional amendments proposed by state legislators.[20] But, as a matter of fact, this is the most minimal form of direct democracy. Twenty-two states allow popular initiation of legislation, while eighteen allow popular initiation (and referendum) of constitutional amendments. Twenty-five states allow so-called veto referenda by which statutes can, upon sufficient numbers of the electorate signing petitions, then be submitted to the electorate for approval or disapproval. This explains why Maine voters were able to override legislation passed by the state legislature and signed by the governor.

It is not inordinately difficult to discover what "We the People" think about specific issues, especially in the modern world of social networks. Rather, the questions posed by direct democracy are primarily ones of *value.* Do we trust "the people" enough to allow them a genuine role in decisionmaking or, on the contrary, do we wish to minimize their role for fear of what the people are like? Recall Hamilton's comment that "the people are turbulent and changing; they seldom judge or determine right." If we agree, we will scarcely be devotees of direct democracy.

One often hears "American politics" described as uniquely "representative" in form, but the slightest acquaintance with the extremely important realms of American politics carried out at the state level puts the obvious lie to any such assertion. Indeed, if one looks at these constitutions both across time and space, one might well conclude that the "American way" is indeed to reserve some possibility for direct democracy. From this perspective, it is the U.S. Constitution that represents the outlier within the fifty-one American constitutions. It is easy enough to explain this difference; one need only emphasize the degree to which those who drafted the Constitution in 1787 were deeply suspicious of what we might today call "democratic politics," including the possibility of "direct democracy," compared to those who drafted state constitutions. The U.S. Constitution was created at almost the last moment in which it was possible to draft and gain acceptance for a constitution that so completely rejected any iota of direct democracy. The early nineteenth century, as Gordon Wood has emphasized in his copious writings, featured a far warmer embrace of popular rule, as illustrated in the spate of state constitution-drafting throughout the United States.

A quite different question is whether this difference between state constitutions and the national foundational document can be justified. There are at least two different paths down which such a question might lead. One is to treat all constitutions as equal; if some component of direct democracy is good in one constitution, it is presumptively good in all foundational documents. Conversely, if we agree with the vision underlying the U.S. Constitution—that direct democracy is a bad thing, perhaps fatal to the very enterprise of constitutionalism itself—then, presumably, it is equally bad wherever adopted. A way of bringing this down to earth is to ask whether we can legitimately believe that direct democracy—to at least some extent—is desirable for Maine, Massachusetts, Iowa, Texas, and California, but not for the United States at large.

If one differentiates between state constitutions and the national constitution, it is presumably because they represent, in some significant sense, quite different enterprises. But one would have to explain what these differences are and why they entail such striking variations in basic political structures. Consider that thirty-two of the states apparently include in their constitutions the requirement that state budgets be balanced, unlike the national Constitution.[21] Though some in fact call for a "balanced budget amendment" that would apply similar strictures to the U.S. Congress, most analysts oppose such proposals, not least because of the strikingly different role that the national government plays in the national and international economy and the concomitant freedom over budgets that presumably is helpful (whatever some admitted costs). Would similar arguments help to justify some measure of direct democracy in almost all of the states and none at all at the national level?

Perhaps one wants to address issues of size: the United States may just be too geographically large with too great a population to allow direct democracy. But what about Texas and California, each many times the population of the United States at the time of its formation (and rejection of direct democracy), and also quite large in territory? With regard to the territory size, is it relevant that Australia has no trouble conducting referenda? And, for what it is worth, Brazil and Russia have resorted to referenda on occasion, the former on whether to continue to allow the sale of firearms—122 million Brazilians participated—the latter concerning ratification of its 1993 constitution—58 million of a potential electorate of 106 million participated (of whom approximately 33 million gave it their approval). And, as noted earlier, approximately 55 percent of the almost twenty-nine million French who voted in a referendum on a draft European Constitution rejected it, which doomed it because the drafters—wisely or not—chose to require unanimity in order for the draft to take legal affect. An important recent referendum involved the new Kenyan Constitution, which was approved by more than six million voters, almost 70 percent of the voting population. Earlier, the Iraqi Constitution was ratified as the result of a popular referendum. The point is that the resistance to direct democracy by those who drafted the U.S. Constitution has become a distinctly minority position not only in the contemporary United States but also in the world at large.

It should be emphasized that the development of the American version of initiative and referendum is profoundly rooted in the actualities of American political history. No one can understand California's embrace of direct democracy in the early twentieth century, for example, without recognizing the influence of the widespread (and basically accurate) perception of people at the time that the California legislature had become completely dominated by particular economic interests, particularly the railroads. Thus, as Stephen Griffin has written in a powerful recent study of California government, the "standard" story concerning "the origins of direct democracy [in that state] suggests strongly that the citizens of California had lost confidence in the normal workings of representative democracy. Accounts of the origins of direct democracy often say that its advocates believed their political system was corrupt."[22] From one perspective, then, the turn-of-the-century Californians, like the citizens of a number of other particularly Western states of the time, were good Madisonians who had indeed learned the "lessons of experience." One of these lessons was that representative democracy could not bear the weight that Madison placed on it, precisely because it was all too subject to factious capture by the non-virtuous who would try to use the powers of government to line their own pockets. Californians did not *replace* representative government with direct democracy, but they clearly offered the processes of such direct involvement by the general public as an important *supplement* to the Madisonian model that would correct what had proved to be its deficiencies.

An especially interesting form of direct democracy is the ability offered in fourteen state constitutions of the electorate to mandate a new constitutional convention within a given state. Voters in Maryland, Montana, Iowa, and Michigan, for example, were asked in November 2010 to vote yea or nay on a new convention to consider revising the existing state constitution. The invitation was sharply rejected in Montana, Iowa, and Michigan, and the 54 percent level of support reached in Maryland was not sufficient to meet the requirement that it be supported by a majority of the total number of voters, many of whom "blanked their ballots" on the convention referendum after voting for one of the candidates in the hotly contested gubernatorial race. Ohio will have the opportunity to vote in 2012 on calling a new convention. If the electorate *does* call for a new convention, one of the issues that would inevitably arise is whether a revised constitution should continue to include some measure of direct democracy or even to expand it—for example, by making Ohio more similar to California, with its initiative and referenda and the ability of the electorate to "recall" state officials, including its governor. Wisconsin also permits the recall of its governor and legislators. In 2011 there were several recall elections involving state legislators of both parties, and it is quite likely that Governor Scott Walker will face a recall election in 2012.

Questions about direct democracy arise with regard to the drafting of any new constitutions, throughout the world. At the very least, in the modern world one doubts if drafters of a new constitution would be able to exclude the general public from a defining role in ratifying any new constitution. Is it fair to describe the U.S. Constitution (though not most American *state* constitutions) as hopelessly anachronistic in its disregard of any role for direct decisionmaking by whoever constitutes "We the People"? Or, on the contrary, should we be proud of the 1787 Constitution in this regard and chastise all those states and foreign countries that have chosen more democratic possibilities?

VIII. ARE ELECTIONS NECESSARY?

We are assuming that the choice facing us is the one Madison set out, that is, between "pure democracy," which relies on the participation of almost all citizens, and "representative democracy," which calls on the citizenry only to select those who will actually make the relevant governmental decisions. What both of these have in common is that each involves the ballot box, whether to make first-order decisions, as in direct democracy, or only to select the representatives empowered to act. But perhaps the problem is thinking in terms of the ballot box at all, whether to select officials or to register views about particular issues.[23]

A number of political theorists have recently sparked renewed interest in an important feature of Athenian democracy, which is widely—and often critically—described as the paradigm of direct democracy.[24] That feature is the selection of public decisionmakers by lottery. There are no elections and therefore no "campaigns" in which candidates try to persuade electors to vote for them. Selection is by chance. Anthony Gottlieb begins an excellent review of voting systems in *The New Yorker* by describing the role played by multiple lotteries in the extraordinarily complicated Venetian system, which was explicitly designed to reduce—ideally to eliminate—the possibility of corruption, which seems endemic in most electoral systems.[25] One need no longer worry about sleazy campaigns or the inordinate role played by campaign contributions or the ability to gain the support of powerful media. All of these are instantly rendered irrelevant if selection is in fact a function of sheer chance.

Think of the modern jury, a very important governmental body, as Tocqueville pointed out long ago in *Democracy in America*.[26] Decisions quite literally of life or death (in states like Texas that allow the death penalty) are made by ordinary citizens who have been called to jury service. The ballot box is wholly irrelevant, as is "appointment" by the presiding judge. Instead, jurors are initially selected through a process that emphasizes the element of chance. There is, however, a winnowing process before they are actually seated that can focus on specific attributes that render a particular person unsuitable for service.

Yale professor Akhil Amar has been one of the most important defenders of not only the jury system but also the wider vision of "lottery selection" that it signifies.[27] There is something satisfying about lottery selection to anyone who is a strong proponent of equality, inasmuch as almost everyone has an equal probability of being chosen for the office or duty in question. One must say "almost" because there will always be some exemptions; no one, for example, would place children in the pool (even if there might be some debate about the age at which someone is no longer a child). So consider the possibility, with regard to any given issue, that the decision is made by a group of citizens large enough to be plausibly "representative of the public" according to the norms of public opinion polling (this would usually mean five to seven hundred persons), selected at random and then given the opportunity to hear "experts" make their various pitches about how best to solve a given problem. British Columbia extensively assessed its own electoral system through a provincewide "citizen jury," though its members weren't randomly selected.

Stanford political theorist James Fishkin has conducted what he calls "deliberative polls" literally all over the world, including in China, in which persons selected at random have offered their views about significant public issues. None of these "polls" or "deliberative assemblies"—my own preferred description—has involved actual decisionmaking; rather they offered "advice" to those charged with making the ultimate decisions. Some of Fishkin's critics have been very critical of his arguments on just this point. But one doesn't have to adjudicate the disputes among various theorists trying to work out the meaning and institutional implications of what has come to be called "deliberative democracy." Rather, the central question is whether we share the view that our present system of "representative government" accords too well with some of the critical descriptions of "faction" offered by Madison in *Federalist* 10.

Fishkin emphasizes that a robust conception of popular government in the twenty-first century cannot stop with "going to the ballot box" (and, presumably, having one's votes counted honestly).[28] That may be a necessary condition of democracy, but in no sense should it be viewed as even close to a sufficient condition—even in a regime that features an honest police force and civil service, which President Obama has emphasized as a necessary supplement to the ballot box. Rather, a model of "competitive democracy" that focuses almost exclusively on the occurrence of elections by which oppositional political parties can mount plausible challenges to the maintenance of power by current political insiders, "keeps the mechanism of democracy without its soul." Though this critique is especially powerful if elections "are won by manipulation or deception, by bamboozling an inattentive public,"[29] even "fair" and uncorrupted electoral processes have their problems. Any democratic republic worthy of the name should accord "the people" a real opportunity to "speak," where such public speech is the product of some genuine deliberation about the relevant issues facing the given polity.

He is attempting to build genuinely new institutional structures designed to fundamentally transform both the conceptions and practical possibilities of politics within a given society. Paradoxically or not, one of his inspirations models is James Madison, who had the advantage of being at the very center of the efforts in 1787 to design a brand new constitution for the fledgling United States of America. "Constitutional design" offers just the occasion for thinking both most broadly and most deeply about the conceptualization of political order and the creation of institutions commensurate with those conceptualizations.

It is obviously far more difficult to engage in such efforts when a political order is already established. At that point, it is often tempting to define the most basic goals of the order in terms of fidelity to the visions of a "founding generation" rather than to emulate those Founders by asking whether we ourselves should engage in what may be viewed as audacious projects of institutional reform. Or, from a less normative perspective, one might simply emphasize the almost tyrannical force of "path dependence," by which even quite "rotten compromises" become structurally embedded and basically impervious to change.

Although emulating Madison's interest in basic issues of institutional design, Fishkin rejects Madison's generally dismissive views of the capacity of ordinary Americans to exercise genuine political autonomy. He writes in a distinctly Jeffersonian spirit of confidence in ordinary Americans and rejection of a desiccated version of "elite democracy." But there is an obvious problem with mass participation that is at the heart of the book. As the American political system has over the decades (at both state and national levels) adopted a more inclusive suffrage and various mechanisms of direct democracy (in the states), "the result of these well-intentioned efforts to move government and policy closer to actual, raw public opinion has been a lessened impact of deliberation."

There are, Fishkin notes, "normally strong disincentives for mass public opinion to be very deliberative." These can range simply from what economists would call the "search costs" involved in becoming suitably informed about public issues to the collective action problems, also much emphasized by economists, that promote "free riding" by most of the public on the relatively small number of individuals who are willing to invest their scarce time and energy (and money) in the demands of genuine republican citizenship. Some use these economistic insights to discredit the very project of popular democracy. This last issue turns us to another crucial aspect of James Madison's thought, his defense of the possibility of the "extended republic" as against those theorists—most importantly Montesquieu—who believed that republicanism was closely correlated with the relatively small size of the territory (and presumably population) in question. I noted earlier the problems presented by making sense of Madison's notion of the "extended republic" in our own time.

To be sure, if the only criteria for such a republic involved the holding of competitive elections and the protection of certain basic rights (coupled with a relatively uncorrupt civil service), then one might proclaim we have achieved this, so there is nothing further to say. And one might even envision such a notion of republican government making further headway in places like India and eventually China. But then we must address the justified concern about the limits of such a vision of popular government. It is one that has little or no role for deliberation or what Fishkin terms "public consultation." At best, we have a facade for manipulation by political elites; at worst, we will see the further rise of a basically plebiscitary form of politics, in which leaders rely on charisma or the talents of demagoguery to gain office and the prerogatives that come with positions of leadership.

There is also the serious problem, as many political scientists have demonstrated, of being able to discern any concrete "meaning" from elections other than the tautological selection of a winner to occupy an office. But the notion of elections as "mandates" presents its own difficulties, beginning with the simple fact that most candidates present views on a multiplicity of issues and any given voter therefore has to decide *which* given issue or set of issues is most important and vote on that basis. One may vote for given candidates *in spite of* their views on issue X because one is so impressed by their commitment to one's favored issue Y. If the winning candidate gets the bulk of support from those who jointly disdain X and prefer Y, then it is simply wrong for the winner to claim a mandate to do X.

So the question is whether we can have a more ambitious notion of popular government that doesn't fall victim to these telling objections? Fishkin himself focuses on an analytic "trilemma" that limns the challenges facing us. Here the focus is on the tensions produced when we try to maximize what have become, in the modern world, three basic notions of "democracy." First, there is the principle of political equality—captured in the notion of one person, one vote—which obviously rejects at the outset many traditional notions of elite rule. The notion of democracy as government by consent almost necessarily leads to a conception of mass participation, by which literally millions of voters cast their ballots and thus "choose" their governments. Finally, there is the desideratum of some genuine deliberation by those voting, lest the election turn into an almost mindless plebiscite empowering what are often demagogic, even Caesarist, leaders chosen by a basically ignorant electorate.

Fishkin is no utopian. Indeed, a very important part of his argument is that one must choose among the horns of his trilemma. There is, therefore, the sad realization that "the fundamental principles of democracy do not add up to such a single, coherent ideal to be appropriated, step by step. Achieving political equality and participation leads to a thin, plebiscitary democracy in which deliberation is undermined. Achieving political equality and deliberation leaves out mass participation. Achieving deliberation and participation can be achieved for those unequally motivated and interested, but violates political equality." He is no magician who can make the trilemma disappear with the wave of a conceptual apparatus. But he clearly believes that we can achieve both better (in terms of policy results) and more legitimate (in terms of meeting contemporary criteria for democracy) governance than is now the case, even as we recognize that there will still be costs to one or another leg of the trilemma.

"Reviving the Athenian ideal," Fishkin argues, "with the best modern technology available, provides a practical method for bringing deliberative democracy to life." That ideal rests on a mixture of both the capacity and the equal probability of each citizen's taking an active part in the deliberations about public policy. Capacity refers to basic attributes that are desired in any citizen, captured in modern polities by such criteria as age or a suitable level of intellectual competence. Some might wish to add explicit educational qualifications, including literacy (and the ability to function in the dominant language of the community). To be sure, all of these can generate controversy, but there is no one who would support genuinely "universal suffrage" if it meant, for example, giving a vote to a six-year-old or a severely mentally disabled adult. The real issue is how to construct a polity in which the millions of competent citizens can in fact function together as part of a "republican form of government."

As the reference to ancient Athens suggests, one answer is to adopt a form of lottery representation whereby only *some* of the citizenry actually participates (and deliberates), but those who are excluded accept the legitimacy of both that procedure and the resulting policies. The legitimacy arises from both the equal probability that any given person (discounting for minimal baseline qualifications) might have been chosen *and* the perception by those not chosen that the system of lottery selection assures the relative "representativeness" of the sample chosen. The deliberative assembly will look sufficiently "like America"—or the given state or locality adopting this form of governance—to provide necessary confidence that one's own views are not absent from the assembly. At the very least, this requires a great deal of sophistication on the part of ordinary Americans with regard to the social science of sampling and representativeness. Those who are comfortable with statistics may be at ease with the notion that a sample of seven hundred probable voters can predict, within a margin of error of 4 percent, the outcome of a national election or the "public opinion" on some controversial subject. However, many of our co-citizens may be skeptical of such statsistically based reassurance, and would be even more so if what Fishkin calls "deliberative polls" became more truly identifiable as "deliberative assemblies" with the power to make actual decisions instead of simply supply unusually reliable information about public opinion to those actually charged with making decisions.

If one is truly persuaded by such arguments, though, one might well prefer decisionmaking by the deliberative assemblies over decisionmaking by the elected representatives, who are less likely to be truly representative than the group chosen by lot. Consider the challenging argument presented at the 2010 American Political Science Association convention by a distinguished political scientist at a panel assessing the impact and legitimacy of filibusters in the U.S. Senate. He argued that there is no particular reason to believe that a majority of Congress or of the Senate will necessarily track American public opinion. After all, electoral success is in substantial measure an artifact of the method by which we choose representatives in the first place, not to mention the independent problems presented by the distribution of voting power in the Senate, the distorting impact of campaign finances, and the impact of differential turnout rates.

One of my favorite political dicta is John Roche's emendation of Lord Acton's famous adage: "Power corrupts, and absolute power corrupts absolutely." Roche's version was "Power corrupts, and the possibility of losing power corrupts absolutely."[30] One thing that almost all electoral systems do is create "ins" who wish to retain that status against "outs" who are challenging their hold on power. Perhaps term limits can control this to some extent, though that reform also appears to have significant consequences for the actual quality of governance—as demonstrated most vividly in California. The call for term limits was a major part of American politics in the 1990s but has diminished since then. One reason may be the realization that term limits may actually reduce the practical capacity of representatives to gain a sophisticated understanding of complex issues of public policy. As a practical matter, this can put ever more power in the hands of the permanent—and obviously unelected—bureaucracy. But if the officials are loyal adherents of a given political party—what Madison might well have viewed as a faction—there will still be a strong incentive to stack the deck in favor of one's partisan compatriots even if one will not be able to remain in office. Once again, choice by lottery significantly diminishes, if it does not out-and-out eliminate, possibilities for partisan manipulation.

The most truly commendable thing about Madison and other Founders was their willingness to look unflinchingly at their political realities and to offer the "lessons of experience." In that spirit, we must first ask ourselves what these lessons are and then what kinds of changes might bring us closer to the most attractive vision of a republican form of government or constitutional democracy today. Do we like the picture of republican government sketched by Madison, with its critiques—both implicit and explicit—of democracy, or do we share a belief that more power should be placed in the hands of ordinary Americans, either through a broadened franchise or the possibility of direct citizen participation in the decision-making process? If we do find credible what I have called the "democracy project" that is embraced—at least rhetorically—by Democratic and Republican presidents alike, then we have to wrestle further with how to achieve it in a twenty-first century whose realities would truly be mind-boggling to anyone from the eighteenth or nineteenth centuries.[31]

6

Bicameralism

Bicameralism is a structure of government that can easily be analyzed along (at least) two different dimensions. The first has to do with various theories of representation. But the second has to do with assessing the degree to which bicameralism contributes to effective government (or, on occasion, contributes to ungovernability). If one opposes otherwise persuasive arguments for proportional representation on the grounds that its adoption would hinder the creation of effective governance, then one might come to the same conclusion about bicameralism, even if its rationale is attractive.

The Court in *Reynolds v. Sims* was obviously aware that forty-nine of the fifty states were bicameral, and most of them had adopted what was sometimes called "little federalism" by which membership in the "upper house" was allocated equally by county. Thus, in North Carolina, each of its 100 counties sent one representative to the state senate. Henderson County, where I lived as a boy, had about 30,000 people, but enjoyed equal representation with Mecklenburg County, of which Charlotte, with its then roughly 120,000 people, was the county seat. This came to an end following *Reynolds*. The main consequence of its decision was to disallow any significant variation in the voting systems for selecting members of the two houses in order to prevent violations of the new one person, one vote rule. As Chief Justice Warren wrote, the hope of "equal representation" would be fatally frustrated if bicameral "states could effectively submerge the equal-population principle in the apportionment of seats" by adopting a variant principle "in the other house. If such a scheme were permissible, an individual citizen's ability to exercise an effective voice…might be almost as effectively thwarted as if neither house were apportioned on a population basis." Although deadlocks between the two houses might be resolved by "compromise and concession on some issues...in all too many cases the more probable result would be frustration of the majority will through minority veto in the house not apportioned on a population basis."¹ Thus the *entire* state legislature, and not only one house, must be apportioned "on a nondiscriminatory basis."

There would be no threat of deadlock or frustration of majority will if the second house of a particular bicameral system had no effective power, even to delay legislation. It might, for example, be limited only to offering commentary or advice on pending legislation and completely powerless to delay or stop it. But that doesn't describe any of the bicameral systems within the United States, where each house at the national and state levels has absolute veto power over legislation proposed by the other. There is no way to break deadlocks unless one or the other house capitulates.

Political scientists George Tsebelis and Jeannette Money, who are among the most careful students of bicameralism, note after examining bicameralism in fifty countries around the world that a number of them have more effective means of breaking deadlocks than the United States. Thus, for example, the German *Bundestag*, the lower house, can pass legislation in specific instances by two-thirds vote, regardless of the wishes of the *Bundesrat*, the upper house (though in some instances, the upper house retains its veto power). France similarly gives final decisional authority to its lower house. Depending on the content of the legislation, Spain gives final authority to either its upper or lower house. Norway breaks deadlocks by bringing its two houses together in joint session and then allowing a collective two-thirds majority to rule. As one would imagine, there are yet other variations.² The United States is not unique; Belgium, the Philippines, Nigeria, and others also have what Tsebelis and Money laconically call the absence of "stopping rules."³ However, these countries are definitely the minority among the systems they study.

Presumably, our views on such matters are a function of what we believe the point of bicameralism to be. It is useful to return to Chief Justice Warren's answer to this question in *Reynolds*:

A prime reason for bicameralism, modernly considered, is to insure mature and deliberate consideration of, and to prevent precipitate action on, proposed legislative measures. Simply because the controlling criterion for apportioning representation is required to be the same in both houses does not mean that there will be no differences in the composition and complexion of the two bodies. Different constituencies can be represented in the two houses. *One body could be composed of single-member districts while the other could have at least some multimember districts.* The length of terms of the legislators in the separate bodies could differ. The numerical size of the two bodies could be made to differ, even significantly, and the geographical size of districts from which legislators are elected could also be made to differ. And apportionment in one house could be arranged so as to balance off minor inequities in the representation of certain areas in the other house. In summary, these and other factors could be, and are presently in many States, utilized to engender differing complexions and collective attitudes in the two bodies of a state legislature, although both are apportioned substantially on a population basis. (emphasis added)

This rationale for bicameralism seems, in the language presented by Tsebelis and Money, to emphasize *efficiency gains* in legislation, that is, the benefits that presumably attach to assuring a greater degree of "mature and deliberate consideration" of proposed legislation. After all, two heads are better than one. But too many cooks spoil the broth! Can both be correct? Although Warren emphasizes various ways of differentiating the two houses, he does not argue that they will necessarily represent significantly different groups or interests.

I. BICAMERALISM AND SELF-CONSCIOUS PLURALISM

So this brings us to considering why, both historically and at present, we might consider bicameralism to be a compelling way of organizing legislative systems. Tsebelis and Money begin their book by quoting the comment of Abbe Sieyes, made during the heated days of the French Revolution: "If the second chamber agrees with the first, it is useless; and if not, it is bad."[4] Constitution-revering Americans probably disagree with Sieyes, but why?

Most serious students of the subject agree that the historical origins of bicameralism have little to do with an abstract commitment to the general virtue of seeking second opinions on important decisions and the consequent efficiency gains of "better" legislation. Instead, bicameralism arose from a belief that *mixed government* was desirable. What sort of "mix" were these initial proponents thinking of? An answer is suggested by the very names of the English houses of Parliament, the House of Commons and the House of Lords. Nothing could be clearer about the basis for the two houses. Until the great voting reforms of the mid-nineteenth century, very few commoners actually got to vote, yet no members of the nobility served in the House of Commons. Instead, they could be found in the House of Lords, which was set aside for the peerage, who were thought to instantiate an interest entirely different from commoners (who rarely owned vast landed estates). It was not that a lord "represented" his fellow aristocrats, for *all* members of the aristocracy at a certain level were entitled to membership.

It was unthinkable, at least until some time in the nineteenth century, that commoners might actually rule Great Britain. Recall Aristotle's (or Hobbes's) typology of governments based on the number of people selected to rule. Great Britain was a model aristocracy (or, if one "misliked" it, an oligarchy) inasmuch as rule was firmly held by a minority of the country based largely on blood descent.

The great difference between Great Britain, at least historically, and the United States is that Great Britain has never been committed to the popular sovereignty suggested by "We the People." Sovereignty resided in the Crown or, following the Glorious Revolution of 1688, in the "Crown in Parliament." But Parliament still consisted for at least two more centuries of two houses, each of which had effective veto power over the other. It was not until the early twentieth century that the House of Lords lost its right to permanently block legislation passed by the House of Commons. A century later, the House of Lords lost the right to control its own effective membership; in 2010, the House of Commons was given the right to choose ninety-one persons from among the over seven hundred peers, both hereditary and appointed by the Crown, who would compose the actual voting membership of the House of Lords. The remainder were relegated to the role of onlookers. At the same time, the British adopted a formal supreme court to replace the group of "law lords" who had served that functional role for centuries.

If one is interested in the self-conscious representation of varied "interests" rather than simply assuring a multiplicity of voices that might well be roughly similar in background and interest, there are a number of possibilities as to which "interests" or "orders" of society might demand (or deserve) representation. Many early Americans agreed with Madison that property constituted an essential source of division in society. A well-organized state would therefore make sure that those with significant property were well represented in at least one house of the legislature. We would not call them "lords," but we would, nonetheless, recognize that possession of property brought with it certain prerogatives, including some special role in governance.[5] This was an especially important consideration given the movement of the various states within the United States toward a broader electorate. This movement would likely bring to power representatives eager to curry favor with the majority of (relative) have-nots (the kinds of people who promoted debtor-relief legislation in Rhode Island in the 1780s, for example, or the passage of bankruptcy laws in the early nineteenth century). If the rights of the propertied were to be protected, they needed an effective veto power over redistributive legislation that sought to transfer resources from haves to have-nots. Thus the requirement in many states that senators own more property than members of the lower houses or the restriction of suffrage with regard to electing members of the upper house. Gouverneur Morris of New York forthrightly advocated limiting the U.S. Senate to men of "great personal property" who were animated by what he called "the aristocratic spirit." He was certainly not alone in this regard, although his proposal failed.

Akhil Reed Amar goes out of his way to praise the Constitution precisely because it included no such property qualifications and "open[ed] its doors to the unpropertied."[6] Opening doors, in this context, may be an ambiguous notion, especially if we look at political actualities rather than pure theory. Could the "unpropertied" in fact walk through the door, whatever their formal right to do so? As Amar himself notes, one motivation for the Seventeenth Amendment, which requires direct popular election of senators instead of continuing their appointment by state legislatures, was to limit the ability of millionaires to buy their appointments from acquiescent state legislators.[7] If diminution of the number (and role) of millionaires in the Senate was the aim of the Seventeenth Amendment, it can be pronounced a notable failure. A December 2006 article in *Forbes Magazine* entitled "Meet Senator Millionaire" noted a number of interesting factoids about some of the senators who were arriving for the new session beginning in December 2007:

> Bob Corker, [Republican] senator-elect from Tennessee, boasts an estimated $64 million to $236 million fortune, according to the financial disclosure he filed to the Senate. Claire McCaskill, the [Democratic] senator-to-be from Missouri, has a portfolio worth roughly $13 million to $29 million. And [Democrat] Sheldon Whitehouse, who ousted the fifth-richest member of the Senate, Lincoln Chaffee of Rhode Island, is hardly hurting for cash himself: He has $4 million to $14 million parked in various trusts and funds.[8]

The least affluent senator at that time was apparently Vermont socialist Bernie Sanders, who had no more than $115,000 in addition to a condominium in Burlington.

A 2009 blog post in the *New York Times* entitled "Your Senator Is (Probably) a Millionaire" reported that a full two-thirds of senators were millionaires.[9] The 2010 congressional elections, viewed by many as a "populist insurgency" against elites, brought a number of newcomers to both the House and Senate. The Center for Responsive Politics found that "sixty percent of Senate freshman and more than 40 percent of House freshmen are millionaires."[10] As it happens, the two richest members of the 2011–2013 Congress are Mike McCaul of Texas and Darrel Issa of California, Republicans who come in ahead of the richest senator, John Kerry, a Democrat.[11]

On the other hand, about two dozen representatives, and possibly two senators, have negative net worth, no doubt because of the general economic collapse after 2008. So to some extent it continues to be true that the House is more representative than the Senate of "We the People," at least with regard to income and wealth. But "more representative" is scarcely the same as what is sometimes called "mimetic" representation, where the representative body really does "look like" the wider polity it is ostensibly representing. Neither the House nor the Senate easily qualifies under this standard, even if the Senate is even more disproportionately a forum for multimillionaires. Yet it is not self-evident that one will be upset by this disparity between the House and the Senate if one accepts some of the arguments made in the eighteenth and nineteenth centuries for separate houses and the self-conscious representation of the special interests of the wealthy. In the modern world, however, one rarely sees such crass arguments made on behalf of the propertied.

To be sure, one often sees demands that constitutions include explicit protections of property rights, though it is hard to explain exactly why one should expect that such protections won't become what Madison dismissed as "parchment barriers" in the absence of "real" political power guaranteed to the propertied. This brings us back to the importance of structural protections, which depend not at all on the goodwill of judges and other would-be enforcers of constitutions, but instead on making sure that institutions are filled with people who can be counted on to protect one's favorite interest.

As Madison recognized, there are divisions besides those predicated on property. Members of disparate groups make similar demands for effective veto power regarding legislation that might be threaten their interests. Consider only the complex relationship among ethnic or religious groups in various polities around the world, where great care is taken to ensure "adequate representation" to various groups. If the groups are dispersed geographically, this offers one set of possibilities, as we see in decennial fights over so-called racial gerrymandering. If they are dispersed more generally throughout the society, then one might be much more likely to see calls for forms of proportional representation, as with the Liberal Democrats in Great Britain. But the point is that the constitutional designer is aware of the implications for the various groups that make up the polity of any chosen and the potential for instability, perhaps even civil war, should given groups feel themselves to be insufficiently represented. One might say that this is simply part of what it means to take "pluralism" or "multiculturalism" truly seriously.

None of this entails the choice of bicameralism. One might instead prefer a unicameral legislature that requires supermajorities in order to pass certain types of legislation, thus enabling minorities (with at least one-third of the vote, for example) to veto proposals they do not like. This is similar to the theory spelled out in John C. Calhoun's notion of the "concurrent majority," created to defend the interests of slaveowners. As Mark Graber points out in his brilliant book on slavery in American constitutional history,[12] the original theory of the American political system was *not* predicated on unalloyed majority rule but rather a bi-regional consensus. Political scientist Arend Lijphart has coined the term *consociationalism* to refer to any system aimed at making sure governmental decisions require the coming together of almost all major, and even some relatively minor, groups with a stake in a given social order. It should be obvious that this differs from majority rule, even if a given election system assigns a majority of the seats to a political party that gets a majority of the vote. But if, in fact, it takes significantly more than a majority of legislators to pass important legislation, the advantage of having a simple majority of the votes is obviously dissipated. One case in point is the "filibuster" in the U.S. Senate, under which most issues require sixty votes to even be brought to the floor for debate and vote, but many states operate under similar procedures. Although Texas for many years operated under the political convention that twenty-one of the thirty senators had to agree in order to bring a matter to the floor for consideration, that custom was shredded in the 2011 legislative session by the Republican majority determined to pass their programs against united Democratic opposition in the state senate. If one believes in majority rule, it is hard to be overly critical of the Republicans, even if one opposes their programs. This might even give hope to Democrats that should they ever regain control of the Texas senate, they could govern without being blocked by a Republican minority.

But we still have to ask ourselves what constitutes the value of bicameralism, especially in the American states after the great transformation caused by the Supreme Court's one person, one vote decision in *Reynolds v. Sims*. The maverick former governor of Minnesota, Jesse Ventura, once called for the abolition of that state's upper house on the ground that it was a needless public expense that contributed nothing to the overall legislative process. Ventura tacitly rejected the argument that bicameralism provided Minnesota with "efficiency gains" by producing better legislation than would have been the case with a single-house legislature like Nebraska's. If Ventura had been willing to look abroad, he might have pointed to New Zealand, a country with a varied and decidedly multicultural population of approximately 4.3 million that seems to operate very well with its unicameral House of Representatives. There is no evidence that Nebraska or New Zealand pays a significant cost for its unicameralism.

The may well be some value to bicameralism for sufficiently large states with varied populations. It is doubtful that either California or Texas, for example, should emulate Nebraska. But the point is to figure out what the precise value of bicameralism is, once one recognizes that the ostensible benefits—such as added voices—may be outweighed by costs ranging from sustaining a second house and its staff to the more serious costs imposed by institutional vetoes that make difficult the passage of what a majority might well view as "necessary" legislation, especially, as is discussed in Chapter 7, if governors themselves possess a veto power to block ostensibly unwise legislation.

Do states necessarily benefit from an upper house composed of members who may well represent only somewhat larger districts than do lower-house representatives? Do longer terms commonly associated with upper houses guarantee the kind of independence from the vagaries of campaigning that will predictably produce better legislation? Perhaps, in some states and some instances, but this is a decidedly empirical question. In the era of the "permanent campaign" and—more precisely—"permanent fund-raisers," one may doubt the necessary value of second houses in most of the American states, and, even in large states and the United States itself, the particular form that these second houses take.

One might take a leaf from Australia's book, which retains a senate (with each of the six Australian states entitled to twelve senators) that is elected by a decidedly different system than Australia's lower house. Instead of single-member districts and first-past-the-post elections, senators are elected by proportional representation. By definition, this means that the senate is more likely to have at least one or two quirky voices who can gather a significant measure of support though not enough to win under a standard-form majoritarian or first-past-the-post system. Even if an exclusive emphasis on geography is thought to make sense for one house, it is hard to see its merits for the second house as well. Most of us are defined in ways that go well beyond geographic loyalties; this may be especially the case for members of groups (or economic interests) that are dispersed throughout the given polity rather than concentrated in particular geographic locations where it might be relatively easy to elect a representative.

II. THE U.S. SENATE AS A PARTICULAR
(AND PECULIAR?) EXEMPLAR OF
BICAMERALISM

Even if one concedes that bicameralism has some value, especially for large and diverse polities, that obviously does not mean that all forms of bicameralism are equally tolerable. In *Reynolds*, the Supreme Court clearly rejected any form of bicameralism resting on the premise that farmers or other relatively small groups deserved a form of entrenched power (and, with it, the entrenched ability to veto legislation cutting against their own interests).

So let us turn now to the particular body known as the U.S. Senate. If we look at bicameral systems around the world, we find that the United States has an unusually "strong" form of bicameralism: Each house has the constitutional power to kill any legislation passed by the other simply by refusing to pass it in an identical form.[13] The refusal of one house to join in dotting a single *i* or crossing a single *t* of the text of a bill is enough, as a formal matter, to doom it, regardless of the degree of its support in the other house, among the general public, or by the president. Given this feature of American bicameralism, there may be no a priori reason to be more critical of the Senate than the House, since each has the same veto power over the other.

As I argued at length in *Our Undemocratic Constitution*, the Senate is clearly less "democratic" than the House, given the rejection of equal representation by population in favor of equal representation by state. But this reality, however important it may be to political theorists, does not necessarily correlate with political ideology or the confidence we might put, at any particular point in our history, in the collective judgment of the House compared to the Senate. Political liberals, for example, should acknowledge that there was once a thriving literature on why the Senate was more liberal than the House;[14] the explanation, at least prior to the reapportionment revolution of the 1960s, lay in the fact that many House districts were firmly in the hands of relatively small numbers of people living in rural areas. That revolution firmly placed the political power in the House far more in the hands of urban and, increasingly, suburban populations. Still, there are particular sessions of Congress when one can easily differentiate between the two houses in terms of their political tilt, most clearly when Democrats control one house and Republicans the other, as was the result in the 2010 election.

Still, as David Mayhew notes, criticism of the Senate seems to be an American tradition. He quotes David Graham Phillips's 1906 essay "The Treason of the Senate," in which that body was described as "the eager, resourceful, indefatigable agent of interests as hostile to the American people as any invading army could be, and vastly more dangerous; interests that manipulate the prosperity produced by all, so that it heaps up riches for the few."[15] Phillips was obviously writing before the Seventeenth Amendment transformed the way that senators are selected, putting that choice in the hands of the electorate rather than state legislatures. As a matter of fact, though, many states had already turned the decision over to the electorate by having elections whose results legislators pledged to honor. Movement to popular election has clearly not sufficed to eliminate doubts about the contribution of the Senate to American politics. Mayhew quotes a variety of journalists writing between 1994 and 2009, who used such terms as "ominously dysfunctional"; "the chamber designed to thwart popular will"; a "dysfunctional and undemocratic partisan hothouse"; and "a body that shuns debate, avoids legislative give-and-take, proceeds glacially and produces next to nothing."[16]

Norman Orenstein and Thomas Mann—the former affiliated with the conservative American Enterprise Institute, the latter with the more liberal Brookings Institution—in 2006 co-authored *The Broken Branch: How Congress Is Failing America and How to Get it Back on Track*. Nothing that has happened since 2006 would rectify their indictment. Indeed, in April 2008, Ornstein published an article titled "Our Broken Senate."[17] Two years later, George Packer published a devastating portrait of the Senate in the *New Yorker* titled "The Empty Chamber: Just How Broken Is the Senate?"[18] It begins as follows: "'Sit and watch us for seven days,' one senator says of the deadlocked chamber. 'You know what you'll see happening? Nothing.'"

Chapter 1 noted the dismal approval rates for Congress held by most Americans. Polls examining popular approval or disapproval of Congress unfortunately do not distinguish between the House and the Senate. One might readily predict that in 2011, Democrats would be considerably more approving of the Senate than of the House, and vice versa for Republicans. But approval of one house scarcely translates into approval of American bicameralism itself. One presumes that everyone in 2012 who approves of the House of Representatives is furious at the Senate for failing to submit to the House's Republican majority; whereas Democrats who approve of the Senate are happy to excoriate the House. Only those satisfied with the status quo—and who properly believe that bicameralism contributes to its maintenance—could be genuinely fond of bicameralism itself.

III. (RE-)TURNING TO MADISON

James Madison once more offers a useful analysis of bicameralism in his three essays on the Senate in *Federalists* 62–64. Madison was appalled by the principle of equality of state voting, though he had no objection to the concept of bicameralism per se. What, then, are his arguments in favor of having two legislative houses? And how well do they resonate with us today, over two centuries later? We should also ask if the arguments resonate differently depending on whether we are talking about *national* institutions of governance or *state* institutions. Might one, for example, support Ventura's plea for Minnesota to follow Nebraska's lead into unicameralism, or the suggestion by an unsuccessful candidate for the Republican nomination for governor of New York in 2010 that the Empire State abolish its senate, while resisting any such suggestion for the U.S. government? Concomitantly, if one finds Madison persuasive with regard to the Senate, does this entail a belief that Nebraska made a mistake in adopting unicameralism (and that other countries drafting constitutions today should reject it as well)?

A. Qualifications for office

We should begin where Madison begins, with the "qualifications proposed for senators, as distinguished from those of representatives." Qualifications are especially interesting in the context of bicameralism; one defense of having separate houses is that each one will be occupied by interestingly different types of people with their varying perspectives. This could be true, as an empirical matter, even if one has rejected classical theories of *mixed* government that provided the initial foundation for bicameralism (and upper houses consisting of "upper classes").

One qualification we have already discussed is age: one has to be thirty to serve in the Senate and twenty-five to serve in the House. But consider also another requirement, which is the *duration* of one's citizenship if one is not a native-born American. To be a representative, one has to have been a citizen for at least seven years; service in the Senate requires nine years of citizenship. Because resident aliens must live in the United States for at least five years before becoming eligible for citizenship, this effectively translates into a requirement that prospective candidates for the House or Senate live in the United States for at least twelve and fourteen years, respectively. This was no idle requirement early in our history. Swiss émigré Albert Gallatin, who would serve with distinction in the House of Representatives before becoming the longest-serving secretary of the treasury of our history under Thomas Jefferson and James Madison, was denied a seat in the Senate in 1793, on a straight party-line vote, because it was alleged that he had not been a citizen for nine years. (He was then elected to the House in 1795.) There was also a fascinating controversy in 1870 about the seating of Hiram Revels, a Mississippian who became the first African American member of the Senate.[19] Democrats claimed that he had become a citizen of the United States only in 1868, with the passage of the Fourteenth Amendment and its reversal of the 1857 decision in *Dred Scott*, which had held as a matter of constitutional law that no descendant of slaves *could* become an American citizen. He was seated, however, also as the result of a vote by party affiliation. Some of his supporters argued that *Dred Scott* had simply been wrong, so its holding was inconsequential. But even some people horrified by *Dred Scott* accepted the premise that the Supreme Court was in fact the authority on constitutional meaning, which is why it required a constitutional amendment, and not merely a statute, to override the limitation on citizenship enunciated by Chief Justice Taney and his colleagues. (A "reformed Court" might have overruled *Dred Scott*, but that would have taken time, whereas the Fourteenth Amendment settled that particular conversation.)

In the modern world, perhaps we can imagine an "ethnic rights activist" who becomes a citizen and immediately files to run for the House or (far less likely) the Senate. Presumably, she would be told to wait seven or nine years (and perhaps to count herself lucky that she's eligible for national public office at all, given the absolute bar against running for the presidency). There's no doubt here what the Constitution *means*; we are clearly talking about the Constitution of Settlement and not the Constitution of Conversation, at least as a subject of litigation. But that doesn't foreclose a different kind of conversation, which focuses on wisdom instead of meaning.

Madison seems to have no trouble with the duration of citizenship requirement. After all, he argues that the powers of a senator "ought to be exercised by none not thoroughly weaned from the prepossessions and habits incident to foreign birth and education." One reason greater length of citizenship is required of senators than representatives is the fact that senators are more involved in foreign affairs because of the Senate's exclusive role in ratifying treaties. Still, we need to address this as a *current* part of our Constitution and not simply to explain why it was made part of the Constitution of Settlement in 1787. Were we rewriting the Constitution today, would we maintain a durational requirement? Moreover, if we got rid of the absolute bar on a naturalized citizen becoming president, would we be tempted to require that he or she had been a citizen for, say, at least eighteen years—twice the duration required to serve in the Senate?

If you do support such requirements, then why not prevent newly naturalized citizens from voting or serving on a jury for, say, three years? Or is this just one more example of the radical distinction we make between voting, as a relatively minimal form of participation in government, and actual service in public office, for which the standards are properly more restrictive? Ask yourself, moreover, how you would respond in the twenty-first century to a *state* constitution that tracked the national one by distinguishing between U.S. (and state) citizens on the basis of the duration of their citizenship or, indeed, whether their citizenship accompanied them at birth or had to be earned later. One can imagine requiring that a person be a citizen of the United States for five years or a citizen of the particular state in which one was running for at least three years. These might be viewed as the "no carpetbaggers need apply" provisions. Full discussion would take us well into the realm of the Constitution of Conversation, particularly the Equal Protection Clause of the Fourteenth Amendment and the (il)legitimacy of such distinctions when adopted by *state* govern-ments.[20] I italicize "state" in order to ask if such criteria survive at the *national* level only because of the forcefulness of the language that does appear to have "settled" the matter, at least for lawyers. But we have already seen that there is no reason to associate the Constitution of Settlement with moral goodness or otherwise necessarily defensible propositions. All one can say is that, for whatever reason, including the political exigencies of the moment, a given policy was adopted and entrenched by being given constitutional status instead of being implemented by a statute that could simply be repealed at a future date if majority sentiment shifted.

B. *Selecting senators*

Far more important as a practical matter is the mechanism by which senators were originally selected, by state legislatures. Here, too, Madison seems to register no objection. Indeed, he suggests in *Federalist* 62 that it provides a "double advantage." First, this is a "select appointment" process, which nicely complements selection by the voting public with regard to the House of Representatives. If an advantage of bicameralism is provid-ing significantly different tracks to public office, then the original House and Senate certainly qualified. The skills needed to win popular elections were presumably somewhat different from those needed to gain the sup-port of state legislators. The second advantage, though, is that "giving to the state government such an agency in the formation of the federal gov-ernment" will help to "secure the authority of the former," that is the state governments. The reason is the important "link between the two systems" of government. It is not simply that senators will be expected to feel some measure of gratitude to the state officials who appointed them. It is also the case that, should they want re-appointment, they will take some care to *represent* the interests of state officials and their presumed desire to main-tain a significant degree of independence from the national government.

So here we come to the great importance of the Seventeenth Amendment, which eliminates this connection. Once senators are elected in the same manner as representatives, by popular vote, they presumably have the same incentives as representatives to serve—or pander to—their constituents. There will be no particular concern to preserve state autonomy unless, by happy accident, that is a deep concern of their constituents. One might have plausibly argued that the pre-Seventeenth Amendment Senate honored the principle of federalism by recognizing the importance of the autonomy of state governments themselves with regard to selecting senators. The post–Seventeenth Amendment Senate has nothing to do with federalism in any deep sense. Rather, the modern Senate is best conceived of as an affirmative action program for the residents of small states, inasmuch as their elevated levels of representation contribute to their being especially well served by national programs that involve the distribution of tax revenues from populous states to far smaller, but equally represented, states. (This helps to explain our contemporary agricultural policies, attacked as wasteful by both Democratic and Republican presidents.) As noted in Chapter 1, some conservatives are advocating the repeal of the Seventeenth Amendment in order to bolster the clout that state officials might be able to exercise in the Senate. One may doubt the likelihood of repeal, but the theory underlying its support is worth taking seriously. At the very least, opponents of repeal should indicate why popular election is highly desirable instead of simply condemning proponents of repeal for calling for amendment of our sacred Constitution. Underlying any such debate is the view one has about the strengths and weaknesses of federalism itself, the subject of extended discussion in Chapter 14.

C. Equality of vote

One might doubt that the Seventeenth Amendment is of much practical significance, just as one might even more plausibly doubt that the age and duration of citizenship clauses, however interesting they might be with regard to the theoretical issues they raise, are of any practical importance. This is surely not true when we come to what is most distinctive about the American Senate, whether in 1789 or 2012: the equality of voting power granted each state.

Here, to be sure, the U.S. Senate is not unique. Australia gives an equal twelve votes to Tasmania and New South Wales, which is roughly fourteen times as large in population as the island-state. There is a connection between such voting allocations and both the extent to which the country in question is federal and the political circumstances at the time the constitution was written. We saw in Chapter 2 that the compromise over voting power in the Senate was key to getting the Constitution adopted, and one might well expect similar situations to arise in other countries that are trying to create a single polity out of formally independent entities. Tasmania might have refused to join the Australian Federation in 1901 had it not been granted equal voting power in the senate. In 1901, the population dispararity between New South Wales, the largest state, and Tasmania was approximately 7:1, whereas today it is around 14:1. I have already noted that the state senators are chosen by proportional representation, as against single-member districts for the Australian house of representatives, which means that there is significantly more diversity of views represented in the senate than in the house. Imagine, for example, if the U.S. Senate consisted of three hundred senators, with even three senators per state chosen by proportional representation every four years. This means that any political party that could get 25 percent + 1 of the popular vote would be guaranteed a seat.

It should be clear that Madison had no liking for equal representation of states in the Senate. As the late English historian J. R. Pole notes in his edition of *The Federalist*, the expression used by Madison to describe the principle of equal voting power—"It does not appear to be without some reason"—"is an expression notably lacking in enthusiasm." Both Madison and Hamilton had resisted the Great Compromise that created the Senate and acquiesced to it only because the alternative appeared worse. Madison is astonishingly frank about this in *Federalist* 62:

> But it is superfluous to try, by the standard of theory, a part of the Constitution which is allowed on all hands to be the result, not of theory, but 'of a spirit of amity, and that mutual deference and concession which the peculiarity of our political situation rendered indispensable.' A common government, with powers equal to its objects, is called for by the voice, and still more loudly by the political situation, of America. A government founded on principles more consonant to the wishes of the larger States, is not likely to be obtained from the smaller States. The only option, then, for the former, lies between the proposed government and a government still more objectionable. Under

this alternative, the advice of prudence must be to embrace the *lesser evil*; and, instead of indulging a fruitless anticipation of the possible mischiefs which may ensue, to contemplate rather the advantageous consequences which may qualify the sacrifice. (emphasis added)

Perhaps the Senate *is* a lesser evil than retaining the Articles of Confederation or, even worse, simply dissolving back into thirteen constituent units, but a lesser evil remains an evil, unless one adopts a form of utilitarian reasoning that describes *any* policy that is better than existing alternatives as positively good.

Madison also seems to suggest that it is an advantage that "no law or resolution can now be passed without the concurrence first of a majority of the people, and then of a majority of the states," and he can use this latter locution because one could make a reasonable argument that senators were in fact the representatives of state governments rather than the people of the given states. What he is describing is something like the present German *Bundesrat*, which is composed of state officials. But, as already suggested, there is no reason to use such language once the Seventeenth Amendment severs the connection between senators and state officialdom, and even the pre-Seventeenth Amendment version of the Senate did not include persons serving as state officials. (Louisiana's would-be dictator Huey Long served simultaneously as that state's governor and its *elected* senator in the 1930s.)

What are the practical consequences of the way that voting power is allocated in the Senate? The most obvious is that states with a majority of the American population will collectively have a remarkably small percentage of the votes within the Senate. Thus over 50 percent of the total population is concentrated in the ten largest states, beginning with California, which alone has about 12 percent (one in eight) of all residents of the United States. One crosses the 50 percent mark with the tenth largest state, North Carolina, which contains around 9.5 million residents. Obviously, these ten states will be able to elect a grand total of 20 percent of the Senate. On the other hand, the smallest twenty-six states, which together have approximately 17 percent of the national population, can elect a majority of the Senate. This means that in any given congressional session the minority party within the Senate could represent more of the American population than the so-called majority party.

It should be clear that this is defensible only if one believes that the particular minorities who are benefited by the allocation of power in the Senate *deserve* the ability to veto legislation that may be enthusiastically backed by the more population-sensitive House and the president. One of the most obvious examples would be legislation changing our present program of agricultural subsides, which may be described as a transfer of resources from largely urban consumers of food to predominantly rural producers—increasingly, large agri-corporations—with a variety of side consequences, including contribution to national obesity because of the advantages given to corn syrup. Such legislation, supported in the past in the House and by Democratic and Republican presidents alike, has always failed in the Senate because of the number of senators from the upper Midwest and their intense commitment to protecting their constituents.

One can hardly defend the Senate as a barrier against "majority tyranny," given the basic arbitrariness of the Senate's overprotection of a limited number of political minorities who live in small states while leaving most minorities to the tender mercies of majority rule. Although I myself fear "tyranny of the minority" at least as much as "majority tyranny," those who are especially concerned about the latter should explain why the better solution is not, for example, simply to require supermajorities for passage of certain—perhaps all—legislation.

D. Madison's qualms about "activist" legislating

Here we reach what may be the crux of the matter. Consider the implications of Madison's suggestion that the real advantage of the Senate is its role in preventing the "excess of law-making [that] seems to be the disease to which our governments are most liable." Hamilton, incidentally, strikes the same note in *Federalist* 73, which concerns the presidential veto power; he supports the veto precisely because of its utility in "restrain[ing] the excess of law making." And presumably we have the most to fear, with regard to pressures for such "excess," from the most popular branch of government. Madison was no fan of what might be called *actual* government "by the people," even in its representative rather than direct form. He is a big fan, at least in his *Federalist* persona, of indirect election, whether by state legislatures or electoral colleges. As he writes in *Federalist* 64, selection by state legislatures of senators is "vastly" superior to "elections by the people in their collective capacity, where the activity of party zeal, taking advantage of the supineness, the ignorance, and the hopes and fears of the unwary...often place men in office by the votes of a small population of the electors." This is congruent with his praise of the American government in *Federalist* 63 for its "*total exclusion of the people in their collective capacity* from any share"—and the emphasis is Madison's—in the actualities of governmental decisionmaking beyond choosing (for one house) their representatives. Madison has only minimal confidence in what we might today describe as democratic politics.

It is not surprising, then, that he likes the fact that there are "two distinct bodies," one of them not accountable to the public in any direct manner, because he believes this will help to reduce "schemes of usurpation or perfidy." He was more fearful of such schemes emanating from the House than from the Senate, partly because the latter's smaller size would reduce the "propensity of all single and numerous assemblies, to yield to the impulse of sudden and violent passions, and to be seduced by factious leaders, into intemperate and pernicious resolutions."

We return yet again, though, to a central theme of this book: to what extent is one generally skeptical of governmental power and/or generally skeptical of the specific dispositions of those who seek and are elected to public office, so that you believe there is a significantly greater likelihood of any given legislature producing truly bad rather than good legislation? Or, on the contrary, do you believe both that government must with some frequency act to regulate society *and* that public officials are likely to be able to distinguish good legislation from bad and to, with some exceptions, pass the former and defeat the latter? The first tests your basic preference for what might be described as libertarianism or acceptance of a more robust role for government as a fundamental participant in the social order. The greater the fear of governmental overreaching, the more veto points one will presumably wish for, even at the cost of presumptively desirable legislation failing to pass. On the contrary, if one has some significant degree of trust in government, the existence of these veto points, including that extreme veto point called the U.S. Senate, might be more frustrating.

An independent issue is the degree of trust one has in governmental officials. One basis for preferring direct democracy, after all, is that one prefers decisions made by oneself, as part of a general electorate, over decisionmaking by presumptively less trustworthy "representatives." Political economists often talk of the problem of "agency costs," which involve the monitoring of those one hires as employees or agents to make sure they do not shirk or outright violate their duties. There is no contradiction in rejecting libertarianism and therefore supporting a very active government while at the same time being very suspicious of the particular agents who purport to represent their constituents.

The point is not really whether Madison was correct in 1787–1788 that equal voting power in the Senate really was a lesser evil and perhaps served to hinder the passage of unwise legislation. Rather, it is whether such a compromise made on entirely instrumental grounds—recall that Madison is really quite unwilling to offer a "principled" and "theoretical" defense of the allocation of voting power in the Senate—should be compelling to us today. And by "compelling" I mean something other than a resigned acceptance to the likelihood that nothing can be done about the Senate. After all, that might be true of our attitude toward an incurable disease we might be afflicted with. Do we truly embrace our fate and say that we prefer it to imaginable alternatives even if we concede, as a practical matter, that nothing can be done? It is one thing to say, "If it isn't broken, it doesn't need fixing," and quite another to say, "Because it can't be fixed, therefore it isn't broken." The first makes perfectly good sense; the latter may represent a form of truly dangerous denial. A third formulation, "It's broken, but unfixable," may send one into despair.

Moreover, as already suggested, the fact that the national government may be stuck with the Senate in its present form because of the near impossibility of amendment does not entail that the states must be similarly accepting of their own bicameral systems. The Court's reapportionment decisions obviously transformed the nature of upper houses in the forty-nine bicameral states, and states can far more easily amend their constitutions. Even if one believes that bicameralism offers some genuine advantages, one might still support more imaginative design of second houses at the state level, which in turn might inspire one to think of alternative possibilities for the national Senate.

E. Number of senators and duration of appointment

Madison seems more than happy to support the smaller number of senators and their longer term of office as aspects of the "dissimilarity in the genius of the two bodies." How, though, do we decide on an optimal number of representatives or senators? Does our answer have anything to do with the actual workload of Congress? Political scientist Larry Sabato, for example, has noted that the number of representatives and senators has not increased since 1959, when the addition of Hawaii to the Union meant the filling out of the current Senate at one hundred members.[21] The population of the United States was then approximately 180 million; today it is approaching 310 million. But the fact that we are more than two-thirds larger may not even be the main point.

Certainly as important is the fact that Congress in 1960 had far less on its plate than is the case today, for reasons independent of population. Congress fifty years ago spent little or no time thinking about national health, education, or general environmental policies, to name only three obvious examples.[22] All these would come with the arrival of the Kennedy, Johnson, and Nixon administrations. Nor was "climate change" even potentially a topic of congressional interest until the twenty-first century. And the international situation—whether as a result of the development of modern weaponry, globalization, or the breakdown of the bipolar world that structured international relations until the end of the Cold War in 1989—calls for greater expenditures of legislative energies. Acceptance of the desirability of "strong bicameralism" requires that members of both houses, ideally, should be equally knowledgeable about the grave matters they address. The House can spread its "knowledge-gathering" duties among 435 members, many of whom are genuine experts in given policy domains. The Senate, on the other hand, has only one hundred members, which means that senators must spread themselves more thinly. Can this possibly be desirable?

Sabato believes that *both* houses need additional members. And, although one could achieve this in the Senate simply by giving each state a third senator, he believes that the additional members of the Senate ought *not* necessarily come from specific states. After all, the territorialism of the Senate, like that of the House, generates strong incentives toward parochialism. Unless a senator contemplates running for the White House, there is little incentive to think in terms of some "general interest" if that might impose some costs on one's own constituents, who are presumably looking out for their own "factional" interests. One might imagine the election of "national" senators. A quite different response might be naming to the Senate all former presidents and vice presidents, speakers of the house, members of the Supreme Court, heads of the joint chiefs of staff, and the like, precisely in order to supply a more "national" perspective than is likely to be held by constituency-oriented senators. This has the advantage of guaranteeing the presence of almost uniquely experienced former national leaders; its great disadvantage is that it might be thought to violate the basic tenet of democracy that "We the People," however defined, should choose our representatives and senators.

It seems clear that Madison assumed that members of the House would serve not only shorter terms, but will also be much less likely to be re-elected, whether because they simply will not wish to spend much of their life in the House of Representatives or because they will be defeated in their bids for re-election. Thus he describes members of the House as "called for the most part from pursuits of a private nature, continued in appointment for a short time, and led by no permanent motive to devote the intervals of public occupation to a study of the laws, [and] the affairs and the comprehensive interests of their country." Senators, on the other hand, because they are guaranteed six years of service—and also because of their presumptively greater distinction than representatives—will devote far more of their time and energy to considering what the public good requires. In *Federalist* 63, Madison offers several encomia to the benefits of "sufficient permanency" of service. He notes that some persons had suggested appointing senators for life—perhaps for reasons similar to those that allegedly justify the lifetime appointment of federal judges. We obviously did not go that route, but our six-year terms, with staggered elections that assure far less volatile turnover in the Senate than in the House, presumably provides some needed protection against what he calls "mutable" government. Less sympathetic people might describe this as opposition to government that is overly sensitive to public opinion, though the response to this view would be that the Senate is more likely to act based on what might be termed "durable" public opinion, reflected over several election cycles, than what Madison refers to in *Federalist* 63 as "irregular passion" generated by the "artful misrepresentations of interested men."

In short, it is Madison's view that the House of Representatives is likely to be made up of amateurs. Even if one accepts his arguments in *Federalist* 10, so that we might hope that representatives are "wise" and "virtuous," it's still the case that they'll just not be around long enough, leaving them relatively unlikely to develop a necessary long-term perspective. Senators, on the other hand, will be much more likely to take a longer-term view.

Did Madison turn out to be right with regard to what one might call the greater "professionalization" of the Senate than the House? Historian Jack Rakove suggests that Madison's predictions were reasonably congruent with the first century of Congress, when the average term of service was roughly three years. This changed in the twentieth century, perhaps as the result of the "professionalization" of many occupations, including that of politician. Thus, according to the Congressional Research Service, the "average length of service for Representatives at the beginning of the 111th Congress was 11.0 years (5.5 terms); for Senators, 12.9 years (2.2 terms)."[23] Senator Kennedy died in his forty-seventh year of service, and he was not the longest-serving senator; that was West Virginia Senator Robert Byrd, who spent well more than half of his ninety-two years (57.5 years) as a U.S. senator. As of 2011, John Dingell of Michigan has served in the House of Representatives for fifty-six years (since 1955), while Hawaii Senator Daniel Inouye has been in the Senate "only" since 1963 (having earlier served briefly as Hawaii's first representative following 1959 statehood). Fewer than half of the currently twenty longest-serving members of Congress are senators. One may or not be cheered by this datum, but it scarcely seems to accord with Madison's predictions as to the character of the two houses.

One might also consider the fact that in 2008, which was viewed as a relatively volatile election, 339 (of 435) members of the House sought re-election, of whom 328 (almost 96 percent) were successful. Thirty senators sought re-election, of whom four failed to win, which means that over 85 percent were successful. The year 2010 was obviously a far more volatile year; fifty-four incumbents lost their re-election bids to the House, (fifty-three of them Democrats), though this represents less than 15 percent of the entire House. Interestingly enough, only two Democratic incumbents lost in 2010 (Blanche Lincoln in Arkansas and Russell Feingold in

Wisconsin). Other Republican gains came in so-called open-seat elections, as in Pennsylvania (though the unsuccessful Democratic candidate had earlier defeated incumbent Senator Arlen Specter, who had switched from the Republican to the Democratic party in the party primary).

In any event, career politicians dominate both the House and Senate, and the tendency of seniority to count in the allocation of practical power in both houses gives added weight to such long-term careers. It helps to explain, for example, why at least one Massachusetts representative decided not to run to replace Ted Kennedy, given that he would start off as a fledgling in the Senate but had many years of accrued seniority, and the prerequisites to go with it, in the House. It may be that "amateur" multimillionaires are far more tempted to try to begin their political careers in the Senate than in the House, given the possible reluctance of such persons to accept being a "backbencher" in the House (particularly of the minority party) instead of occupying a far more public role as one of only one hundred senators.

One response to the professionalization of national legislative politics has been the call by some, including the Republican Party in the 1990s, for term limits. An attempt by Arkansas to impose term limits on election to Congress was ruled unconstitutional by the Supreme Court, which held that the listing of qualifications in the Constitution in effect settled the matter and could not be supplemented by additional qualifications of the states (such as not having already been in Congress for more than a given number of years). Such constitutional limitations do not apply to the organization of state legislatures, however, and several states have adopted term limits. The most notable example is California, though that may be yet another pathological feature of the California political system: term limits assure the non-existence of any legislators with long-term institutional memories or the policy expertise that comes through years of experience and hearings and the concomitant shift of actual power to long-term administrative officials. Analyzing contemporary California politics, Michael Lewis has written that term limits in that state assure that "no elected official now serves" in the California legislature who can "fully understand" the state's government. This relative dumbing down of state politicians—even if they are in fact very smart by conventional measures—helps to generate, he says, "maximum contempt for elected officials."[24]

The Constitution does contain such a term limit for the president, however. So an obvious question is why not for senators or members of Congress. And if we reject term limits for the latter, does this suggest that the Twenty-second Amendment was a mistake? We will have occasion for a longer discussion of that amendment when we turn to the presidency.

III. JOHN JAY MAKES A BRIEF APPEARANCE

The Federalist was largely written by Hamilton and Madison. Indeed, after writing *Federalists* 2–5, John Jay reappears only once, when discussing the treaty power in *Federalist* 64. This may well be appropriate, inasmuch as Jay was a noted diplomat (as well as the first Chief Justice of the United States). The point he makes is an important one. The House and the Senate do not in fact have completely equal powers. Only the House can initiate revenue legislation. Far more important is the exclusive role assigned to the Senate with regard to confirming federal officials, in which the House plays no role at all, and in the ratification of treaties. And, note very well, the Constitution does far more than simply assign treaty ratification to the Senate; it also requires a supermajority—a two-thirds vote—in order for a treaty negotiated by the president to become a binding commitment (and the law of the land). This is no small feature, as many majority-supported treaties have in fact failed as a result of an inability to gain the needed two-thirds vote.

Perhaps a supermajority rule is a good idea, though one could have that just as easily in the House of Representatives. And it is important to know that "executive agreements," developed since the 1930s, in effect negate the importance of the Treaty Clause by allowing such agreements to become operative by majority consent of both houses. The most famous example is probably the North American Free Trade Agreement (NAFTA). In any event, why assign the assessment of treaties to the Senate? Again, the answer lies in the perception that senators will be different from representatives in ways that will make them more trustworthy. Compared to the House, "composed of members constantly coming and going in quick succession," the Senate offers the prospect of "able and honest men" who will have "continue[d] in place a sufficient time to become perfectly acquainted with our national concerns." This greater awareness of what truly serves our "national interests" will obviously prove "more beneficial to their country" than would placement of such power in the hands of the vastly less experienced and more unpredictable members of the House. Once again, these seem to be largely empirical propositions, and it would be interesting to figure out ways to robustly test them.

IV. A BRIEF DIGRESSION ABOUT FILIBUSTERS AND "HOLDS"

No discussion of the Senate can avoid mentioning some of the more peculiar institutional practices associated with that institution (and not at all with the House of Representatives). The first is the filibuster, in which a minority of senators (currently forty-one, assuming a full Senate of 100 voting members) can block legislation or other similar matters (such as votes on presidential nominees) from coming to the floor at all. This is linked to the notion of the Senate as a peculiarly *deliberative* body that therefore ought to be extremely reluctant to cut off debate. Given that the modern Senate is scarcely deliberative in any significant sense—no one seriously believes, for example, that senators actually listen to one another's speeches and change their minds on important issues of the day as a result—the filibuster functions almost entirely as a device for a minority veto. If one accepts John C. Calhoun's theory of the "concurrent majority," one might find this a fine idea. If, however, one actually believes in majority rule, it is indefensible, save in the not uncommon situation where the filibustering "minority" in fact represents a majority of the national electorate inasmuch as the ostensible "majority" comprises fifty-one senators drawn largely from small states.

Far more indefensible is the Senate's practice of allowing individual senators to place "holds" on presidential nominees, so that the Senate will not consider actual confirmation until the hold is lifted. Filibusters at least require fairly large minorities in order to veto legislation. Holds allow one petulant senator to delay, perhaps indefinitely, the bringing of legislation to the floor or, most commonly, the confirmation of presidential appointees. The latter, by definition, leaves executive agencies without the leadership that the nominees would presumably provide.

No one argues that the Constitution requires such practices. There are even occasional arguments that they are unconstitutional. What seems to legitimize them and bring them within the Constitution of Settlement that is the focus of this book is the language in Article I, Section 5: "Each House may determine the Rules of its Proceedings." So, the argument goes, if the Senate determines, as it has by Rule 22 of its own rules, that debate is extended unless 60 percent of the voting members vote for "cloture," that is determinative. Interestingly enough, though it is often argued that two-thirds of the entire Senate would be necessary to change Rule 22 itself (including, obviously, to eliminate it), a number of scholars—and members of Congress—suggest that the filibuster could be eliminated at the beginning a Senate session by a simple majority vote. Indeed, there were some suggestions, in 2005–2006, that Senate Republicans might invoke a so-called nuclear option and change the filibuster rule by a simple majority. (This arose during an extremely bitter debate about the refusal of Democrats to allow a number of President Bush's judicial nominees to come to the floor for a vote that they would easily have won, given Republican control of the Senate.) For better or worse, a compromise was reached whereby some of the nominees were confirmed and the nominations of others were dropped. It is an open question whether the compromise served the country's best interests. Similarly, some Senate Democrats attempted at the beginning of the new session of Congress in January 2011 to revise the filibuster rules, but they faced an uphill battle caused not only by adamant Republican opposition but also by the views of many of their Democratic colleagues that they would these rules would prove beneficial if, as appears likely, the Democrats return to being a minority of the Senate after the 2012 elections. As David Mayhew argues, the filibuster, whether or not an attractive feature of American politics, is thought to be "bipartisan" in its long-run operation, so that it has proved impossible to generate a willingness even of ostensibly powerful senate majorities to change the rules.[25]

Senate rules do not explicitly authorize holds. Rather, they follow from the fact that the Senate often relies on "unanimous consent" in order to conduct its business. If a single senator refuses to give such consent, then the legislation can't move forward. As is the case with most institutions, the Senate requires a certain level of good-faith collegiality in order to operate effectively. But if one is opposed to "effective operation" in contexts where that would mean victory for one's opponents, then the temptation to take advantage of procedural technicalities that forestall the Senate from doing its business may be irresistible. To some extent, we are returned to the issues earlier discussed with regard to the (un)willingness to "compromise" core political values. In any event, both political parties are quite willing to take advantage of these possibilities when it serves their political interests. Which is one of the reasons that they remain in effect regardless of who nominally "controls" the Senate, even if the cost is the perception by both citizens and political analysts that the political system is increasingly dysfunctional.

7

If Two Opinions Are Good, Is a Third Opinion (with the Power to Kill the Decisions of the First Two Opinion-makers) Even Better?

The primary defense of bicameralism is the desirability of seeking second opinions and the benefits of the added deliberation that comes from the double scrutiny of both House and Senate. Redundancy, we might say, is "a feature and not a bug" inasmuch as it is likely to discover problems that were overlooked the first time around.

One can certainly agree with this general logic, but it leads to two crucial further questions: How many opinions are optimal? Who should have the last word if the various decisionmakers disagree? On the first question, the U.S. Constitution answers three or four, depending on your view of the role of the judiciary. If one "disaggregates" some of the institutions in question, by recognizing that "Congress is a 'they', not an 'it'"[1] and applying this insight to the executive and judicial branches as well, then one can find many more people and institutions with a quasi-decisive role, at least with regard to the ability to kill suggested policy changes. Think only of the complex committee system within each house of Congress, where the approval of several committees might be necessary for legislation to reach the floor in the first place.

One can well argue that the most resistant party often has the last word, in killing legislation or extracting concessions and compromises that would never be available were there other mechanisms to break deadlocks. Even at the most formal level, agreement between the House and the Senate, though a *necessary* condition for legislation, is most certainly not a *sufficient* condition. The president must assent to the legislation; if the president vetoes the legislation, the vote of two-thirds of both houses of Congress is required to override it. Presidents win such contests about 95 percent of the time. Many state governors, it is important to realize, have even more significant veto power than the president given their privilege to veto only parts of given legislation—the so-called item veto—rather than having to exercise an all or nothing choice.

As with equal voting power in the Senate, there are many arguments that demonstrate the extent to which the presidential veto is yet one more unfortunate feature of our "settled" Constitution, especially when presidents only disagree with the policies endorsed by Congress and do not have deep reservations about the constitutionality of given legislation. (No one argues that *all* such vetoes have been unfortunate. As always, one must assess overall frequencies and tendencies rather than focus on singular or even what political scientists call "low-number" events.) Still, one should acknowledge the fundamental accuracy of describing the American system of government, at both the national and state level, as significantly *tricameral* inasmuch as presidents or governors become major actors in the legislative process itself.

The mere *threat* of a veto, if credible, often leads to reshaping legislation on the floor of the legislature. Members of Congress respond quite differently to the threat of a presidential veto than to a suggestion by one of their colleagues that the courts may find legislation to be unconstitutional. Legislators often modify their commitments if the president makes a credible threat to veto legislation, usually justified by references to the importance of "compromise" and settling for "half a loaf" when the near certainty of a successful veto precludes a "full loaf." But one rarely finds similar changes if the suggestion is "merely" that a court will invalidate a statute several years later. Indeed, there are times when the prospect of such an invalidation would be a plus. Perhaps it would prevent a policy from going into effect that the legislator in fact opposes but is afraid to vote against because of constituent pressures. Another quite different calculus would involve the potential political gains linked to being able to criticize an arguably activist or overreaching judiciary. To be sure, there are times when one might be pleased by presidential vetoes for similar reasons; this only reinforces the importance of the potential for "strategic misrepresentation" of one's actual views in a complex divided structure of government like our own.

Threatened invalidation by some court may also be quite different from the possibility that the Supreme Court in particular will strike down an act of Congress or a state legislature. There are approximately nine hundred federal judges serving as district judges, members of courts of appeals, or as one of the nine members of the U.S. Supreme Court. The actual number is constantly in flux not only because of resignations and delays in filling empty seats but also because many judges can take "senior status," which opens up a vacancy even as the judges themselves can continue to handle a number of cases at their own discretion. An ideologically diverse judiciary will often generate quite different results depending on what particular court hears a case.[2] So one might well be able to predict, as given legislation is being considered, that *some* judge(s) would look unkindly on it even as others would see no problem. This necessary uncertainty as to the ultimate judicial response is far different from the confidence one might have in threats by presidents to erase legislation that one has fought for unless changes are made to their liking.

I. HAMILTON'S DEFENSE OF THE VETO, AND THE DIFFERENCE BETWEEN INSTITUTIONAL SELF-DEFENSE AND PROTECTING THE "GENERAL WELFARE"

The veto is obviously an explicit feature of the national Constitution, just as it is of all state constitutions.[3] Interestingly enough, opponents of the 1787 Constitution did not register objection to this aspect of the document. Thus the Federal Farmer, one of the leading opponents of ratification, wrote that "the third branch in the legislature may answer three valuable purposes, to impede in their passage hasty and intemperate laws, occasionally to assist the senate or people [presumably by noting unrecognized defects in otherwise desirable legislation], and to prevent the legislature from encroaching upon the executive or judiciary."[4] The principal defense of the veto was offered by Alexander Hamilton in *Federalist 73*, where he offered two quite different justifications. Like the Federal Farmer, Hamilton noted the importance of *protecting the institutional prerogatives* of the presidency from invasion by the Congress. It is part of the scheme of institutional checks and balances (which means that each branch is authorized to interfere in the workings of the others, as distinguished from a strict notion of "separation of powers," which leaves each branch fundamentally insulated from the possibility of any such interference). An effective way to prevent congressional "invasions" of "the rights of the executive" is to give the president the right to say no when Congress engages in such attempts. Indeed, if one is *really* concerned about such invasions, one might even support an absolute veto instead of the qualified veto that does, after all, allow a truly militant Congress to prevail if it can amass the two-thirds majorities in each house. Needless to say, any institutionalist theory of the presidential veto depends on knowing exactly what should be regarded as the equivalent of a president's "castle," protected against invasion by alien branches. For better or worse, though, most discussions of the president's "invasion-free" domain quickly take us to the Constitution of Conversation and leave the Constitution of Settlement well behind.

That being said, though, there is certainly something to the argument that if we can agree on what *does* count as the president's protected domain—such as the pardon power, the receiving of foreign ambassadors, or absolute discretion as to whom to invite to state dinners—then the strongest case for the veto arises when the president is attempting to rebuff presumptively illegitimate invasions of that domain by Congress. One might say that the president should have no such option and should be forced to rely on the judiciary for executive protection, but that itself raises a host of controversial questions.

In any event, Hamilton's second defense shifts from a focus on institutional self-defense to protecting the country against "bad laws" presumably generated by "the effects of faction, precipitancy, or of any impulse unfriendly to the public good." Here we no longer have the president protecting the particular domain of the chief executive against illegitimate attack. Instead, the president is ostensibly protecting all of us. Is it completely tendentious to refer to this as the notion of the president acting as the "Great Parent" over us the children?

One kind of bad law might be an "unconstitutional law," though this requires a strong confidence in one's ability to tell exactly which laws are "unconstitutional" rather than merely "unwise." One also ought to recognize that unless one builds a theory of "goodness" into one's notion of constitutionality, it is always possible that one will lament something that was wise or even essential to "establishing justice" being viewed as unconstitutional. Recall in this context one of the essential compromises with slavery, which prohibited Congress from banning American participation in the international slave trade until 1808. Had Congress tried to do that in, say, 1799, it would presumably have been the duty of John Adams, who most certainly did not support slavery as an institution, to veto the legislation as beyond Congress's power.

However, Hamilton does not focus on the propensity of Congress to pass *unconstitutional* legislation and the need to have a president ready to use the veto power as a shield against such laws. Instead, Hamilton appears to refer to laws that are perfectly constitutional but, nonetheless, "bad" or otherwise contrary to the "public good." One cannot emphasize too strongly (or repeat too often) that almost no one identifies all "bad" laws as unconstitutional or all "good" laws as necessarily constitutional. As James Wilson told his fellow delegates to the Philadelphia Convention, "Laws may be unjust, may be unwise, may be dangerous, may be destructive; and yet may not be so unconstitutional as to justify the judges in refusing to give them effect."[5] Interestingly enough, Wilson made his observation in the context of an unsuccessful argument supporting a *Council of Revision*, which would have been composed of federal judges as well as the president, precisely because the judiciary as such would not have had the power to strike down as unconstitutional laws that were only viewed as "unwise," "dangerous," or even "destructive" but not in violation of explicit constitutional prohibitions.[6]

The same questions would face a president who believes that exercise of the veto power requires as a prerequisite a belief that the legislation is unconstitutional *as well as* unwise, unjust, dangerous, or destructive. Legality and wisdom—or even justice—are simply different categories of analysis. To return yet once more to an earlier example, it would be almost lunatic to argue that waiting until January 20 to inaugurate new presidents is "unconstitutional," since it is the text of the Constitution itself that mandates that day. But it is not at all outrageous to say that this is an unwise, perhaps even "dangerous," feature of the Constitution that should be changed, just as the Twentieth Amendment changed the prior inauguration day of March 4. Inauguration Day scarcely raises great questions of justice. For that, we would have to turn to other features of the U.S. (or a state) constitution, past or present, including such obvious issues as slavery or religious discrimination.

So now we imagine a Congress that passes laws that seem perfectly constitutional but, alas, "bad." In that event, according to Hamilton, we will be fortunate to have "a man of tolerable firmness" who will "avail himself of his constitutional means of defense, and would listen to the admonitions of duty and responsibility." The obvious question, though, is why one would expect devotion to "the public good" to be found so much more often in a single president than in an *aggregate* Congress, especially when the Congress itself is subdivided into two different houses. After all, perhaps what the president believes to be a "bad" law is *really* a "good" one. What is it about a president that makes him or her more trustworthy about judgments of "good" and "bad" than others in the polity, or the executive branch, as an institution, more trustworthy in making such judgments than Congress?

Is Hamilton proposing a backdoor theory of "mixed government," in which presidents are deemed to be gratifyingly "different" from members of Congress in the way that lords were different from commoners and the king ultimately different (and better) than either? There were certainly people who felt that way about George Washington. And perhaps there have been some other presidents who are viewed as simply possessing a better character than the rest of us. Many people have this view of Abraham Lincoln, but he is only one of forty-four men to hold the office to date. And even if we have exalted views of the American president, does this translate into similar regard for state governors, who also enjoy the veto power in every state?

David Paterson, the recent governor of New York—assuming the position only upon the fiasco that forced the resignation of the elected Eliot Spitzer—chose in September 2010 to veto a bill that would have raised the levels of punishment following conviction for attacking taxi drivers, whose occupation is perhaps particularly vulnerable to violent attacks. There is no serious argument at all that the bill was unconstitutional, and few people argued that it was unwise. But it just didn't matter, since Paterson had the veto power. As the *New York Times* noted, the bill in question had the "nearly unanimous" support of the New York legislature.[7] An earlier story describing a "veto marathon" began as follows:

> As the Senate sought to negotiate and further delay a late budget to head off 6,900 promised vetoes, Gov. David Paterson rifled through a 2-foot high stack of the Legislature's budget bills, voiding them at a rate of one every 3 seconds Thursday.
>
> "I'm not talking to them," Paterson told reporters during a break in vetoing the Legislature's budget bills that he said the state can't afford. "They sent me a message. They sent that budget that was out of balance."[8]

Governor Paterson may have been absolutely right to eviscerate the budget bill; no one familiar with New York state politics views the state legislature as a repository of Madisonian republican virtue. And perhaps Paterson, whatever his unpopularity among the New York electorate, was a paragon of civic virtue, as has been the case on occasion among the hundreds of men and women who have served as state governors. That really isn't the point; rather, the question involves what social scientists would call the *frequency distribution* of such character traits in any given population.

So how plausible is the model behind Hamilton's defense of the executive's veto power? Moreover, it should be clear that one must presumably believe that there are basically correct answers to questions about the good and evil of proffered legislation. As an empirical matter, there is surely no agreement on the techniques we use to identify goodness or badness. But even if we treat asking questions about goodness or badness as the equivalent of asking who won the 2004 World Series, we must still ask ourselves why we would believe that presidents would necessarily be especially reliable sources of accurate answers. It is rather odd to believe that there is something special about the executive branch that, for example, makes a President Obama (or Harding, Truman, Kennedy, or Nixon) more trustworthy now than he was as a senator.[9]

Why would we place such trust in a single individual, even one who is unusually smart and even wise? There is a whole contemporary literature about "the wisdom of crowds," in other words, the greater likelihood of a collectivity reaching certain "correct results" (when "correctness" can be easily verified) than a given individual, even if we stipulate that the particular individual is smarter or more knowledgeable than any given member of the "crowd." One might argue that the ability to recognize goodness or badness, justice or injustice requires systematic education in a way that knowing the winner of a World Series does not, but that still requires us to believe that presidents are more likely to possess that education than members of the House or the Senate. Perhaps we believe that presidents are not only more intelligent than members of Congress—a question that would be difficult, if not impossible, to verify—but also purer in heart, less subject to various temptations and corruptions generated by the desire to win the next election. These assertions also seem to belie credibility.

Consider in this context South Africa, where the president can indeed veto legislation passed by the parliament, but *only* on constitutional grounds. That is, there is no policy-based veto at all. The parliament then reconsiders the veto that *is* allowed, based on constitutional arguments. If it disagrees with the president, it can simply repass by majority vote the legislation in question, which then goes to the South African constitutional court to render a definitive decision. If the court upholds it, then the president *must* sign it. There is no possibility of the president having the "last word" on the constitutionality of a measure, let alone its political wisdom. Such ultimate judgments are left, respectively, to the constitutional court or to parliament. Were the South Africans mistaken to adopt such a view of presidential veto power, even in a context where practically everyone knew that Nelson Mandela, like George Washington before him, would almost undoubtedly become his country's first president? Perhaps one commends their having done so because of attributes specific to South Africa that do not apply to the United States. But we can still wonder what those attributes might be.

Indeed, if one is especially worried about a legislature passing unconstitutional legislation, Massachusetts and a few other states suggest an alternative: authorizing their supreme courts to issue so-called advisory opinions. (A similar system operates in France.) Opponents of legislation on constitutional grounds can seek an immediate ruling from the court as to its constitutionality. This rests on the view that judgments about constitutionality and unconstitutionality rely on certain professional skills that are far more likely to be found in judges than in executives. This simply returns us to figuring out *who* is most likely to possess what we are willing to call "accurate knowledge" about disputed matters of "fact." Most presidents have not been lawyers, and not one so far has been a biologist. So why should we trust presidential judgment about constitutionality of legislation any more than we would necessarily trust a president to resolve disputes about the mechanisms of evolutionary selection? It may be important that presidents take seriously their oaths of office and therefore refuse to sign bills that are deemed unconstitutional. But this scarcely entails that presidents themselves make the judgment as to what is or is not constitutional, especially if we suspect that their own judgment may be highly influenced by what will best serve the political interests of their own party.

One of the themes of this book so far has been the emphasis placed by defenders of the U.S. Constitution on a certain vision of virtuous disinterestedness. But the snake in this particular garden is the political party. After all, at least since 1796, the President of the United States has run as the candidate of a defined political party and—more to the point—has been treated as the leader of that party, with commitments to its members and to its electoral fortunes. One would scarcely expect a political party pick a candidate who could not be trusted to support the party's priorities and stand up for its interests. We are used to candidate selection systems by which hopefuls go directly to the voters in primaries, thus sidestepping party leaders. That is a distinctly modern development, taking genuine wing after the disastrous Democratic convention in Chicago in 1968. Until then, even though there were a few primaries, party leaders played a dominant role. Indeed, conventions often were the ultimate decisionmakers, taking multiple ballots to decide. The last time a convention selected a candidate in one of the two major parties, however, was 1952, with the ultimate nomination of Adlai Stevenson as the Democratic candidate.

One might well believe that the development of political parties changes the analysis in Hamilton's defense of the presidential veto; he seems to require a president "above politics" who would think only of the national interest and never of "factional" party interests. To be sure, *all* major public officials are now fully involved in political parties and presumably devoted to their specific welfare. This entails the almost automatic critique and rejection of policies associated with the "other" party or parties, but one has to explain why presidents are less likely to submit to partisanship than is Congress as a whole.

Most dramatic is the situation when the majority in Congress and the president come from different parties, defined in part precisely by conflicting notions of what constitutes the public good. Even the belief that presidential policy-based vetoes are useful because they force continued conversation scarcely requires accepting the proposition that the president prevails unless two-thirds of both houses disagree. As a practical matter, this guarantees that the president will in fact prevail in any policy showdown. By reducing the percentage of votes needed to override a veto, one diminishes at least to some extent the president's power in our tricameral system. At the extreme, an absolute majority of both houses—that is, 218 members of the House and 51 members of the Senate—might be able to overcome a presidential veto. But the Constitution compels two-thirds to overcome a veto. As with so much else about the Constitution of Settlement, one can ask whether it is a strength or weakness of the constitutional order bequeathed us in 1787.

II. LINE-ITEM AND "REDUCTIVE" VETOES

Even a brief look at the variety of American state constitutions makes it absolutely clear that there is no single veto system within the United States. Political scientist John Dinan notes the prevalence in most American state constitutions of the line-item veto, which allows governors to veto only specific parts of legislation without having to kill an entire bill. Such veto power is often confined to spending bills, where one might be especially concerned about the ability of "factional interests" to use their political power to engage in what economists call "rent seeking." Some states allow their governors simply to reduce specific dollar amounts spelled out in legislation; for example, a governor can with the stroke of a pen change an initial $100 million appropriation to $50 million and sign the revised bill.

Interestingly enough, a Republican Congress in 1994 was willing to grant Bill Clinton line-item veto power, but the Supreme Court declared that unconstitutional. Were this a different book, we could discuss at some length the merits of the Court's decision as an exercise in constitutional interpretation. However, it is enough for purposes of this book that we ask only whether it counts for or against the U.S. Constitution that it is not perceived as authorizing such vetoes even where the Congress in good faith believes that assigning such power to the president would produce "better" legislation overall.

Incidentally, one might well wonder if it is possible to both oppose the assignment of a wide-ranging veto power to the president and support granting line-item veto authority. One might argue that the skepticism about Congress is most justified with regard to what have come to be called earmarks, the assignment of federal funds to favored interest groups or constituencies. And, clearly, just as individual senators have an incentive to support tools like holds—even if they agree that particular holds are dreadful—there are strong incentives for individual members of Congress to support their constituents via earmarks and therefore demonstrate an ability to "bring home the bacon." If Congress is unable to discipline itself, the argument goes, the president (or a governor) must step in and blow the whistle. But do these arguments apply to broad policy judgments that cannot so easily be reduced to exercises in narrow, constituency-oriented rent seeking?

There are yet other kinds of veto techniques that are part of political systems elsewhere in the world. As noted earlier in the discussion of bicameralism, some upper houses are given the power only of a "suspensive veto," by which the lower house must wait a defined amount of time before attempting to override the veto by repassing the legislation in question. One might imagine presidential or gubernatorial vetoes that generate a similar "cooling off" process, so that the legislature could override the veto immediately by a supermajority vote or wait six months and repass the legislation simply by majority vote.

III. SEGUEING INTO THE ELECTORAL COLLEGE: THE PRESIDENT AS A UNIQUELY "NATIONAL" OFFICIAL

One often hears policy-based vetoes defended via an argument that the president truly represents "the Nation" in a way that Congress does not.

This perspective goes back at least as far as the presidency of Andrew Jackson, with its notion of the president as "tribune of the people." It is also reflected in Theodore Roosevelt's assertion that the president was in effect the "steward of the nation." In his autobiography written after his presidency, Theodore Roosevelt described himself as "act[ing] for the public welfare...for the common well-being of *all our people,* whenever and in whatever manner was necessary, unless prevented by direct constitutional or legislative prohibition."[10] Not surprisingly, most presidents present a similarly ennobling self-portrait. George W. Bush reassured the American public after the 2004 presidential election of his "duty to serve all Americans."[11] One could easily find similar statements in President Obama's speeches. No president publicly promises to support only those who voted for him or those who constitute the base of his political party.

One need not doubt the sincerity of these various presidents and many more who could be similarly quoted. Sincerity is beside the point, especially inasmuch as almost all members of Congress adopt equally self-serving (and quite possibly sincere) descriptions of their own motivation when deciding what votes to cast or policies to support. The question is whether such assertions are *empirically* plausible and how we could possibly test the "comparative virtue" of our various presidents, especially against that exhibited by Congress. One can easily concede that a president represents a larger group of people, across a wider swath of territory, than does any *individual* representative or senator. But the relevance of this concession may well be vitiated once one addresses the peculiar method by which we select our presidents—the electoral college. State governors are chosen by their statewide electorates. Presidents, however, are most definitely not chosen by the national electorate. Let us turn, then, to some of the implications of American "presidentialism" and, at the state level, "gubernatorialism."

8

Presidentialism
(and Gubernatorialism)

What do we mean when we refer to a political system as "presidential" (or, with regard to the American states, "gubernatorial")? Generally, most contemporary political systems around the world can be described as adopting either presidentialism or parliamentarianism as their central mode of governance. Several contemporary countries, the most important being France and Russia, have adopted what some political scientists call "semi-presidential" systems, which feature both nationally elected presidents and prime ministers chosen by parliament, with the actual division of powers depending on whether they are from the same or different parties. The French coined the term *cohabitation* to refer to the political equivalent of a "mixed marriage" in which the two primary officials were the candidates of often sharply conflicting political parties.

So what makes a system presidential or even semi-presidential? The answer is fairly easy: it is the election of someone called "president"—or, in the American states, "governor"—by a process that is *separate* from that for selecting members of the legislature (and where that separate process is not simply the selection of the president *by* the legislature). Germany and Israel, for instance, are systems that any political scientist would describe as parliamentary though they do have someone designated "president." The office in such systems is not entirely trivial. At the very least, it is the president of Germany or Israel who is *head of state*, whereas the chancellor or prime minister is merely *head of government*. And, though Great Britain is certainly the paradigmatic case of parliamentary government, it is important to know that the head of state, for Great Britain—as for

Canada, Australia, and New Zealand—is Her Majesty, Queen Elizabeth II. (Australia, given an opportunity in a national referendum several years ago to ditch the monarchy and become a full-scale republic, voted to retain the connection with the Queen, in large part because of fears about the potential power of a president. There are no such fears about the British monarch, who has no real political power.)

The U.S. Constitution does not speak expressly to the identity of the head of state, but it has been taken as a given that the President of the United States is both the head of government and the head of state. This is why military bands often play "Hail to the Chief" whenever a president appears in public settings (and not only, for example, when he visits military bases, when the tune might be considered appropriate). Nothing similar occurs in Great Britain when a prime minister appears. He is treated—to adopt the terminology of H. Ross Perot when he was running for the presidency in 1992—as an "employee" of the public who can be dismissed, sometimes quite ruthlessly, when he or she is no longer thought desirable.

Great Britain's is the quintessential parliamentary system because the prime minister, who must be a member of Parliament, is elected by his or her fellow parliamentarians and remains accountable to them inasmuch as they can vote him or her out of office. Sometimes this will be via a vote of "no confidence," which may mean that the existing government "falls" and new elections are called. But it is also possible to envision an intra-party revolt in which the party leader is sacked and replaced with someone thought to be more suitable. An especially notable example was the uprising within the Conservative Party in 1990 against the leadership of Margaret Thatcher, who until then was one of the most powerful peacetime prime ministers in British history.

Presidential systems, by contrast, require that the president not only run for office separately but also sever any connection with the legislature. Thus President Obama resigned from the Senate shortly after his election in 2008, as would be the case with a state legislator who was elected governor of one of the states. Moreover, and crucially, the president or governor may be accountable to the public at large—and subject to impeachment by Congress or the state legislature under very special conditions—but there is no mechanism by which unhappy members of Congress, even if they represent a large majority, can replace a president in whose judgment they have lost confidence.

There is an extensive literature on whether presidential or parliamentary systems are "better." Many political scientists argued for some years that parliamentary systems were generally more democratic and more likely to remain so than their presidentialist counterparts, which had, it was argued, an unfortunate tendency to disintegrate into dictatorships. These dictatorships would be generated either by strong presidents who absorbed more and more powers or by military juntas who would overthrow presidents not to their liking. More recently, an important book by Jose Antonio Cheibub has argued that the suggested differences do not stand up under refined empirical analysis.[1] He argues, for example, that the proclivity of Latin American countries—a major focus of "anti-presidentialists" like Juan Linz[2]—to disintegrate into dictatorships is less a function of their having adopted presidentalism than having had a military coup in their historical past. Thus the experience of an initial military coup prepares the ground for later such events, quite independently of a later decision to adopt either a parliamentary or presidential form of civilian government.

Moreoever, Cheibub notes the importance of specifying the *actual* powers held by a president under a given constitution. Consider only the specific aspects of a president's veto power. A president with no veto power at all is obviously far weaker, by any standard measure, than one who has absolute veto power. One of the things that makes the United States describable as having a "strong president" is the relative power the president has over legislative decisions by the two-thirds override rule. The same is true of "strong governors" within the American states. Other more informal features, such as the president's ability to dominate the public agenda, may help to explain the strength of the modern presidency, but one should obviously not underestimate the importance of the formal veto-override rule. Moreover, the president gains considerable power from having an extended tenure in office, which is a major defining characteristic of presidentialism per se. In any event, one should beware of any single-factor approach to understanding the dynamics of presidential, as against parliamentary, systems.

I. CHOOSING PRESIDENTS

If the chief executive is chosen in a separate-track election from members of the legislature, the executive branch of both nation and states can be headed by someone of a different party from the majority of the legislature. One feature of the American system of government is that the national executive is chosen by a quite spectacularly different process than any state governor, all of whom are elected in statewide popular elections, with the popular vote winner (who, as noted earlier, may not have received a majority of the total vote) gaining the prize of public office, save in states with run-off systems. So we now turn to the electoral college, by any criterion one of the truly "exceptional" aspects of the American political system.

A. What explains the 1787 decision to adopt the electoral college?

The delegates to the Philadelphia convention created an unusually complex manner of electing presidents, which in many ways has remained constant (with only one significant change) since George Washington's election in 1789. A basic decision of the delegates was to adopt a presidential form of government. But what best explains their refusal to adopt popular election of the president and instead, through a remarkably complex process, to trust selection of the chief executive initially to specially chosen electors and, should a majority of these electors be unable to agree on a choice, later to the House of Representatives (voting by state rather than individual member)? One might explain the adoption of presidentialism per se to the august presence of George Washington. Had Washington been killed on his way to Philadelphia, one might wonder if there might have been at least some support for a more parliamentary form of government. This might be an anachronistic question, inasmuch as what we today think of as parliamentary government was only in its birth pangs in Great Britain. We can still ask, though, if the Framers might have made a different choice as to the mode of electing presidents if they had been aware that the presidency of Washington would help to stimulate the creation of a national two-party system. "Had they imagined that post–George Washington elections would devolve into a clear contest between two nationally prominent candidates," Jack Rakove has written, "they might have decided not to invent the electoral college in the first place."[3]

But the Framers were not clairvoyant. Many of their leading lights, including Madison, seemed to possess an almost desperate desire to prevent the development of "factional" parties. Such parties, after all, would negate the promise of at least one version of a "republican form of government" that depends on apolitical leaders devoted to a politics of the common good. It would also require clairvoyance for the Framers to have genuinely considered parliamentary government in any modern sense. That simply was not "on offer" at the end of the eighteenth century. Historians can legitimately describe Great Britain as moving toward such a system even at that time, but what Americans perceived was a monarchy headed by King George III, even if Parliament played a significant role as well. As Rakove has also written, "eighteenth-century ministerial government" in Great Britain continued to have "a strongly monarchical cast," not least because "popular political parties simply did not exist."[4] Only in the twentieth century could constitutional designers genuinely imagine parliamentarianism as an alternative to the separation-of-powers system notionally headed by a president. It is, therefore, no surprise that "the task of establishing a national executive on republican principles puzzled the framers."[5]

It was, then, almost certainly overdetermined that the Framers in Philadelphia would choose some form of a presidential system. The central question was how the president would be chosen, and the answer was through the electoral college. As before, it is worth starting with what might be termed the "official" defense of this decision, found in Alexander Hamilton's *Federalist* 68.

1. Hamilton's defense

Once more we see the strong preference for representative government over any kind of direct decisionmaking by the people. The electors in their way are a very special legislature, with only one item on their agenda, the choice of a president and vice president. Hamilton associates popular election with the threat of "tumult and disorder." These dangers would presumably be minimized if the role of the people was limited to choosing only "a small number of persons, selected by their fellow citizens from the general mass, [who] will be most likely to possess the information and discernment requisite to so complicated an investigation," that is, determining who is best suited to take the highest office in the land. "Information" refers to relevant knowledge, but "discernment" is presumably a capacity for sound judgment in addition to that knowledge.

Moreover, for Hamilton it is an advantage that the chosen electors will never gather together in one place, which might be the focal point for "heats and ferments"; instead, they will meet in their own state capitals to cast their votes, which will then be transmitted to the nation's capital for the final count (and, if there is no majority, decision by the House of Representatives). It is also worth noting Hamilton's seeming embrace of the Constitution's exclusion of all officials of the United States, including representatives and senators, from serving as electors. This, he suggests, will lessen the possibility of what he calls "sinister byass" [*sic*] entering into the final deliberations.

All of this, Hamilton argues, "affords a moral certainty, that the office of president, will seldom fall to the lot of any man, who is not in an eminent degree endowed with the requisite qualifications...It will not be too strong to say, that there will be a constant probability of seeing the station filled by characters pre-eminent for ability and virtue." And note, incidentally, that the Constitution initially mandated that the vice president would be the person who came in second when the votes were tallied (assuming that the person first past the post in fact received a majority). Presumably the electors, each of whom could cast two votes, would vote for the two persons deemed most "pre-eminent for ability and virtue." The most able and virtuous person would be president; the second most able and virtuous person would become vice president. One should note as well the Constitution's bar against electors voting for two candidates from their own state. This meant that Virginia's electors, for example, could not vote for two Virginians, but they could certainly vote for two New Yorkers. This relatively modest bar on electoral choice was thought to be a valuable protection against any tendency to overly favor local notables inasmuch as it forced the electors to go out of state for at least one of their two choices. Although one can readily doubt the continuing importance of this bar, it re-emerged in 2000, when some lawyers suggested that Texas electors could not vote for both George W. Bush and Dick Cheney because both could be considered inhabitants of Texas. In fact, Cheney, well aware of the Constitutional bar, transferred his residence from Texas to Wyoming, his original home state, immediately after receiving the Republican nomination. A federal court quickly dismissed a suit that attempted to enjoin Texas electors from voting for both.

2. Akhil Amar's functionalist explanations

It is useful to supplement Hamilton's justification with a set of basically functionalist explanations offered by Akhil Amar.[6]

A. LACK OF POLITICAL PARTIES AND OTHER MECHANISMS GENERATIVE OF A NATIONAL "PUBLIC OPINION"

The Constitution was drafted before the organization of systematic political parties (even if they would follow within the decade). One obvious and important role of political parties is to select its champions for national office and thus to coordinate choices that might otherwise be made by people living in very different areas far from one another. In the absence of such coordinating institutions, the desirability of turning to presumptively sophisticated local elites—in other words, presidential electors—makes some sense, especially if one is also skeptical of the existence of other national communications systems that might supply relevant knowledge to ordinary citizens. Rakove writes that "popular election," which was proposed by some Framers, "was a casualty not of the Framers' fear of demagoguery but of an information problem for which they had no obvious solution."[7] So an obvious question is whether the development of modern political parties, as well as systems of mass communication that were truly inconceivable in 1787, affects any arguments made at the time about the unlikelihood that ordinary Americans would possess the knowledge needed to make an informed choice as to who should become president and vice president.

B. THE IMPORTANCE OF STATE AUTONOMY CONCERNING VOTING RULES

The rise of political parties and the development of modern communications systems do indeed render irrelevant at least one justification or explanation for the electoral college mechanism. But this is far less true regarding a second factor that Amar emphasizes, which is the reality of differences among the states regarding who can vote. Even today, when a variety of constitutional amendments (primarily to the U.S. Constitution) and Supreme Court decisions have made the states somewhat more homogeneous in this regard, there are still some dramatic differences, such as rules regarding the (in)ability of convicted felons to vote or the use of stringent registration systems or election-day mechanisms to limit the number of actual voters.

One might well believe that popular elections, then and now, would have generated a large incentive for states to become more inclusive in dispensing the right to vote. This would maximize the number of Texans, Indianans, or citizens of any other state in determining the final outcome. It is a perhaps peculiar feature of the electoral college system, where the number of electoral votes is a function only of general population and is totally unrelated to the number of actual voters, that there is no "cost" to restricting the number of voters, at least from the perspective those who control state politics. Those in control might be especially eager to keep the number of voters down if they fear that those deprived of the ability to vote—whether through formal exclusion or informal mechanisms to diminish the turnout of certain voting blocs—might have views perceived as threatening to existing elites. Such manipulation of voting rules to reinforce hegemonic power would presumably be less likely if the number of electoral votes were a function of actual participation in elections, let alone if we shifted to a national popular vote.

The electoral college system that came out of Philadelphia certainly did not discourage manipulation by sophisticated political elites. The first genuinely contested election was that between Thomas Jefferson and John Adams in 1796, very narrowly won by Adams in part because he won single electoral votes in North Carolina and Virginia. This was possible only because neither state had adopted the "winner-take-all" system that freezes out anyone who votes for the loser from receiving any representation at all in the so-called college of electors; instead, electors were chosen by districts. Not surprisingly, Virginia changed the rules prior to the 1800 election to eliminate the district method of choosing electors, substituting winner take all. Equally unsurprising was the decision by Massachusetts,

Adams's home state, to follow suit, though "rather than take any chances with the electorate, the legislature arrogated the appointment of electors to itself," as allowed by the Constitution.[8] As Rakove writes, "no fewer than six states changed their electoral law for the occasion [of the 1800 election]. They acted not in response to deep constitutional values...but from purely strategic calculations of partisan interest."[9] Among other things, this meant that all states had an incentive to adopt the winner-take-all method of allocating electoral votes, lest they in effect lose clout in the final vote by more accurately reflecting the actual distribution of the local citizenry's preferences. None of this, it should be emphasized, involves "interpreting" the electoral college or having long conversations about its "meaning"; it simply entails taking advantage of the clear assignment of power to state legislatures to decide how electors would be chosen. "Each State shall appoint, *in such Manner as the Legislature thereof* may direct, a Number of Electors" (emphasis added).[10]

C. SLAVERY

But Amar reminds us once more that one simply cannot understand the 1787 Constitution, and thus that part of the Constitution of Settlement that structures our polity even today, without recognizing the importance of slavery. *Only* the electoral college allows the Three-Fifths Compromise that gave slaveowners extra influence in the House of Representatives to translate into a bonus when choosing the president as well. Popular election would simply wipe out the bonus. Indeed, it would even offer an incentive for free states to allow free blacks to vote. So, Amar argues, this is a major, if not the principal, explanation for the electoral college. To be sure, one could scarcely have expected Hamilton, who opposed slavery, to offer this as a defense to wavering New York delegates who were the target audience for *The Federalist*.

One should not think, though, that the bonus disappeared with the addition of the Thirteenth Amendment, barring slavery. The "slavery bonus" may have disappeared after 1865, but it was replaced in substantial measure by a "Jim Crow" bonus, whereby former slave states that successfully suppressed African American political participation nonetheless gained additional power in the electoral college. This is, after all, the meaning of counting former slaves as full persons instead of only three-fifths of persons in computing total population, members of the House of the Representatives, and therefore votes in the electoral college.

B. The Twelfth Amendment as the legitimation of the party system

The electoral college initially reflected the Framers' presumed belief that the United States, though not without "factions," would at least be lacking political parties. Whatever one thinks of this vision of politics, its utter collapse was certainly illustrated by the fiasco of the 1800 election, which brought the country to the brink of civil war. Jefferson was the clear popular vote winner over Adams, with 41,330 votes to Adams's 25,962. It's not clear, though, what to make of these figures, since the total population of the United States in 1800 was 5,304,716, of whom, according to the census bureau, one million were "other" than Caucasian; we can be confident that most of them were slaves. So the total vote of approximately 67,000 was a bit more than 1 percent of the total population and less than 2 percent even of the Caucasian population. Even eliminating women, who were deprived of the vote, would only roughly double the overall percentage of white males. Moreover, recall that the legislatures of several states—including Pennsylvania, Connecticut, and Massachusetts—chose the electors, bypassing the electorate entirely.

Jefferson also carried eight states compared to the seven won by Adams. The electoral vote difference between the two, however, was far narrower than the popular vote difference: seventy-three votes (for both Jefferson and Burr) to sixty-five votes for Adams. Adams would have won were it not for the "slavery bonus." Virginia, which gave its native son all of its twenty-one electoral votes, was only 55 percent Caucasian, while South Carolina, which split its twelve electoral votes 8–4 in favor of Jefferson, was still 57 percent white. (By the 1820 census, South Carolina would be majority black.)[11] South Carolina's vote in 1800 is explained by the cleverness of Adams in picking South Carolinian Charles Cotesworth Pinckney as his running mate in the election. The tie between Jefferson and Burr was a function of the inability of the Jeffersonians to coordinate and make sure that at least one of the electors voted for someone other than Burr as his second choice.

How were deadlocks broken? The answer as laid out in the original Constitution was again deceptively simple: the House of Representatives would choose. Had neither Jefferson nor Burr received a majority, the House would have chosen among the top five candidates; since both in fact did receive a majority, the choice was between the two. But here other bizarre features of the Constitution came into play: the newly elected Jeffersonian House of Representatives would not begin meeting until thirteen months after its election, which meant that the deadlock would be broken by the "lame-duck" Federalist House of Representatives, which by and large despised Jefferson. Moreover, the decision rule mimics the allocation of voting power in the Senate; each state has a single equal vote in breaking such deadlocks, and a majority of the states is necessary to name the winner. Many Federalists were tempted to vote for Burr, some simply because they detested Jefferson, some because Burr was anti-slavery, and some because Burr was viewed as more opportunistic than Jefferson and therefore likely to endorse at least some Federalist programs in return for the presidency. Alexander Hamilton joined in detesting Jefferson, but he loathed Burr even more—precisely because of his perceived lack of civic virtue—and he refused to support any such schemes. (This may help to explain why Burr later killed Hamilton in the most notorious duel in American history.) It took until the thirty-sixth ballot, less than a month before the March 4 inauguration, for Federalist James Bayard, the single representative from Delaware, to vote reluctantly for Jefferson. Bayard, of course, had voting power equal to the entire delegations of larger states like Virginia and Massachusetts, given the one state, one vote rule set out in the Constitution. For what it is worth, moreover, the Jeffersonian governors of both Pennsylvania and Virginia had threatened to call out their state militias and to march on Washington should the Federalists deprive Jefferson of what they perceived to be his rightful victory. Had Bayard stood firm, the American Civil War might have been hastened by sixty years.[12]

The Twelfth Amendment was proposed and ratified in 1803 in response to the crisis. It "solves" the particular problem presented by the election of 1800—or, for that matter, by the election of 1796, which produced John Adams as president and his increasingly bitter rival Thomas Jefferson as vice president—by splitting the electors' votes into distinctly separate tracks for the presidency and vice presidency. In effect, this is the tacit recognition in the Constitution's text that party politics had come to America. Moreover, it acknowledged that there might be significant differences with regard to the merit of presidents and vice presidents, who would often be chosen for geographical balance or for other party-oriented reasons.

There was one other change buried in the Twelfth Amendment: whereas the original Constitution gave the House the right to choose from the top five candidates, the Twelfth Amendment changed it to the top three. This became important in the 1824 election, also thrown into the House, when Henry Clay came in fourth, by four votes (41–37) behind William Crawford (though Clay got almost seven thousand more popular votes). Both were well behind the two leading candidates, Andrew Jackson, who won ninety-nine electoral votes and 41.3 percent of the popular vote, and John Quincy Adams, who was awarded eighty-four electoral votes with approximately 31 percent of the popular vote. In the House, Clay might actually have emerged as president, but he was eliminated by the Twelfth Amendment rule. What did not change was the necessity to win the votes of a majority of the states. Clay threw his support to Adams in return, it was alleged, for a promise to name Clay as secretary of state; the majority of states was procured and Adams moved to the White House.

C. Why does the electoral college survive?

One can well wonder why the electoral college survives. After all, the first of Amar's three explanations for the original institution, relating to the absence of relevant information on the part of the electorate, collapsed once national parties are organized, as happened in 1796. Mass media in our own world, including contemporary "social media," provide almost instant information about what a candidate may be saying to an audience thousands of miles away. The slavery-bonus rationale collapsed after 1865, though one might argue that the former slaveowning states were the big winners from the Civil War inasmuch as their "non-Caucasian" populations now counted as whole persons instead of merely three-fifths of persons. There was only a relatively brief period, however, when African Americans fully participated in Southern politics. One could describe the electoral college in most of the South from 1877 to 1965 as a "segregation bonus" that continued to give the South an inordinate role in choosing American presidents, especially when they were Democrats. After all, as late as 1952, Adlai Stevenson, the darling of most liberals, chose Alabama Senator John Sparkman as his running mate. When Stevenson once again won the nomination in 1956, he was decidedly cool toward *Brown v. Board of Education*, the Supreme Court decision that ostensibly invalidated school segregation. Still, one might argue that in the aftermath of the Voting Rights Act of 1965, there is little or no residuum of the "slavery" or "segregation" bonus. Perhaps state political elites believe privately that it is a good thing that they can minimize local electorates, whether to serve partisan political ends or because of a belief that there are some otherwise mature citizens who simply ought not be invited to participate in choosing their leaders. Few state leaders are willing to express such views publicly, which suggests that they have become unacceptable as part of the "American creed" in the twenty-first century. So we must continue to ask what explains the survival of the electoral college?

A less cynical explanation for its survival is that Americans really like it, much as they like other features of American government that might be hard to defend from a particular academic (or political) perspective, including the presidential veto and the two-thirds vote requirement (in both houses of Congress) to override it. The problem with this answer is that the evidence seems very much to cut the other way. In the sixty-five years that the Gallup organization has been polling the American public about the desirability of substituting direct popular election for the electoral college, the highest disapproval response—which in this context means support for the electoral college and opposition to moving to direct election—was 37 percent in December 2000. Prior to 2000, the highest disapproval response was 22 percent. Perhaps the 2000 poll reflects Republican approval of a system that placed in the White House a Republican who did not in fact win the popular vote. Still, as Table 8.1 shows, the polling evidence is rather dramatic.

Especially interesting is a 1968 poll immediately after the November election, when Richard Nixon attained the White House with approximately 43 percent of the national vote. Eighty-one percent of the public supported direct elections at that time. Unfortunately, the Gallup organization didn't take a similar poll in November 1992, when Bill Clinton was

Table 8.1 *Gallup Direct Election Polls Since 1944*

	APPROVE %	DISAPPROVE %	NO OPINION %
2004 Oct 11–14	61	35	4
2000 Dec 15–17	59	37	4
2000 Nov 11–12	61	35	4
1980 Nov 7–0	67	19	14
1977 Jan 14–7	73	15	12
1968 Nov 9–4	81	12	7
1968 Sep 1–6	76	13	11
1967 Oct 6–1	65	22	13
1967 Jan 26–1	58	22	20
1966 Jan 21–6	63	20	17
1944 Jun 22–7	65	23	13

Source: FairVote, http://www.fairvote.org/assets/Uploads/npv/GallupPolls.pdf.

elected with a roughly similar percentage. Whatever explains the retention of the electoral college, it certainly is not a demonstrable desire by the American public for that outcome. One could simply offer this as a leading illustration of the imperviousness of the Constitution even to widely supported change—at least in an abstract sense, given that almost no one has organized marches against the electoral college or stood at street corners passing out leaflets supporting direct election.

There are, to be sure, defenders of the electoral college, two notable examples being Professor Dan Lowenstein of the University of California, Los Angeles, and Northwestern Law School professor John McGinness.[13] Although both Lowenstein and McGinness defend the failure to turn to a national popular vote to elect presidents, it is significant that neither is eager to defend the entire electoral college system, including, for example, the one state, one vote process by which the House breaks deadlocks or the possibility of so-called faithless electors who would reject their party's candidate in favor of their own idiosyncratic choices. The latter has happened 156 times, beginning with the 1796 election, though never changing the outcome.[14] McGinness is particularly forthright about his rejection of the importance of democracy or majority rule, privileging instead what he perceives as the relative stability provided by the electoral college, including the distortion whereby the choice of a de facto minority of the electorate may gain impressive majorities of electoral votes. Lowenstein is less of an anti-democrat and instead emphasizes the ostensible advantages of a procedure emphasizing "stateness" as a constitutive element of the United States rather than collapsing us into one undifferentiated electorate. He is also unbothered by the phenomenon of "battleground states" that invariably gain excessive attention during the presidential campaign, viewing them (implausibly I believe) as proxies for other relatively similar states. I am unpersuaded by such defenses, however heartfelt they may be. We should ask, after all, not only why no foreign country chooses its president in such a byzantine way but also why all American states elect their governors by direct vote of the people. To be sure, the national government is federal in a way that no state is, but does this justify the peculiarity of the electoral college?

D. Proposed modifications of the electoral college

1. Eliminating winner-take-all assignment of votes

Some people advocate *modifying*, rather than eliminating, the electoral college and substituting a nationwide popular vote. One proposal would eliminate the winner-take-all feature that most states—all but Maine and Nebraska—adopt. This plan would instead assign electoral votes to the winners of each congressional district, with the statewide winner getting the "senatorial bonus" of two electors. Among other things, this brings up the issue of "partisan gerrymandering," the intentional drawing of political boundary lines in order to maximize the interests of a given political party. If one (properly) fears the consequences of such gerrymandering when selecting presidents, one could move to a more "mechanical" form of proportional representation, whereby each candidate would be assigned a number of votes equal to the percentage of the vote actually received in a given state. We would have to decide whether "thresholds" should in effect eliminate marginal candidates and whether we would allow "fractional" electoral votes or require whole numbers that would inevitably deviate from the presumptive idea of proportional allotment. Still, these modifications would presumably not require a Constitutional amendment, which is attractive, given the prohibitive difficulties of Constitutional change in the United States.

2. The FairVote proposal

Another suggestion, advocated by FairVote, a group devoted to reforming the system by which we elect presidents, is that the eleven largest states simply agree with one another to order that their electoral votes be cast for the winner of the national popular vote, which would effectively eliminate the electoral college. But it should be obvious that this proposal, even if it eliminates the "non-plurality winner" problem (e.g., George W. Bush), does nothing at all to eliminate the "non-majority-supported" problem exemplified by Clinton, Nixon, and—further back in our history—Woodrow Wilson and Abraham Lincoln. Is it important to have a president who can plausibly claim to be supported by a majority of Americans? If we think the answer is yes, how do we assure that the winner can make such a claim? Consider the possibility of a French-style runoff if no one gets a majority, or the Alternative Transferrable Vote, which would allow the voter to rank-order the candidates and thus more likely produce majority-acceptable winner than is the case with our present system.

It is hard to imagine such systems being adopted in the absence of a constitutional amendment. And, as a technical matter, it is not clear that the eleven states currently needed to produce the requisite 270 electoral votes could enter into a truly binding agreement, which, as an "interstate compact," would require the consent of Congress in order to be enforced by a court. Otherwise, one might imagine that California would decide that it really did not wish to direct its electors to vote for the Republican national popular-vote winner or Texas the Democratic winner. At the end of the day, the electoral college, perhaps like the specific day the Constitution specifies for the inauguration of a new president, simply exemplifies the importance of *path dependence,* the inertial force possessed by past decisions whether or not we believe they make much sense for us today. One can well doubt that "We the People" would maintain the electoral college if the U.S. Constitution were as easy to amend as most state constitutions. That it persists tells us almost nothing about actual public opinion and much about the difficulty of formal amendment.

9

So What, Precisely, Does One Get, as a Constitutional Matter, Upon Being Elected President?

We turn now to Article II of the U.S. Constitution, which sets out the executive powers of the president, just as analogous articles in state constitutions set out specific powers attached to the governor and, often, other executive branch officials. For those interested in the notion of "separation of powers," here is where we might find domains of action that are protected against legislative or judicial intrusion. Article II is substantially shorter than Article I, perhaps because in 1787 there was more fear of the legislature as "the most dangerous branch" and thus a felt necessity to stipulate more carefully what it could—or could not—do. So what does the Constitution settle about presidential powers and duties as *chief executive*?

I. THE EXECUTIVE POWER

One should read carefully the beginning of Article II: "The executive Power shall be vested in a President of the United States of America." It is worth comparing the language of Article II with the language at the outset of Article I, even if this takes us away from the Constitution of Settlement into the Constitution of Conversation. Some analysts think it is extremely important that Article II refers to "the executive Power," in contrast to Article I, which begins by stating that "all legislative powers herein granted shall be vested in a Congress of the United States." It is precisely the "herein granted" phrase that provides the basis for arguing that Congress possesses only "assigned powers" that are more or less explicitly "granted" in the text of the Constitution. James Madison actually told his fellow members of the House of Representatives during one of the first great debates on congressional power that it was fortunate that the Constitution specifies a procedure for entering into treaties, as the absence of such a clause, however "deficient" it would have made the Constitution, would have been rectifiable only by proposing and ratifying an amendment granting Congress such a power. One may or may not find this a plausible argument; the important thing is that Madison, often termed the "Father of the Constitution," felt free to make it and to expect it to be taken seriously. It was his commitment to this view that presumably led him, in his last act as president, to veto a "public improvements" bill passed by the Congress as beyond congressional power, however desirable as a matter of policy.

But the executive power is *not* limited to those powers "herein granted" later in Article II. This is obviously a very important issue when interpreting the Constitution and, more particularly, the scope of presidential power. A later chapter focuses on the subject of "emergency powers" and the president's ability to engage in extraordinary—perhaps even "illegal"— action when thought "necessary" to save the country. But first we should look at the undeniably "assigned" powers.

II. SPECIFIC ASSIGNMENTS OF POWER

A. Commander-in-Chief of the armed forces

The specific powers of the president are set out in Sections 2 and 3 of Article II. The first section details the procedures for choosing the president, limitations on eligibility for office, and the details of the oath that must be taken prior to assuming office. Section 4 sets out the standards for impeachment. However important Sections 1 and 4 may be, Sections 2 and 3 better answer our question of what power, exactly, the president gets upon assuming office.

Section 2 opens by assigning to the president the power (and duty) to serve as "Commander in Chief of the Army and Navy of the United States, and of the Militia of the several States, when called into the actual Service of the United States."[1] One aspect of this clause certainly counts as coming under the Constitution of Settlement, while another is at the heart of many contemporary conversations, often acrimonious, about constitutional meaning. The first, settled aspect concerns the fundamental principle, within the United States, of civilian control of the military.

As we have seen in reports about the wars in Iraq and Afghanistan, under both the Bush and Obama administrations, there is no doubt that generals are not the persons making the final decisions on the deployment or withdrawal of troops, though their advice is certainly being asked for. The final decisions are made by civilians, ultimately the president as commander-in-chief of the armed forces. The principle of civilian control is so fundamental that Congress could not, for example, pass legislation under the "war power" granting "supreme authority" to the head of the Joint Chiefs of Staff or any other military officer, even if Congress had completely lost faith in the judgment of the president and his civilian advisers, including the secretary of defense. It would be clearly unconstitutional to shift authority because it would so obviously violate the Constitution's unequivocal command that the president, as the top civilian official, exercise authority over any and all military personnel.

So what is there left to discuss? It is whether the Commander-in-Chief Clause awards a *substantive power* to the president that precludes congressional command or whether the clause is only procedural in terms of limiting the ultimate power of the military. After all, Congress is composed of civilians and not full-time military personnel. This is ensured by another obscure clause of the Constitution, in Article I, Section 6: "No Person holding any Office under the United States, shall be a Member of either House during his Continuance in Office." This means not only that persons who wish to serve in a presidential cabinet must resign their membership in Congress, but also that anyone "holding office" as a member of the armed forces must also resign to be eligible to serve in Congress. (There is, you should know, some debate about the status of those members of Congress who are reserve officers; the Supreme Court dodged ruling on this issue in 1974.[2] It is clear, though, that a full-time military officer is prohibited from serving in Congress.) So, returning to the possibility that Congress had completely lost faith in the judgment of the president, would anything bar Congress from engaging in micromanagement by passing legislation—perhaps over the veto of an angry president—ordering or preventing certain actions by the armed forces? Would *that* constitute a law that the president would be under a constitutional duty "faithfully to execute"?

If the Commander-in-Chief Clause is simply meant to ensure civilian control, then it would seem that Congress could in fact limit the president's ability to order the military to do certain things, whether sending troops to foreign countries or using torture as a means of interrogation during otherwise authorized wars. On the other hand, if the clause grants substantive power, a president can legitimately refuse to obey certain congressional statutes because they illegitimately attempt to limit his power as commander-in-chief to make any and all decisions about the use of the armed forces. There is no doubt that Congress possesses the ultimate "power of the purse" and can refuse to fund the military, but this is an extreme measure. Congress might be more than happy to fund particular military expeditions so long as it could place certain conditions on how the missions were carried out. As already suggested, this broad issue is very much a part of the contemporary Constitution of Conversation, where one can find esteemed advocates taking what have come to be called either the "congressional" or "presidentialist" positions.

B. The pardon power

The next named power is that of "Grant[ing] Reprieves and Pardons for Offences against the United States, except in Cases of Impeachment." It gives the president the power to suspend the ordinary operation of law, including the restraints it imposes on lawbreakers, by offering both a figurative and at times quite literal "get out of jail free" card to those who run afoul of the law.[3] Indeed, it is enough that the beneficiary of a pardon *might* run afoul of the law, for nothing prevents a president from pardoning someone in advance of a trial or even an indictment. The most (in)famous such example is surely President Ford's pardon of Richard Nixon for any crimes he might have committed prior to his resignation, which occurred on the brink of his probable impeachment by the House and conviction by the Senate for his role in the cover-up following the break-in by Republican operatives into the Watergate offices of the Democratic Party. Is this a wild card in the national constitutional system?

We can well wonder if contemporary constitutional designers would give a president such power. John Dinan, as part of his well-justified insistence that the "American constitutional tradition" includes what can be learned from our state constitutions, notes that a "majority of the states have chosen…to deviate in some fashion from the federal model."[4] Many states require their governors to share the pardoning power with other officials, in the belief that "ill-advised pardons would be prevented" by the requirement of multiple approval. As Dinan notes, governors in a number of states have been impeached or have faced criminal charges for selling pardons. Like the governors of ten other states, the Massachusetts governor can pardon only if it is first recommended by a "council." Interestingly enough, governors of these states are free to exercise unilateral decisions *not* to pardon. While running for the Republican nomination for the presidency in 2008, former Massachusetts governor Mitt Romney "often proudly point[ed] out that he was the first governor in modern Massachusetts history to deny every request for a pardon or commutation during his four years in office. He says he refused pardons because he didn't want to overturn a jury."[5] Six states—Alabama, Connecticut, Georgia, Idaho, South Carolina, and Utah—place the power to pardon entirely in a pardoning board in which the governor plays no role.

Although there is a special pardon attorney within the U.S. Department of Justice who has the responsibility of assessing petitions for pardons, presidents are not bound by any determinations made by that office. A recent book by Jeffrey Crouch, *The Presidential Pardon Power*, is severely critical of Presidents George H. W. Bush, Bill Clinton, and George W. Bush for what he terms the "abuse" of the pardon power. Both Bushes pardoned or otherwise reduced the sentence of persons who had been convicted of participating in legally questionable actions during their service to the president issuing the pardon, while Bill Clinton issued a pardon before trial to an alleged felon whose former wife had been a major Clinton contributor. In none of these cases did the pardons go through the process established for what might be termed "ordinary" supplicants. When Gerald Ford offered his extraordinary pardon to Richard Nixon, Ford suggested that Nixon had "suffered enough"; more serious, perhaps, was the argument that the country, in a fragile condition after the collective scandal known as Watergate, could not psychically or politically afford the spectacle of a former president being tried in front of a jury and, if convicted, perhaps sentenced to jail. There are many analysts who believe that continued outrage over the pardon cost Ford the election in 1976. Interestingly enough, when Ford died in 2005, many eulogists declared that he had done the right thing because, they said, it *did* serve the national interest.

In the great scheme of things, the pardon power is scarcely as important as, say, the veto power, let alone the president's foreign policy and military powers, whether such powers are constitutionally based or simply accepted by a Congress unwilling to seriously challenge a president. Still, the pardoning power raises not only deeply interesting theoretical issues but also, at least on occasion, practical ones with significant implications both for the pardoning president and the society that must live with the consequences of any such decisions.

The theoretical issues can be addressed by asking what we really mean by "the rule of law." To what extent do we acknowledge that adherence to legal rules may on occasion cause significant problems? One problem may be summarized in terms of "mercy," where we believe that there are good reasons (i.e., the "suffered enough" rationale for pardoning President Nixon) for exempting particular *individuals* from the law's seemingly clear command that they be punished in certain ways or for certain times. Just as important, though, are arguments that look less at the attributes of particular individuals than at general *public* interests that may be served by issuing pardons (such as the argument that the country as a whole would be better off if Nixon went quietly into the sunset rather than to a federal court as a defendant).

Public considerations may be especially important with regard to pardons or amnesties issued to perhaps thousands of individuals in an effort to restore some kind of national unity. As always, we should begin with the "quasi-official" justification for the pardoning power, set out in Hamilton's *Federalist* 74. He begins his discussion by referring to "the benign prerogative of pardoning." Two things are worth noting: The first is the use of the word "prerogative," which resonates with a famous chapter in John

Locke's *Second Treatise on Government* that defends the monarch's ability to go beyond the law, even to break it, when the "public good" requires. The second is the assumption that this is a "benign" power, nothing really to be concerned about.

So why should presidents have this power? The first justification touches on discrete individuals who, even if guilty, might be subject to unnecessarily severe punishment. Criminal codes must necessarily think in "wholesale" terms, considering defendants (and then persons convicted) as a whole. But if one thinks in more "retail" terms, one can quickly realize that there are times to dispense with what the law might require. "The criminal code of every country partakes of necessary severity," Hamilton writes, "that without an easy access to exceptions in favor of unfortunate guilt, justice would wear a countenance too sanguinary and cruel." Thus, an 1833 decision written by Chief Justice John Marshall defined a pardon as "an act of grace, proceeding from the power intrusted with the execution of the laws, which exempts the individual...from the punishment the law inflicts for a crime he has committed."[6] What occasioned controversy is whether there ought to be any literally "unpardonable" acts, such as treason, and the Constitution quite clearly says no. Presidents have free rein with regard to dispensing the "grace" of a pardon; they are restricted only from undoing the consequences of a congressional impeachment.

As Dinan notes, some of the concerns that led state constitutional designers to reject unilateral gubernatorial pardon authority also led them to place substantive limits on the pardoning power within their state constitutions. Particularly controversial were pre-conviction pardons, which thirty-seven state constitutions prohibit. Half of the states require that governors issue opinions justifying their decisions to pardon, while an additional fourteen states require advance notice to the public that a pardon is under consideration.[7]

A central point of this book is that one should ask whether we have something to learn from the often quite different decisions made by states when structuring their own constitutions of settlement. But the question goes both ways: perhaps the national-level decisions are better than those made by given states. Consider in this context those presidential pardons that include general "amnesties." These are best defended under Hamilton's second justification, where pardons involve a calculation by a president that the public interest is best served by the state refusing to exact the full measure of legal liability that it may well be entitled to. Ironically enough, this point is most clearly made with regard to traitors.

After all, Hamilton notes that "in seasons of insurrection or rebellion, there are often critical moments, when a well timed offer of pardon to the insurgents or rebels may restore the tranquility of the commonwealth; and which, if suffered to pass unimproved, it may never be possible afterwards to recall." Hamilton is a big proponent of "energy" in the executive, which often requires quick and decisive action. "The loss of a week, a day, an hour, may sometimes be fatal." Thus the president should have close to absolute power to make such decisions when the "public tranquility" may require it.

It should occasion no surprise that the first important pardons in American history were those by George Washington of participants in the so-called Whiskey Rebellion of 1795, two of whom had been sentenced to death for treason. In pardoning them, Washington noted that the rebellion had been successfully put down and that "the principal end of human punishment [is] the reformation of others." John Adams shortly thereafter emulated Washington with regard to the even more obscure Fries Rebellion, an armed tax revolt led by Pennsylvanian John Fries, who was sentenced to death with two of his compatriots. Adams pardoned them and issued a general amnesty to all of the revolt participants. Presumably, only the most vindictive of Americans might have preferred Fries's death to the generous display of mercy by the president.

Probably the most important pardons in our history were those issued after 1865 to many Confederate leaders who arguably deserved maximum punishment for treasonously precipitating (and then participating in) a war that caused the death of 2 percent of the entire population of the United States. They avoided even minimal legal punishment because both Lincoln and his successor Andrew Johnson believed that pardons and amnesties would be conducive to restoring some notion of unified nationhood. One can doubt whether a Republican Congress would have authorized such generous amnesties as these presidents did, but that reservation does not matter. That's just what presidential "prerogative" entails in this context. Similarly, one of Jimmy Carter's first acts as president in 1977 was to issue a general amnesty (and, therefore, a "welcome home" invitation) to those who resisted induction into the armed forces during the Vietnam War by fleeing to Canada. All of these examples illustrate the political implications of the presidential power to pardon.

Things get even more complex when presidents pardon their own associates accused or convicted of illegal acts while serving the presidential agenda. Gerald Ford's pardon of Richard Nixon was mentioned earlier. Less dramatic, and perhaps less defensible, was the pardon by George H. W. Bush of several of his associates who were accused of taking part in an illegal cover-up involving the shipment of arms to Iran and financial and other aid delivered to the Contras then at war with the leftist regime in Nicaragua. There were allegations that Bush himself, as Ronald Reagan's vice president, had been part of the illegal conspiracy, and a special prosecutor was appointed to look into these allegations. During the Christmas period of 1992, just weeks before he left office, Bush pardoned former secretary of defense Caspar Weinberger and others who were the target of an investigation by a special prosecutor. More recently, George W. Bush's commutation reprieve of Vice President Dick Cheney's loyal aide Lewis "Scooter" Libby from serving any time in jail after conviction for perjury was viewed by many as a payoff to a loyal associate, though the former vice president was reportedly angry that Bush did not in fact pardon Libby.

Some of the anti-Federalist opponents of the Constitution suggested that presidents would take part in cabals against the public interest and then use the pardoning power to escape any accountability. Whether the actions of the two Bushes meet this description, they do point to one of the things that makes the pardoning power so rich as a topic for discussion. Indeed, the anti-Federalist concerns raise one further theoretical issue, which has never been tested in practice: can a President engage in *self-pardon?* Did Richard Nixon have to wait for Gerald Ford's "gracious" act, or could he—on August 7, 1974, the last night of his presidency—have issued himself and all his Watergate confederates a blanket pardon?[8] The Constitution's text certainly does not specify an answer to the question, though one might argue that this would be the ultimate violation of the principle that no one should be allowed to judge his or her own case.

A final point: as Professor Crouch notes in his book on the pardon power, modern presidents are far stingier in issuing pardons than their predecessors. Woodrow Wilson, for example, issued almost 1,750 pardons in his second term, and Wilson's successors through Jimmy Carter granted at least 500 pardons each. Since then, however, only Bill Clinton (in his second term) exceeded even 250. George Bush was notably unwilling to issue pardons as a general matter. A Web site that specifically follows pardons by the president and state governors noted that, as of September 23, 2010, President Obama had gone a full 612 days without issuing a single pardon. Only three presidents had gone longer, beginning with George Washington, who waited 1,811 days—almost six years into his nearly eight-year term—before issuing his first (of a few) pardons. Interestingly enough, second and third place are held by George W. Bush and Bill Clinton, respectively. President Obama finally issued his first pardons on December 2, 2010, 682 days into his presidency, which allowed his immediate predecessor to retain second place to George Washington by approximately two weeks. Still, as the *New York Times* emphasized in its story on the pardons, the recipients had committed only "small-scale" offenses many years ago that garnered most of them only sentences of probation.[9] One might contrast these presidents with Harry Truman, who issued his first pardon eight days after succeeding to the presidency; Woodrow Wilson, who took nine days to issue his first pardon; and John F. Kennedy, who granted his first pardon nineteen days after his inauguration in 1961.[10]

2012 began with a huge controversy in Mississippi: its outgoing governor, Haley Barbour, granted pardons in his last days in office to 215 convicted felons, more than two dozen of whom had been convicted for murder or manslaughter. It was widely agreed that he had in effect declared his retirement from elective politics. As one political observer put it, "With the 200 pardons and 25-plus being for murder or manslaughter, that door's not open anymore." Defending his actions, Barbour told a news conference that "Christianity teaches us forgiveness and second chances. I believe in second chances, and I try hard to be forgiving. The historic power of gubernatorial clemency by the governor to pardon felons is rooted in the Christian idea of giving second chances."[11]

There are presumably few people who would wish to strip presidents of *any* pardoning authority at all, given the presence of circumstances where it seems quite clearly (even if controversially) to serve public interests. And even emulating the practices of many states by requiring the approval of some special commission or board might prove unwise if one accepts the Hamiltonian point that speed is sometimes essential. But consider the far

more common case of "merciful" pardons. One might be nervous about placing that power in the hands of a president and thus trust in what Madison
called the requisite "virtue" not to abuse the power. But it is also possible
that the contemporary reluctance to pardon, whether by presidents or state
governors, is a manifestation of insufficient virtue; fear of political consequences from those who interpret practically any pardon as being "soft
on crime" leads to unjust treatment of persons who can be said to deserve
mercy. Reviewing Crouch's book, Bernadette Meyler observed that the
"refusal to pardon may—just as much as an improvident grant of pardon—
reflect self-interest" rather than a genuinely disinterested reflection on what
either mercy or the public good might require. "A thoroughgoing effort to
hold the president to a standard of character involving acting in the public
interest would necessitate addressing the instances in which he failed to
pardon as well as those in which he seemed to pardon too liberally."[12] It
should be clear that "addressing" in this context, as is generally true with the
Constitution of Settlement, does not require standard-form conversations
about the scope of presidential power—everyone agrees that it is basically
plenary—but rather about the wisdom of its use.

C. Making treaties

Presidents also "shall have Power, by and with the Advice and Consent of
the Senate, to make Treaties, provided two-thirds of the Senators present
concur." This is obviously no small power, especially if we recognize the clause
as in effect stating that the president also has the power *to refuse to make* treaties. That is, a president alone cannot enter into a binding treaty with another
country; *that* requires ratification by the Senate, which raises yet further questions about the Senate's powers, given that the one-third-plus-one senators'
votes sufficient to kill a treaty might theoretically come from the seventeen
states with a total of less than 8 percent of the entire U.S. population.

As a matter of fact, in the decades following the Senate's 1919 rejection of
the Versailles Treaty, presidents increasingly started using so-called executive agreements, which many scholars have described as functionally similar
to treaties, though they were not submitted to the Senate for ratification.
Some agreements were submitted to Congress, but, unlike treaties, to *both*

houses where majority vote in each sufficed for passage. NAFTA is perhaps the most famous example. Bruce Ackerman and David Golove published a fascinating book *Is NAFTA Constitutional?*, in which they argued
that NAFTA is indeed a treaty in every functional respect, but that since
Versailles, the United States has come to tolerate the practice of executive
agreements lest the Senate put fatal roadblocks in front of international
accords thought necessary by the president and most of Congress. Indeed,
Ackerman and his colleague Oona Hathaway were critical of President
Obama's decision in 2010 to seek Senate ratification of the New Start treaty
with Russia, given the fear that there would be insufficient Republican support to reach the magic number of sixty-seven votes.[13] They would have
preferred describing it as an "executive agreement" that could therefore
avoid the supermajoritarian hurdle. President Nixon had taken this path
in 1972 after negotiating the first arms control arrangement with the Soviet
Union. Much more could be said about this, but it is enough simply to note
that any understanding of contemporary international agreements needs to
consider both executive agreements *and* formal treaties that are indeed submitted to the Senate and made liable to the two-thirds ratification rules.

Still, the critical point is that whether one is thinking of treaties *or* executive agreements, neither can take place without an affirmative decision by
the president. So, for example, the United States really was not interested
in negotiating treaties on the environment or international human rights
during the Bush Administration, and there was, as a constitutional matter
at least, nothing that Congress could do about it. On the other hand, the
Kyoto Accords that *were* negotiated by the Clinton Administration never
even came to a vote because of obvious opposition in the Senate. That has
been the fate of a fair number of other treaties "made" by the president.

The justification for placing this power in the hands of the president has
to do with the desirability of having a single person at the helm of foreign
relations. When Hamilton discussed the treaty power in *Federalist* 74, he took
care to defend the Senate's participation in ratifying treaties, even though, like
John Jay in *Federalist* 64, he had no real use for the prospect of participation
by the House of Representatives, which he perceived as unlikely to possess
"those qualities which are essential to the proper execution of such a trust."

D. "He shall nominate, and by and with the Advice and Consent of the Senate, shall appoint Ambassadors, other public Ministers and Consuls, Judges of the supreme Court, and all other Officers of the United States"

The power of nomination is obviously among the most important powers given to a president. Once again, the requirement that the Senate confirm appointments is no small matter. Most dramatic, surely, is the frequency with which nominations for the Supreme Court have been rejected. Over our entire history, for example, the Senate has flatly rejected only twelve nominees to the U.S. Supreme Court while affirming a grand total of 123 nominations, including justices already on the Court who were elevated to the position of chief justice. The Senate's refusal to take action on or postponement of votes on eight other nominations led to their withdrawal. In 1795, the Senate rejected George Washington's nomination of John Rutledge to succeed John Jay as the chief justice of the United States. Washington then nominated Oliver Ellsworth, who was already a member of the Court (and who, therefore, had already been once confirmed by the Senate). Interestingly enough, Rutledge had in fact served for a year as chief justice under a recess appointment, a topic to which I shall turn presently. The most recent formal rejection of a presidential nominee occurred in 1987, with regard to Ronald Reagan's nomination of Judge Robert Bork. George W. Bush's nomination of Harriet Miers to succeed Sandra Day O'Connor was derailed by strong opposition from conservatives and withdrawn before the Senate took any action at all.

Rejection of cabinet or low-level officials is far rarer. None was rejected in the first forty-five years of our history under the Constitution. The first to be rejected was Roger Brooke Taney, nominated by Andrew Jackson to serve as secretary of the treasury and rejected by the Whig-controlled Senate in 1834 by a vote of 28–18. Indeed, Taney was also rejected by the Senate when Jackson first nominated him for membership on the Supreme Court. Needless to say, Jackson was ultimately successful in gaining both positions for Taney, who was secretary of the treasury before succeeding Marshall as chief justice.

Certainly the most unsuccessful president in our history with regard to cabinet nominations was John Tyler, who had two nominees for secretary of the treasury rejected, as well as nominees for secretary of the navy and secretary of war. It is not at all coincidental that Tyler, whom some called "his accidency," was the first vice president to succeed to the presidency on the death of a president, and his politics were strikingly different from those of William Henry Harrison, who had been elected as the Whig candidate. The most recent cabinet nominee to be rejected was former senator John Tower of Texas, nominated by George H. W. Bush in 1989 to serve as secretary of defense.

Opponents of the president can attempt to derail presidential nominations either by filibustering or, more likely, placing holds that may result in endless delay of bringing nominations to the floor for a vote. This happened, for example, when President Obama nominated Indiana University law professor Dawn Johnsen to serve as the head of the extremely important Office of Legal Counsel within the Department of Justice. Although she had the declared support of more than a majority of the Senate, her name was never brought to the floor for a vote even though it appeared that there were (barely) enough votes, in part because of the support of Indiana Republican Richard Lugar, to overcome a threatened filibuster.

How important is this power of the Senate, though? The Senate can certainly make life hard for particular nominees, who may be tempted simply to withdraw, as did Professor Johnsen, rather than continue to face what seems like political torture. And, obviously, the Senate can embarrass presidents by rendering them powerless to place particular favorites in office. But the president always has the last word with regard to placing another name in nomination, and the replacement may be little more palatable to the opposition than the rejected nominee. So we have a game of political chicken in which the president dares the opposition to keep rejecting nominees until he capitulates. Consider, for example, the fact that the replacement for the rejected John Tower, who lost his nomination in part because of accusations of alcoholism and sexual misbehavior, was Dick Cheney. One suspects that many political liberals, in retrospect, lament this turn of events! Yet one can also point to instances where the confirmation fights might be deemed to have been "worth it," from the perspective of the political opposition. Robert Bork was replaced by Anthony Kennedy, who was easily confirmed and has been far less conservative by any account than Bork likely would have been. More recently, the political conservatives who derailed George W. Bush's nomination of Harriet Miers were amply rewarded by the replacement nomination of Samuel Alito.

E. Recess appointments

So how might a president respond to a filibuster or a hold that delays consideration of a nomination? One response is taking advantage of an obscure clause of the Constitution granting to the president the "Power to fill up all Vacancies that may happen during the Recess of the Senate, by granting Commissions which shall expire at the End of their next Session." A "literal" reading of this clause might suggest that the vacancies themselves must "happen during the Recess of the Senate," which would mean that a vacancy that occurred while the Senate was meeting could not be filled by a recess appointment. Rightly or wrongly, this literal reading has not become accepted. Presidents are deemed authorized to make recess appointments anytime the Senate takes a "recess," as by taking a spring "vacation" during which they can return to their home states and/or engage in trips abroad. The president can then make an appointment that might be good for close to four years, at least the remainder of the present session plus the entirety of the "next Session." As noted earlier, George Washington took advantage of the Recess Appointment Clause to name John Rutledge as chief justice, though he had to leave the Court upon the Senate's affirmatively rejecting his nomination. Indeed, five of the nominees to the Supreme Court by our first five presidents were recipients of recess appointments. The most recent recess appointment to the Supreme Court was of then-Circuit Judge Potter Stewart, named to the Supreme Court by President Eisenhower in October 1958, though not formally nominated until January 1959 and confirmed by the Senate the following May. This was actually Eisenhower's *third* recess appointment to the Supreme Court, after former California governor Earl Warren in 1953 and New Jersey Supreme Court Justice William J. Brennan in 1956 (named to the Court just before the election in order to appeal to northeastern Roman Catholics).

Early recess appointments are easily explainable: Until the Civil War, Congress met relatively briefly, with recesses of six to nine months being altogether common. This functionalist explanation mirrors the defense of recess appointments offered by Alexander Hamilton in *Federalist 67*—that "it might be necessary for the public service to fill without delay." This is undoubtedly a fine argument for 1787 and, perhaps, for the U.S. system of government at least through the Civil War. But one can question its applicability in the modern world, where Congress is in session most of the time and recesses are relatively short.

So consider the fact that President Clinton made 139 recess appointments during his eight years in office, 95 to full-time positions. George W. Bush made even more such appointments, 171, of which 105 were to full-time positions.[14] In both cases, such appointments included members of the federal judiciary, though not Supreme Court justices. On March 27, 2010, President Obama made fifteen recess appointments, the most significant of whom was a pro-labor lawyer whose nomination to the National Labor Relations Board had been blocked by presumptively pro-management Republicans.

There are those who defend the Recess Appointment Clause as a valuable arrow in the quiver of presidential powers, precisely to overcome a Congress recalcitrant to even bringing nominees to the floor for a vote. For example, one of President Bush's most notable recess appointments, that of John Bolton to be U.S. Ambassador to the United Nations, was caused by a Democratic filibuster. There was little doubt that he would receive the approval of a majority of the Senate, then controlled by the Republican Party, if his nomination could be brought to the floor, but that was impossible given Rule 22 and the requirement of sixty votes in order to close off debate.

Some critics of the modern operation of the clause view it as far more a vehicle for abuse of presidential power than a needed corrective to the problem of long recesses by the Senate that now never occur. A special problem with recess appointments to the federal judiciary is that the judges are in fact "auditioning" for permanent jobs on the bench, given the need for Senate confirmation for permanent appointment. One might well believe that this calls the judges' "independence" into question, as they might be fearful of making certain decisions that could rankle the senators on whose votes they depend for lifetime office. This is an excellent example of the Constitution of Settlement's serving a very different function in contemporary America than was contemplated by those who wrote this particular power into the Constitution in 1787.

F. Special sessions

Section 3 of Article II contains another clause that is of relatively little importance today, given the quasi-permanence of congressional sessions, but was certainly crucial at at least one time in our history. What if Congress is *not* in session? Well, the president "may, on extraordinary Occasions, convene both Houses, or either of them." Prior to the passage of the Twentieth Amendment in 1933, which not only changed the date of Inauguration Day but also the time that a new Congress would begin meeting (from thirteen months to approximately seven weeks after the election), there were forty-six special sessions.[15] Sometimes both houses would be called back, if passage of legislation was crucial; sometimes calling only the Senate back would suffice if the issue was confirmation of presidential appointments or ratification of treaties. Not surprisingly, there have been far fewer special sessions—four—since 1933.

The most important special session in our history was surely the one called by Abraham Lincoln following the attack on Fort Sumter on April 12, 1865. Though called on April 15, Lincoln specified, as authorized by the Constitution, that it not begin until July 4, 1861. Lincoln clearly had the power under the Constitution to stave off Congress; he could have refused to call a special session at all. The Constitution provides no way for Congress to call itself into session. But Lincoln has not escaped significant criticism for his delay in bringing Congress back. Thus Giorgio Agamben has written that "in the ten weeks that passed between April 15 and July 4, Lincoln in fact acted as an absolute dictator."[16] Clinton Rossiter, the author of an important book *Constitutional Dictatorship*, basically agrees: "The eleven weeks between the fall of Sumter and July 4…constitute the most interesting single episode in the history of constitutional dictatorship. The simple fact that one man was the government of the United States in the most critical period in all its 165 years; and that he acted on no precedent and under no restraint, makes this the paragon of all democratic, constitutional dictatorships." Yet Rossiter also writes, "If Lincoln was a great dictator, he was a greater democrat."[17] Whether this makes conceptual sense will be considered at greater length in the penultimate chapter.

G. "Tak[ing] Care that the Laws be Faithfully executed"

Ironically or not, closely following the special session clause is the injunction upon the president to "take Care that the Laws be faithfully executed." It may be that part of the Constitution of Settlement is that this is the president's overarching duty, but what this really means is distinctly part of the Constitution of Conversation (which is why this section is so short). As Lincoln himself asked with regard to his extremely controversial—and, according to Chief Justice Taney, unconstitutional—suspension of habeas corpus in the early days of the Civil War, "Are all the laws, but one, to be unexecuted, and the government itself go to pieces, lest that one be violated? Even in such a case, would not the official oath be broken, if the government should be overthrown, when it was believed that disregarding the single law, would tend to preserve it"?[18] We shall have the opportunity to look further at such arguments, almost invariably made during "emergencies," at the conclusion of this book.

10

Executive Duration in Office, the Possibility of Impeachment, and the Role of the Vice President

I. DURATION IN OFFICE

In some ways, the most important grant to a president by the Constitution is the certainty of a four-year term in office, and the same may be true with regard to governors and their state constitutions. Prime ministers in parliamentary systems, in contrast, have tenure in office only so long as they maintain the confidence of enough members (usually, but not always, a majority) of parliament. Depending on the particular political system, a vote of no confidence will trigger either new elections or an often lengthy process of renegotiation among the multiple parties in parliament regarding the identity of the new prime minister and the division of the relevant ministries. But either new elections or a dramatic change in government can be avoided by the prime minister's own political party, which might decide that the time has come for the prime minister to go. (One can identify the arrival of such a time by polls or other relevant information indicating that sticking with the incumbent would prove fatal to party prospects at the next election, coupled with the mounting of a challenge by a would-be successor.) Thus Margaret Thatcher, one of the most important peacetime prime ministers in the entire history of Great Britain, was turned out of office in 1990 by a revolt within her own Conservative Party, which unsentimentally replaced her with John Major (who went on to win the next election). And Tony Blair may well have felt pushed out of office in 2008 by his fellow members of the British Labour Party, who replaced him with Gordon Brown (who notably did not win the next election). One can only wonder if George W. Bush would have been subjected to similar treatment by the Republican Party after 2006, if such an option were available. Perhaps Barack Obama would have had similar worries in early 2011 about the level of support from his ostensible Democratic compatriots in Congress. But, of course, neither Bush nor Obama had any such worries, and that is precisely the difference between a presidentialist (or gubernatorial) system and any parliamentary (or even quasi-parliamentary) alternative.

There was much debate in Philadelphia about the "ideal length" of a presidential term. A few, including Hamilton, liked the idea of a basically lifetime tenancy. Not surprisingly, this earned him the accusation of being a monarchist. Few people, interestingly enough, seemed to suggest a term as short as four years. One rationale for that relatively short term was the desirability of holding the chief executive accountable, through the electoral mechanism, with some modest frequency. After all, at least two-thirds of the Senate would have to face their electoral masters—even if, originally, these were their state legislatures—within a given four-year period, and one could dismiss the harm that any particular disappointing senator might do over a six-year term. Given the importance of the presidential office and the emphasis placed, especially by Hamilton in his *Federalist* essays, on the desirability of having only one person at the helm, charged with making fundamental decisions at times of peace and war, there would be a far greater price to pay for long-term tenure. But originally, the president could seemingly run for repeated terms of office, so that a satisfied electorate could presumably reward an achieving incumbent with renewed mandates. It was not until the Twenty-second Amendment, ratified in 1951 and arguably the last truly significant change to the Constitution, that presidents were limited to two terms in office.

Hamilton happily defended these features of the Constitution. The long term, at least when compared to members of the House of Representatives and most governors of the time, would help to assure the election of individuals committed to the "PUBLIC GOOD" [capitalization Hamilton's] who can presumably resist "every sudden breeze of passion" or the "transient impulse" that may lead individual voters to place in the House less virtuous or truly publicly spirited people. (Again, we see both the relative disdain for what might be termed "democratic politics" and justification for the veto as an important check on such a politics.) Thus, as Hamilton writes in *Federalist* 71, "when occasions present themselves in which the interests of the people are at variance with their inclinations, it is the duty of the persons whom they have appointed to be the guardians of those interests, to withstand the temporary delusions, in order to give them time and opportunity for more cool and sedate reflection." A president can do this, presumably, not only because of the special mechanism of selection, which Hamilton earlier assured us would produce persons of unusual virtue and ability, but also because of the security of holding a four-year tenure in office. "Cool and sedate reflection" would presumably validate what a president had done, however unpopular, several years before. But what about presidential decisions made during a period of popular "temporary delusions" shortly before the next election?

Indefinite re-eligibility would only reinforce these happy tendencies, according to Hamilton, not least because of "the love of fame, *the ruling passion of the noblest minds*, which would prompt a man to plan and undertake extensive and arduous enterprises for the public benefit, requiring considerable time to mature and perfect" (emphasis added). It would be disadvantageous if presidents were forced to "quit the scene" before "accomplish[ing]" such great work. It is worth noting Hamilton's assumption that presidents, however "virtuous," also be directly motivated by the desire to enter the history books and be remembered and revered—and perhaps memorialized in great monuments—by generations afterward. We assume that presidents are constantly thinking of their "legacies," from the first day they enter office. According to Hamilton, this is a good thing.

So one obvious question is what led us ultimately to reject Hamilton's heartfelt argument by proposing and ratifying the Twenty-second Amendment. Do we think he was wrong even in 1787, so that it was *always* a good idea that presidents remove themselves from the scene after a maximum of eight years, as George Washington himself so notably did and Franklin D. Roosevelt so notably did not? We might instead point to the changes in American culture since 1787; perhaps opportunities for presidential overreaching and even demagoguery have significantly increased over time because of the developments in mass communications and the nature of the party system, where presidents increasingly take center stage. It is easy enough to *explain* the amendment, originally proposed by Congress in 1947 when Republicans controlled Congress for the first time since 1930, as partisan revenge upon the dead Franklin Roosevelt, though that scarcely counts as a *justification*. Roosevelt died decades ago, and there has been no truly serious effort to repeal the amendment since then. Why has it become a presumably settled part of our constitutional fabric, not only in the sense that there is no serious argument as to what the amendment "means," but also in that it has *not* generated public controversy—unlike the Seventeenth Amendment providing for the popular election of senators, which became a subject of popular debate in the 2010 and 2012 elections?

One possible reason that has already been suggested is that by the mid-twentieth century, and certainly in the twenty-first century, we (properly) fear the rise of more Caesarist presidents than the Constitution's drafters ever envisioned and wish to limit the possibility of their developing a cult of "indispensablitly" that would promote lifetime quasi-emperorship, especially given the vastly wider range of powers available to a contemporary president. Akhil Amar does not explain the amendment but seems to justify it in part because it has purportedly led presidential candidates to pick stronger vice-presidential running mates, who themselves are increasingly viewed as future presidential timber.[1]

Perhaps both of these are true, but it is possible that Hamilton might have been right in *Federalist* 72. He wrote there that an "ill effect" of excluding presidents from indefinite re-election would be "banishing men from stations, in which in certain emergencies of the state their presence might be of the greatest moment to the public interest or safety." If the country has an unusually gifted commander in chief, who possesses remarkable gifts as a diplomat both with our allies and even our enemies with whom we must eventually make peace, why should we not be allowed to keep him or her in office? Perhaps the problem with the Twenty-second Amendment is not its existence as such, but instead that it admits of no potential exemptions. After all, even the writ of habeas corpus, perhaps the most fundamental of all civil liberties, can be suspended in perilous times such as "invasion" or "insurrection," according to the Constitution. And there are powerful traditions justifying other suspensions of constitutional norms in times of emergency. So, even if one likes the Twenty-second Amendment as a valuable protection against demagogues, it might be even better if, for example, Congress could suspend the amendment by a two-thirds vote when "the national interest requires it."

One might express similar skepticism about the value of absolutely rigid fixed-time elections. Or, with regard to both the Twenty-second Amendment and fixed-term elections, is the proper response that there is good reason to fear an unscrupulous "factional" alliance between a president and partisans in Congress? In that case, we are certainly better off with an absolutely rigid rule.

It is usually thought to be a shining example of Lincoln's commitment to democratic norms that he never counseled the suspension of the 1864 election, even though he knew that he could well lose to his opponent, General George McClellan. According to Lincoln, this might have meant dissolution of the Union inasmuch as McClellan would be willing to make peace with the Confederacy. Imagine, though, that Lincoln had been in his *second* term of office in 1864 and that the Twenty-second Amendment were part of the original Constitution. If we do believe that he would have properly stepped down rather than run for an (unconstitutional) third term, then is it obvious that he should have remained in office until the next Inauguration Day, March 4, 1865—several months after the electoral college had designated his successor? Perhaps we should instead have expected him to work with leaders of Congress to amend the Succession in Office Act, making possible the quicker succession of his replacement.

All of these questions implicate a basic feature of constitutions of settlement, which is their "rule-like" aspect, as contrasted with the far more indeterminate language that invites not only endless conversation but also a certain malleability of interpretation that makes it possible to adjust to circumstances. Rules often lack, in their linguistic formulation, any such malleability; indeed, their very purpose is to forestall conversations initiated by persons who chafe at particular rules and ask for "special treatment."[2] There is obviously much to be said for rigid rules, but it should be obvious, as economists often insist, that even the greatest benefits—including those of "settlement"—are rarely without attendant costs.

II. IMPEACHMENT

The above suggestion of a potential defect in the Twenty-second Amendment presupposes that we are blessed with a president everyone truly admires and whose loss of leadership we would bewail. But consider a distinctly less happy possibility, which is a president who behaves in such a way as to dishonor the office or simply to lose the confidence of the American people. One of the ill-concealed tensions in American thought, amply revealed in the debates at the constitutional convention and afterward, is the general confidence expressed in the special virtue of the person chosen by electors to be president, coupled with fears that he would in fact turn out to be corrupt or even treasonous, eager to use his various powers, including those of pardon, to enter into cabals against the public interest. What is, or should be, our potential response to such a president?

The impeachment system provides a mechanism of accountability. The obvious question is whether it has actually served that function over the past two centuries. Or might it be that it has served to embolden presidents who have learned one lesson from the "experience" of our system, which is that, as a practical matter, they either cannot or will not be impeached save for the commission of flagrant crimes leaving "smoking gun" evidence (and possibly not even then)? Akhil Amar emphasizes the importance of holding presidents responsible for their *misconduct*. We could get into a long discussion at this point whether misconduct, to be impeachable, must also be a sufficiently serious crime to meet the "high crimes and misdemeanors" requirement. But why, exactly, should we focus *only* on misconduct? Should simple incompetence or bad judgment be enough to warrant dismissal through a vote of no confidence? Why, exactly, should we think that it makes sense to assure a president an unbroken tenure in the Oval Office for four years, however bad his judgment turns out to be and whatever misfortunes are visited on the nation because of that misjudgment?

The record of the debates in Philadelphia and during ratification reveals how little attention was given to such questions. Most of the debate concerned the propriety of the Senate sitting as the "court" that would assess the bills of impeachment drawn by the putative grand jury, that is, the House of Representatives. Some of the debates take on nearly a paranoid character, exemplified by the fear that Congress would move to impeach not only federal officials but state officials, thereby gaining malign control over the entire American political system. There are, however, nuggets buried within what is often an unhelpful (at least to modern readers) debate that are worth emphasizing. On September 12, 1787, George Mason of

Virginia importantly moved to add "maladministration" as a potential justification for impeachment, along with "Treason, Bribery, and other High
Crimes and Misdemeanors." This was quickly withdrawn, however, perhaps
because of James Madison's expressed fear that "so vague a term" would in
effect lead to the president's being able to serve only with the "pleasure of
the Senate."[3] And in a fascinating speech to the North Carolina ratifying
convention, James Iredell, who would become an initial member of the U.S.
Supreme Court, strongly argued against the possibility of impeachment for
what one might regard as bad judgment in decisionmaking. "Whatever
mistake a man may make, he ought not to be punished for it, nor his posterity rendered infamous…We're a [public official] punishable for want of
judgment, he would be continually in dread, but when he knows that nothing but real guilt can disgrace him, he may do his duty firmly, if he be an
honest man" However, "if a man be a villain, and willfully abuse, his trust,
he is to be held up as a public offender, and ignominiously punished."[4]

It is possible that both Madison and Iredell were absolutely correct,
in 1787. Perhaps there was good reason to fear that Congress would too
easily establish supremacy over the president by abuse of a latitudinarian
impeachment clause. This possibility posed a serious problem for those who
viewed Congress as likely to be "the most dangerous branch" because it was
most likely to reflect the passions and even "delusions" of the public. Why
would one be eager to put the president in peril from such representatives,
unless true "villainy" could be proved? The question is whether fears that
made sense in 1787 need control us today. Is it true that Congress, whatever one may generally think of its institutional performance, constitutes
the "most dangerous branch"? Or is there reason, as Arthur Schlesinger
argued a generation ago and Bruce Ackerman argues at present, to fear
an "imperial" or "plebiscitary" president who is increasingly indifferent to
constitutional norms and enabled in that indifference by "going over the
head of Congress" to the American public and by "winning" Gallup polls
instead of elections, therefore gaining seeming legitimacy for ever greater
aggrandizements of power?[5] Would we be better off if we supplemented
impeachment, which would continue to be reserved for genuine misconduct or criminal behavior, with a system by which we could fire a president
through a vote of no confidence based not on bad behavior but on demon-
strably bad judgment that leads most Americans, including congressional

leaders of both parties, to lose confidence that the president will make sufficiently wise decisions, particularly about life and death matters, in the future?

Note an important difference between impeachment for bad behavior, however defined, and being tossed out because of a lack of confidence in judgment. In the former instance, it will almost always be sufficient to have the vice president—who will always be from the same political party as the president, thanks to the Twelfth Amendment—simply take over, assuming that he or she isn't tainted by the same misconduct. Think only of Bill Clinton in this respect. Nobody angry at Clinton because of his reckless and undignified (and almost certainly criminal in some respects) personal misconduct could possibly object to Al Gore's becoming president. On the other hand, if it is an administration's quality of *judgment* or *wisdom* that's at issue, then one might well believe a current vice president viewed as a major participant in the administration's decisionmaking would be no better. This would certainly describe most people who objected to President George W. Bush; it is hard to believe that any of Bush's opponents would have been comforted or otherwise thought the country was better off with the replacement by Vice President Cheney, who was widely perceived as the *éminence grise* behind many of the most controversial decisions of the Bush Administration.[6] So it is possible that a vote of no confidence would be directed at both the president *and* vice president.

Amendment of the Constitution would be necessary in order to institute a no-confidence system. That is what it means for something to be part of the Constitution of Settlement. It is worth examining how such a system might work. One possibility often found in parliamentary systems is that a vote of no confidence, whether by majority vote or a supermajority vote, topples the government and requires new elections. A two-thirds vote by both houses of Congress meeting together, which would at least somewhat correct for the gross malapportionment of the Senate, could correct that problem; in addition, save in extraordinary situations, requiring such a supermajority would guarantee some significant degree of bipartisanship. One might well adopt a leaf from the German or Israeli notebooks, both of which require so-called constructive votes of no confidence in which the opponents of a sitting chancellor or prime minister must also simultaneously agree on the identity of the replacement. Neither country can vote the existing prime minister out of office and then wait around for negotiations to decide on the successor. Given the impossibility in the modern world of discussing no-confidence systems without paying some attention to the role played by political parties, I would also require that the successor of a repudiated president—and vice president, if appropriate—be chosen by the congressional caucus of the displaced president's own party, in order to prevent a "coup" of the White House without that party's actually winning an election.

The presence of a no-confidence system would obviously change our concept of presidential "accountability," which now depends on a mixture of the presumed desire to be re-elected (once) and the desire to not be impeached. Election as an accountability mechanism vanishes once a president is re-elected for the second and final term. And if impeachment is indeed highly "legalized" and requires criminality rather than incompetence to trigger its sanction, then it is functionally useless.

But it is not only presidents who might change their behavior, for good or for ill. One consequence of the present American system of government is that senators and representatives are "stuck" with presidents of their own party. This means that the legislators have every incentive to "stand by their man," not least because the president will continue to possess all legal powers of office, which will invariably include the ability to make life difficult for anyone who goes into unseemly opposition. If, on the other hand, votes of no confidence were a real possibility, then representatives and senators would have to explain to their constituents why they were not attempting to remove someone in whom the electorate had lost confidence, especially if the issues involved life and death, peace and war, or economic collapse or recovery.

It is not that impeachment is a terrible feature of our Constitution per se. Most constitutions, both within the United States and around the world, contain some mechanisms for impeaching errant presidents or governors. What is terrible is that impeachment is the *exclusive* means of firing presidents midterm and that the clause has, in effect, become captured by lawyers who shout at each other only about theories of criminal behavior, thereby forestalling the altogether necessary public discussion—requiring no legal training at all—about what attributes we should expect of our presidents in the twenty-first century.

Another possibility, known as *recall*, is worth mentioning. The no-confidence system assumes retention of an exclusive procedure of *representative democracy* that was the focus of debates (and design) in Philadelphia, given the general disdain for truly popular rule and any semblance of *direct democracy*. But consider the fact that the widespread presence of direct-democracy mechanisms in the states also includes the possibility that the electorate, by its own efforts, can displace a governor (or other state official) in whom they lose confidence. As a matter of fact, recall mechanisms are almost exclusive to the United States, though Venezuela also apparently includes such a possibility at least for the president inasmuch as Hugo Chavez survived such an election in 2004.[7] Even in the United States, they exist only in a few states.[8]

Such mechanisms were a result of the Progressive Era critique of the actual behavior of ostensibly "representative" institutions, which were viewed all too often as falling under the domination of "the interests." Los Angeles led the way in 1903, and California followed statewide in 1911. (Oregon adopted recall procedures in 1908.) Eighteen states now grant their voters such an option, though almost such efforts have occurred at the local level. A *New York Times* article on September 22, 2010, was headlined "Recalls Become a Hazard for Mayors."[9] "Over the last two years," the article informs readers, "failed recall campaigns have sought the ouster of mayors in Akron, Ohio; Chattanooga, Tenn.; Flint, Mich.; Kansas City, Mo.; Portland, Ore.; and Toledo, Ohio, among other cities. Next month the voters of North Pole, Alaska, 140 miles south of the Arctic Circle, will vote on whether to recall their mayor." Two governors were faced with recall elections: Evan Mecham in Arizona in 1987, whose recall "almost certainly would have succeeded had Mecham not already been impeached and removed by the Arizona legislature,"[10] and the far better known Gray Davis in California in 2003, who was replaced by Arnold Schwarzenegger. It appears likely that 2012 will see gubernatorial and state legislative recall campaigns in at least Wisconsin and Michigan. One might predict that, if at all successful, they will become a more standard part of the American political arsenal, especially in an age of sharply divided electorates.

Lest one believe that the recall is simply another illustration of the political idiosyncrasies of the American west, it is worth noting that Rhode Island in 1992 and New Jersey in 1995 (also Georgia in 1975 and Montana in 1976) adopted the recall as part of the arsenal of tools for keeping public officials accountable to the electorate. In any event, it should be clear that the U.S. Constitution is near one end of a spectrum with regard to exercising effective accountability over problematic presidents.

III. THE PARTICULAR PROBLEM OF DISABLED PRESIDENTS

Consider the possibility that President Kennedy had only been grievously injured and not instantly killed on November 22, 1963. What would have happened? The fact is that the 1787 Constitution provides no semblance of an answer. We might well have profited from the presence of clear answers during the times immediately following the ultimately successful assassination attempts on two of our presidents, James Abram Garfield, who survived until September 19, 1881, after having been shot on July 2, and William McKinley, who lingered for six days before succumbing (at which time Teddy Roosevelt took over). Woodrow Wilson, who suffered a significantly debilitating stroke in October 1919 while campaigning for ratification of the Versailles Treaty, insisted on serving out his term until March 4, 1921. (Wilson was sufficiently megalomaniacal—a common condition, one might believe, of political leaders in the modern era—to believe that he could run for a third term in 1920.) There is no reason to believe that the country was well served by Wilson's unwillingness to leave office, save that Vice President Thomas Marshall, a former senator from Indiana, was, like many vice presidents, almost certainly unqualified to take charge.

Imagine that Kennedy, who was serving in a world substantially different than McKinley's or Garfield's (or even Wilson's), had survived for six weeks while slipping in and out of consciousness. Fortunately, the country was spared the additional trauma of Kennedy's lingering in various hospitals. Because Kennedy died instantly, Vice President Lyndon Johnson, who had been a serious rival of Kennedy's for the Democratic nomination, was able to take over immediately and exhibit his considerable talents of public leadership. That did not, however, eliminate the "What if?" question.

Consider Article II, Section I: "In Case of the Removal of the President from Office, or of his Death, Resignation, or Inability to discharge the

Powers and Duties of the said Office, the Same shall devolve on the Vice President, and the Congress may by Law provide for the Case of Removal, Death, Resignation or Inability, both of the President and Vice President, declaring what Officer shall then act as President, and such Officer shall act accordingly, until the Disability be removed, or a President shall be elected." For whatever reason, to my knowledge no one has proposed that Congress pass legislation relating to the determination of "inability" and thus obviating the felt need for actual amendment of the Constitution. Instead, the response to the potential "Kennedy problem" was the Twenty-fifth Amendment, which does set out a procedure for responding to a disabled president or a president who simply faces even relatively minor surgery that will incapacitate him or her for several hours. Presidents now commonly acknowledge such incapacity by designating the vice president as "acting president" until the anesthesia wears off. Far more serious is the possibility not only of a debilitating stroke like Wilson's but also mental illness or the onset of Alzheimer's disease. There seems little doubt, for example, that President Reagan's affliction with Alzheimer's disease, a disease that correlates significantly with age, began no later than sometime in his second term of office. Yet there was never a hint of recourse to the Twenty-fifth Amendment, which suggests that it will take something truly extraordinary for the amendment to take on real life, as it were. Perhaps that point will come when the United States has a president widely known to have been diagnosed by relevant specialists as suffering from a long-term disease that impairs mental functioning or the ability to make sound decisions.

Professor Brian Kalt has noted that the Twenty-fifth Amendment is linguistically ambiguous with regard to one extraordinarily important political possibility, which is resistance by a president to the determination by the cabinet that he or she is no longer able to exercise the powers of the office.[11] Can the president *immediately* resume the powers of office, including the ability to fire the cabinet (though not the vice president) that declared him unable to function, or does the "new regime" have at least four days in office to elaborate their objections to the resumption of powers by the now-displaced president?[12] As Kalt points out, we have never had a true test of the application of the Twenty-fifth Amendment in what the 1787 Framers might have called "exigent circumstances," including resistance by a deluded president. Perhaps we will continue to be blessed by the only "theoretical" importance of the present amendment. As Kalt well argues, though, the amendment concerns a topic for which one might believe that a constitution of settlement is especially necessary and that there be, concomitantly, no "conversation" possible about potentially alternative meanings of the text.

A curious feature of the Twenty-fifth Amendment is that it applies exclusively to the president. What if, however, it is the vice president who exhibits unsuitability for office of the kind that would properly allow the invocation of the amendment in the case of a president? One might ask the same question with regard to members of the Supreme Court, especially given the well-documented fact that several members clearly stayed on well beyond their period of maximal mental functioning.[13] Does it make sense to say that we have to await a vice president's actually becoming president before taking notice of significant (and disqualifying) debilities? And we might ask similar questions with regard to a vice president who is perfectly healthy, but has displayed such bad—though not criminal—judgment that we might be fearful about the prospect of succession to the Oval Office.

IV. THE VICE PRESIDENCY

Why have a vice president at all? One potential answer to this question is that it is always useful to have a "designated successor" waiting in the wings, should anything happen to the president. There's something to be said for this, but that answer simply raises two additional questions: First, how should the vice president be selected? Secondly, should he or she necessarily be as "entrenched" as the president, with the same constitutionally guaranteed four-year term, regardless of any doubts that might emerge about his or her judgment (or mental or physical condition)? Even if one rejects the arguments for firing presidents in midterm via votes of no confidence, do the considerations that lead to that conclusion operate equally with regard to the (un)desirability of allowing either the president or Congress to "fire" the vice president should either come to feel uncomfortable with the thought of the vice president ascending to the Oval Office? The South African Constitution, for example, establishes a "deputy president," but that person serves at the pleasure of the president. Would that be unacceptable in the United States?

Still, it is worth asking why we need a vice president at all. What precise benefit do Americans get from this constitutionally ordained office? The vice president can break 50–50 votes in the Senate in his or her capacity as president of the Senate, though—as some senators grumbled back in 1803—this appears to give one state three instead of two senators. One suspects these senators would not be amused by the fact that the two most recent vice presidents of the United States, Dick Cheney and Joe Biden, have come from among the least populated states, Wyoming and Delaware.

Many organizations simply treat tie votes as a rejection of the motion under question. Presumably, though, the vice president can be counted on to vote as a presidential loyalist, which suggests no genuine inquiry into whether the president's program actually serves the public interest. This is very different from what might have been expected from John Adams's vice president, Thomas Jefferson, who we can be sure would never have submitted his own judgment to that of the Federalist Adams, his rival for the presidency both in 1796 and 1800. Perhaps the vice presidency made a great deal of sense under the assumptions in 1787 of no political parties and the capacity of electors to identify individuals of unusual civic ability and virtue. Do arguments for the office survive the rise of political parties? How has the post–Twelfth Amendment system worked out? What "lessons of experience" might we draw from that history?

Two nineteenth-century presidents died in office (William Henry Harrison and Zachary Taylor), while two others were assassinated (Abraham Lincoln and James A. Garfield). They were succeeded by John Tyler, Millard Fillmore, Andrew Johnson, and Chester A. Arthur, respectively—at best nonentities, and at worst, as with Tyler and Johnson, disasters. Tyler was insistent on doing whatever he could to strengthen what was called the "slavocracy," while Johnson devoted most of his energies as Lincoln's successor to torpedoing any significant "reconstruction" of the defeated Confederacy.

The twentieth century is better on this score, giving us as successors to the Oval Office Teddy Roosevelt, Calvin Coolidge, Harry Truman, Lyndon Johnson, and Gerald Ford. But consider some of the other possibilities had events taken a different course: we might have gotten as president John Nance Garner, a former speaker of the house bitterly opposed to many aspects of Roosevelt's New Deal; the amiable but otherwise unqualified former Kentucky senator Alban Barkley (Truman's vice president); Spiro Agnew, who resigned in disgrace as Richard Nixon's vice president and was replaced by Ford; or Dan Quayle, George H. W. Bush's mysterious choice as running mate in 1988 and 1992. More recently, one can certainly wonder about John Kerry's choice of John Edwards as his 2004 running mate or John McCain's pick of Sarah Palin in 2008.

Furthermore, a look at the historical record demonstrates that "We the People" have, in fact, gone many years with nobody occupying the vice president's office. (Succession-in-office acts have always designated the next in line to the presidency in the event of a tragedy.) It was only in 1967, with the ratification of the Twenty-fifth Amendment, that a procedure was established to assure that there would always be a vice president. Prior to that, the office simply remained vacant if a vice president succeeded to the presidency or, more commonly, if the vice president died in office. Succession to the White House by Tyler, Fillmore, Johnson, Arthur, Teddy Roosevelt, Coolidge, Truman, Johnson, and Ford accounts for twenty-seven years of vice-presidential vacancies.

In addition, a surprising number of vice presidents died in office; indeed, serving as vice president was almost a kiss of death throughout the nineteenth century. For example, both of James Madison's vice presidents (George Clinton and Elbridge Gerry) died remarkably early in their terms in office. Running mates chosen by Franklin Pierce, Grover Cleveland, and William McKinley—William R. King, Thomas Hendricks, and Garrett Hobart—also died so quickly that all of these presidents basically served their entire terms without a vice president. Other vice presidential deaths came later in presidential terms. In sum, we have been without a vice president for about forty-five years since the inauguration of George Washington—approximately 20 percent of our national history—and no one has seemed to notice or believe the nation in peril.

Even if one believes that we are well served by having a vice president at the national level, questions can still be asked about the present method of selecting him or her. We earlier looked at the Twelfth Amendment with regard to its revising the presidential electoral system by splitting off the candidates for president and vice president into separate tracks and thus eliminating the "Jefferson-Burr" problem of a tie vote for the two undifferentiated candidates. However, the amendment, as "common-sensical" as it may appear to most of us today, was scarcely without opposition. Delaware's Senator White gave an extended speech to his colleagues in opposition. "The Vice President," he told them, "is not only the second officer of Government in point of rank, but of importance, and should be a man possessing, and worthy of, the confidence of the nation."[14] One may doubt whether the vice president is in fact all that important a position. But it seems hard to deny that anyone in that position should indeed possess, and be "worthy of, the confidence of the nation." White feared that splitting off the two candidates would make that far less likely. Presidential candidates would become zealous to procure election to the highest office and therefore be unable to resist the temptation to choose as running mates persons who would help them attain that goal rather than be first-rate presidents themselves. Presidential candidates would no longer ask, "Is he capable? Is he honest?", but rather, "Can he by his name, by his connexions, by his wealth, by his local situation, by his influence, or his intrigues, best promote the election of a President,"[15] who will scarcely be contemplating his own death or removal from office? Another senator asked, "Will the ambitious, aspiring candidate for the Presidency, will his friends and favorites promote the election of a man of talents, probity, and popularity for Vice President, and who may prove his rival? No! They will seek a man of moderate talents."[16] Senator Tracy also bewailed the likely consequences of no longer requiring electors "to select two men qualified to be President."[17]

One may well wonder if the concerns expressed by these opponents of the Twelfth Amendment have not been amply vindicated to make us properly cautious about sticking with the present procedure of choosing vice presidents. This basically boils down to the ability of newly designated Democratic and Republican candidates for the presidency to engage in an almost monarchical prerogative of designating running mates, secure in the knowledge that no convention is likely to repudiate their choices. (Though it is alleged that John McCain did not choose his actual first preference, Connecticut Senator Joseph Lieberman, because he feared just such a public humiliation. Instead, he chose Alaska Governor Sarah Palin.) There can be no doubt that *some* vice presidential candidates are certainly equipped to become president, as has occurred either by direct succession upon the death or resignation of the president, or by winning elections on their own, as George H. W. Bush did in 1988 (though he was the first such candidate to be successful since the 1837 succession of Martin Van Buren to the presidency following Andrew Jackson's term in office). So the question is one of *frequency distribution*. how often are we gratified by the selections and how often are we dismayed, independent of our political agreement or disagreement with the officials in question? How much risk do Americans wish to run that ambitious presidential candidates will be insufficiently imbued with what might be called "Madisonian virtue" when trying to figure out who will best help them win the general election?

Here, again, a look at American state constitutions may be illuminating, for one discovers that in most states there is no necessary link between governor and lieutenant governor. They run separately; victors, therefore, may come from different political parties. Thus the Texas lieutenant governor during the governorship of George W. Bush was a Democrat, Bob Bullock, and it was Bush's ability to work well with his opposite-party counterpart that enabled him to run a plausible campaign for the presidency in 2000 on the basis of being "a uniter, not a divider." Ironically, if Texas were more like the national government, then Bush, precisely by being able to select his lieutenant governor, would have been deprived of the considerable assets that Bullock provided him. A recent lieutenant governor of California was a Republican, Abel Moldanado, who was appointed by Governor Arnold Schwarzenegger in April 2010 to succeed a Democrat, John Garamendi, who was elected to the U.S. House of Representatives. Such a split executive may have interesting consquences: under California law, the lieutenant governor takes on the powers of the governor whenever the latter leaves the state, which has led several Republican governors to "stay home" rather than risk what the Democratic lieutenant governor might do even in a brief absence. A similar rule led New York Governor David Paterson, who succeeded to office on Eliot Spitzer's resignation, to remain within the Empire State lest the thoroughly corrupt president of the New York senate, a former Democrat who gained that office as the result of a bargain with senate Republicans eager to gain majority power, exercise his power. As it happened, Paterson read the New York Constitution to allow appointment of a new lieutenant governor, a reading that was upheld by New York's highest court.

The primary justification of having a vice president is indeed to have a designated successor should something happen to the president. But what if we were faced with the novel situation of having neither a president or a vice president? The Constitution acknowledges such a possibility and gives Congress the power to declare "what Officer shall then act as President" should there be no vice president ready to step in. Congress has done so in the Succession in Office Act of 1947, which establishes as successors the speaker of the house, and then the president pro tempore of the Senate, who is typically a grizzled and aged veteran of many terms of service. Let me respectfully suggest that no rational person would seriously believe that any of the presidents pro tempore would qualify to be president of the United States. No serious polity would include them in the line of succession. One can easily argue that it is equally unwise to include the speaker of the house, for reasons ranging from the obvious fact that speakers are often from a different party than the president to the critical fact that the skill set that leads one to be chosen as speaker may have no overlap at all with the skill set needed to be president of the United States.

The fraternal law professors Akhil and Vikram Amar have also offered a constitutional critique of the Succession in Office Act, based on the legal point that members of Congress are not correctly described as "officers of the United States," and the Constitution appears to require that the succession go to such officers (like cabinet members, for example). Some of the more arcane discussions of the impeachment clause were based on just this point, for the Constitution gives Congress the power to impeach *only* officers of the United States, which means that representatives and senators cannot be impeached precisely because they are not officers. We can ignore the merits or problems with the Amars' critique,[18] since it obviously doesn't fall within the Constitution of Settlement (else we wouldn't have the Succession in Office Act that we do). Still, one might well believe that it would be better if succession went to the secretary of state, which was the law prior to 1947. This would not only be a safeguard against changes in party, should a speaker of the house be an opponent of the president, but also a relative guarantee that the new president would be more likely to have relevant experience, especially given the inevitable international turmoil that would surround circumstances generating such a succession.

There is also the practical point, emphasized by the Amars, that a speaker would have to resign from the House if he or she became president even for a day (while, say, the president underwent surgery). That surely makes little sense, but it is required by another arcane but important part of the Constitution of Settlement, the Incompatibility Clause that prevents members of Congress from service as officers of the United States. However, Seth B. Tillman has argued, counterintuitively, that the president and vice president are *not* such officers, precisely because "officers" are those who owe their office to presidential appointment. Presidents and vice presidents are *elected*, not self-appointed, at least save for a future Gerald Ford who is, like an ordinary "officer," nominated by a sitting president to fill a vice-presidential vacancy.

These discussions, as with those surrounding the Twenty-fifth Amendment, might sound "academic" in the pejorative sense, but they point to possibilities that could certainly roil our politics should they occur. Tillman, for example, has suggested that placing succession only in cabinet officials would leave the United States vulnerable if something happened to both the president and vice president prior to the confirmation of a newly elected president's cabinet. This is, to be sure, an extraordinarily unlikely possibility, but anyone who has lived through the last decade, with such events as September 11, Hurricane Katrina, major earthquakes, and two devastating tsunamis should be aware that low probability is not impossibility. One might well believe that a function of a well-designed Constitution is to provide firewalls against even very low-probability events.[19] We shall have further opportunity to discuss problems posed by "continuity in government" in the final chapter on emergency powers.

One should mention a final conundrum with regard to the peculiar office of the vice presidency as constructed by the U.S. Constitution: in which branch is the vice president actually located? Vice President Cheney raised this mind-bending question during his own term of office, when he argued that he was either a member of both branches or, in some sense, of neither. After all, the one and only duty assigned to the vice president by the Constitution is to preside over the Senate (with a vote in case of a tie), which would suggest that the correct answer to the conundrum is "the legislature." On the other hand, the vice president is selected by the very same electors charged with choosing the president. And, especially in recent decades, presidents almost always treat the persons they choose to serve in the office as trusted associates, often with explicitly assigned responsibilities. So is the answer "the executive"? In any event, the vice presidency instantiates, more than any other office within the national government, the utter impossibility of viewing the United States as being committed to a hermetically sealed version of "separation of powers" and branches of government. The vice presidency should perhaps be viewed as akin to the duck-billed platypus of Australia, an egg-laying mammal that defies our typical classification systems.

11

Divided Government

I. THE SHIFTING MEANING OF "DIVIDED GOVERNMENT"

A. The Madisonian vision of institutionally divided government

One should begin by emphasizing the radical change in the notion of "divided government" between 1787 and the present. With the original Constitution, divided government was basically synonymous with what we call "separation of powers" or, even more to the point, "checks and balances," though there are actually profound differences between these two notions. Still, one might say that the very aim of the Philadelphians was to create a complex system of government that was indeed divided both horizontally, within the national government, and vertically, between the national government and the states. Many eighteenth-century materials, including various *Federalist* papers, discuss the divided nature of governmental power. Consider only bicameralism, the presidential veto, the role of the Senate in confirming presidential nominees, or the role of the Senate in ratifying treaties. This is just more proof that the basic structures established by the 1787 Constitution remain extremely important in the twenty-first century.

The most famous delineation of the divided government created by the Constitution comes in Madison's *Federalist* 51, the first sentence of which sets out the central theme: "the necessary partition of power among the several departments." Why is this "necessary"? The answer is (deceptively) simple: recall the Madisonian political psychology and sociology that we saw spelled out particularly in *Federalist* 10, which focused on the anxiety generated by the inevitable and ubiquitous existence of factions organized to take advantage of others for their own interests. It is therefore "necessary" to create a system of government that, as much as possible, protects us against the ravages of faction. Recall also that the only way to eliminate faction would be either to radically transform human beings or to suppress political freedom entirely. After all, as Madison writes in oft-quoted sentences in *Federalist* 51, "What is government itself, but the greatest of all reflections on human nature? If men were angels, no government would be necessary. If angels were to govern men, neither external nor internal controls on government would be necessary." But human beings are distinctly *not* angelic.

There is, then, no escaping our fallen selves. Thus, Madison tells us, we must "contrive[e] the interior structure of the government as that its several constituent parts may, by their mutual relations, be the means of keeping each other in their proper places" and limit, as much as possible, their inevitable tendencies to overreach and transgress. He suggests that the best way to create truly separate or divided governmental structures is by hermetically sealed systems of selection, though this is especially difficult in a system predicated on popular sovereignty. Classical theories of mixed government usually dispensed with any sentimentality about popular sovereignty and were separated into institutions composed of the monarchy, the aristocracy, and then the common citizenry. In classical mixed systems, though, the monarch and aristocrats were selected by blood, though there were more lines to draw on with regard to the House of Lords than the monarchy itself. This is not to say, for anyone familiar with the tangled history of British kings and queens, that such bloodlines did not come to some rather abrupt terminations followed by sometimes remarkable replacements from abroad, as occurred most notably in 1688 with William of Orange and Mary and then again in 1714 with the importation of the Hanoverian monarch George I (who spoke little or no English) from Germany to resolve the problematics of succession that monarchical systems are prone to.

But the most basic meaning of the first three words of the Preamble is that mixed government had been decisively rejected in the name of popular sovereignty. The demise of mixed government and the replacement by theoretical sovereignty of the people means that *all* public officials trace their authority back to some aspect of popular selection, even if attenuated.

Thus the state legislators who picked senators, in the original scheme, were themselves chosen in popular elections, as is true, in most cases by the early nineteenth century, of presidential electors (though the South Carolina legislature selected electors until 1876). Even federal judges can plausibly claim some linkage to "the people," given their nomination by the president and confirmation by the Senate, and most state judges must face the electorate at one or more points in their judicial careers.

Still, one should, according to Madison, applaud a Constitution that, as much as is reasonably possible, provides measures of genuine (even if ultimately limited) independence of the various institutions from one another. One symbol of this are the "emoluments" clauses in the Constitution, which guarantee that neither presidents nor judges ever face the prospect of their salaries being cut by a vengeful Congress. Another is the prohibition of members of Congress from serving as "officers" of the United States, which means that members of Congress would have to resign their seats upon joining the president's cabinet.

"But the great security against a gradual concentration of the several powers in the same department," Madison argues, "consists in giving to those who administer each department the necessary constitutional means and personal motives to resist encroachments of the others." By providing for a measure of institutional autonomy for each of the basic structures of the American polity (these are "the necessary constitutional means"), persons elected to serve within any given structure will develop the requisite "personal motives" to defend particular institutional interests against others within the American government who would encroach on them. In two of the most famous sentences within the entire body of *The Federalist*, Madison writes that "ambition must be made to counteract ambition. The interest of the man must be connected with the constitutional rights of the place."

Members of the executive branch will be jealous to protect whatever Article II means by "the executive power," and they will often be challenged in the exercise of this power by members of Congress who are equally jealous to preserve the prerogatives of *that* branch. "The constant aim," Madison insists, "is to divide and arrange the several offices in such a manner as that each may be a check on the other." One can conceive of "checks" along multiple dimensions. The most obvious is that it will be far harder to pass unwise or otherwise illegitimate (because unconstitutional, even if politically desirable) legislation because of the various barriers we have already examined. But one can also think of "checking" in terms of *oversight*, in other words, mechanisms by which overreaching officials will be held *accountable*. The most obvious example is impeachment, which has been defined as the "grand inquest of the nation."

Federalist 51 serves as the indirect refutation of those who would endorse parliamentary systems of government, which reject the institutional separation of legislature and executive in favor of a prime minister who serves entirely at the legislature's pleasure. But what anyone who buys fully into Madison's argument must address is the fact that most political systems in the world have rejected the American version of separation of powers in favor of parliamentarianism or what has come to be called "semi-presidentialism" (the system most prominent in France and Russia, which has both reasonably strong presidents *and* prime ministers elected by and formally accountable to the legislature).

Proponents of American-style separation of powers suggest that parliamentary systems in effect appoint quasi-dictators, at least inasmuch as popular prime ministers can be assured of pushing their legislative program through a compliant parliament. Though formal accountability is maximal—prime ministers can, after all, lose their jobs with the negative vote of a parliamentary majority—other forms of accountability may be minimal. It is relatively unlikely, for example, that parliamentary committees will engage in close scrutiny of governmental programs initiated and managed by a government that is the choice of the parliament itself. And most notoriously, the prime minister in some systems is given the authority to schedule what in Great Britain are called "snap elections" at a time most favorable to his or her own party. This obviously has not prevented leadership from being ousted, but it arguably makes it at least a bit more difficult than in a system with fixed elections like our own.

Yet proponents of parliamentarianism claim not only that it is more democratic—at least if one defines "democracy" by sensitivity to majoritarian political preferences—but also less likely to slide into actual dictatorship. Thus critics of presidentialism, led for many years by Yale professor Juan Linz, who specialized in the study of Latin American polities, claimed that the decision of most Latin American countries to emulate the United States contributed to the frequency with which presidents became *caudillos*, often collaborating with the military to engage in coups that would entrench their joint power. Recall the critique of the Linz view by Antonio Jose Chiebub, who holds that the propensity of Latin American polities to engage in military coups and establish dictatorships is linked to the occurrence of a military coup in the past. There seems to be an enormous difference between systems that have never had a coup and those that have. As with most objects of temptation, the key seems to be the first try. It is far easier to go from one to two to X than from zero to one. This reminds us that political culture may often be at least as important, if not more important, than formal political structures.

B. Party and the Madisonian system

But the most obvious reality is that our political system, though formally similar to what was created in Philadelphia in 1787, has been transformed beyond recognition in terms of Madison's arguments. And the reason is simple: political parties. Whether one views political parties as the snakes in the Madisonian Garden of Eden or the saviors of a Byzantine political system that could not possibly operate without them, there is no escaping their fundamental importance. We saw earlier, with regard to the Twelfth Amendment, that the only real explanation for the proposal and ratification of that amendment in 1803 was the recognition that one could no longer understand presidential elections within the 1787 framework. So the response was to establish separate voting tracks for president and vice president, legitimizing the fact that candidates would be running as representatives of nationwide political parties rather than as virtuous and wise individuals free from any such encumbrances.

There has, however, been no such recognition in the rest of the formal Constitution of the manifest importance of political parties in our system of government, unless one interprets the effort of the Twentieth Amendment to limit lame-duck Congresses as an indirect recognition of the role of parties and the value of turning over control of the House and/or the Senate to the former minority party. Otherwise, the Constitution—and the American state analogues—remain formally unaware of the reality of party government.

So thus we come to the modern notion of "divided government," by which emphasis is placed far less on the "creative tension" and "ambition counteracting ambition" among the various branches and far more on the party identity of the president and House and Senate majority leaders, or, for that matter, members of the federal judiciary. Most political scientists register deep skepticism about the contemporary applicability of the Madisonian argument. In his extremely influential book *The Electoral Connection,* David Mayhew argues that most representatives are motivated primarily by the urge to be re-elected, not by maintaining the prerogatives of their particular institution. And re-election may well be a function of what presidents are doing while in office. Thus, members of the president's own party generally have a strong incentive to rally around their party leader, just as members of the out party have an incentive to limit presidential successes. It is this aspect of divided government that best explains the behavior of Senate Republicans during the Obama Administration, given that Republican Minority Leader Mitch McConnell has publicly acknowledged that his principal agenda is to defeat President Obama in 2012. Having observed the contribution that the late Democratic Senator Ted Kennedy made to the re-election of George W. Bush in 2004 by co-operating in passing Bush's signature bills on education ("No Child Left Behind") and providing prescription drugs to the elderly, McConnell altogether rationally has concluded that Republicans have nothing to gain, as a political party, from collaborating in anything that the president could then claim as an achievement.

This does not guarantee that even "unified" government, with the same party controlling both president and Congress, will necessarily be able to enact its domestic programs. Bicameralism and supermajority rules in the Senate put obstacles in the way. But it surely means that the minority party will be able to pass none of its preferred programs, even if it will have the occasional pleasure of blocking programs favored by the majority.

One consequence of divided government, though, is that accountability of the executive branch may be enhanced, for the simple reason that Congress, when controlled by the opposition, has strong incentive to investigate the executive for potential misconduct. At the extreme, an opposition Congress may even move toward impeachment, as occurred with Richard Nixon in 1974 and President Clinton in 1998. Daryl Levinson has written an important article criticizing the assumptions underlying *Federalist* 51, and he went on to co-author an important article with Richard Pildes emphasizing the importance of thinking in terms of what they called "separation of parties" rather than "separation of powers," precisely because the actual relationship between the executive branch and Congress is explained far more by the variable of party than by Madison's conjectures about institutional allegiance.

It is easy enough to delineate the indices of "divided" government. All one needs is at least one house of Congress and the executive being in the hands of different political parties. What is far more difficult is *assessing* divided compared to unified government, especially given its frequency in post–World War II American politics. Some argue that divided government is indeed an advantage inasmuch as it tends to make less likely the passage of sweeping legislation. If one believes the status quo is likely to be preferable to most suggested changes, then any system that promotes stasis is an advantage rather than a disadvantage. Others, such as David Mayhew, challenge the assertion that divided governments produce less significant legislation that unitary ones. Just as Cheibub criticizes those who overestimate the importance of the choice between presidential and parliamentary systems, Mayhew attacks those who view divided government as a bug. He offers lists of laws passed under conditions of divided political control of White House and Congress and suggests that there is nothing really to worry about. *Note well, though, the inevitable political criteria that are necessarily involved in deciding whether the legislation produced is sufficient to meet national needs.* It is not a "scientific" question, to be decided simply by reference to "data," but requires the application of one's own political views. No Child Left Behind was a signature achievement of George W. Bush's first term, and it was supported by the late Senator Edward Kennedy and what was then a Democratic Senate. There is no consensus on the merits of the bill and whether it would have been a "better" or "worse" bill had it been crafted more or less entirely by Republicans or by Democrats.

Mayhew notes that unitary government produces far less oversight than divided government, precisely because legislatures are unlikely to closely scrutinize an administration of their own party. If one assumes that such oversight is desirable, is there a way to get the benefits of divided government even in a situation of party unity across the branches? Levinson and Pildes refer to the German solution, which places leadership of key parliamentary committees in the hands of the opposition. This means that they can easily undertake investigations should appropriate occasions present themselves, presumably with requisite powers to compel testimony. This proposal works, however, only if one recognizes the importance of political parties in the modern state. It is also easier to envision such a scheme in a two-party system than a multi-party system. How does one decide who constitutes "the opposition" in the latter situation?

The failure to think adequately about the reality of party government is especially pronounced with regard to our rules involving succession in office should both the president and vice president die or otherwise prove unfit to serve. The current law provides that the speaker of the house, who can readily come from the opposition party, will be the new president. Thus, if anything happened to both Barack Obama and Joe Biden prior to 2013 (and perhaps even through 2017), Republican John Boehner would become president, with attendant powers to fire the existing cabinet and do whatever he could to reverse the policies of his predecessor.

C. Should we move away from divided governance?

James Sundquist, the author of a 1986 book tellingly titled *Constitutional Reform and Effective Government,* laments the consequences of divided government and wishes to lessen its likelihood. He was not alone. Lloyd Cutler, President Carter's (and later President Clinton's) White House Counsel and a leading figure of what used to be thought of as "the Washington Establishment" had written in a 1980 issue of *Foreign Affairs* an article entitled "To Form a Government" that bewailed the extent to which the United States lacked "a government" in the sense that Great Britain did. Indeed, Cutler began his article with an anecdote told by Winston Churchill about his being summoned to Buckingham Palace on May 10, 1940: "His Majesty received me most graciously and bade me sit down. He looked at me searchingly and quizzically for some moments, and then said: 'I suppose you don't know why I have sent for you?' Adopting his mood, I replied: 'Sir, I simply couldn't imagine why.' He laughed and said: 'I want to ask you to form a Government.' I said I would certainly do so."¹ And so he did! No such story could be told within the United States, whether at the national or state level, given our commitment to separate branches that must come together—or not, as the case may be—in order for effective governance to take place.

One possibility, suggested Sundquist, is changing the terms of members of the House to four years, with their election possibly coinciding with that of the presidency, thus encouraging more party-line voting than would otherwise be the case. Another proposal is to give the winner of the presidential election the right to appoint a certain number of members of the House and Senate sufficient to provide a "working majority" and thus increase the likelihood of the "party program" being adopted. Indeed, one rationale, albeit weak, for having the vice president serve as president of the Senate is to give the president's party the tie-breaking vote should the Senate be equally divided.

Is it the case, though, that Americans actually "like" the Madisonian system, with the possibility and frequent enactment of divided government? We saw earlier that it is hard to make this case with regard to the electoral college, which has consistently had less than majority support in Gallup polls since 1944. So what might be said about divided government? To a significant extent, divided government is the result of *ticket splitting*, in other words, the casting of a vote for the presidential candidate of one party and the congressional candidates of the other party. Given the way our system operates, it is not clear that one can infer from a given voter's preference for a representative or senator of the "other" party that the same voter would actually prefer a Congress controlled by that party. Still, at the very least, it means that the such voters accept that their preferred candidates for the House or Senate will vote to organize the respective house of Congress on a partisan basis different from that of the president. What we know from observing voting behavior is that significant majorities do *not* split their tickets. Ticket splitting is a decidedly minority approach to politics.²

The highpoint of ticket splitting, at least since 1952, appears to have been in the 1970s and 1980s (see Table 11.1). One explanation is that Americans were becoming more "independent." Another is simply that many "Reagan Democrats" were in the process of leaving their traditional

Table 11.1 *Split Ticket Voting Presidential/Congressional 1952–2008*

	'52	'54	'56	'58	'60	'62	'64	'66	'68	'70	'72	'74	'76	'78	'80	'82	'84	'86	'88	'90	'92	'94	'96	'98	'00	'02	'04	'08
Dem. Pres./ Dem. Congr.	39	**	39	**	45	**	59	**	40	**	31	**	42	**	35	**	36	**	40	**	48	**	44	**	43	**	43	46
Dem. Pres./Rep. Congr.	2	**	2	**	4	**	9	**	7	**	5	**	9	**	8	**	6	**	7	**	10	**	13	**	10	**	7	9
Rep. Pres./ Dem. Congr.	10	**	13	**	10	**	6	**	11	**	25	**	16	**	20	**	20	**	18	**	12	**	4	**	9	**	10	8
Rep. Pres./ Rep. Congr.	49	**	45	**	41	**	26	**	42	**	40	**	34	**	38	**	39	**	34	**	30	**	38	**	39	**	40	38
N	1009		1151		1187		947		776		1293		1280		762		1144		1030		1124		855		814		674	1286

Source: Split Ticket Voting Presidential/Congressional 1952–2008, http://www.electionstudies.org/nesguide/toptable/tab9b_2.htm.

political party behind but remained loyal to long-term representatives and senators who were more conservative than the Democratic presidential candidates. Thus 20 percent of Reagan voters in both 1980 and 1984 voted for Democratic candidates for Congress. By the 2004 election, only 10 percent of Bush voters voted for Democrats (while 7 percent voted for Kerry and Republican congressional candidates).

Thus Jonathan Rauch was manifestly incorrect in a column published shortly after the November 2010 elections when he declared that that "the public strongly prefers divided government."[3] There is not an iota of empirical evidence that a majority of Americans actively prefers divided government when engaging in their most fundamental opportunity to choose such a government in presidential election years. Instead, the evidence appears overwhelming that most Americans would prefer a unified government, at least if their own party controlled both branches. Only a small minority reveal a preference for divided government.

That being said, one can plausibly argue that most Democrats would prefer a divided government to one controlled by the Republicans and vice versa. And, presumably, both Democrats and Republicans might therefore oppose such proposals as those involving "bonus seats" for the president's party, precisely because this would increase the likelihood of a unified government controlled by their dispreferred party. The ultimate question is whether they might prefer a government that made it considerably more likely that *either* party could in fact pass significant domestic legislation after winning a presidential election or if, when all is said and done, persons are so risk averse that they prefer a system biased to the status quo and structured to make the passage of such legislation difficult. It is just such a political system that is currently described, across the political spectrum, as "dysfunctional" or even "pathological."

II. DIVISIONS WITHIN THE BRANCHES THEMSELVES: DO WE WANT A "UNITARY EXECUTIVE"?

An earlier chapter discussed bicameralism, which is nothing more than a "divided legislature." What about a "divided executive"? Is there something compelling about a vision of a "unitary executive," where the president does indeed appoint all executive branch officials, even if many of them require Senate confirmation? Whatever one thinks of the U.S. Constitution, it is easily demonstrable that it does *not* in fact instantiate "the American way" of organizing executive branches. As professor William Marshall notes, for example, forty-eight of the fifty states do *not* give their governors the authority to name the attorney general, perhaps the most important single executive branch official in terms of providing potential oversight of the executive branch with regard to criminal misconduct.[4]

Most Americans therefore live in states with more or less divided executive branches. Consider only the two largest states, California and Texas. The sample ballot for the 2010 election in Texas listed no fewer than fifteen executive branch offices to be selected by voters, including, in addition to the attorney general, eight members of the State Board of Education. California voters selected twelve executive branch officials, including four members of the Board of Equalization—"the nation's only elected tax commission," according to its Web site. Voters of the third largest state, Florida, chose "only" five executive branch officials, including "tied" candidates for governor and lieutenant governor, one less than Massachusetts, which elected six of its executives. New Jersey looks a lot like the United States with regard to the powers held by the governor to appoint state officials, but it is a definite outlier among the American states.

It is worth focusing for a moment on the attorney general. The attorney general is in some real sense the chief law-enforcement official of the particular polity, though at the national level the president is supreme, able both to hire (with Senate confirmation) and to fire the attorney general. This is impossible in almost all of the states, where the attorney general is independent of the governor. Forty-seven states elect their attorneys general, while the Tennessee Supreme Court appoints that state's attorney general. Indeed, even though New Jersey attorneys general are appointed by the governor, they do not, unlike other executive branch officials in that state, serve at the pleasure of the chief executive. Once appointed, the attorney general is entitled to remain in office for the entire term of the governor.

Madison's arguments in *Federalist* 51, with their emphasis on the political psychology of "ambition," provide a basis for fearing that attorneys general who owe their appointment and job retention to a president will have incentives to subordinate their independent judgment to the political imperatives of the White House. We might be most concerned when, for example, presidents appoint their brothers, as with John F. Kennedy's appointment of Robert Kennedy; their campaign managers, as with Richard Nixon's appointment of John Mitchell; or hyper-loyalist protégés, as with George W. Bush's appointment of Alberto Gonzales. Interestingly enough, Gonzales's predecessor, former Missouri senator John Ashcroft, had a quite distinguished career prior to his appointment, and there is some evidence that he was less the servant of White House interests than the far more pliable Gonzales. Still, Ashcroft, and almost all other national attorneys general, can scarcely be described as strongly independent, at least if presidents are willing to pay the political costs of firing them. Thus Richard Nixon notably fired Acting Attorney General William Ruckelshaus when he refused to obey Nixon's command to dismiss Special Prosecutor Archibald Cox. Attorney General Eliot Richardson had earlier that day resigned when ordered to dismiss Cox. Robert Bork, next in the line of succession to become acting attorney general, famously agreed to fire Cox, partly, it is said, because Bork feared the disintegration of the American government—or at least its executive branch—if he, too, defied the direct orders of the ostensible "chief executive." (Interestingly enough, Bill Clinton was never able to dismiss Janet Reno, even though, by all accounts, they had a basically terrible relationship.)

One of the most important developments in twentieth-century American government was the creation of so-called independent agencies whose heads, though appointed by the president and confirmed by the Senate, do *not*—unlike all cabinet and sub-cabinet officials—serve at the pleasure of the president. The most important example of this phenomenon is almost certainly the head of the Federal Reserve Board, at the time of this writing Ben Bernanke, who was reappointed to a new four-year term by President Obama in 2010. The argument is that economic policy should be distanced from crass political considerations that pervade any White House, particularly as elections near.

Some lawyers believe that all independent agencies, beginning with the Fed and going through the Federal Communications Commission and the Securities and Exchange Commission, are unconstitutional because of the purported commitment of the Constitution to a "unitary executive."

That view, however, has been decisively rejected by the Supreme Court, with the acquiescence of Justice Scalia himself, who had been thought to be sympathetic to such arguments. Even "non-independent" agencies are staffed by lower-level officials who are protected by civil service laws going back to 1886, passed precisely in order to limit the possibility of retaliation by political officials, including the president, against underlings who might exhibit undesired independence. Moreover, whatever the status of the president as commander in chief, elaborate procedures within the Department of Defense are in place to insulate the promotion of military officers from undue presidential influence.[5] For better or worse, one simply cannot understand the contemporary American executive branch through the lens of "unitary executive" theory.

So the question is this: *if* we like the idea of an "independent" Federal Reserve Board, should we be equally attracted by a (more) independent Department of Justice? To be sure, the president still retains a significant power to shape the Fed because of the power of appointment. So perhaps the real question is whether we would prefer to have an elected attorney general, or one appointed by a bipartisan group of congressional leaders or by the Supreme Court (or a specially chosen committee of retired federal judges). An elected attorney general increases the likelihood that the president and attorney general would come from different parties, with whatever awkwardness (or additional oversight) that would bring. And even if they belong to the same party, it is quite likely in many of the states that the attorney general has ambitions to attain the governor's mansion him or herself. This was the case, for example, in New York in 2010, where Andrew Cuomo was successful in dissuading Democratic Governor David Paterson from attempting to remain in office.

One final issue is especially important when considering the status of the attorney general. Does it matter that the attorney general will invariably be a lawyer, whereas chief executives, whether presidents or governors, are only sometimes lawyers? And even if the presidents or governors have legal training, it may be difficult at times to separate their duties to "take care" that the law be faithfully executed from their judgments, as heads of political parties and persons very much concerned with re-election, as to what kinds of law enforcement best serve their political interests. We saw this drama being played out almost immediately upon President

Obama's taking office, with regard to potential prosecution of those who developed and implemented American interrogation policies, including the use of torture. It is fair to say that almost no one has been held legally accountable for various depredations that occurred (and, indeed, the Obama Administration has fought vigorously to stifle any civil suits that have been brought against those alleged to have been complicit in torture). Who—Attorney General Holder or President Obama—should make the final decisions to prosecute or not to prosecute, to accommodate civil litigants or to put up barriers in their way? And what constitute proper criteria when making such decisions? President Obama *is* a lawyer, a former professor of constitutional law at the University of Chicago. How relevant is this, though? Is it important that Jimmy Carter, Ronald Reagan, George H. W. Bush, and George W. Bush were *not* lawyers, while Richard Nixon, Bill Clinton, and now Barack Obama were legally educated and either practiced law or, as was the case with Clinton, served as a state attorney general? I shall address the importance of legal training and expertise in the context of a judiciary, but the question obviously emerges with regard to organizing the executive branch itself.

Perhaps the ultimate point is this: Just as the experience of myriad other countries has demonstrated the limited applicability of James Madison's specific defense of separation of powers and checks and balances in *Federalist* 51, so has the experience of over 90 percent of the American states demonstrated the possibility of functioning at least reasonably well without a "unitary executive." Again, one might want to argue that the national government is fundamentally different from those of California, Texas, and forty-six other states, but at the very least, one would like to know precisely why.

There is another point about the unitary executive that is worth mentioning: giving the president the power to appoint all executive branch officials lends a winner-take-all partisan character to presidential elections (and to the gubernatorial elections in the two unitary executive states). This will be true unless a particular president or governor chooses, for political purposes, to offer an appointment to someone from the opposite party. President Obama did this with the secretary of defense, a holdover from the Bush Administration, and secretary of transportation (and attempted to do with regard to the secretary of commerce, but New Hampshire Republican

Senator Judd Gregg rejected the offer). What Jacob Gerson calls the "unbundled executive" that exists in most states allows the possibility that the major parties will in fact end up sharing the tasks of governance.[6] This same result can be produced in many parliamentary systems, when a given party fails to secure a majority of the seats in the legislature and therefore must enter into a coalition with what would otherwise be an "opposition" party. Among other things, this allows members of various parties to gain valuable experience that can presumably be put to good use in the future, whereas the American national system assures that very talented members of the opposition are in effect frozen out of participation in the executive branch unless and until their party wins back the presidency.

One might well argue that the Constitution of Settlement just requires a unitary executive, in the same way that it requires inaugurating a new president on January 20 of the year following election. As with changing Inauguration Day, perhaps it would take a constitutional amendment to disaggregate our present executive branch, but so what? The question is not what the current Constitution mandates or prohibits but whether we are necessarily well served by the Constitution established in 1787; concomitantly, we should also be engaged in a national conversation as to whether most of the states are well served by state constitutions that so dramatically reject the design preferences reflected in the 1787 Constitution.

Although some partisans of the national system defend it in terms of maximizing "accountability," by placing on the president the responsibility for defending whatever is done by his or her executives whenever he or she seeks re-election, Gerson argues that the "unbundled executive" might in fact enhance accountability by allowing voters to hone in on those executives whose policies they support or oppose. It is highly unlikely, for example, that one will actually choose to cast one's vote for governor of New Jersey on the basis of whom he appointed commissioner of veterans' affairs or transportation, at least if one finds generally tolerable his appointees as attorney general and treasurer. Voters always rank-order priorities when assessing candidates for office, and they might even vote for someone with whom they disagree on a host of matters because they agree on one big matter. It is no easy matter to figure out what "accountability" means in such a context.

12

How "Independent" a Judiciary Do We Really Want?

The last chapter discussed the desirability of building some "wall of separation" between a president and attorney general. The reason to build such a wall with regard to the attorney general is the perception that law—and its enforcement—should be truly distinguishable from what we ordinarily call "politics." "Political justice" is usually a term of opprobrium, referring to the self-conscious use by political authorities of the machinery of law to go after or intimidate one's political opponents.

If there are those who are concerned about the "independence" of attorneys general, there are many more people who emphasize the importance of "judicial independence" as part of the very definition of "the rule of law." Judges should be accountable, it is often asserted, only to the law, not to the wishes of a president or of Congress, whatever role they may have played in the initial appointment process. But the appointment process is scarcely free from political overtones. Various appointment processes, including those established by the United States and state constitutions, have been criticized as injecting too much politics into what ought to be a non-political institution, the judiciary.

That being said, readers can test their own intuitions about what they mean by independence and whether it is in fact a good thing. Independence is primarily a notion of autonomy and, therefore, basically of non-accountability to those possessing particular political (or what Madison might call "factional") interests insufficiently embraced by the independent decisionmaker. "Brutus," one of the leading anti-Federalists, was harshly critical of the Constitution with regard to the independence accorded the judiciary, especially the Supreme Court.[1] The Philadelphians, Brutus argued "have made the judges independent, in the fullest sense of the word. There is no power above them, to control any of their decisions. There is no authority that can remove them, and they cannot be controlled by the laws of the legislature. In short, they are independent of the people, of the legislature, and every power under heaven. Men placed in this situation will generally soon feel themselves independent of heaven itself."[2] So for Brutus, "judicial independence" was a bug rather than a feature. Let me offer an example of a maximally "independent" institution and ask if it offers a desirable model for designing a judiciary.

Consider the French Academy, which is remarkably "independent" in the particular sense that it is a self-perpetuating body. When a vacancy occurs among the forty "immortals" who comprise the Academy, the remaining academicians select a new member. Outsiders may express some interest in who is chosen, but the one certainty is that the surviving members will cast their votes and make whatever selection they want. Now put this within the context of judges and judiciaries. Would any readers endorse a judiciary that operated under the rules of the French Academy? Whenever a vacancy occurred in the Supreme Court, it would be filled following selection by the remaining justices. In addition, one might give to the members of the Supreme Court the prerogative of selecting all members of "inferior" courts, as they are labeled by the Constitution.

This is not an entirely fanciful notion. For many years, Aharon Barak, the former president of the Israeli Supreme Court, played what many considered a dominant role in selecting new members of his court, though, at least formally, he was only one among several members of a judicial selection commission in Israel. Students of the Indian political system have concluded that the Indian Supreme Court basically selects its own successors, even if the formal appointment is by the president of India. Similarly, the Danish Supreme Court is said to have a de facto, even if not constitutionally specified, right to veto any judicial appointments. These may all be informal, but they are very real practices. Moreover, as Tom Ginsburg notes in his invaluable book *Judicial Review in New Democracies*, a number of political systems assign some formal appointing authority to current members of the judiciary. In Bulgaria, Italy, Georgia, and Ukraine, members of the highest court get to name some designated percentage of the total membership of the court, with no possibility of veto by the president (in presidential systems) or the legislature. Many other systems, including in many of the American states, include some form of "nominating commissions," also designed to restrict political discretion. Interestingly enough, attorneys general or ministers of justice often are members of such commissions, but this depends on the perception that persons filling those offices are in fact apolitical in some important sense.

So, to summarize, one form of independence involves an appointment process that is designed to limit the play of "political" considerations in any decisions that are made. One may also take a desire for independence into account when deciding how long judges shall serve. If independence fundamentally means "non-accountability," one might be tempted by life tenure, coupled with constitutional barriers against the reduction of salary. But the central question is how tempted we are by what might be termed "maximal non-accountability" to political considerations.

Such considerations can take multiple forms. An appointing authority might be eager to curry favor with a particular demographic constituency by appointing one of their own. Or the primary consideration might instead be a commitment by the appointing authority to only one constitutional vision among many that have contended with one another throughout our history. One might even describe such a singular commitment as an attempt to shut down important aspects of the Constitution of Conversation by suggesting that there is only one legitimate answer to the questions posed by the Constitution.

But judicial independence remains a mysterious notion even after any questions presented above are resolved. A valuable collection of essays, *Judicial Independence at the Crossroads*,[3] is rife with challenges to the very utility of the concept. Thus Lewis Kornhauser titles his own contribution *Is Judicial Independence a Useful Concept?* His answer is a resounding no. He concludes that "legal debates over adjudication, debates about the design of judicial institutions, and the explanation of the emergence and performance of various judicial institutions would be clearer and progress more rapidly if we abandoned the concept."[4] Part of the problem is empirical: how, exactly, do we measure independence in a way that allows us to determine that a particular court or an overall judicial system is more independent than another?[5] As already suggested by reference to the French Academy, even if we can confidently define what constitutes "autonomy" or "independence," we must still engage in the normative task of evaluation. It is easy enough to assert that a court with life tenure, maximum freedom to take any and all cases brought before it, and the ability to choose its own successors free of any participation by elected political officials is more "independent" than one at the other end of the spectrum with regard to all these attributes. But does that tell us anything useful about whether that degree of independence is to be applauded or lamented?

After all, it is a settled reality that almost all judges face the prospect of their decisions being appealed to higher authority. As the Canadian scholar Peter Russell has written, "the influence of the decisions of higher courts on lower court judges is surely not to be regarded as a violation of judicial independence."[6] By any measure, members of the U.S. Supreme Court—or of state supreme courts in certain contexts—are more autonomous than the members of what the Constitution in Article III deems "inferior" courts. Every judge on one of these lesser courts must always be looking over his or her shoulder and wondering what a reviewing court might say about any given decision. Indeed, built into our standard definition of the rule of law is precisely the notion that "inferior" judges will feel bound by the decisions of their "superiors," *even if the "inferior" judges believe, perhaps with good reason, that the hierarchically superior judges are deeply mistaken on what "the law," best interpreted, really is.* Why would anyone describe such judges as "independent" if they are forced to acquiesce to decisions they believe to be mis-statements of the law? With regard to statutory interpretation, an ever-more-important aspect of the contemporary judiciary, judges must always be aware of the possibility that legislatures might overturn their decisions should they deviate too far from legislative preferences.[7] In any event, even if judicial independence is not completely useless as an analytical concept, it is in fact a truly complex notion. Few, if any, people are truly committed to what I have termed "maximal" judicial independence.

I. WHAT DOES THE U.S. CONSTITUTION SAY (AND NOT SAY) ABOUT THE JUDICIARY?

Consider what the U.S. Constitution specifies about the about the federal judiciary: "The judicial power of the United States, shall be vested in one Supreme Court, and in such inferior courts as the Congress may from time to time ordain and establish. The judges, both of the supreme and inferior courts, shall hold their offices during good behaviour, and shall, at stated times, receive for their services, a compensation, which shall not be diminished during their continuance in office." Also relevant is Article II, Section 2: "[The President] shall nominate, and by and with the advice and consent of the Senate…judges of the Supreme Court, and all other officers of the United States, whose appointments are not herein otherwise provided for, and which shall be established by law."

A. The Supreme Court

1. Size

Congress, it appears, *must* establish a Supreme Court—one can scarcely imagine the Supreme Court "constituting itself" in the absence of such congressional authorization—but Congress remains free to decide whether there shall be any "inferior" courts at all. It is theoretically possible that the *only* federal court would be the Supreme Court, and that all other courts would be state courts. That is obviously not the way things worked out, but it is worth recalling that the nation didn't have a separate tier of appellate courts between district courts and the Supreme Court until 1891. To be more precise, an appellate judiciary *was* established by an act passed by a lame-duck Federalist Congress on February 13, 1801, three weeks before the inauguration of their hated adversary Thomas Jefferson and the shift of power in Congress that would reflect the elections of 1800. Not at all surprisingly, outgoing President John Adams appointed only Federalists to fill the positions that were created, and the Federalist Senate quickly confirmed them. The newly empowered Jeffersonians did not take this lying down; the Judiciary Act of 1801 was repealed on April

29, 1802. Some might describe this as a "purge" of the federal judiciary based entirely on politics, but the creation of those courts and the identity of those appointed to places on them can also be explained only by reference to the deep and bitter politics of the moment.

But consider a question about which the Constitution is completely silent. How large should the Supreme Court be? Does it count as a bug or a feature of the U.S. Constitution that there is no answer provided in the text, which implies that the number will basically be a joint political decision of the Congress and the president? If one looks at a variety of American state constitutions, one usually finds the number of supreme court justices specified in the text. The Virginia Constitution, for example, says that the supreme court shall consist of seven justices; the New York Constitution specifies a chief justice plus six other justices. California's constitution also specifies a total of seven justices, while the Texas Constitution names nine as the constitutionally required number. Texas is unique among the states, incidentally, in having *two* supreme courts, one that handles only civil appeals, the other hearing only criminal appeals. Smaller states, not surprisingly, make do with fewer judges. Thus the supreme court of our smallest state, Wyoming, "shall consist of five (5) justices," and, interestingly enough, "the justices shall choose one (1) of their number to serve as chief justice." North Dakota is also satisfied with a constitutionally designated supreme court "consist[ing] of five justices, one of whom shall be designated chief justice in the manner provided by law."

National constitutions seem somewhat more prone to leave the number out, though one can certainly find many counterexamples. Thus the initial Constitution of India specified that "there shall be a Supreme Court of India consisting of a Chief Justice of India and, until Parliament by law prescribes a larger number, of not more than seven other Judges." It appears that the current number of members of the Indian Supreme Court is twenty-nine.[8] One might ascribe this to the sheer population of India, which is approaching four times the current U.S. population of approximately three hundred million, but it could also be explained by the fact that it is far easier to gain access to the Indian Supreme Court than it is to the U.S. Supreme Court (or, for that matter, *any* federal court). Tom Ginsburg, in his review of recent constitutional developments throughout the world, notes that numbers of supreme court (or "constitutional court") judges range from eighteen in the Ukraine and seventeen in Estonia and Guinea-Bissau down to five in Cape Verde, El Salvador, Senegal, Tanzania, and Uruguay.

In any event, the U.S. Constitution is silent as to number, and the number chosen by the First Congress, when passing the Judiciary Act of 1789, was six.[9] The Federalists who passed the Judiciary Act of 1801 reduced the number to five, hoping to limit Jefferson's ability to appoint his own preferred candidates to the bench, but that was also repealed by the Judiciary Act of 1802. Congress increased the number to seven justices in 1807 and then to nine justices in 1837. These additions could easily be justified on the basis of the rapidly increasing size, whether defined by population or acreage, of the United States. The greatest number of justices was ten, as the result of a statute passed in 1863 by a Republican Congress in order to give Abraham Lincoln an extra appointment. (The tenth justice appointed by Lincoln was Stephen J. Field, a Democrat Union loyalist, unlike many Democrats.) In 1866 Congress passed an act providing that the next three justices to retire would not be replaced, thus reducing the size of the Court to seven. Apparently, the Court itself requested the diminution. But this act also had the no-doubt desirable effect, for Republicans, of depriving Andrew Johnson of the opportunity to appoint anyone to the Court. "Court packing" (or, in Johnson's case, "unpacking") is therefore as American as apple pie, at least if one looks at the first century or so of our history.

Thanks to the 1867 Act, the Court's membership temporarily dipped to eight, but the Judiciary Act of 1869, passed after Ulysses H. Grant succeeded the widely despised Johnson, raised the number back to nine, giving Grant an immediate appointment. The Court's composition has remained at nine justices ever since, though Franklin Roosevelt very controversially tried to raise it to fifteen as part of his so-called Court-packing plan in 1937, when he was battling a Court still controlled by five conservative justices who were invalidating as unconstitutional key aspects of the New Deal. The Court ultimately backed down—some still speak of the "switch in time that saved nine"—and due to human mortality and resignation, Roosevelt had by 1942 appointed seven of the nine justices, who were now regularly upholding, often by unanimous votes, extraordinarily expansive regulatory legislation passed by Congress and signed by the president.

The events of the 1860s especially underscore the importance of the Court's size and the potential for manipulating it in order to achieve political ends. Anyone who believed in serious regime change in the South as a part of "Reconstruction" should have welcomed depriving Johnson of the opportunity to place someone with his anti-Reconstructionist sympathies on the Court, though this may obviously discomfort those who view the judiciary as "above politics."

One might well argue that by 2012, the nine-justice Court has become part of our "unwritten Constitution," as revealed by the remarkable failure of President Roosevelt, even after his overwhelming victory in 1936, to gain sufficient support for raising the number to fifteen.[10] Equally telling is that no one suggested, in the days immediately after President Obama's inauguration in 2009, that Democrats should increase the number of justices to eleven in order to overcome the current majority of five conservative Republicans (which, because of the ages of the justices, could outlast even a two-term Obama Administration). To the extent that one thinks keeping the Supreme Court a nine-member body is a good thing, perhaps it was a weakness of the 1787 Constitution that it didn't specify Court size and that American state constitutions provide a better guide of judiciary size to those designing constitutions today in other countries. One the other hand, India (and all other countries that do not fix the size of the court in their constitutions) may provide a better model because the size can be adjusted to take account of population changes. Recall the critique of the Constitution's limiting each state to two senators, which means that we have not been able to "hire" additional senators despite the significant increase in population and senatorial work load over the past half century.

2. How does someone get to the Supreme Court (or, for that matter, to any federal court)?

The formal answer to this question is that one gets to the Supreme Court by being nominated by the president and then confirmed by the Senate. There are no formal constraints on the president in nominating persons. Unlike many constitutions around the world, ours does not require that judiciary nominees have any particular level of experience. Many constitutions require that nominees be "learned in the law," which is taken to mean many years in legal practice, an extended career as a legal academic, or service on the lower judiciary. There is no such constitutional requirement in the United States, although Congress by statute requires that the solicitor general of the United States be "learned in the law." But there are certainly many examples in our history of appointees to the federal judiciary who would not meet the definition of "learnedness" established in these other constitutions. As a technical matter, it is not necessary to be a lawyer at all, though no non-lawyer has ever been nominated for the federal judiciary.

Justice Joseph Story was nominated at age thirty-two, and William O. Douglas and Clarence Thomas were nominated while in their early forties. Not surprisingly, Story served for thirty-four years and Douglas holds the current record for length of service at thirty-six years and 209 days, followed closely by John Paul Stevens, who retired in 2010 at the age of ninety, two years before he would have replaced Douglas as the longest-serving justice.

Compared with many other political systems, we have a decidedly less "professional" judiciary. In contrast to the European process, students here do not train to become judges and accept, upon graduation, employment as low-level judges, with expectation of promotion as experience accrues over the years. It is important to realize that most of these European countries have generally, following World War II, established "constitutional courts" with special responsibilities for enforcing constitutional limits against other branches of government, and the appointment process for these is far different than for lower courts. Still, by any measure, the process by which federal court judges in America are selected maximizes the role of political considerations. Whether this is a strength or weakness of the American system depends on the functions one envisages for the Court.

It should be clear that there is remarkable variation, both at home and abroad, in how people get to the judiciary. Most other systems appear to try to constrain appointments by limiting the discretion of the nominally appointing authorities.[11] Such constraint can be achieved either by requiring the authorities to be deferential to other participants in the process, through "nominating commissions" and the like, or by carefully specifying criteria that any nominee must meet, including age, prior experience, region, political party, language, or whatever.

Consider, for example, that half of the Belgian constitutional court must be former legislators. This guarantees what is notably absent on the current U.S. Supreme Court, which is the presence of even one judge who has successfully run for elective office and thus has some hands-on experience with legislating. Only Justice Thomas has had experience managing even a mid-level federal agency—in his case, the Equal Employment Opportunity Commission. Otherwise, his colleagues are almost spectacularly devoid of high-level governmental experience (save for having been federal judges prior to their appointment). Compare this, for example, with the Court that decided *Brown v. Board of Education* in 1954, which included as chief justice a former governor of California, three former senators (Black, Minton, Burton), two former attorneys general (Clark and Jackson), two former solicitors general of the United States (Jackson and Reed), a former head of an important federal agency (William O. Douglas), and one of the leading law professors of his time (Felix Frankfurter). Does this tell us something important about the changes in the composition of our Supreme Court over the past fifty years? If so, we should decide which kind of Court we find preferable.

Several countries informally require a certain amount of diversity on their highest courts. The French constitutional court, for example, usually has at least one Protestant among its members, just as Ireland seems to take care to have at least one non-Catholic. Germany apparently is attentive to maintaining a balance between its Protestant and Catholic members as well. Israel traditionally has had on its supreme court at least one Orthodox Jew who is knowledgeable about traditional Jewish law; in 2004 Salim Joubran, a Christian Arab, became the first non-Jew to be appointed to the Israeli Court. The current U.S. Supreme Court, as of 2011, consists of six Catholics and three Jews. To be sure, Protestants apparently no longer constitute a majority of the American population,[12] though one still might find their absence from the Supreme Court to be quite remarkable.

Canada's Supreme Court Act requires that three of its nine justices be from Quebec.[13] Although the Canadian House of Commons passed a law requiring that all the justices be bilingual, the minority government engaged in what the Toronto *Globe and Mail* described as the "constitutionally controversial practice" of killing the bill in the Canadian Senate through what Americans would call a filibuster.[14] Article 107 of the previous

Swiss Constitution required that parliament, when choosing members of the federal court, be attentive to maintaining a balance in the representation of the country's three primary language groups; interestingly, that requirement did not become part of the brand new constitution adopted by referendum in 1999 that went into force on January 1, 2000. Geographic considerations appear to play a role in other polities as well. In Austria, a fourth of its high court justices must live outside of Vienna. Within the United States, Tennessee's constitution requires that its supreme court include justices from the three geographic regions of the state.

One may have mixed opinions about the "diversity" of the current U.S. Supreme Court, but one measure of its non-diversity is really beyond argument: the last justice (successfully) appointed while living west of the Mississippi River was Anthony Kennedy, in 1987. The current Court basically consists of people from the East Coast, in terms of where they either spent their adult lives prior to appointment (Stephen Breyer was in fact born in California and attended Stanford as an undergraduate, though his principal career was as a professor of law at Harvard and member of the federal circuit court based in Boston) or where they have lived since appointment. There is no reason to believe that any current member of the Court knows much, if anything, about the American West, including, for example, issues surrounding access to and control of water or the complexities of American Indian life and law. Given that all of the current justices (as of 2011) attended the Harvard and Yale law schools (though Ginsburg, having transferred from Harvard for her third year, received her degree from Columbia), there is no reason to believe that attention to such legal issues was an important part of the curriculum.

Perhaps the maximum constraint on political appointments is to take appointment authority entirely away from elected officials, as is a common practice particularly (and basically uniquely) in the American states, many of which have chosen to select judges by election. As legal historian Jed Shugerman demonstrates in an important study of the rise of elected judiciaries in nineteenth-century America,[15] this was a deliberate attempt to make judiciaries *more* rather than less independent, given the widespread perception that appointment by governors (and confirmation by the legislature) simply assured the presence in office of judges who would basically legitimate whatever it was that these institutions wished to do.

Thus election was designed to liberate judges from such influences and to make more likely the exercise of judicial review that would invalidate over-reaching by given governors or legislatures.

Many people, including sitting state court judges, were shocked by the decision of the Iowa electorate in November 2010 to remove three of that state's seven state supreme court justices—presumably because they had joined in a unanimous decision holding that the Iowa legislature's ban on same-sex marriage violated the state constitution. The Iowa constitution provided the voters an opportunity to determine whether to "retain" judges at the end of their eight-year terms of office. One can well believe that there will increasingly be retention election battles in the future should judges be perceived as antagonizing public opinion. This is obviously dif-ficult to square with protecting the independence of judges, though it is an excellent example of making judges accountable to the public whom they ostensibly serve.

Election of judges horrifies almost all non-Americans and, to be fair, many Americans as well. In Texas, for example, where every judge is elected, running as Democrats or Republicans (or members of other par-ties) for terms of four or six years, there are often calls, led by members of the judiciary themselves, for the abolition of the elected judiciary in favor of gubernatorial appointment. Such calls are sparked in part because of pressures to raise money for increasingly expensive political campaigns, not least because business interests have strongly invested in attempt-ing to place "friendly" judges on the bench. So far such efforts have been unavailing, and there is no reason to believe they are likely to be suc-cessful in the future. Why not? One answer was provided by the author of a 2009 letter to the editor of the *Austin American Statesman* that sug-gested that replacing the popular election of judges would not guarantee "merit selection" but rather a less transparent form of continuing *partisan* selection. The author could well have been mimicking some of the argu-ments offered in the 1846 New York state constitutional convention that established judicial elections in that state and influenced many other states when the latter designed (or redesigned) their own constitutions. Some contemporary political scientists, moreover, vigorously challenge the cri-tiques of elected judiciaries, which tend to be offered most strongly by elite lawyers and judges themselves. The co-authors of the leading defense of judicial elections almost flamboyantly assert that "contrary to the claims of judges, professional legal organizations, interest groups, and legal scholarship, judicial elections are democracy-enhancing institutions that operate efficaciously and serve to create a valuable nexus between citizens and the bench."[16]

A leading critic of judicial elections is former justice Sandra Day O'Connor, but consider her own description of her selection by Ronald Reagan in 1981.[17] The president was, said Justice O'Connor, looking for a *Republican* woman who had plausible qualifications, and she was the most compelling person on what was a very short list. At the time, she was serving as an intermediate judge in the Arizona state judiciary. There were many *Democratic* women who might have been equally compelling, but they obviously were of no interest to the Republican Reagan. It is a given that presidents will seek appointees to the Supreme Court exclusively from their own parties,[18] something that is overwhelmingly true for appointees to inferior courts as well. George W. Bush did appoint some Democrats to the bench, and Barack Obama will undoubtedly appoint some Republicans, but these appointments will be the result of political deals carefully worked out with opposite-party senators representing given states (within given circuits). For example, a deal cut with New York Democratic Senator Daniel Patrick Moynihan led George H. W. Bush to nominate Sonia Sotomayor to serve as a federal judge in that state.

3. Length of term

Is the length of a judicial term simply a "technical" consideration or is it instead deeply infused with political overtones? I begin with one of our favorite family stories, involving our then three-year-old daughter, whom we took out for a special dinner the night before my wife was scheduled to give birth via induced labor to our younger daughter. Our daughter first asked how the baby was going to arrive, and my wife painstakingly explained, once more, the miracle of birth. Then came the killer question, "And how long will the baby stay?" That was when we delivered the very "bad" news: the baby would indeed stay forever; she would not "return home" after a suitably brief visit, at which time our older daughter could revert to her privileged status as the only child.

So, even after we fix on a method of appointing justices, there remains the altogether important question of how long the judges will be staying. Again, there is striking variation within the states and around the world in answering this question. Many states and countries have age limits; others have term limits, sometimes allowing re-election or re-appointment, sometimes not. Extraordinarily few, however, emulate the Constitution of the United States by granting life tenure. Among our fifty states, only Rhode Island and New Hampshire grant life tenure;[19] of the "selected new democracies" canvassed by Tom Ginsburg, only Brazil, Ecuador, Cape Verde, and Guinea-Bissau seem to have chosen life tenure. All others have either limited appointments or age limits. Basically, the only people left in America who have true lifetime tenure are federal judges and university professors. One can doubt whether the respective institutions are really well served in either case—though I can testify personally to the joy of having such tenure!

Needless to say, life tenure does not mean that one *must* serve forever. Presumably, most judges (like most professors) will in fact choose to retire. But the point is that it is up to them to time their retirements. Sometimes purely personal considerations, such as the desire to keep doing something really interesting rather than move out to pasture, explains a refusal to retire. In other instances, and for men especially, a premature death ends service. But, as one might expect, politics may also play a role in a justice timing their retirement.

Recall Justice O'Connor's comment about her own selection, early in the Reagan Administration. Potter Stewart, a Cincinnati Republican named to the Supreme Court by President Eisenhower in 1958, almost certainly chose to outlast the Carter Administration in the (successful) hope that the next president would be a Republican who could name a fellow Republican as his successor. (As a result, Carter became the only elected single-term president to have no opportunity to make an appointment to the Court.) One may suspect similar motivation—with party identity reversed—in Byron White's decision to retire early in Bill Clinton's term, thus paving the way for Justice Ginsburg's accession to the Supreme Court.

In addition to problems regarding exiting the court, it has also become obvious that lifetime tenure has created an incentive to appoint relatively young men and women to the Supreme Court, precisely so they can continue their support of the appointing president's (and his party's) broad agenda well into the future. Increasingly, if you haven't made it to the Supreme Court by age fifty-five, you should develop other aspirations.

4. How does the Court speak?

A final topic worth at least brief mention is the voice in which a Court speaks. Consider the initial rule of the post–World War II German Constitution, which prohibited dissents, as remains the case in Greece and on the European Court of Justice. In contrast, there is the traditional practice of the House of Lords in England, in which each of the five Law Lords hearing a case would deliver an individual opinion.[20] That was also the original practice of the U.S. Supreme Court. One of John Marshall's signal accomplishments was to replace this custom of *seriatim* opinions whenever possible with a single "Opinion of the Court," though the name of the author was given. Almost all constitutional opinions were written by Marshall himself, and for many years there were no dissents at all. The modern Supreme Court is often sharply divided, with a significant number of 5–4 opinions or even more fragmented decisions in which there is *no* Opinion of the Court but rather a collection of opinions that end up in a particular result as to who wins or loses.

We are obviously used to our own way of doing things, but it is worth asking why some countries or courts have chosen to suppress dissent and issue only impersonal opinions of the court with no attribution of individual authorship. The answer is simple: some people believe that this adds to the perception that "the law" is impersonal and not dependent on the particular identity of the judges who happen to be members of the court. Moreover, dissents (and even concurrences) underscore the view that equally competent judges can disagree, often heatedly and even bitterly, as to the correct legal result. An obvious question is why those who disagree with the result should be particularly respectful of the court if, for example, it appears to be the result of a cleavage in the court that is easily describable in political terms, whether liberals versus conservatives or Democrats versus Republicans. The most (in)famous example of such a cleavage, for many, is the 2000 decision in *Bush v. Gore*, in which a majority consisting of five conservative Republicans shut down the Florida recount and therefore gave the White House to George W. Bush, against the vehement dissent of four justices who could, if you wish, be described as two Democrats and two disgruntled Republicans.

II. CONCLUSION: ON IDENTIFYING COURTS AS "DEMOCRATIC" OR "REPUBLICAN"

A fundamental reality of the Supreme Court, obviously, is that everyone who seriously follows the Court—and many others as well—identifies the judges in terms of their political party backgrounds or ideology. Political scientists refer to the post-1938 Supreme Court as "the Roosevelt Court," by which they also mean that it was a distinctly Democratic Court. Today's Court might be called "the Roberts Court," under the less-than-useful convention of naming courts after their chief justices, but many would identify it simply as a conservative-Republican Court, although there are now four Democrats nipping at the heels of the Republican majority.

In the famous debate between Senator Stephen A. Douglas and Abraham Lincoln, Douglas noted that Lincoln professed his mistrust in the "Democratic" Supreme Court that gave us the *Dred Scott* case. Lincoln said that the proper response to *Dred Scott* was the future appointment of Republican justices committed to the constitutionality of barring slavery in the territories. Douglas then spoke as follows:

> Suppose you get a Supreme Court composed of such judges, who have been appointed by a partisan President upon their giving pledges how they would decide a case before it arise, what confidence would you have in such a court? ["None, none."]…It is a proposition to make that court the corrupt, unscrupulous tool of a political party. But Mr. Lincoln cannot conscientiously submit, he thinks, to the decision of a court composed of a majority of Democrats. If he cannot, how can he expect us to have confidence in a court composed of a majority of Republicans, selected for the purpose of deciding against the Democracy, and in favor of the Republicans? [Cheers.] The very proposition carries with it the demoralization and degradation destructive of the judicial department of the federal government.[21]

Whatever else one thinks of Douglas, who was in effect defending slavery against the anti-slavery Lincoln, his question was a very powerful one. It goes to the heart of what we mean by the notion of government "under" law. What are the consequences for any such notion of the ability of self-interested political officials—or, for that matter, the general electorate—to select the judges who give content to ostensible legal norms? It is thus appropriate to turn specifically to issues raised by the practice of judicial review.

13

On the Judiciary (and Supreme Court) as Guardian of the Constitution

There are many reasons to want courts as part of any political system, and there is no political system that lacks institutions that can be denominated "courts." Even the worst tyrants have found "courts" and "judges" useful as agents of the state. Perhaps they find courts useful as legitimation mechanisms; that is, they think that more of the populace—or perhaps outside observers—will give greater credit to criminal punishments and the like if handed out by people called judges rather than directly ordered by the tyrant. To the extent that this doesn't work, it is precisely because the judges are thought to be insufficiently *independent* of the tyrant.

But even in a tyranny, one might find courts performing a variety of agreed-upon useful functions, such as enforcing ordinary private contracts or handling divorces. Courts arise, anthropologists and political scientists both suggest, initially as an alternative to private revenge or other inefficient methods of "self-help." When *A* and *B* can turn to some ostensibly neutral party *C* to adjudicate the dispute, there is likely to be a greater degree of overall "domestic tranquility" than if *A* and *B* are left to their own devices. This obviously does not mean that all private disputes are settled in legal institutions. No society could operate that way. But, to use a phrase famous among lawyers, much private bargaining takes place "in the shadow of the law." Even if disputes are settled outside of courts, as the overwhelming majority are, it is nonetheless often important that at least one of the parties can convey a meaningful threat to seek formal legal redress and that the consequences of doing so are sufficiently predictable—otherwise, why not simply flip a coin?—to lead to a settlement. In any event, one could find courts in Nazi Germany and Stalin's Soviet Union that, at least some of the time, were functionally providing a more or less neutral third party to resolve disputes. Perhaps a Jewish merchant, assuming any existed in Germany after around 1936, could expect no "justice" from a German court, but a Nazi merchant suing another Nazi merchant had no reason to reject the legitimacy of the decision handed down.

So one thing that courts do is adjudicate disputes between private parties. But they also adjudicate disputes where the two parties involved are the state and private individuals. Most commonly, the state will claim authorization to make its demands on the citizen by reference to legislative statute. This, after all, is the principal function of legislatures—to make laws. And the executive then "enforces" them. But what if the law passed by the legislature is less than self-evident in its meaning, as is usually the case? Does the executive branch get *carte blanche* to interpret statutes however it likes? Generally speaking, the answer is no. The state and the private party turn to a third party for a decision as to how the statute in question is best interpreted. To quote again the preamble to the 1780 Massachusetts Constitution, which is still in operation, "It is the duty of the people, therefore, in framing a constitution of government, to provide for an equitable mode of making laws, as well as for an impartial interpretation, and a faithful execution of them." Why not rely on the executive for "impartial interpretation"? Or should one even rely with confidence on judges who are not only appointed by the executive, but also serve at his pleasure (as was the case with British judges in the American colonies)?[1]

The answer that most people would give, plausibly enough, is that this would lead to inevitable overreaching by the executive. A standard maxim is that we don't allow people to be judges in their own cases. This applies not only to private parties A or B, but also to suits between the state and A. These rather banal points help to explain why no political theorists who accept the legitimacy of the state advise doing without courts. Everyone seems to benefit, at least to some extent. But, obviously, the decision to have courts in the first place does not begin to answer the question about the scope of their power. Are courts good for *some* things or for *every* thing? And to what extent do one's answers depend on a variety of background assumptions relating to the issues examined in the last chapter: how are judges selected; what qualifications must they have; and for how long do they serve? Hovering over all of this remains the question of how much independence we really wish to accord judges. It is clear that one cannot understand governance in America (or many other countries) without paying attention to the role played by judges, so one must inevitably wonder also about the circumstances under which judges contribute to the governability of their societies. Perhaps, at least on occasion, they help instead to explain perceptions of "ungovernability."

As suggested in the last chapter, judicial independence is scarcely a "monolithic" notion.[2] It is possible to distinguish between, on the one hand, *institutional independence*, which relates to the degree to which non-judges—whether presidents, legislators, police chiefs, or large campaign contributors—can directly affect the decisions made by judges and, on the other hand, *individual independence*, which refers to the extent to which any given judge is truly autonomous, unaccountable to any other decision-maker. Even in systems that feature a high degree of institutional independence, there can be many limits on the individual independence of a judge. Every judge of an inferior court knows that his or her decisions can be appealed to a higher court. In the federal system, federal district courts are subordinate to courts of appeals, and courts of appeals must, at least in theory, worry about the Supreme Court. Yet well over 99 percent of all appellate decisions in fact receive no direct oversight from the Supreme Court. This leads many political scientists to wonder exactly how significant the Supreme Court is for most inferior judges if they do not in fact have to worry very much about being reviewed.

What one discovers, however, is that most discussions of judicial power focus on the U.S. Supreme Court or the highest courts in other political systems, inasmuch as a distinguishing feature of all high courts is that no appeal can be taken from their decisions to a yet higher court (or else *that* court would become the new high court). Moreover, most discussion of the Supreme Court—or of analogous high courts in the American states and in other countries—focus on the specific issue of *judicial review*, that is, the authority of a court to invalidate acts of the legislature when, according to the court, such acts violate the Constitution itself.

The U.S. Constitution nowhere explicitly grants the power of judicial review, and there has been a long and ultimately fruitless debate about whether the Supreme Court's exercise of judicial review is legitimate. Two things can be said with some confidence: First, it is quite easy to read the Constitution's text as implicitly authorizing judicial review. Consider Article VI:

> This Constitution, and the Laws of the United States which shall be made in Pursuance thereof; and all Treaties made, or which shall be made, under the Authority of the United States, shall be the supreme Law of the Land; and the Judges in every State shall be bound thereby, any Thing in the Constitution or Laws of any State to the Contrary notwithstanding.

We can infer from this two important lessons. The first is that the Constitution is "the supreme Law of the land," which logically entails it trumps all laws that contradict its terms. The second is that "the Judges in every State" are obligated to enforce the Constitution even in the face of particular terms of the judge's own state constitutions or the laws passed by state legislatures. In case they fail to get the point, they have all taken the oath specified by a later clause of Article VI "to support the Constitution." This obviously refers only to state judges and the supremacy of the national Constitution over conflicting state constitutions or laws, but it is easy enough to suggest that this notion of constitutional supremacy applies to laws passed even by Congress.

But even if there were not such apparent textual authorization, a second thing that can be said with confidence is that, for better or worse, judicial review has become an accepted practice within the United States. There are occasional calls for abolishing judicial review, but these are exercises in futility. Even those persons who are furious at the Supreme Court for one exercise or another of judicial review usually present their criticisms in terms of "judges on a rampage" rather than assert that the moral of the story is to emulate the Dutch by adopting an analogue to Article 120 of the Constitution of the Netherlands stating that "the constitutionality of Acts of Parliament and treaties shall not be reviewed by the courts." New Zealand, which does not have a formal written constitution, nonetheless passed a sweeping Bill of Rights Act in 1990 that also specified that its terms did *not* authorize the judiciary to invalidate laws passed by the New Zealand House of Representatives that contradicted the Bill of Rights Act. Among the questions raised by such examples—and there are others—is whether judicial review is a necessary condition for a country that wishes to call itself a constitutional democracy. The answer seems to be no, unless we wish to exclude the Netherlands and New Zealand from the list of such countries. But even if one might advise another country to do without judicial review, there is no likelihood that the United States will eliminate the practice. So it is worth looking at what is undoubtedly the most famous and influential defense of judicial review, Alexander Hamilton's *Federalist* 78.

I. *FEDERALIST* 78 AND HAMILTON'S DEFENSE OF JUDICIAL REVIEW

A. Complete independence of the judiciary?

Hamilton writes that "the complete independence of the court of justice is peculiarly essential in a limited constitution." By this he means a constitution that in one way or another is designed to *limit* the power of government, and *Federalist* 78 is devoted to defending the importance of the judiciary in maintaining such a constitution.

Still, we have to ask if Hamilton, or anyone else, really supports the *complete independence* of the federal judiciary, including the Supreme Court. Does he endorse, for example, the French Academy model of self-perpetuation, which maximizes *institutional autonomy*? He does not. It is interesting to note, though, how quickly he passes over the first of his three concerns at the outset of the essay, "the mode of appointing the judges." He believes that it is sufficient to say that "this is the same with that of appointing the officers of the union in general," and he declares that it would be "useless" to repeat the arguments he has offered in *Federalist*s 76–77 defending presidential selection of such officers. But there he was discussing the process by which presidents would pick their cabinets and staff the executive branch, and one can easily believe that it is altogether proper for politics to dominate those decisions. It is banal to say that the president wants executives who share his or her view of sound public policy, not to mention executives whose appointments might curry favor with key political constituencies and voting blocs. Do we have a similar view with regard to judicial appointments?

One might say that Hamilton, like Madison, was writing in a pre-party world, so that he envisioned a wise and virtuous president standing "above politics" making appointments, which a similarly disinterested group of senators would then confirm. But we obviously do not occupy that world, though one might suggest that neither did Hamilton as a practical matter. One can be certain that he enthusiastically supported the appointments of the Federalist "midnight judges" in the waning days of the Adams Administration; their role would be to stymie, as much as possible, the Jeffersonian program. Turning to more contemporary times, is one disturbed or gratified to discover that since 1956—when President Eisenhower appointed William J. Brennan because he was looking for a northeastern Catholic to shore up his re-election—there has been a perfect correlation between the political commitments of an appointing president and the basic ideological commitments of those appointed to the Supreme Court?

Nor are the data strikingly different if one looks at appointments to inferior courts.

As of 2011, there is congressional authorization for 179 federal circuit judges and 678 federal district court judges (and, of course, 9 Supreme Court justices).[3] When Barack Obama took office in January 2009, most judges were Republican, reflecting the Republican domination of the presidency since 1980 (save for the eight years of the Clinton Administration). The Supreme Court, for example, contained seven Republicans and two Democrats. Republicans Stevens and Souter (admittedly perhaps not in synch with the contemporary Republican Party) have left the Court, replaced by Democrats Sonia Sotomayor and Elena Kagan.

At the level of intermediate courts of appeal, 56 percent of all circuit judges were Republican and 36 percent were Democrats (with an 8 percent vacancy rate).[4] There were dramatic differences among the thirteen intermediate appellate courts within the federal judiciary. Thus the Ninth Circuit, which comprises California and other West Coast states (plus Arizona) had a 16–11 Democratic majority (with two vacancies), while the Eighth Circuit, which includes most of the upper Midwestern states, had a 9–2 Republican majority, and the Fifth Circuit (Texas, Louisiana, and Mississippi) had a 13–4 Republican majority. (Neither had any vacancies.) As of April, 2011, President Obama had successfully appointed (i.e., received Senate confirmation for) eighteen appellate judges, though seventeen vacancies remained.[5] Four of those appointees were to the Fourth Circuit (Maryland, Virginia, West Virginia, North Carolina, and South Carolina), which created a new Democratic majority. Similarly, the appointment of three new judges to the Second Circuit (New York, Connecticut, and Vermont) also affected a shift in party domination. However, the extraordinarily important District of Columbia Circuit, which handles a disproportionate number of administrative law and "war-on-terrorism" cases, had a 6–3 Republican majority with two vacancies, neither of them filled by President Obama two full years into his term.

At the beginning of the Obama Administration, 371 federal district judges had been appointed by Republican presidents and 264 by Democrats, with 41 vacancies. Because of deals made with Democratic senators, it was altogether likely that at least some Republican appointees were Democrats or that some of Clinton's fifty-five appointees were Republicans, even if one can be confident that appointees will generally be from the president's party. President Obama has made fifty-nine successful nominations to the district bench, but there are sixty-six vacancies as of January 2012. In recent years, as the importance of inferior federal courts has increasingly been recognized, confirmations have become more difficult, with both parties engaging in filibusters or other delay tactics regarding nominees who are viewed as too conservative or liberal for their tastes.

Hamilton also writes about the importance of the "good behavior" standard as a guarantor of judicial independence, but that topic was addressed in the last chapter. It is important to note that part of his argument involves a relatively modest view of the judiciary. It is, he tells us, "the least dangerous" of the branches of the national government, with regard to threatening popular liberty, because it possesses neither the power of the purse—it cannot levy taxes—nor of the sword. "It may truly be said to have neither FORCE nor WILL, but merely judgment: and must ultimately depend upon the aid of the executive arm even for the efficacy of its judgments."

B. Does judicial review entail judicial supremacy?

So let's take a deeper look at what Hamilton has just said. It's undoubtedly true that the judiciary does not possess its own police force. It does indeed depend on the decisions of other branches, whether in the national government or in the states, to *comply* with its judgments. What brings about this compliance?

Consider a key paragraph from what is probably the most famous veto message in our history, Andrew Jackson's July 10, 1832 announcement that he was vetoing the decision of the Whig Congress to renew the charter of the Bank of the United States. We need not review the fascinating history of the Bank. It is enough to know the following: George Washington signed the initial charter over the protests of James Madison, Thomas Jefferson, Edmund Randolph, and others that Congress was acting beyond its powers. The charter expired in 1811, during Madison's first term as President. Madison, however, signed an 1816 bill chartering the Second Bank of the United States, saying *not* that he was wrong in his initial arguments against the Bank in 1791 but that the country had clearly accepted its legitimacy and he therefore would no longer enforce his previous views. From one perspective, one can view this as an argument that the Constitution had in effect been *amended* by practice instead of by the passage of a formal Article V amendment, which Madison would have thought necessary in 1791.

The second charter was due to expire in 1836, but the Whigs mistakenly believed they had a winning issue and forced the renewal four years early, just before the 1832 election. Among the arrows in their quiver was the fact that the Supreme Court, in the 1819 decision *McCulloch v. Maryland*, unanimously held that Congress did indeed have the power to charter the Bank. This did not stop Jackson, who defended his veto on the grounds that not only was the Bank bad public policy but it was also—just as significantly—unconstitutional. But what about *McCulloch*? Jackson responded as follows:

> If the opinion of the Supreme Court covered the whole ground of this act, it
> [still] ought not to control the coordinate authorities of this Government. The
> Congress, the Executive, and the Court must each for itself be guided by its own
> opinion of the Constitution. Each public officer who takes an oath to support

the Constitution swears that he will support it as he understands it, and not as it is understood by others. It is as much the duty of the House of Representatives, of the Senate, and of the President to decide upon the constitutionality of any bill or resolution which may be presented to them for passage or approval as it is of the supreme judges when it may be brought before them for judicial decision. The opinion of the judges has no more authority over Congress than the opinion of Congress has over the judges, and on that point the President is independent of both. *The authority of the Supreme Court must not, therefore, be permitted to control the Congress or the Executive when acting in their legislative capacities, but to have only such influence as the force of their reasoning may deserve.*[6] (emphasis added)

So now we see the central issue. Does the Supreme Court serve as the *definitive* interpreter of the Constitution, so that the discussions attached to the Constitution of Conversation simply come to an end once the Supreme Court speaks? Or, on the contrary, is the Supreme Court simply one conversational partner among many, with its particular opinions "hav[ing] only such influence as the force of their reasoning may deserve"?

This issue was at the center of the legendary debates between Senator Stephen A. Douglas and Abraham Lincoln during their heated struggle for the designation as Illinois's senator in Washington in 1858. For Douglas,

the right and the province of expounding the Constitution, and construing the law, is vested in the judiciary established by the Constitution...When the decision is made, my private opinion, your opinion, all other opinions must yield to the majesty of that authoritative adjudication...What security have you for your property, for your reputation, and for your personal rights, if the courts are not upheld, and their decisions respected when once firmly rendered by the highest tribunal known to the Constitution?...I respect the decisions of that august tribunal; I shall always bow in deference to them.[7]

He was suggesting that Lincoln had insufficient respect for the Court. How would Lincoln respond?

The answer was given the next day.

I have expressed heretofore, and I now repeat, my opposition to the *Dred Scott* decision, but I should be allowed to state the nature of that opposition...What

is fairly implied by the term Judge Douglas has used "resistance to the decision"? I do not resist it. If I wanted to take Dred Scott from his master, I would
be interfering with property...But I am doing no such thing as that, but all that
I am doing is refusing to obey it as a political rule. If I were in Congress, and
a vote should come up on a question whether slavery should be prohibited in
a new territory, in spite of that *Dred Scott* decision, I would vote that it should.
[Applause; "good for you"; "we hope to see it"; "that's right."]

    We will try to reverse that decision...Somebody has to reverse that decision,
since it is made, and we mean to reverse it, and we mean to do it peaceably.[8]

My first book, *Constitutional Faith*, set out a rather elaborate analogy between our constitutional "civil religion" and the various cleavages
we see in our more traditional religions, especially Christianity. Just as
Christianity can be divided, broadly speaking, into its "Catholic" and
"Protestant" components, so can constitutional interpreters. The divisions lie along two quite different dimensions. Thus, Catholicism is distinguished first by its supplementing an emphasis on the Gospel with at
least as great an emphasis on the traditions and teachings of the Church,
and secondly by its possessing a clear institutional hierarchy with the
Pope at the top, claiming (at least since 1870) the attribute of infallibil-
ity in matters of faith and morals when speaking *ex cathedra*. Dissenting
Protestants are notable for emphasizing the importance of scripture
alone—*sola scriptura*, in the words of Martin Luther—and, just as importantly, rejecting *any* institutional hierarchy. Another phrase associated
with the Reformation is the "priesthood of all believers." So translate this
into the terms of American constitutionalism. Along the first dimension we can distinguish between those who emphasize the *text* of the
Constitution and those who give at least equal priority to the traditions,
which include cases handed down by courts and even seminal speeches
such as the Gettysburg Address. Along the second dimension, we can
distinguish between those who emphasize the supremacy of the Supreme
Court with regard to what the Constitution means and those who view
the Court as simply one participant in a community in which *all* citizens
can proclaim their status as "constitutional lawyers" in a non-trivial sense.
One does not need to be a lawyer to have informed and creditable views
about constitutional meaning.

Akhil Amar emphasizes the relevance to such discussions of the jury trial provisions in the Constitution. It is not simply that juries are an important way for ordinary citizens to participate in testing the state's allegations as to *facts*, so that no one is punished for doing something that he or she did not do. In addition, Amar argues, juries in the late eighteenth century had the freedom to come to their own decisions about the very laws under which people were being tried. They could say that someone did indeed do X and that X was "against the law," but that it was "unconstitutional" to criminalize X (say, criticizing the president) even if Congress had passed such a law and even if the judge presiding over the trial informed the jury that the law was perfectly acceptable and that it was ultimately up to the judges to decide questions of law. It should be clear that anyone accepting the propriety of what its opponents call "jury nullification" is very much a "protestant" along the second dimension. More to the point, it is equally obvious that Jackson and Lincoln were also protestants, at least so far as judicial supremacy was concerned. Neither rejected *constitutional supremacy*; rather, they rejected the proposition that the Constitution necessarily meant whatever the Court, even if unanimous (as was the case in *McCulloch*), said it did.

What of Hamilton? He writes that "interpretation of the laws is the proper *and peculiar* province of the courts" (emphasis added). Nobody denies that it is proper for courts to interpret the law. But does "peculiar," in this context, mean that *only* courts can interpret the laws—which makes little sense—or that courts necessarily prevail should there be a difference of opinion between them and other interpreters?

This book is structured around the difference between the Constitution of Settlement and the Constitution of Conversation. One can easily believe that judicial review inevitably relates almost exclusively to the latter. But one can still ask which of these "two Constitutions" is relevant to determining the ability of the Court to bring conversations to an end by asserting its own authority to say what the law is.

Readers should be aware that the Supreme Court itself, especially over the last half century, has articulated a highly "catholic" notion of its own supremacy as the "ultimate interpreter" of the Constitution, in a number of opinions written by both liberal and conservative justices. This is precisely what has led some scholars to credit the anti-Federalist "Brutus" with some degree of prescience in describing the Court created by the Constitution as "invested with such immense powers, and yet placed in a situation so little responsible"—that is, *accountable* to the other branches—that there is reason to fear what we might today call a "runaway" judiciary. Recall from the previous chapter the stinging criticisms—and fears—expressed by "Brutus," which concluded that the Supreme Court as structured by the new Constitution would be "independent of the people, of the legislature, and of every power under heaven."[9] Needless to say, his full critique applies only to the Supreme Court, and political scientists and lawyers point to the various ways that Congress and the president might respond to a Court matching Brutus's worst fears. Still, a pervasive reality of American politics over the past half century is the charge that the Supreme Court—and the federal judiciary more generally—has made its own contribution to the perception of a political system that is, in important ways, increasingly beyond the control of electorates and their representatives and is instead in the hands of the judiciary. As one would expect, the sharpest anguish is felt by those who disagree with the decisions issued by the courts.

The most important decision in generating such accusations is surely *Roe v. Wade*, the Court's 1973 decision striking down the abortion laws of all fifty states insofar as they unduly limited a woman's right of reproductive choice. Although later decisions modified *Roe* in important respects, the basic right remains on the books and continues to structure much American political conversation (and animosity). It is not my aim in this book to offer any evaluation of *Roe* and successor cases. Presumably both proponents and opponents of the decision—whether they define themselves as "pro-choice" or "pro-life"—can easily agree that the Court has *not* brought that conversation to an end. Justices Souter, Kennedy, and O'Connor famously wrote, in a 1992 opinion justifying the refusal to overrule *Roe*, that "the Court's interpretation of the Constitution calls the contending sides of a national controversy to end their national division by accepting a common mandate rooted in the [the Court's interpretation of the] Constitution."[10] But, as with Lincoln's rejection of the Court's authority to end the conversation about the legitimacy of slavery in its *Dred Scott* decision, opponents of *Roe* are uninterested in ending our "national division" until they prevail. The debate over slavery triggered the ultimate in ungovernability: civil war. Though no one suggests that is a possibility with regard to the "abortion wars," it reminds us of the limits on any and all courts when faced with fundamental cleavages in which any compromise appears "rotten" rather than "prudent."

C. The scope of judicial review

Let it be agreed, though, that the other branches have no authority to violate the Constitution and that all judges, both state and federal, are authorized to enforce the supreme commands of the Constitution when public officials transgress them. "No legislative act...contrary to the constitution can be valid." Hamilton states. "To deny this would be to affirm that the deputy is greater than his principal; that the servant is above his master; that the representatives of the people are above the people themselves." That is, "We the People" have ordained *this* constitution, which is a limited one; it is a given that those we elect as our representatives have only the same powers *we* have; and we have agreed to limit our own collective power at least in the absence of formal amendment under Article V. To allow representatives to judge the scope of their own power would be to allow "the most dangerous branch" to make self-serving decisions. The only feasible alternative, asserts Hamilton, is judicial review and reliance on the judiciary to keep the legislature (even if supported by the president) in check.

This leaves open the question as to the *clarity* of the Constitution. After all, one basis for distinguishing between the Constitution of Settlement and the Constitution of Conversation is that certain clauses of the Constitution speak so clearly that good-faith conversation about meaning—though not about wisdom—appears impossible. This is altogether different from the situation presented when we readily concede the availability of even two reasonable views as to what the Constitution means.

Consider Hamilton's own examples of a Congress that passes bills of attainder or ex post facto laws in violation of the clear prohibition of Article I, Section 9. Bills of attainder are legislative pronouncements of the guilt of persons; in addition, Parliament had often "tainted" the bloodline of the ostensibly guilty party by prohibiting his descendants from enjoying certain rights or owning property. Ex post facto laws declare criminal what one did in the past, at a time when the behavior was legal. It is one thing for the state to say that you can't smoke after January 1, 2014. It's another to say that you committed a criminal offense by smoking on January 1, 2009, even though there was no law then prohibiting smoking. Most lawyers would say that the meanings of the two clauses are relatively clear. They are, in that sense, far closer to the Inauguration Day Clause, unequivocally part of the Constitution of Settlement, than to the Equal Protection Clause, which is just as unequivocally part of the Constitution of Conversation.

The "problem," though, is that Congress has rarely attempted to violate those parts of the Constitution that come under the Constitution of Settlement, though there are several significant cases that invalidate congressional actions as violations of the Bill of Attainder Clause. Still, the controversy about judicial review concerns not the enforcement of those provisions but rather who is entitled to give authoritative pronouncements concerning what is undoubtedly within the Constitution of Conversation.

Hamilton is concerned that the judiciary be available to "guard…the rights of individuals from the effects of those ill humours which the arts of designing men…sometimes dissemble among the people themselves," including the "oppression of the minor party in the community." The judiciary, he suggests, will consist of "virtuous and disinterested" judges, whose "moderate" opinions presumably enforcing the Constitution against those who would ignore it would gain the applause of similarly "virtuous and disinterested" citizens. Once more we see significant reservations expressed about the actual operations of representative government and the professed need for further methods of reining it in. Nothing could be more dangerous, Hamilton suggests, than judges who might be concerned with "popularity"; it is precisely to prevent such concerns that he so applauds life tenure. So why does the role of the American Supreme Court continue to generate such controversy and, on occasion, elicit criticism even from those who might be described as "virtuous and disinterested"?

Part of the answer comes from the fact that sharply different examples can be offered of the "minor party in the community" that has reason to fear what later generations learned to call "tyranny of the majority." Today we are most inclined to think of racial or religious minorities, though many readers would properly add those whose sexual orientation differs from the heterosexual majority. Gender could also be added, though one difficulty is that one has to adopt a special definition of "minority," inasmuch as women constitute a majority of the population. One would focus on the fact that until relatively recently, men could be said to exercise hegemonic power and that even today men occupy positions of power far in excess of their percentage of the population. If this were a different book, we could profitably explore at great length the extent to which the Supreme Court, over the past 220 years, has in fact been receptive to the claims of these groups regarding alleged denial of constitutional rights. Among other things, one would have to explain why one would expect judges nominated by presidents and confirmed by the Senate to hold significantly different views from those two bodies with regard to protecting what are by definition unpopular minorities. In fact, we only sporadically find the Supreme Court willing to reach out and protect genuinely unpopular minorities. As Lucas Powe and Barry Friedman have argued in recent overviews of its history,[11] the Court has served, generally speaking, either as the relatively faithful agent of the political coalition able to establish a measure of hegemony over the national political order (Powe) or as a reasonably accurate mirror of the so-called median voter within the national electorate (Friedman). Neither presents a picture of a Court that will be likely to reach out to protect beleaguered minorities.

Hamilton, however, was not defining "minority rights" the way we may be inclined to today. For him, the central "minority" comprised property owners and persons of means. Recall Madison's expression, in *Federalist* 10, that property is the most pervasive dividing force in any given society. One of the things we can be confident of is that there will *always* be more (relative) "have-nots" than "haves" in any given social order. This means that as a political system develops ever greater sensitivity to the political preferences of majorities, perhaps by extending the franchise or by shifting the selection of senators from state legislators to popular majorities within the states, there will be ever more inclination to pass laws that redistribute property from the well-off to the less well-off. This is obviously one of the ways of understanding the great debates provoked by the Obama presidency and the Democratic Congress of 2009–2010. Whether or not the President's proposals were "socialistic," they were certainly "redistributive" in a variety of ways, but this is no different from much other legislation since the triumph of the New Deal in the 1930s.

The Constitution clearly includes protection of property among its delineated rights. The most specific protection is found in the Fifth Amendment, which states not only that no one shall be "deprived of life, liberty, or property, without due process of law," but also that "private property be taken [only] for public use [and with] just compensation." The original Constitution, in Article I, Section 10, states that no state shall pass any law "impair[ing] the obligation of contracts," which means that states can't emulate Rhode Island and pass debtor relief laws that stipulate, for example, that a contract in which the debtor agreed to pay 6 percent interest is now reduced to 4 percent or that a sum of money due on January 1, 1788, would now not be due until two years later.

As a matter of fact, the Contracts Clause was the most heavily litigated clause throughout the nineteenth century, given recurrent political pressures to aid deserving debtors by rewriting existing contracts. That might well be the case even now if the Supreme Court had not decided in a 1934 decision (by a 5–4 vote) that "reasonable" impairments were acceptable and that the legislature was the best judge of when they were in fact reasonable. It would take us far afield to examine what the Court has been willing to deem "reasonable." The major point is that the apparently unequivocal language of the Constitution, which contains no modifier and invites the question "what part of 'no law' do you not understand?" was modified by the Court. What *is* relevant to this book is that the 1934 case arose during the Great Depression and challenged a so-called moratorium on mortgages imposed by the Minnesota legislature to prevent further public disorder generated by banks foreclosing on homes. In some states, aroused farmers had threatened judges enforcing foreclosures with lynchings. Chapter 16, on emergency powers, discusses this case further.

So, inevitably, the greatest questions about judicial review concern controversial issues within the United States at a given time. It is just as inevitable that skillful lawyers will be found on both sides of any controversy (assuming there are only two sides). And it is also inevitable that the many of these controversies will involve basic (and conflicting) visions of what Justice Robert Jackson called the "majestic generalities" of the Constitution,[12] including the aspirational goals enunciated by the

Preamble. And the final inevitability is that judges themselves will have been selected on the basis of what particular vision of high politics they are likely to possess.

D. An excursus into explaining why courts are special

Consider what precisely is thought to make courts "special," as well as the ramifications of any particular answer for *designing* judicial systems within given constitutional orders. As we have already seen, there are dramatic variations in such design among the American states and foreign countries. So how might we assess these various systems? Surely the answer would depend on what we think constitutes the special attributes of judges.

1. Judges as "experts" (or "legal scientists")

One response is that judges are special because they have distinct expertise in discerning what the law "really" means or requires. Whether or not law is the equivalent of "rocket science" (it is not), it is a highly technical domain that requires specialized education and a high level of competence in discerning and applying what "legal science" requires. Among other things, this view amply justifies according a monopoly to lawyers with regard to becoming judges, just as we would easily assign a monopoly to rocket scientists in designing trajectories for astronauts to reach the moon.

Formal legal education is highly relevant to performing well as a lawyer or judge. However, it is less than clear whether "legal science" offers a satisfying explanation of the power we grant to judges on the *highest* courts of state or national judiciaries. At the very least, one is forced to confront the fact that members of the U.S. Supreme Court, for example, often disagree with one another, sometimes in very harsh language. It is difficult to adhere to the "rocket science" conception of judging in the face of repeated 5–4 decisions, unless one possess the happily self-serving belief that the judges one agrees with are simply more competent than the judges one disagrees with.

Few serious students of the judiciary adopt the "legal science" view. There is general agreement that judges bring with them to the bench ideological presuppositions that are reflected in the decisions they make and the opinions they write. Yale law professor Jack Balkin and I have described such presuppositions as constituting the "high politics" of judges, in contrast to a "low politics" that might focus simply on whether one's favorite political party or candidate prevails in a given lawsuit. Though the latter can surely be found among some judges—even a decade after the Supreme Court's decision in the 2000 case of *Bush v. Gore*, many analysts are inclined to describe it simply as a decision in which five conservative Republican justices decided to make sure that their personal favorite, George W. Bush, would become the forty-third president of the United States—such episodes are relatively rare at the highest level of the judiciary. Drawing on "high politics," however, is not only not rare, it is also difficult to imagine how one can even participate in the Constitution of Conversation without drawing on deep ideological pre-commitments that necessarily implicate one's definition of a "majestic generality" like "equal protection of the law." During a program honoring former justice Lewis Powell, Chief Justice William Rehnquist noted that "a judge's background might have as much to do with the way he went about deciding a case as would his legal education."[13] Rehnquist echoed what then Harvard law professor, later Justice, Felix Frankfurter wrote in a 1930 essay on the Supreme Court. Commenting on the admonition by many that judges should not "read their economic and social views into the neutral language of the constitution," Frankfurter observed that "the process of constitutional interpretation compels the translations of policy into judgment," and what generates these judgments are the judges' "'idealized political pictures' of the existing social order."[14] These "pictures"—which function as ideological templates used to organize complex realities—constitute the "high politics" that all judges necessarily bring with them to the consideration of any significant constitutional dispute. Any justification of judicial independence and power must confront such realities and offer justifications that do not depend on the analogy between "legal" and "rocket" science.

2. Judges as possessors of wisdom

The picture of the judge as "legal scientist" depends on specialized *expertise*. But one could defend a special role on the basis that they are simply likely to be *wiser* with regard to resolving the complex social and political issues that come before them. Many of the eighteenth-century debates are rife with skepticism about the capacities for such wise judgment among ordinary people, including, for that matter, those likely to be elected to office. So might it not be better to have the equivalent of wise "Platonic guardians" to make important judgments in circumstances where we would doubt the capacities of elected leaders?

The most obvious problem with this rationale is simply that there is no reason to believe that judges, whether appointed or elected, as a group possess superior wisdom with regard to the issues of public policy that come before them. One can easily agree with Justice Oliver Wendell Holmes, one of the chief critics of "legal science," who famously proclaimed that "the life of the law is not logic, but experience," but still question whether judges necessarily have the kinds of experiences that bring wisdom in their wake. Or, at the very least, one might want to make sure that there is adequate *diversity* of experiences on any given court to which we would extend our own confidence regarding the wisdom of their judgments.

3. Judges as liberated from "political" constraints

There is one other possible justification for treating judges as special. Most high-ranking public officials are politically accountable, often concerned with facing the electorate in relatively short order. Again, one of the recurrent themes of the debates during the founding era was the potential danger of having leaders with insufficient virtue to prefer the public good over the particular demands of constituents susceptible either to the passions of the moment or by the general propensity to prefer their own selfish interests over the public interest. Federal judges, on the other hand, because of their presumptively lifetime tenure, are liberated from any such considerations and therefore can be trusted to decide in the public interest.

One should not confuse this last justification with the second one, which emphasized the wisdom of the judiciary. Wisdom is a cognitive capacity, whereas the disposition to decide in the public interest is a matter of *character*. But Madison and other Framers accurately recognized that character could be effectively molded by given institutional designs that would generate all-important incentives to follow one set of judgments

rather than another. Life tenure and the liberation from political accountability would remove certain incentives that lead ordinary leaders to betray
the public good. There is certainly a plausibility to such arguments, though
one should note two consequences. The first is that it casts a certain pall
over *all* politics precisely inasmuch as it causes one to fear that any and
all politically accountable leaders will, at the end of the day, be exposed
as panderers to private interests rather than adherents of the public good.
The second is that it calls into question the practices in most states of
making judges politically accountable through various election scheme.
In any event, it should be clear that one's view of how best to organize the
judiciary—and therefore to pick with confidence among the many different models available within the United States—is a function of how one
imagines the defining strengths and weaknesses of judges as a group.

E. Access to the judiciary

But let's assume that courts do (and *should*) play a special role in enforcing
constitutional norms, for whatever reason. Then, an important question is
how easy it is for ordinary people, including people possessing unpopular
political views, to actually gain access to courts. People with popular views
may not really need judicial access; they can depend on legislatures to be
sympathetic, though it is still necessary to gain access to enforce legislation. But, with regard to judicial review, what we are really talking about is
the ability to mount an *attack* on popular legislation or executive actions.

Again, it is instructive to realize that there are many answers to this
question as we look at courts around the world or in the United States.
Apparently one can initiate a case in the Indian Supreme Court by sending in a postcard outlining one's complaint.[15] The Israeli Supreme Court
is also notable for granting almost everyone what lawyers call "standing"
to raise legal complaints against the state. The Israeli judges have declared
that "closing this Court's doors before [any] petitioner...who sounds the
alarm concerning an unlawful government action, does damage to the
rule of law. Access to the courts is the cornerstone of the rule of law."[16]
In an article contrasting the United States and Israeli high courts, Professor

Kaufmann notes, the U.S. Supreme Court has adopted ever more restrictive "standing" restrictions with regard to those who would challenge American conduct during the now decade-long military and clandestine response to those suspected of terrorism. Moreover, because the Supreme Court can establish standing rules for the entire federal judiciary, it can in effect limit access, not only to itself, but also to any of the federal courts. That has been the ramification of several decisions over the past two decades, in which conservative justices have tried to cut back the greatly enhanced standing established during the far more liberal "Warren Court" era of the 1960s. Standing limitations, which are often regarded as "technical" and thus rarely receive extensive press coverage, are often especially important with regard to such substantive areas as environmental litigation and to claims that the state is violating the Religious Establishment Clause of the First Amendment.

In addition, the Supreme Court has almost complete authority to decide which among the six thousand or so petitions for review it receives each year it will actually grant. It hears extremely few cases each year; the current number is around seventy-five. This refusal to take many seemingly important cases, among other things, puts the lie to the model of the Court as in fact providing answers to vital legal questions. It frequently adopts what the late Alexander Bickel famously labeled the "passive virtues" to refrain from engaging with political hot potatoes that might prove damaging to the Court's own institutional interests.[7]

Finally, there is the question of the *timing* of access. Many courts worldwide—and about eight within the United States, including the Massachusetts supreme court—will issue so-called advisory opinions concerning proposals currently before a legislature. Usually legislators themselves petition the court for a declaration as to the constitutionality or unconstitutionality of the legislation in question. Federal courts within the United States will not accept such petitions. Instead, those who object to legislation are forced to pay often significant costs to challenge it, which itself may lead to the "under-enforcement" of constitutional norms. And even if one could predict that a court would strike down one's conviction for violating a given federal law, one would still have to be willing to bear the cost of a criminal trial and to pay the legal costs involved in defending oneself.

II. A LAST COMMENT ABOUT JUDICIAL "VOICE"

The last chapter concluded with a brief discussion of whether courts will (or should) speak with a single voice or with multiple voices. But one can also ask about the *strength* of that voice. The governing rule in all multimember federal courts, including the Supreme Court, is "majority rule." That's why 5–4 decisions are often so dramatic. But consider that North Dakota requires four out of five justices to agree before they can apply the North Dakota state constitution against a legislative statute, and Nebraska requires five out of seven. One might regard it is as odd that a majority of justices would agree that a given statute is unconstitutional, but it would be of no effect because they comprise *only* a majority and not the requisite supermajority.

No doubt this seems extraordinarily odd, perhaps because only two small, relatively ignored, states have chosen this supermajoritarian option. Perhaps we might be less dismissive had Ohio retained at least some version of a clause adopted as part of the new 1912 state constitution drafted during the Progressive Era.[18] The convention rejected an appeal by former president Theodore Roosevelt to allow the overruling by popular referenda of unpopular judicial decisions. But a judge, interestingly enough, "introduced a proposal that would have required an unanimous vote of supreme court justices to declare an act unconstitutional." This proposal was triggered in part by the fact that the Ohio supreme court "had a reputation of striking down legislation that protected workers' rights." A compromise, proposed by the convention and approved by the electorate, "required the concurrence of all but one supreme court justice to reverse an appellate court judgment upholding a law as constitutional. However, if the appellate court found the law unconstitutional," a majority of supreme court justices could uphold *that* decision. This might have been designed by the cartoonist Rube Goldberg, famous for his fanciful inventions, inasmuch as it created the possibility (and reality) that the very "same law could survive a constitutional challenge in one case and be found unconstitutional on another by the same court voting the same way," depending on what the court below had ruled. It can come as no surprise that Ohio ultimately changed its constitution and reverted to ordinary majority rule.

The Ohio procedure might be thought to be bizarre rather than simply odd, but it, like those of North Dakota and Nebraska, forces us to wonder if they are any less defensible than the other anti-majoritarian features in the U.S. Constitution we have seen so far in this book. These include not only the two-thirds rules regarding overriding presidential vetoes, convictions for impeachment, or ratifying treaties, but also the anti-majoritarian aspects of the American form of bicameralism, given the allocation of power in the Senate or the ability of the electoral college to generate minority presidents. Recall as well that the original size of the Supreme Court in 1789—six—meant that two-thirds of the judges would have to agree on an outcome in order to prevent a tie vote. At the very least, one might believe that deviations from the principle of majority rule require some special justification that adoption of majoritarianism does not, at least in a society that professes to be democratic (instead of republican). Some of these deviations may be easily defensible; others, as I have argued in earlier chapters and in my earlier book *Our Undemocratic Constitution*, are not. The central question is what presuppositions underlie either conclusion, and North Dakota and Nebraska provide good test cases for understanding our own idealized political pictures and their implications for assessing any given structure of judicial power.

One of these pictures, idealized or not, involves federalism and the opportunity a federal structure provides for quite different solutions to a given issue. Much of this book has been devoted to setting out the sometimes dramatic differences between the national government and particular states with regard to some quite basic issues of government and, possibly, the prospects for governability when faced with special challenges. Thus we now turn to some of the specific issues raised by federalism.

14

Federalism

I. WHAT *IS* FEDERALISM?

According to a recent book by Jenna Bednar,[1] between 1990 and 2000 there were roughly twenty-five countries that could be described as "federal," of which she labeled seventeen "democratic federations" and nine "authoritarian federations." Those numbers add up to twenty-six, because she places Mexico in both groups. These countries range, alphabetically, from Argentina and Australia to Yugoslavia, which became a federation consisting of Serbia and Montenegro in 2000. In fact, Montenegro declared its independence in 2006, so that presumably reduces the number of federal countries by one. It also illustrates a problem—secession—which will be the focus at the end of this chapter. For a variety of reasons, federal systems may be prone to secessionist impulses, and an obvious question is what, if anything, a constitution (including our own) says or should say about such tendencies (and whether what a constitution says is actually relevant in controlling any such impulses).

We should begin, though, with a basic question: how should we *define* federalism? A very interesting book, *Designing Federalism*, begins by acknowledging that there is no truly canonical definition of the term accepted by political theorists or social scientists engaged in more empirical analysis. "Federalism," the authors write, "is not a concept amenable to an unambiguous descriptive definition."[2] One might believe that that is true of many of the terms that arise in constitutional discourse, including the notions of a "republican form of government" or "representative democracy." We might well believe that, because of all the ambiguities attached to the term, "federalism" will naturally become part of the Constitution of Conversation rather than serve as the kind of fixed point linked with the Constitution of Settlement. Whatever definitions we adopt, however, will necessarily be pragmatic; one important criterion will be their utility in covering enough countries that we're prone to recognize as "federal." Bednar supplies a three-part test.

A. Geopolitical division

A distinctively federal "territory is divided into mutually exclusive states (or provinces, *lander*, etc.)," the existence of which are "constitutionally recognized and may not be unilaterally abolished" (unlike the boundaries of counties or school districts within states). One could imagine non-territorial forms of federalism, in which the state is divided not into distinct geographical units but rather ethnic or religious groups whose members share certain important political rights to communal self-governance even if they happen to live across the country. This might have captured an important reality of the "millet" system in the Ottoman Empire, where Jews, for example, were given a degree of autonomy by their Islamic rulers. Modern Israel, inasmuch as it delegates control over family law to religious institutions, including Islamic ones, may be said to be following this practice.[3] The possession of strong rights to at least some form of self-governance would distinguish this kind of "non-geographic federalism" from nationwide systems of proportional representation that allow geographically dispersed groups to coalesce around given candidates for national office strongly committed to pursuing their specific interests. Still, all systems accorded the status of *federal* are indeed geographically divided.

B. Independence

"The state and national governments have independent bases of authority," according to Bednar.[4] Another recent book defines federalism as "a grant of partial autonomy to geographical subunits of a nation."[5] Though these two recent books offer sharply different evaluations of federalism, both agree that federalism requires that the subnational geopolitical units have real control over some matters of genuine importance, whether one's favorite word is "independence" or "autonomy." As Bednar puts it, "Each level of government is sovereign in at least one policy realm."[6] Subnational units, in particular, must have the ability to perform at least some essential functions of governance without being overruled by institutions of the national government that disapprove of their choices.

C. Direct governance

Bednar labels as "direct governance" the ability of each of the levels of government, both national and subnational, to make legal demands on the individuals comprising the federal union (or, for that matter, even non-citizens). Thus, anyone in the United States is subject to at least two governments and must obey the laws of both. Most obviously and importantly, one almost certainly pays taxes to both, as, for example, when one purchases gasoline. To be sure, if a state passes laws that contradict the U.S. Constitution, such laws are subject to invalidation. But that is simply to say that the states are not fully independent, autonomous, or sovereign. It does not establish that states must submit to national institutions on all issues across the board.

Moreover, at least in the United States, the "direct governance" at the subnational level is provided by officials who are electorally accountable to the state's citizens. Filippov et al. make this a defining criterion.[7] Indeed, many state officials, such as judges and heads of departments within the executive branch, are far *more* electorally accountable than are national officials. Some readers may note (or protest) that they are effectively subject to at least *three* levels of government, if one adds local governments to the mix. Thus, for example, we often pay both state and local sales taxes on the same transaction. But such local governments, at least in the United States, do not partake of what might be called "constitutional status." In the United States, cities are, legally speaking, entirely creatures of the state governments.[8] The one exception, Washington, D.C., continues, in important ways, to be under the thumb of Congress even after having been granted a degree of "home rule" by Congress. Thus, part of the last-minute deal President Obama made with congressional Republicans in 2010 to keep the national government functioning involved Congress's overriding the District of Columbia's ability to spend its own funds aiding poor women who wish to exercise their constitutionally guaranteed right to receive abortions. (It is absolutely clear that Congress could not prevent a state from choosing to spend its own funds in such a manner.) Cities in general may certainly possess the attributes of geographical division and even direct governance, but they generally lack the vital characteristic of constitutionally guaranteed autonomy, save for those states whose constitutions provide for some degree of "home rule."[9] This is also true, incidentally, of the over five hundred recognized American Indian tribes, which enjoy such autonomy as they have at the sufferance of Congress.

It is essential, after defining basic criteria of federalism, to realize what does *not* fall under that heading. Federalism is in no way synonymous with decentralization or the political principal of subsidiarity, which is the commitment to locate political decisionmaking at the level that makes the most sense in any given situation, which may often be local.[10] It is worth emphasizing, incidentally, that the principle of subsidiarity supports allocation of decisionmaking responsibility to the center as easily as to the periphery, depending on which one believes is most suited to confront the issue at hand.[11] Decentralization is a completely sensible institutional technique that a rational central government will often choose both to design and to implement public policy. One can look at countries around the world that have so-called unitary (i.e., non-federal) governments and find a great deal of decentralization, sometimes because in that instance the principle of subsidiarity commends local rather than national decisionmaking. The question is what degree of decentralization is truly possible, given the challenges presented by particular issues. One may also be interested in who gets to decide whether these possibility conditions are in fact met. It makes all the difference whether national or state governments have the final word in any such arguments. But decentralization describes a *choice* rather than a legal necessity. Only if the latter is present can one speak of federalism in the strongest legal sense.

II. WHY FEDERALISM?

People often disagree about the desirability of federalism. So we must ask why a country would ever adopt federalism, which is ultimately a legal or constitutional concept. The alternative is to embrace what might be called a political presumption in favor of decentralization, but leaving those in charge of a unitary government to decide when any such presumption is overcome because of the advantages of more centralized government.

A. Is Federalism a positive good or a tragic compromise?

One answer, not surprisingly, is that federalism is a highly desirable way of organizing societies. For such theorists, federalism is much like principles of freedom of speech or religion, racial non-discrimination, and the like; these would be adopted by any rational person when designing the basic institutions of the polity, whether because they provide what might be termed affirmative public goods—for example, a vigorous and robust exchange of ideas identified with theories of freedom of speech—or necessary constraints whose violation would trench on central norms of human dignity, such as "invidious discrimination." But other analysts, including Feeley and Rubin, lament federalism even as they applaud the wisdom of decentralization. This is why they title their book *Political Identity and Tragic Compromise.* They see the explanations for choice of a federal structure as *always* explicable by the existence of certain facts on the ground and the felt necessity to engage in tragic, perhaps even rotten, compromises. These are necessary in order to achieve the goal of adopting a new constitutional order designed to pursue some measure of peace and stability within a geographical area rent by significant cleavage generating the threat or actuality of violent conflict among the contending groups. It's not that federalism is an "irrational choice." Far from it. Rather, the rationality in question is highly responsive to given contexts. But the point is that it is *always* a second-best choice, for the truly best outcome, if it were possible, would be to overcome such cleavages while avoiding the foreseeable problems attached to federalism.

Political scientist Alfred Stepan has helpfully suggested that we distinguish between what he calls "coming together" and "holding together" forms of federalism. American federalism is a classic illustration of the former, for federalism was part of the bargain by which the thirteen quite disparate states were willing to come together in a radically transformed new

Union (when compared with the far weaker confederation established in 1781 and scrapped by the Framers in Philadelphia). In contrast, "holding together" federalism arises in countries that already exist but are threatened with centrifugal, regionally concentrated sociopolitical forces, at least some of which might be tempted to secede and form their own independent country. He cites India, Spain, and Belgium as examples, though one might well add Canada.[12] The only way to keep such countries together is to offer deals to the regions that recognize significant autonomy with regard to certain pressing issues, such as language. Whether to bring together or hold together, one can easily understand the etiology of many federal systems. That does not, however, dispose of the normative questions linked with constitutionalizing such autonomy.

The reason for Feeley's and Rubin's antagonism to federalism, for example, is quite simple: autonomy that seems to make sense at time *A*, and is constitutionally locked in via the grant of final authority to states, might make much less sense at time *B*. We have seen this problem of unwise "lock-ins" throughout this book, even with regard to something so relatively minor as the determination of Inauguration Day. A fundamental critique of constitutionalism is precisely that it engages in too many lock-ins that prevent "We the People" from making our own choices as to what would best serve our collective interests at any given time. Thus one might argue that a rational designer, even one who supports decentralization, would be disinclined to accept permanent, locked-in, subnational autonomy on given matters of "real importance" precisely because this limits needed flexibility as situations change. Yet, if this is true, why do we have federalism in so many countries, including the United States?

The answer is that lots of political systems, at their formation, involve societies that are fundamentally divided along certain lines, usually involving race or ethnicity, religion, or language. These divisions are especially pressing if the groups in question have a longstanding attachment to particular lands, as distinguished from immigrant ethnic groups who have left their historical lands in favor of an aptly named "new world."[13] The United States is unusually rich in its diversity of ethnic groups, but the only historically rooted "nationality groups" that might make claims about their treatment by the United States consist of American Indian tribes. Even the Mexicans and Spaniards who were politically displaced by the results of the Mexican War were themselves settlers in lands that had been the home territories of various Indian tribes. The constitutional status of aboriginal natives—a major issue in Canada and Australia, for example—remains very much on the back burner of American constitutional politics. Few proponents of American federalism, with its emphasis on "state's rights," go on to suggest that Indian tribes should have greater autonomy, including explicit representation, comparable to that granted states, in the House or Representatives or the Senate. One can point to the obvious centrality of race in American society and politics, with its historical linkages to slavery, but very few analysts have suggested a "federal" solution by which, for example, African Americans would get their own state with linked abilities to engage in the legal regulation of its members.

One should also be aware of the implications for social cohesion of significant differentials in economic resources, including all-important access to natural resources such as fertile soil, coal, oil, water, or diamonds. In some cases, such resources might be necessary to physical nurturance or even survival. Others, such as diamonds or other precious metals, may serve as instruments to amassing great wealth, so that it becomes of dominant importance whether the state or the nation at large controls the export (including the collection of relevant taxes) of such goods.

As already suggested, in order to make federalism a likely option, these divisions must take geographical form. It should be obvious that there is a huge difference between a society divided between Catholics and Protestants along geographical lines and one in which Catholics and Protestants who may mistrust one another nonetheless live in the same communities (though in separate neighborhoods, as in Belfast, Northern Ireland). Territorial federalism makes no sense as a solution to the problems in Northern Ireland or Lebanon, but it may be a possibility in a place like Iraq, especially if there is a certain amount of "resettlement" of populations along ethnic or religious lines.

If one is presented with the phenomenon of significantly "divided societies,"[14] then the principal problem facing those interested in creating a new political order will be getting agreement from the various geographically divided communities as to the terms of the deal underlying the new order. One way to do this is to guarantee the communities that they will indeed retain significant autonomy about the things that matter most to them. With regard to the United States, slavery explains important features of American federalism, even if it is not the *only* explanation for our federalism. After all, we *were* significantly divided on religious grounds as well, as Madison noted in *Federalist* 10. Massachusetts, for example, had an established church until 1833, and one reading of the First Amendment is that its prohibition of Congress's establishing a religion was a tacit acceptance of the legitimacy of states making their own decisions as to establishment or disestablishment and, if choosing the former, their own decisions as to which church would receive the preferential treatment.

And, although it might not have been a central focus in 1787, it is also clear that key resources are not evenly distributed across the United States; today, for example, it is all too easy to distinguish between "coal" and "non-coal" (or "oil" and "non-oil" or "breadbasket") states. Even in 1787, though, it was easy to distinguish the rice- or cotton-producing states from the others, and this distinction would become key to understanding developments in American (and even world) politics in the nineteenth century. It was over-determined that the United States of America would be organized along "federal" lines if it was to exist at all under a new constitution. But any complacence about the success of American federalism has to be significantly discounted not only by the rotten compromise necessary to "seal the deal," but also by the fact that it kept the country together for only about seventy years, at which point eleven states attempted to secede and over 600,000 persons lost their lives in a struggle over preservation of the Union. Moreover, the explanation for the dissolution of the Union in 1861 in significant part flows from federalism-protective aspects of the Constitution.

So one explanation for federalism, particularly from those who are basically skeptical of its merits, is that it is a response to deep pre-existing cleavages within a given society or, as William Riker especially insisted, simply an opportunistic solution for small entities faced with military threats who correctly believed that "in union there is strength" and thus came together in what is basically a glorified military confederation. But Jenna Bednar and other proponents of federalism instead point to "positive goods" that federalism will bring and thus its appeal even to conflict-free societies. What are these ostensible goods?

1. Protecting diversity

If one recognizes the presence of multiple legitimate answers to certain important political questions, then federalism, by permitting subnational units to make their own decisions on such matters, allows persons to settle in a state that adopts their own preferred solutions to these question.[15] And, have no doubt that decisions might differ state by state precisely because, as the Federal Farmer[16] wrote in 1787, during the ratification debates over the new Constitution, "different laws, customs, and opinions exist in the different states."[17] Indeed, one might rewrite this slightly to say that *because* different states may be distinguished by the significantly different "customs and opinions" among their particular populations, one would expect that "different laws" would be the result. And, suggests the Federal Farmer, "a uniform system of laws would be unreasonably inva[sive]" of such diversity. Much may be anachronistic about many of the arguments underlying the U.S. Constitution, but surely this one continues to resonate, for good and for ill.

The minimum wage is higher in some states than in others, though none can go below the "floor" set by the national minimum wage. Environmental regulations or taxation policies can differ significantly by state. Often these policies are motivated by a self-conscious desire to establish a "business-friendly" atmosphere that will help to attract new businesses into the state, including those that may relocate from less "friendly" states.[18] States, with Delaware in the vanguard, compete with one another over the terms offered to corporations that will choose them as places of incorporation. Looking more to "social" policy, we find wide variation among the states. Nevada became (in)famous in the twentieth century, for example, with regard to its legal toleration of gambling and prostitution, as well as its lax divorce laws. There is increasing diversity among the states with regard to the regulation of drugs, particularly marijuana, just as there is concerning the rights of same-sex couples to marry or adopt children. Even with regard to heterosexual couples , some states have begun offering the option of "covenant marriages" that place significant restrictions on the possibility of later divorce. Most recently, we have been made aware of the states' quite different policies regarding their treatment of immigrants who entered the country illegally, including, especially, their children. California and

Texas, for example, have eased the way for children who have grown up in the United States, whatever their legal status, to attend their state universities. On this matter, at least, California's Democratic governor Jerry Brown and Texas's Republican chief executive Rick Perry agree. Alabama and Georgia, on the other hand, are among the states that have chosen to pass far more punitive policies. In Alabama these have led to a massive exodus of Hispanic children from several public school systems.[19] All these examples involve the ostensible legitimacy of diverse approaches to economic and social life (including what domains of individual choice will be left basically unregulated).

The question is how much diversity we find acceptable with regard to what issues. There can be little doubt that since the Great Depression the American economy has seen a substantial move toward national regulation limiting (though certainly not eliminating) the range of variation among the states. Similar nationalization has occurred with regard to social and cultural diversity inasmuch as state legislation in these areas is often successfully challenged as violative of the Bill or Rights or the Equal Protection guarantees in the Fourteenth Amendment. But, as with the economy, space for some degree of state autonomy remains, and we still must confront the question of what kinds of diversity we find desirable and what kinds we would wish to stifle. Literary theorist Stanley Fish has written of "boutique multiculturalism,"[20] by which he means that we are willing to accept cultural diversity only when we are not deeply offended by given practices. Many cultural differences can be not only tolerated, but even accepted by others as "charming" and exotic, perhaps like strange animals at a zoo. But "honor killings" of daughters who stray from parental desires for most of us go far beyond any such line. At that moment, our ostensible commitment to multiculturalism or diversity is dropped and such behavior is (properly) criticized in terms of either fundamental American values or more universal conceptions of human rights. The same considerations might apply with regard to how much latitude we are willing to give parents who refuse to provide medical treatment for their children on religious grounds.[21]

The complexities of diversity are well exemplified in the practical application of another section of Article IV of the Constitution, which concerns the admission of new states to the Union. The last such event took place in 1959, with the admission of Hawaii, so the relevant clause is scarcely the topic of contemporary discussion. It should be, for it raises extremely interesting issues that could roil the country in the future. The decision to admit a new state is ultimately left to Congress, as reflected in the fact that Congress refused *six* applications for citizenship from residents of the Utah Territory prior to 1890. Why? The reason was simple: the Mormon Church, which essentially controlled Utah, still viewed polygamy as a divinely required practice.[22] Yet polygamy had been described by the 1856 Republican platform as constituting one of the "twin relics of barbarism" (along with slavery), and Congress outlawed it in 1862. The Supreme Court in 1879 unanimously upheld the imprisonment of Mormon leader George Reynolds for violating this federal law, against his claim that his own polygamy should be protected under the Free Exercise Clause of the First Amendment. Utah was in fact finally admitted to the Union in 1896, but only after the Mormon Church changed its policy in light of what was described as a new revelation, and the Utah Constitution was written to include a flat ban on polygamy. This scarcely seems to be a ringing endorsement of "diversity."

Similarly, Congress was hesitant to admit Arizona or New Mexico in 1912 until each firmly rejected the possibility that Spanish would have equal status with English within the states. Even if one takes the position that polygamy is morally unacceptable (which, frankly, does not seem a self-evident proposition), that conclusion could hardly apply to speaking a non-English language or organizing a political system with more than one official language. Yet the issue of language is volatile politically, often going to the heart of the very notion of national identity and raising the all-important question of the relationship between the political *state* and any given *nation* within the state.

This latter issue could certainly arise if Puerto Rico, acquired by the United States in 1898 and today the world's largest remaining colony, ever petitioned for statehood. About 90–95 percent of its populace is divided roughly equally between proponents of statehood and those who prefer the present "commonwealth" status, which, among other things, allows Puerto Rico to have its own team in the Olympics. The remaining percent support independence. Imagine, though, that the "statehood party" gained true majority approval and petitioned for admission. On what grounds, if any, could Congress refuse to grant statehood? Is it relevant, for example, that the official language of the commonwealth is Spanish and that most Puerto Ricans speak only Spanish? If one looks at many federal countries around the world, beginning with the country immediately to our north, one discovers that linguistic pluralism is one of the most important realities of those countries, though there would be sharp dispute as to whether that is for good or for ill.

Canada and Belgium are "merely" bilingual, though both countries have been threatened by movements that would dissolve the existing federations.[23] Switzerland has four official languages, though the divisions among the respective monolingual cantons seem far more stable than is the case in Canada or Belgium. India is notable for many things, including the sheer diversity of languages that are officially part of its federal system. Sujit Choudhry notes that the Congress Party in India since 1920 "had consistently been committed to the creation of linguistic provinces" consisting of "clear linguistic majorit[ies] whose language would be the sole official language" of the given province. "The champion of this move was Gandhi, who regarded it as essential for transforming the Congress Party from an elite-led English-speaking organization into a mass political movement, which would only be possible if it operated in regional vernaculars." Following independence, the Congress Party basically reversed its position "out of a fear that the creation of [such provinces] would fuel secessionist mobilization in India's border states and doom the country to disintegration."[24]

Interestingly enough, those who drafted the initial Indian Constitution in 1947 quite deliberately avoided making any definitive decision about India's "official language" and, in effect, kicked that issue down the road, hoping that later developments would make it easier to confront what is obviously such a volatile issue. As a matter of fact, India has never directly confronted, as a constitutional issue, the role of English. That being said, many of the individual states *do* have their own official languages that are quite different from English or Hindi. And one author has suggested that the creation in 2000 of two of the three youngest states within India was at least partly motivated by linguistic considerations.[25] Choudhry has pointed out that the differential language policies on the part of the Indian states have profound consequences for eligibility for state civil service positions, a matter of both theoretical and practical importance.

Although the United States is not now, and never has been, a truly "English-only" country—Benjamin Franklin, otherwise a beacon of tolerance, was concerned in 1751 that "Pennsylvania, founded by the English, [would] become a Colony of Aliens, who will shortly be so numerous as to Germanize us instead of our Anglifying them, and will never adopt our Language or Customs"[26]—English has remained dominant by any measure. Whatever gestures of bilingualism exist in the United States by virtue of congressional statutes, there is no serious possibility that the United States will emulate Canada by becoming officially bilingual and thus requiring, for example, that all government documents be written in both English and (presumably) Spanish.

Puerto Rico also raises potential questions of religion (it is predominantly Catholic), of race (most Puerto Ricans would almost certainly be classified as "non-white" or, even more certainly, "non-Anglo") and of class (Puerto Rico would instantly become America's poorest state, most in need, therefore, of a variety of federal transfer payments that, by definition, would come from the taxpayers of other states). And Puerto Rico, because of its size, would be entitled to roughly seven members in the House of Representatives (and, of course, two senators). Unless the number of representatives was increased by at least seven, to 442 instead of the present 435, this means that seven existing states—and not the smallest, whose one representative is constitutionally guaranteed—would lose representation. Moreover, it is highly likely that all seven Puerto Rican representatives and two senators would be Democrats, with obvious implications for the balance of power in the Congress. Would *any* of these considerations be legitimate to vote against Puerto Rican statehood? And, incidentally, would the denial by Congress of full rights of membership in the Union serve automatically to legitimate a move by a majority of Puerto Ricans, should they so desire, to declare independence from the United States and become a "sovereign state" within the international system?

Within the United States, the most important "diversity" historically involved what is euphemistically described as control of the labor system—slavery—a topic that fully re-enters the moral realm. Even after slavery was formally abolished as the result of war, it was succeeded by racial segregation and other forms of oppression whose effectuation was made far easier by acknowledging the principle of state autonomy. Perhaps it is unfair to tag contemporary "diversity-oriented" proponents of federalism with having to defend slavery and segregation, but it should still be obvious that diversity cannot possibly be thought to be a good in itself, even if one accepts the proposition that it may often be attractive. To defend "communal autonomy" requires both defining who is within the relevant community and deciding the scope of their purported autonomy. At least on occasion, "communal autonomy" may be part of a rotten compromise that acquiesces in the local majority's oppression of minorities within given states.[27]

It is worth noting that one way of preserving diverse communities is to give them substantial control over their borders. Such control has traditionally been recognized as a central attribute of "sovereignty" within the international system. Although the United States has historically been open to vast immigration, its history also features decided limits on precisely *who* has been welcome to come to the United States and join the American community as citizens. The first naturalization act, in 1790, limited the privilege only to whites. The aptly named Chinese Exclusion Act of 1882 expressed the American attitude at the time toward Asians, who were not allowed to become citizens until 1952 (although the ban on naturalizing Chinese immigrants was lifted in 1943, presumably because we were allied during World War II with the Republic of China). American states have occasionally attempted to exercise similar control over their borders with regard to such potential "threats" as free blacks, who were legally prohibited from settling in antebellum Indiana, Illinois, and Oregon.[28] During the Great Depression, California attempted to deny entry to impoverished refugees from the Oklahoma "dust bowl," but the Supreme Court intervened and stripped states of control of their borders.[29]

Just as the Constitution is viewed as creating a "free trade" zone among the states, prohibiting any attempts by states to place tariffs or their equivalents on outside competitors to local industries, it also has created a "free movement" zone by which anyone legally in the country—citizen or noncitizen—is free to move to and settle in any state within the Union. There are good reasons to applaud both notions of freedom, but one should recognize that the second makes it more difficult to maintain strongly "diverse" states. It should occasion no surprise that the European Union faces something of a backlash from member countries who are having second thoughts about the practical demise of borders and the concomitant duty to welcome anyone legally within that vast territory.[30]

There is also the reality that perhaps the central narrative of American constitutional development over the past century has been the steady demise of state autonomy in the name of national interests and values. This is true whether one thinks of state ability to regulate its economy free of national intervention, one of the great subjects of the New Deal; the maintenance of such practices as racially segregated schools or the injection of prayers into the public school day; or a variety of idiosyncratic practices regarding the treatment of criminal defendants. The list goes on and on, but one constant is the relative diminution of the diversity of American state practices. Whatever justifies contemporary American federalism, it is scarcely a truly robust diversity of the kind seen, for better and for worse, in other federal countries ranging from Canada to India.

2. Local control (civic republicanism)

A second defense of federalism is predicated on the benefits of placing as much political control as possible in the smallest political units. This, it is thought, will generate the kind of "active citizenship" that "civic republicans" in particular consider so important to human flourishing. According to such arguments, "liberty" consists not only in being left alone by a possibly intrusive state, it also involves what Justice Breyer, borrowing from arguments going back to ancient Athens, has recently called "active liberty," the ability to engage in the task of *self-governance* by participating in the making, and even enforcement, of the laws.

There is a great deal that is attractive about this argument. One does not have to be particularly alienated from our national government in order to feel a striking lack of personal efficacy as we recognize our identity as only one among millions of voters, let alone the far larger number of citizens or residents. It is this impulse that underlies the attraction of subsidiarity, which bears a resemblance to the call by many radicals in the 1960s for "participatory democracy," that is, the ability of people to participate meaningfully in decisions about issues that fundamentally affect their lives. Moreover, federal systems inevitably generate leadership cadres of persons who run for local office, whether to serve as governors, legislators, or members of state boards of education. Service in such positions helps to prepare people for more national public positions. But the existence of state governments may also mean that even relatively hegemonic national political parties will be assured of "oppositions" that arise in selected state governments. All of this, generally speaking, is desirable.

Recognizing this, one can still ask what it has to do with *federalism* compared to *decentralization* as a general political desideratum. Consider the introduction to a recent comprehensive overview of federalism around by world by Daniel Halberstam:[31]

> Even France now values local government. Over the past thirty years, top-down appointment of regional prefects and local administrators has given way to regionally elected councils and a revision of Article 1 of the French Constitution, which proclaims that today the state's "organization is decentralized." The British Parliament, too, has embraced local rule by devolving powers to Scotland, Wales, and Northern Ireland. And in China, decentralization has reached a point where some scholars speak of "de facto federalism."[32] A systematic study of the distribution of authority in 42 Democracies found that over the past 50 years, regional authority grew in 29 countries, remained stable in eleven, and declined in only two.[33]

But return to the point that "federalism" as a legal concept almost always involves states, *not* localities. So what one repeatedly sees is the concentration of power in *state* legislatures and governments to the severe detriment of major cities (and other areas) of the state. Those of us who live in Austin, Texas, for example, are well aware that the state legislature is often hostile to the city—and quite willing to limit its local autonomy—because of its relative liberalism. *Federalism has nothing whatsoever to do with acceptance of the principle of "home rule,"* which is decidedly *not* a constitutionally recognized principle, even if some state constitutions do acknowledge the principle as a way of limiting the power of state governments over localities.

So if one is genuinely attracted by a strong notion of subsidiarity, or "participatory democracy," then one might wish for a far more radically decentralized form of governance than that provided by "two-tier" American federalism even at its strongest, especially if one takes into account the fact that the United States today has seventy-five times the population as the United States in 1788, not to mention a vastly greater expanse of territory. It is significant not only that California alone has almost ten times the population as all the United States two centuries ago, but also that Los Angeles County itself, which is nearing a population of ten million people, has 250 percent of the total population of the United States in 1790. So anyone truly committed to the "civic republican" rationale for federalism might well wonder about the desirability of centralizing power in state legislatures, relative to cities.

Or perhaps the "solution" is to create many more states, since the existing fifty are all artifacts of earlier moments in American history. At the same time, one might force some "under-populated" states into union with one another. If one believes, for example, that six million is an optimal size for a state, then one might blend Wyoming, Nebraska, the two Dakotas, Idaho, and Montana into a single new state even as one divides California into six separate states. It is obvious that this will not occur, not least because part of the Constitution of Settlement is that existing states have the right to veto any such proposals. Nonetheless, it is a worthwhile thought experiment, inasmuch as such basic realities of American life as the number and geographical shape of the states—just as is true of counties and other sub-state units within the states—play a great role in determining the actualities of successful governance within the United States.

Still, before embracing "local control" too enthusiastically, one might carefully reread Madison's arguments in *Federalist* 10. They hardly provide any great support for the virtues of local government. Instead, Madison emphasizes that it is far easier for factions to gain control of state governments than of the national government. This may help to explain why Madison fought, unsuccessfully, for a provision in the Constitution explicitly allowing Congress to override state laws whenever it deemed them antagonistic to national interests. Indeed, though Madison became a primary supporter of the Constitution, as evidenced by his authorship of many of the *Federalist* essays, he also wrote privately to Thomas Jefferson on September 6, 1787, as the Constitution was taking final shape—the Convention would finish its work on September 17—that if the Constitution was adopted it would "neither effectually answer its national object nor prevent the local mischiefs which every where excite disgusts ag[ain]st the state governments."[34]

One might wonder what Jefferson, who was in general far more favorably disposed to local control, thought of this statement. But one should be aware, at the very least, that this basic fault line in American political thought and politics has been there from our beginning as the United States of America.

3. Fiscal efficiencies relative to preferences of people

Another appeal of federalism has to do with "fiscal federalism," by which localities can decide on their own mixture of goods and services, including levels of taxation necessary to pay for them. This clearly has some linkage with the diversity defense, though what is diverse now is the relative preference for, say, educational facilities rather than prisons, or environmental conservation instead of exploitation of natural resources like gas or oil.

A famous argument linked to economist Charles Tiebout suggests that the difference in such mixtures among the states will lead members of the general society to sort themselves out relative to their own preferences. One explanation for the "red state, blue state" phenomenon—whatever its exaggerations—is that people who dislike the political cultures and linked patterns of expenditures associated with Massachusetts or Alabama will "vote with their feet" and move to more compatible states. One problem, as one might expect, is finding adequate empirical support for this proposition, not least because most people have mixed preferences and can relatively rarely find a community that offers the "just right" mix of services instead of a blend of "too hot" and "too cold" ones. The same issues that make if difficult, if not impossible, to interpret the results of a given election, given the multiple positions of any candidate and the necessity that the voter choose the candidate who emphasizes issue X even as she prefers the other candidates positions on issues Y and Z, make interpretation of a person's settlement decision the equivalent of assigning a given meaning to an ink-blot test. Moreover, there appears to be a great deal of evidence that people will put up with a fair amount of what would otherwise count as grief to surround themselves with others who are engaged in similar work. This may help to explain, for example, why Silicon Valley continues to draw outstanding talent even though its taxes and housing costs are far higher than most other places in the United States. Thus one scholar has written that "the existence of agglomerative gains means that individuals are making location decisions for reasons other than matching their preferences for public policies. Agglomeration therefore causes a reduction in the efficiency of sorting."[35] "Agglomeration" is a form of sorting, but it may have little to do with the sensitivity to public policies that is at the heart of the Tiebout hypothesis and defenses of federalism based on it.

So-called foot voting depends, among other things, on the notion that individuals are almost fanatically concerned about tax rates or particular public policies. These individuals also are presumed to have relatively few, if any, constraints on mobility among states and localities that offer an optimal blend of taxes and services. Moreover, as one scholar has noted, it ignores the fact that movement often takes place by family rather than individually, and one spouse may wish to remain in the original location while the other demands to move because of the attractions of a new job.[36] None of the presumptions underlying a strong theory of "foot voting" is very plausible or, more to the point, supported by empirical evidence, even if we can readily concede that *some* individuals do have both the inclination and the freedom to pick locales, usually *within* a given state rather than *among* states, on the basis of such considerations as tax rates and public services such as schools for their children.

Once one starts applying standard-form economic analysis to federalism, however, a host of questions present themselves. After all, one thing we know is that people like to *externalize* the costs of their preferences onto others, while at the same time engaging in free riding, that is, not paying for goods they like. Thus a common defense for the move toward centralized decisionmaking is the propensity of states to adopt policies that push costs onto other states. A pro-environment state may be dissuaded from passing anti-pollution legislation not only because adjoining states would benefit from the policy without having to pay for it but also because other states might be tempted to lure business from the pro-environment state by noting that the businesses would *not* have to pay for new anti-pollution devices in the less regulatory state.

There are also significant debates with regard to certain welfare expenditures by states, whether by "welfare" one thinks of income transfers to genuinely poor people or the kind of welfare instantiated in public universities. Should Texas be expected to welcome residents from adjoining states and thereby leave those states freer than they might be to stint on the taxes necessary to pay for a first-rate public university? It is precisely the desire to limit externalities and/or free riders, which have unfortunate consequences for the making of public policy, that has substantially justified the move toward national resolution of many, if not most, great issues since the early twentieth century. Indeed, it is also such considerations that help to explain, at least in part, the move toward greater unification in Europe.

4. States as "little laboratories of experimentation"

Proponents of federalism will almost inevitably quote from a famous dissent written by Justice Louis D. Brandeis in a 1932 case involving the right of Oklahoma to pass a particular economic regulation of the ice industry. We need not concern ourselves with the details, for what was important was his statement: "It is one of the happy incidents of the federal system that a single courageous State may, if its citizens choose, serve as a laboratory; and try novel social and economic experiments without risk to the rest of the country."[37] There can be no doubt that states—and even more "local" governments—often engage in such experiments. A recent example is the rise of charter schools.

The practical question, according to Feeley and Rubin, is whether "experimentation" would be just as great under a system that included significant decentralization. Does one *need* the added rigidity of legal federalism to get these benefits? Feeley and Rubin suggest that experiments are likely to be far less valuable, even if we applaud the "courage" of a particular state, precisely because of the inability to place certain conditions on the experimentation that would allow social scientists to determine whether they in fact were efficacious for the purposes suggested. Moreover, even if we grant that a particular state experiment is wholly successful in proving that some important social good can be produced by adopting a particular policy, that does not guarantee that other states will adopt it themselves, perhaps because of the presence within these latter states of entrenched "factions" who rely on the status quo. In many instances, only a coercive national government can assure reform.

III. THE "METAPHYSICS" OF THE UNION

Many of these points apply to all federal systems across the world. Our primary concern, though, is the American polity and the contributions or costs of our particular constitutionalized political institutions. Before proceeding further, it is worth a brief digression to discuss what might be referred to as the "metaphysics" of our Union and, therefore, what would constitute its "perfection." Does the United States possess an "essence," either at its inception or today? Consider Madison's discussion in *Federalist* 39 about the *national* and *federal* aspects of the new Constitution. He makes very clear that he conceives the United States, as of 1787–1788, as composed of "the distinct and independent states to which [the people] respectively belong." This is the importance of Article VII, which places the power of ratification in *state* ratifying conventions. Moreover, even though the new Constitution comes into legal being with the ratification of only nine states, no state is to be a member of the Union without its consent. "Each state in ratifying the convention, is considered as a sovereign body independent of all others, and only to be bound by its own voluntary act." This is why Rhode Island and North Carolina were not part of the United States of America when Washington was inaugurated on April 30, 1789. Madison even goes so far as to deny that the acts of the people in these separate states create "one aggregate nation" with a singular national identity. This is no small point, either theoretically or practically.

Madison would a decade later author the "Virginia Resolves," just as Jefferson would pen the "Kentucky Resolutions" that not only protested the Alien and Sedition Act of 1798 but also articulated most vividly the "compact" theory of the Constitution. This described the Constitution as an act, fundamentally, of "sovereign states" that had chosen to contract together to form a new Union. As we shall see presently, some drew from such arguments the message that these states could withdraw from the Union if they perceived a breakdown of the deal entered into in 1787 with regard to maintaining crucial elements of state sovereignty.

Even in 1787–1788, Madison took pains to declare that the new national government was indeed a *limited* one and that states maintained their own significant autonomy. Thus, he writes, "the proposed government cannot be deemed a *national* one; since its jurisdiction extends to *certain enumerated objects only*, and leaves to the several States *a residuary and inviolable sovereignty over all other objects*" (emphasis added). He is invoking a central mantra of the Constitution, that continues to be heard today, that it creates only a *limited* national government of *assigned* (or *enumerated*) powers, particularly those set out in Article I, Section 8, the powers "herein granted" to Congress. "Inviolable sovereignty" is a very powerful term. The question is whether it has any real bite with regard to understanding the actualities of American federalism. As I suggested in the very first chapter, these apparent limits on national power have served as the essential topic of the Constitution of Conversation and what I have also termed the Narrative of Change with regard to the basic history of American constitutional development over the past two centuries. We have witnessed the ever greater assignment of powers to the national government, whatever might have been the "original understanding" of the Constitution. Indeed, one can even argue that many of the opponents of the Constitution, such as Patrick Henry and others who feared that the inevitable tendency of the Constitution was to create a "consolidated" government, got it absolutely right, at least in the long haul. And, after all, it was Madison himself, in *Federalist* 48, who warned against relying on "parchment barriers" to provide reliable defense against those with strong ambitions (and potential power).

But one of the surprises, in a close reading of the Constitution, is that it is not clear whether it even provides much by way of significant "parchment barriers" in favor of robust federalism. This may be one reason that proponents of federalism rely so much on the mantra of "limited government of assigned powers," whatever its problems.

IV. SO WHAT PRECISELY DOES THE CONSTITUTION SAY ABOUT STATE AUTONOMY?

A. *The irrelevance of the Tenth Amendment*

The key question, then is to what extent the Constitution recognizes federalism in the sense of guaranteed autonomy? What constitutes the "residuary and inviolable sovereignty" that allows us to describe the United States as a "federal" system? One point needs to made immediately: reference to the Tenth Amendment is close to irrelevant, as is true of other sections that acknowledge the existence of states. What we are trying to discern is some realm of strongly protected *state power.*

The Tenth Amendment is widely cited by those who would re-energize federalism in America. But there are some problems. Not only was it not part of the original Constitution. But it also provides astonishingly little useful information. It states, "The powers not delegated to the United States by the Constitution, nor prohibited by it to the States, are reserved to the States respectively, or to the people." The Supreme Court once famously described this as a "truism," stating that what is neither assigned to the United States nor prohibited to the states is reserved to the states. It provides no clue at all as to what precisely *is* assigned to the national government or prohibited to the states, especially given the rejection by the First Congress, when debating the words of the amendment, of a proposal to include the magic word "expressly" before "delegated." The best (or worst) one can say about the amendment is that it provides the basis for endless conversation, but contributes nothing whatsoever to the Constitution of Settlement.

Madison simply suggests that inevitable controversies will be decided "impartially...according to the rules of the constitution." We saw Hamilton invoking the same notion of "impartiality" when justifying judicial review. But difficulties remain with regard to defining truly impartial institutions. Thus Madison concedes that "the tribunal which is ultimately to decide"— the Supreme Court—"is to be established under the general government," which may be not altogether reassuring to those primarily concerned about preserving state autonomy from national overreaching. Imagine a Supreme Court in which four of the nine justices were appointed by state governments, through some suitably complex process. Why wouldn't that be more likely to be impartial than a Supreme Court appointed entirely by the national government—or would one grow to expect that every federalism case would be decided by a 5–4 vote?

But Madison and the later "rational-choice" theorists Mikhail Filippov and his colleagues appear to agree that it is a real challenge to design a system that will maintain a complex structure of government consisting of both national and subnational units. Each will have its own incentives to push the envelope on whatever was decided during the negotiating process that produced the constitution in the first place. One might well believe that some of the central things to be determined at a constitutional convention are the autonomous powers specifically reserved to the states. This is thought to be one of the advantages of written constitutions, that the political deals are publicly acknowledged in documents that can be readily distributed far and wide and thus serve as important evidence later when claims of infidelity to the deal are raised, often before courts. Getting guarantees in parchment may not be a sufficient condition, but many people regard it as at least a necessary condition, because of the rhetorical advantage that unambiguous text is thought to provide.

B. So what are the specific guarantees?

So what do we find if we read the Constitution very carefully, looking for the kind of policy autonomy that distinguishes truly federal systems? The surprising answer is not very much, especially if we are motivated to look at the Constitution because of contemporary disputes about the extent of state autonomy.

1. Managing elections

It is no small matter that states are given the responsibility for actually running elections, including elections for national office. Whether this is a feature or a bug of the American system can certainly be debated. Some observers have suggested that a number of our states are in some respects little better than most underdeveloped or third-world nations in the way they conduct elections. One might believe that independence is at least as important with regard to those who conduct elections as to those we hire to judge cases. Yet in many states the elections are presided over by highly partisan officials, sometimes elected, sometimes appointed, but always with clear partisan identities. The most spectacular example was surely Kathleen Harris, the Florida secretary of state who was in charge of that state's recount in the 2000 presidential election even though she had also been state co-chair of the Bush-Cheney election committee. Recall that the national government has no serious involvement in conducting the

elections. To be sure, state autonomy with regard to elections has been significantly limited by a number of congressional statutes and constitutional
amendments, at least with regard to the ability of states to deprive people
of the right to participate in elections, but much autonomy *does* remain, for
better or, quite likely, for worse.

2. The original Senate

The original placement of the power to appoint senators in the hands of
state legislatures (as well as the initial role that state legislatures were imagined by some to play with regard to choosing presidential electors) could be
viewed as an *indirect* protection of state autonomy. After all, those seeking
the approval of the legislatures might be expected to support their claims
to "residuary" powers. Even with regard to the original conception of the
Senate, however, the appointing legislature had no power to set senatorial
salaries, which came from the national treasury, or, more importantly, to
recall senators whose votes were seen as betrayals of the state's interests.
There was, in fact, a lively debate at the end of the eighteenth century
whether "representatives" were subject to "instruction" from their constituents or could instead exercise "independent judgment." One way of enforcing an "instruction" model is to allow the de facto firing of political agents
by recall (instead of waiting until the next election). But that doesn't exist in
the national American system. Moreover, Filippov and his colleagues argue
that one important implication of the extended six-year terms of senators
is that the senators were assured a certain immunity from the response of
those who appointed them because the appointing officials in many state
legislatures would be out of office by the time of the next election. (As a
matter of fact, most senators themselves were content to serve only one
term; it was not until the end of the nineteenth century that senators often
returned for multiple terms.) Even if one antagonizes those who hold current majority power, it is always possible that they will be succeeded by a
new majority more compatible with the representative's views.

But the Seventeenth Amendment and the requirement of popular election substantially "defederalized" the Senate. The excessive weight given
to the interests of small states in the Senate—like the distortions of the
electoral college that similarly benefit specific states—has nothing to do

with protecting what is thought to be important about federalism, which is state autonomy. Pandering to the residents of Ohio is entirely different from pledging to strengthen the powers of the Ohio legislature or, even more strongly, supporting the prerogatives of that legislature against what it might perceive as an overweening national government. If one is really interested in the Senate as a protector of state interests, one might look to Germany, where the second house, the Bundesrat, is composed of state officials, just as one might expect far more "federalism-friendly" presidents if electors chosen directly by state legislatures were charged with picking presidents.[38]

One other aspect of the Senate should be mentioned in this context. There can be no change in the "equal" access of voting power by states in the Senate without the de facto unanimous consent of the states. There is no reason whatsoever to believe that any state would ever consent to having diminished power in that body.

3. The guaranteed status of state boundaries

Article IV, Section 4 provides that "no new State shall be formed or erected within the Jurisdiction of any other State; nor any State be formed by the Junction of two or more States, or Parts of States, without the Consent of the Legislatures of the States concerned as well as of the Congress." This means that California or Texas, to name the two most obvious examples, cannot independently decide that they would be better off splitting into smaller states, for Congress would have to approve that. And why is it almost certain that Congress would refuse to approve such changes? The answer is that they would effectively multiply the representation in the Senate of the geographical territories encompassed by the states. Thus Northern and Southern California would now have a total of four senators, just as the potential states of North, East, Central, South, and West Texas would have ten Senate seats. Why would the rest of the country consent to *that*? It's hard to see this clause, as it applies to the hypothetical (but sensible) desire of California and Texas to split into smaller units, as protecting federalism as such. What *is* protective of federalism is the fact, as noted earlier, that Congress could not force the altogether reasonable joinder of the Dakotas into one state or the dissolution of Delaware into parts of New Jersey,

Pennsylvania, and Maryland, since the affected states (including Delaware) would have a veto over such proposals. In any event, whatever interesting questions might be suggested for classroom discussion, it is hard to view this clause as a truly major protection of twenty-first-century federalism.

4. State militias

States are also guaranteed, by the Second Amendment, the right to have their own state militias. As a practical matter, this might be the most important protection of federalism in the original Constitution, for it involves a recognition of the importance in any political system of the actualities of control of the means of violence. I shall discuss this at far greater length below, with regard to secession (which may suggest that this is far more of historical than of contemporary importance).

5. Extradition and alcohol

Perhaps it's worth mentioning the promise that states make one another, in Article IV, to return certain fugitives who have fled from one state to another. Historically, the most important such commitment involved the compulsory return of fugitive slaves, but the additional promise to return "A Person charged in any State with Treason, Felony, or other Crime, who shall flee from Justice; and be found in another State" upon the "demand" of the governor of the state from which the person fled remains significant. Although not so disruptive to social harmony as the so-called Fugitive Slave Clause, the Extradition Clause can nonetheless generate controversy. This can occur either when the two states differ on the substantive merits of making particular conduct illegal or where there are deep suspicions on the part of the state being asked to extradite someone about the fairness of the procedures that led to the charge. This was most obviously the case in the past with regard to Northern suspicions of the procedural fairness of Southern cases involving African Americans. Thus, from the perspective of the returning state, this may be viewed as a *burden* on state autonomy, a *price* of national union rather than a benefit (until that particular state demands extradition from another state that might have its own reluctance about following the Constitution's mandate).

There is also the Twenty-first Amendment, which on its face seems to guarantee a state absolute control over the regulation of alcohol within its territory, though some recent decisions of the Supreme Court have challenged the scope of state authority in this realm. But even if the ability of the state to regulate alcohol were complete, that would be small beer, as it were, when compared to such issues as education, the environment, or family law—none of which is explicitly "reserved" to the states and all of which are increasingly subject to controversial regulation by institutions of the national government. Imagine, for example, a constitution that specified that such important subject matter areas or policy domains were indeed to be "reserved" to the states. There are *no* such provisions in the Constitution. Still, there are implicit, even if decidedly non-textual, understandings about the nature of the balances struck between the national and state levels of government. How are those deals, whether explicit or implicit, to be maintained?

V. MAINTAINING THE DEAL(S)

A. Trust, mistrust, and federalism

Recall the basic argument that the most plausible empirical explanation of federalism is the presence of conflicting groups who do not sufficiently trust one another to enter into a *unitary* polity that places all relevant power in whatever political coalition can gain control of the national government. That this coalition might even plausibly claim to represent a majority of the entire populace is irrelevant if you are a member of a vulnerable minority worried that the majority will be indifferent to your claims (or will become so as soon as that appears politically costless). Again it is worth recalling Madison's argument in *Federalist* 10 with regard to the greater ease of local majorities to gain power and, therefore, to tyrannize (i.e., engage in offensively "factious" conduct over) local minorities in the *states*. One advantage of moving to the national stage, therefore, would be the stumbling blocks placed in front of such local majorities and, therefore, the overall greater likelihood that the non-factious "common good" would be served by national legislation. Though some people at the time no doubt understood and agreed with Madison's arguments, the far greater likelihood is that most people neither understood nor necessarily agreed with them; the target audience of the *Federalist* was those who were afraid of the enhanced power of the national unit.

All federal constitutions exemplify deals among mistrustful groups, by which they first agree to give the central government some important powers, but then agree as well to "reserve" other powers to the constituent subunits. Along the way, they might also agree to *limit* the powers of state governments in certain respects, but the easiest way to limit such powers is by establishing a unitary government that will be able to pull the plug on decentralization gone wrong.

So what is the most obvious good that a central government provides? It is defense against external threats—"in unity there is strength." But, at the same time, the new, more empowered national government must reassure the subunits that its power won't be used to deprive the states of autonomy on issues of vital interest to them. As the perception of outside threats wanes, one might expect that the enthusiasm of the subunits for a strong national government might diminish as well. This tension was at the core of the call for a new constitutional convention in 1787.

Let's look for a moment at some important political realities of the 1780s that generated the call for reform and the strengthening of the national government. A fundamental reality is that the national government, such as it was, was nearly broke. Under the Articles, all the purportedly national government could do was to issue "requisitions" to the various states, in which the national government basically pleaded with the members to tax its own citizens and then convey the proceeds to the central government. Calvin Johnson has noted that the requisition of 1786, the last under the old regime, asked the states to remit a total of approximately $3.8 million, of which a grand total of $663 was actually received.[39] As Hamilton argued in *Federalist* 15, what were intended to be solemn, even sacred, obligations of the states had been reduced to "mere recommendations," indeed "pompous petitions for charity." 1786 surely represented the utter collapse of the requisition system, but it had never functioned well in the first place. Jenna Bednar includes an illuminating table noting that the thirteen original states paid a range of 64 percent (New York) and 0 percent (Georgia) of the requisitions asked of them. Massachusetts ponied up 42 percent, which put it well ahead of its neighbors—Rhode Island contributed 5 percent, New Hampshire 18 percent, and Connecticut 14 percent.[40] No national government can function in such a condition, which is presumably the very definition of "ungovernability."

It was also the case, incidentally, that the government established by the Articles could not raise its own armies. Here, too, it had to call on the constituent units to send troops (and the money to pay them). Fortunately for the cause of independence, the states complied at a higher rate than with regard to taxes, but the figures still send decidedly mixed messages. Thus, with regard to the requisitions for troops between 1777 and 1783, New York was again in first place with a 77 percent rate, and Connecticut was very narrowly behind at 75 percent. But no other states crossed the 70 percent threshold, and the two Carolinas tied for the lowest rate at 26 percent.

So in many ways the two most important parts of the new Constitution involved the explicit assignment of power to tax (and spend) for the general welfare and to raise a national "standing" army that would not be dependent on the states. It should be clear that the new Constitution was not defended primarily as a device for protecting individual rights but rather as an instrument for creating a new government that could adequately protect Americans against perceived dangers.

There were other, more internal dangers as well. Many of the Philadelphia delegates defined as dangerous the passage by Rhode Island and other states of debtor-relief legislation, which was thought to threaten the economy. This explains the presence of the Contract Clause in Article I, Section 10, designed explicitly to prevent such legislation. And there were other assignments of power to the national government, set out in Article I, Section 8. So what we see is a system that consists, broadly, of a national government with new assignments of powers—some of them quite broad—and states that are at once prohibited from doing certain things (see Article I, Section 10) and at the same time promised that they will retain their traditional autonomy on a variety of issues of special importance, even though almost none are spelled out. The only specific prohibitions on the national government in the original Constitution are found in Article I, Section 9; however important they might be, they scarcely speak to the central concerns of those suspicious of the new government.

The problem, then, is obvious: what assures that the multiple deals necessary to achieve a federation in the first place will in fact be kept? One can obviously write down specific promises, what Filippov and his colleagues call "level-one" protections of a federal bargain. But there are at least two problems. The first is that developments over time will diminish the importance of much that was written down and highlight the importance of other policy domains that were left unaddressed (and where no promises were made). The second was classically stated by Madison in *Federalist* 48: "Will it be sufficient to mark with precision the boundaries of these departments in the constitution of the government, and to trust to these parchment barriers against the encroaching spirit of power?" The answer is no. Part of the problem, as Madison (following John Locke) demonstrated in a remarkable passage in *Federalist* 37, involves the almost inevitable indeterminacies of language, so we are not actually clear about the precise content of the promises. But even if the language *is* on occasion suitably precise, it still constitutes only a mere promise that could all too easily be broken when it was in the interest of one or another government to do so.

Thus even if the Constitution included more explicit reservations of state decisional autonomy than it does, these might turn out to be relatively unimportant. There are two great dangers. The first is the "encroachments" of the national government. But one should be equally concerned about the "shirking" of the states with regard to their own promises of subordination, even if not total, to the new national government. The breakdown of the requisition system is the best example of such shirking. "Free riding" is the favored term among economists to refer to those who wish to enjoy the benefits of deals without actually paying for them. But, in addition to shirking, there is also the danger that states will adopt policies that will impose costs on their neighbors in the absence of a sufficiently strong national government. What sort of arrangements can be counted on to preserve the federal system that exquisitely balances both state and national interests?

As Filippov and his colleagues suggest, above level-one promises spelled out in texts are level-two institutional structures, including a Senate appointed by state legislatures and a judiciary that will presumably be willing and able to monitor both state and national governments to make sure that they are faithfully complying with the deals as originally made. As already noted, though, one problem with looking to the federal judiciary as the "umpire of federalism" is that it seems, by virtue of the appointment process, more likely to have nationalist loyalties than state-oriented ones; relying on state courts would generate the opposite problem.

But there is also a more inchoate body of level-three cultural and ideological values that will reinforce—or call into question—the maintenance of federalism. They are at the heart of James Madison's argument, in *Federalist* 46, as to why opponents of the new Constitution ought not be very concerned about the new national government—and its enhanced powers—that ratification of the Constitution entails.

B. So what will preserve state autonomy, according to Madison? The "political sociology" of Federalist 46

Devotees of state autonomy might be especially worried if they were aware, as we are, of what Madison and Hamilton, and others, had said in the secrecy of the Philadelphia Convention about the (ir)responsibility of state governments and the need for a far-strengthened national government. What could be (and was) said in private and what could be articulated in public, though, might be quite different, especially once the task was not simply writing a constitution but gaining its ratification in thirteen separate state conventions. The *Federalist Papers* are not abstract exercises in political theory presented to a seminar; they are propaganda, even if of an extraordinarily high quality, designed to justify the Constitution to those who might be doubtful. Among the most doubtful were strong proponents of what we would today call "states' rights." *Federalist* 46 is Madison's (and *The Federalist*'s) most extended response to the all-important question of why states should rely on the national government to preserve state autonomy.

Madison insists, plausibly or not, that the new Constitution offers only a limited "sphere of jurisdiction" to the new national government. But his primary argument is one of *political sociology* and not based on the raw text of the Constitution, which scarcely supports, in any unequivocal way suitable to a Constitution of Settlement, a reading of significantly limited national powers. Thus he emphasizes the crucial reality that "the first and most natural attachment of the people will be to the governments of their respective states." That is, ordinary citizens will naturally identify with their state governments and view the national government as a fairly remote, and possibly mistrusted, entity. The image he sketches of the United States in *Federalist* could be applied to the United Nations, which no one would confuse with a "world government" not only because the various states ratifying the United Nations Charter most certainly do not intend to give up much, if any, of their pre-existing legal authority as sovereign states but also, and perhaps more fundamentally, because almost no one identifies him or herself primarily as a "citizen of the United Nations" instead of a citizen of one of the member states. One doesn't need complex social science "evidence" of this last point. You need only look into your own consciousness and ask what constitutes your primary sociopolitical identity.

So, in effect, Madison seems to suggest that what is the case today for almost all of us with regard to the United Nations is substantially true for the United States, at least as of 1787. Perhaps he was reflecting his own knowledge of his home state of Virginia. He could not have known that some seventy-two years after Madison published *Federalist* 46, Robert E. Lee, the West Point-trained general who had been offered command of the Union armies by Abraham Lincoln, would vindicate Madison's sociological observation by giving priority to his identity as a Virginian. Lee was obviously not alone in rejecting national in favor of state identity.

Indeed, Madison should have been unsurprised by the events of 1861 for yet another reason. He predicted, after all, that "ambitious encroachments of the federal government, on the authority of the state governments, would not excite the opposition [only] of a single state or of a few states." Instead, there would be a "general alarm" throughout the country, and "every government would espouse the common cause." This indeed had happened in 1774–1776, when what turned out to be a disastrously overreaching British policy toward the single colony of Massachusetts following the Boston Tea Party in fact incited a revolutionary response in all of the colonies.[41] This kind of "universal" response may have been lacking in 1860–1861, but there was certainly enough to cause reasonable leaders to believe that they had legitimate grounds to withdraw from the Union and that they could make a go of it as an independent Confederate States of America. And, finally, they were encouraged in this perception by the existence of state militias. It is these state militias that, in a very deep sense, comprise the most important level-two reinforcements of the "federal bargain," at least from the perspective of the states, should the national government prove overbearing.

C. Level-two institutional protection

1. The legislature and the executive

Before turning more fully to militias (and, ultimately, secession), one might wonder why other level-two protections broke down by 1860. The Senate, given its mode of selection, might be expected to be attentive to general issues of state autonomy, but this might end up undercutting sufficient concern for preserving the Union itself. If federalism is explicable in part because of the importance of what might be termed "deep diversity," what happens if a particular issue that divides us, culturally and politically, also takes a strongly territorial dimension? This issue, of course, was slavery, which *did* ultimately become strongly defined along territorial lines. For better or worse, the compromise, "rotten" or otherwise, that created the Union in 1787 might have been maintained had there been no expansion of the United States. The five free states that would be created out of the territories that were the subject of the Northwest Ordinance—Ohio, Indiana, Michigan, Illinois, and Wisconsin—would be neatly counterbalanced by the Southwest States that would shortly enter the Union as Kentucky, Tennessee, Alabama, and Mississippi. And, so long as population growth in the new United States was spread relatively equally between North and South, the federal bargain regarding slavery would almost certainly stick, for better or—for millions of people—distinctly for worse.

What changed this? The answer is the 1803 Louisiana Purchase, which, as historian William Freehling suggests, should really be called the "Midwest Purchase," since it more than doubled U.S. territory, ranging from New Orleans, the point of the original negotiations, to what is now eastern Montana. Many new states would be created, and it mattered greatly whether they would be slave states or free states, especially in the Senate, with its principal of equal voting power among the states. Given that every single member of the House and Senate is elected locally, rather than in a truly national (or even regional) election, it is not surprising that senators will represent the views of their constituents, who may be increasingly disinclined to compromise with other states and regions which they view as engaging in immoral conduct. Thus we see the increasing polarization of views in both the Senate and the House throughout the 1850s, when senators were ever more "hard-core" pro- or anti-slavery. What might be called a level-three culture of "bi-sectional accommo-dation" was breaking down. Abolitionists were never more than a minority, but the new Republican Party, created out of the wreckage of the Whigs, did define slavery as one of the "twin relics of barbarism" and pledged to prevent any further expansion into the territories. That would assure that any future states would be admitted as free states.

Just as importantly, it turned out that the patterns of population growth ended up favoring the free part of the United States, with consequences for the House of Representatives. To be sure, the slave states were still far better off than they might otherwise be, because of the Three-fifths Compromise, but they were increasingly nervous about what political sci-entists would call the "self-maintaining" features of the Constitution. The electoral college had worked wonderfully overall to protect the interests of what was often called "the slavocracy," but that came crashing to a dra-matic end in 1860, when Abraham Lincoln gained the White House with a majority of electoral votes while winning less than 40 percent of the popular vote (and, as one might predict, gaining no electoral votes in any of the fifteen slave states, eleven of which would attempt to secede).

2. What about courts?

Let's look once more at courts and their adequacy to maintain the federal bargain. As almost all political scientists recognize, the presence of judicial review is strongly correlated with federalism, for courts are assigned the role of the "impartial" third parties who can adjudicate disputes between the national government and the states when they accuse each other of fail-ing to implement the terms of the bargain. But this requires that one views the courts as genuinely "impartial," worthy of the trust claimed for them.

So consider one of the most famous episodes in the history of the early United States, the Federalist enactment of the Alien and Sedition Acts that made it a crime, among other things, to criticize the president of the United States. (Interestingly enough, it was not a crime to criticize the vice president, who just happened to be the Federalists' adversary Thomas Jefferson.) Jeffersonians uniformly thought that the Sedition Act was an "encroachment" by the national government. There was, after all, the First Amendment, which provided that Congress shall make no law abridging freedom of speech.

Jefferson's response was to float the idea of the "nullification" by states of national legislation that they viewed as violating the federalist bargain; Madison was more moderate. The years 1798–1799 saw the passage by the Kentucky and Virginia legislatures of resolutions challenging the Sedition Act, with accompanying justificatory reports written by Jefferson and Madison. Both states relied, among other things, on the "compact" theory of "essence of Union," which allowed, they argued, the compacting states to declare the offending legislation offensive to the Constitution and—for proponents of "nullification" like Jefferson—null and void. As a matter of fact, "nullification" was rejected as a constitutional possibility by almost all the other states and by almost all constitutional theorists. The presence of "almost" indicates that the doctrine always has had, even now, some adherents.[42] One might place it at the outer boundary of The Constitution of Conversation, but it is safe to say that no "mainstream" lawyer or political figure countenances the possibility.

Why not rely on courts to monitor national overreaching? Madison offered his answer in the Virginia Report defending the resolution of 1798.[43] First, it is possible that there "may be instances of usurped power, which the forms of the Constitution would never draw within the control of the judicial department." That is, if courts have only *limited* jurisdiction, then some issues will not come before them even if they raise deep questions about constitutional fidelity. But Madison also writes of the impropriety of raising "the decision of the judiciary…above the authority of the sovereign parties to the Constitution," that is, the states themselves. "The decisions of the other departments"—in this case the states—"must be equally authoritative and final with the decisions of that department." This is especially important with regard to "those great and extraordinary cases, in which all the forms of the Constitution may prove ineffectual against infractions dangerous to the essential rights of the parties to it.

The [Virginia] resolution supposes that dangerous powers, not delegated, may not only be usurped and executed by the other departments, but that the judicial department also may exercise or sanction dangerous powers beyond the grant of the Constitution; and, consequently, that the ultimate right of the parties to the Constitution, to judge whether the compact has been dangerously violated, must extend to violations by one delegated authority, as well as by another; by the judiciary, as well as by the executive, or the legislature."

And, frankly, why should one put such faith in a judiciary, all of whose members are appointed (and paid) by the national government? The system we have, Madison is suggesting, does not justify the level of trust that some would place in it. These arguments link with those we saw articulated by Jackson and Lincoln in the previous chapter, but they were, most notably, taken up by Jefferson Davis and other proponents of secession.

3. Autonomy and militias

So if national institutions like the legislature and the courts lose their luster with regard to keeping to the federal bargain of only a limited government, what is next? One ominous response is to withdraw from the federation itself, by secession. Before examining the constitutional arguments with regard to any such claimed right, we should look at another level-two autonomy right found at least in the amended Constitution: the apparent guarantee of the Second Amendment that each state may have its own militia.

This is no small matter, even if debates about the right to bear arms today focus more on alleged "individual rights." But why might a state *want* to have its own militia? One answer may be that a militia would be useful in quelling certain kinds of local troublemakers or providing order in a city ravaged by a hurricane. Indeed, one historical analysis of the origins of the Second Amendment emphasizes the relevance of "slave patrols" in the South. But another use for a militia might be as a potential means of defending a local state against what is perceived as the tyranny of the national government. Consider in this context the fact that the governors of both Pennsylvania and Virginia threatened to call out their state militias and send them to Washington if the Federalists didn't acquiesce to the election of Thomas Jefferson to the presidency in 1800 (as they finally did on the thirty-sixth ballot of the House of Representatives within three weeks of the March 4, 1801, Inauguration Day).

The German sociologist Max Weber famously defined the state, among other things, as possessing a monopoly over the legitimate use of violence. It's easy enough to figure out what this means if one is referring to a "unitary" government, defined as one with a clearly supreme authority over any and all territorial subunits (and individual citizens). But it is considerably more difficult to figure out the meaning if we refer to truly federal systems. Given the predictable difficulty, within any federal system, of "securing the bargain," especially with regard to preventing encroachments by the national government, isn't it reasonable for states to believe that having their own ability to maintain armies (called "militias") might be useful in warding off certain kinds of attacks on their residual sovereignty? To be sure, the Constitution is ambiguous on what might be termed the Weberian argument. Thus Article I, Section 10 explicitly prohibits a "State, without the Consent of Congress," from "keep[ing] Troops, or Ships of War, in time of Peace." Yet that same section does in fact empower states to "engage in War" if suffering not only "actual invas[ion,]" but also "such imminent Danger as will not admit of delay," and perhaps one should view Congress's willingness to propose what became the Second Amendment—numerically it was originally the Fourth Amendment, but the first two failed of ratification at the time—as implicit consent that the states should "keep troops."

Consider very carefully a paragraph in *Federalist* 46, written by Madison, on the importance of an armed citizenry and the ultimate protection that offers against even a "federal government [that] may previously accumulate a military force for the projects of ambition." Madison asserts that "the highest number to which, according to the best computation, a standing army can be carried in any country," would lead to a national army of no more "than twenty-five or thirty thousand men. To these would be opposed a militia amounting to near half a million of citizens with arms in their hands, officered by men chosen from among themselves, fighting for their common liberties, and united and conducted by governments possessing their affections and confidence." He evokes "the last successful resistance of this country against the British arms" as evidence of the power of a citizen-militia. So the ultimate tier-two defenses are in effect "the advantage of being armed, which the Americans possess over the people of almost every other nation [and] the existence of subordinate governments, to which the people are attached." Both assure that the "free and gallant citizens of America" are "able to defend the rights of which they would be in actual possession."

There is, incidentally, a side argument as to whether this should be read as requiring that any such militia be firmly in the hands of the states (even if not the national government) or instead under more "communal" control. After all, if one can imagine a potentially oppressive national government that needs the disciplining response from states, one might also imagine state governments that could profit from a similar show of force by aroused citizenry. And Madison in *Federalist* 10 had made the classic argument as to why one might, as a member of a vulnerable minority, feel greater concerns at the state than the national level. These are not pleasant questions to contemplate. But it is a fundamental mistake to view "constitutionalism" as unconnected with the means of violence. After all, the debate about the president's power as commander-in-chief is ultimately a debate about who has the power to inflict violence, maiming, and death (and, in turn, to accept the reality of those events with regard to those defending the United States).

So let me direct the following question to you. Imagine that you are consulting with *any* of the various groups in Iraq, Afghanistan, or Libya regarding the creation of a suitable constitution for those ethnically and religiously divided countries. Would you advise your clients to hand over their arms and disband their militias and therefore place their trust in the new central government that the constitution is creating? Or, on the contrary, would you maintain their right "to keep and bear arms," at least until enough "verification" had taken place—possibly over many years—to engender sufficient trust in a Weberian state? Does whatever answer you give for those three decidedly unhappy countries have any implications at all for the responses you might make with regard to the modern United States or any other countries you might think of? Recall the earlier-quoted comments of Sharron Angle while running for the Senate from Nevada about the potential need "for the people to protect themselves against a tyrannical government" and the beneficial role that by be played by "those Second Amendment remedies."[44]

It is unlikely that many readers of this book agree with Ms. Angle's particular assessment of contemporary American politics and her specific reasons for sharing the widespread dissatisfaction with the direction the country is going.[45] But she makes an important point about the provenance of the Second Amendment. If one *did* agree with her about the "tyrannical" nature of the national government, would it be frivolous to suggest that a given state, committed to the importance of a "non-tyrannical" view of politics, might mobilize itself against the centralized oppression? One might well wonder if there is a truly shared baseline for determining what is "tyrannical" or "non-tyrannical," but that raises yet other problems when trying to assesss *any* political institutions for their propensity to achieve the "public good."

4. Secession

And so we come to secession and its constitutional status. In the context of this book, perhaps the overarching question is whether secession is best treated as part of the Constitution of Settlement or the Constitution of Conversation. And, whatever your answer, has that *always* been true, since the ratification of the Constitution in 1787–1788, or has it changed since then, for whatever reason? It should be clear that there is no hard-and-fast piece of text that provides a yea-or-nay answer to the question, "Do states in the United States have a constitutional right of secession?" Is this lack a bug or a feature? That is, should the Constitution have explicitly addressed the potential tension between a "more perfect Union," as an aspiration, and the possibility that the national government would not honor the rights "reserved" to the states and thus warrant the possibility of their withdrawal? Cass Sunstein argues that a well-drafted federal constitution should *never* legitimize secession; one assumes that he would endorse the explicit prohibition of secession even if this makes it marginally less likely that the parties will agree to a constitution in the first place. Legitimate secession, by definition, allows what the economist Albert Hirschman famously labeled the option of "exit" from a trying political situation, instead of remaining and exercising "voice." One reason to contemplate exit, whether from a marriage or from a state, is that one feels totally ignored, even if one is "allowed," as a formal matter, to speak. If, however, no one genuinely listens or, even more to the point, responds adequately to one's complaints, why can't one choose to leave the no longer functional relationship?

On February 11, 1861, while traveling from Springfield, Illinois, to his inauguration, Lincoln spoke to an audience in Indianapolis and derided the secessionist argument in the following way: "In their view, the Union, as a family relation, would not be anything like a regular marriage at all, but only as a sort of free-love arrangement [laughter] to be maintained on what that sect calls passionate attraction [continued laughter]." Let me suggest, though, that this is no laughing matter, or perhaps it is best described as "gallows humor." After all, how many of us, in the twenty-first century, have a view of "regular marriage" that precludes divorce, particularly if "passionate attraction" has disappeared? It is undoubtedly better if both sides agree to the divorce, but what if one of them does not, whether because still hopelessly attached to the marriage or out of sheer malice? At that point, would we support what might be termed "unilateral secession" from the marriage, based on the logic of individual consent and the illegitimacy of the state's forcing a continuing relationship upon someone who might even view it as akin to slavery?

An interestingly different argument was presented in the concluding paragraph of James Buchanan's final State of the Union message to Congress in December 1860. The hapless Buchanan agreed with Lincoln that secession was illegal, but he also believed that the national government was without practical power to prevent it beyond pleading with the states in question not to do it:

> The fact is that our Union rests upon public opinion, and can never be cemented by the blood of its citizens shed in civil war. If it can not live in the affections of the people, it must one day perish. Congress possesses many means of preserving it by conciliation, but the sword was not placed in their hand to preserve it by force.[46]

This book is being published during the commemoration of the sesquicentennial of the war that began in 1861 and killed 600,000 Americans in the next four years. Lincoln obviously did not start the war, but his decision to respond to the attack on Fort Sumter certainly helped to cause the conflagration. Was it worth it? If so, is it justified by the simple preservation of the Union, against the desire of eleven states to go their own way, as had the then-British colonies in 1776, or must one emphasize the importance of eradicating slavery? If it is the latter that justifies the war and its costs, what does that suggest about accepting the particular form of American federalism that was proposed and ratified in 1787? Were the anti-slavery anti-Federalists correct, after all?

VI. CODA

Federalism is an unusually complex concept. As noted at the outset, there is no universally accepted definition of the term. Moreover, and perhaps more importantly, there is no easy way to determine the relationship between federalism, however defined, and governability. The German political scientist Franz Neumann (who, after fleeing Germany, had an illustrious career at Columbia) wrote a notable article in 1955 on the relationship between "federalism and freedom" in which he ultimately concluded: "It all depends." Thus, he wrote, it "seems impossible to attribute to federalism, as such, a value; or to assert that the federal state—as contrasted to the unitary state—enhances political and civil freedom by dividing power among autonomous territorial subdivisions...There are no values that inhere in federalism as such, and federalism cannot be defended successfully on the grounds that the inevitable tendency of a unitary state is toward political repression."[47] Perhaps the key word is "inevitable." Neumann certainly does not denounce federalism and proclaim that it has its own inevitable tendencies, whether fortunate or unfortunate. In some countries, among them the United States, federalism, at least historically, is impossible to disengage from slavery and racism. Thus, William Riker, an eminent political scientist, once declared that "if in the United States one disapproves of racism, one should disapprove of federalism."[48] On the other hand, those who analogize discrimination against gays and lesbians to racism can point to the lead taken by a number of states, including New York, in legalizing same-sex marriage.

It is impossible to credit federalism with enhancing the "governability" of the United States in the run-up to the conflagration of 1861–1865. Perhaps federalism *did* contribute to governability and the reunion of the country following that war, but only by placing African Americans, by and large, at the tender mercies of local whites. Federalism raises the same basic questions as do the other institutional settlements examined in this book:[49] how—and under what circumstances—do they enhance the admittedly broad notion of "governability"? However broad and inevitably contested, "governability" presumably includes at least the ability of governments, at both the national and state levels, to make decisions that both receive the requisite amount of public approval within relevant political constituencies (and thus have some "democratic" warrant) and as well contribute in some sense to what the Preamble terms the "general Welfare" of the United States and the creation of a "more perfect Union." To the extent that federalism, in its own way, at least on occasion, contributes to the inability of government(s) to do this, then it must at least be described as part of the problem rather than the potential solution.

15

Amendment

I. CONSTITUTIONAL "(IM)PERFECTION" AND THE POSSIBILITY/NECESSITY OF AMENDMENT

Let's assume that one believes that a weakness of the U.S. Constitution is that it doesn't speak clearly, one way or the other, to the possibility of secession. One obvious solution is to amend the Constitution to specify whatever position you think best, whether to allow secession under carefully laid-out procedures or to reject the possibility categorically. But at that point one necessarily confronts the reality of the U.S. Constitution with regard to the difficulties it places in the way of amendment.

This, however, generates a seeming tension in the Constitution: the only reason to desire a provision allowing constitutional amendment at all is belief that the Constitution, however admirable as drafted, might display "imperfections" in the future that need to be changed. As a logical matter, all one need do is imagine a single imperfection that one might like to see changed, even if it's not tremendously important and does relatively little to lessen one's overall esteem for the Constitution. But one might be less than admiring of *many* initial features of a constitution, especially if some of them can be explained by the felt need for (rotten) political compromise rather than genuine conviction that fidelity to basic principles required them. At that point, one might be much more concerned about amending the Constitution inasmuch as much more is perceived to be at stake. In either case, though, one is presented with a basic question: how easy or difficult should it be to amend a constitution?

If it is too easy, then one might be tempted to deny the designation of "constitution" to whatever it is we're talking about. We might instead refer to it simply as an "initiating statute" that, like any other statute, can be changed by the ordinary political process. Perhaps this should be our view of the Austrian or Swedish Constitutions, which are the easiest-to-amend constitutions of those studied by political scientist Donald Lutz, who has devised the metric of an "amendment rate" to determine the practical (non)amendability of any given constitution.[1] So consider that the amendment rate of Austria is 7/year, of Sweden, 4.72/year. Interestingly, Malaysia, which has a higher "index of difficulty" with regard to the formal procedures necessary to amend its constitution, beats out Sweden in that it had, at least up to when Lutz was writing his essay in 1994, just over five amendments per year. These countries also have impressively (or, perhaps, depressingly) long constitutions: Malaysia's was, as of 1994, over 90,000 words, while Sweden came in fifteenth in the world at just over 40,000 words, and Austria's constitution had 36,000. The United States has an extraordinarily low amendment rate (.13/year) and an unusually short constitution, approximately 7,400 words.

American states are all over the map. As of 1994, California and South Carolina led the pack with a rate of over four amendments per year. Vermont had the lowest rate, less than .25/year, though Indiana, Kentucky, Tennessee, and Illinois were also under .33/year. In absolute numbers, the Texas Constitution, adopted in 1876, has been amended more than 450 times, while the California Constitution, adopted in 1879, has seen over five hundred amendments. The record for amendments is held by Alabama, whose constitution, the longest in the world at 340,136 words, has been amended since 1901 an astounding 821 times as of 2011. Even the "youngest" of the state constitutions, the Rhode Island Constitution of 1986, has been amended twenty-one times in its first quarter-century of existence.[2] And Vermont, even with the lowest amendment rate among the states, has nevertheless amended its constitution fifty times.

It is worth noting that all of these states have had multiple constitutions over their histories. South Carolina leads that particular race with seven constitutions, the most recent adopted in 1895. Kentucky and Illinois have each had four, and the Land of Lincoln is living under one of the newer state constitutions, dating only to 1972. Tennessee and Vermont have each had three constitutions, though Vermont's current constitution dates back to 1793, when an obvious early spate of constitution drafting and revision came to an end. California and Indiana have each made do with only two constitutions, though in California especially there have been recurrent (and unsuccessful) calls for a new constitutional convention that might address the glaring dysfunctionalities of the Golden State's existing foundation. Other states present their own colorful histories, including Georgia and Louisiana, with their ten and eleven constitutions, respectively.

One might believe that what is special about constitutions is that they take certain issues out of ordinary politics by proclaiming that some very particular process will be necessary in order to change things. From this perspective, a high amendment rate—or, even more striking, a high number of constitutions—can be quite damning. After all, there is an old joke about someone going to the French National Library and asking for a copy of the French Constitution, only to be told that it is available in the periodicals division. Now that the French Constitution that formed the Fifth Republic in 1958 is a full half-century old, one can wonder when the joke loses its punch.

Surely *some* change is desirable. But *some* obviously doesn't mean *all.* Perhaps certain things should be unchangeable, truly off the table not only of ordinary legislation but even of the extraordinary (and usually supermajoritarian) procedures attached to amendment in most political systems. The post–World War II German Constitution offers a model of limited changelessness. Article 79 of the German Constitution states, "Amendments to this Basic Law affecting the division of the Federation into Länder, their participation on principle in the legislative process, or the principles laid down in Articles 1 and 20 shall be inadmissible." Article 1 states: "(1) Human dignity shall be inviolable. To respect and protect it shall be the duty of all state authority. (2) The German people therefore acknowledge inviolable and inalienable human rights as the basis of every community, of peace and of justice in the world." Article 20 provides that the state, "mindful also of its responsibility toward future generations...shall protect the natural bases of life by legislation and, in accordance with law and justice, by executive and judicial action, all within the framework of the constitutional order."

Some observers have taken this to mean that not only is it unconstitutional to allow abortion in Germany, which the German Constitutional Court held was the case in 1975, but also that it would be unconstitutional to attempt to amend the German Constitution to allow abortion. This notion of an "unconstitutional constitutional amendment," which has also become part of Indian constitutional discussion, raises fundamental theoretical issues. It doesn't mean that the constitution in question can, as an empirical matter, never be changed in these areas. It *does* mean, though, that it would be necessary to engage in a political *revolution* to bring that change about.

So with regard to the U.S. Constitution, we might ask ourselves if Article V allows any and all amendments, so long as they surmount the supermajoritarian hurdles the article establishes. Or are there are *any* features of our own Constitution that are, as a legal (and not merely empirical) matter, impervious to amendment?

Many people offer the guarantee of equal membership in the Senate, at least insofar as it requires the unanimous consent of all the states. But unanimous consent is only a presumably insurmountable procedural hurdle to amendment. If states *would* consent to their diminished representation in the Senate, Article V would not prevent that. Consider, though, the other protection offered by Article V, which is the guarantee that Congress would not be able to bar American participation in the international slave trade until 1808. One might read this as protecting individual slave-traders in a way that the Senate protected "only" the states. States could, at least in theory, waive the protection against unequal votes in the Senate. But, perhaps, not even the unanimous consent of the states would have authorized an amendment allowing the abolition of the slave trade earlier than 1808. This is not worth further discussion because it is clearly only of academic interest.

But the Senate as such is another matter. Given the practical impossibility of modifying the distribution of power in the Senate, what of Akhil Amar's suggestion that it would be perfectly legitimate to amend the Constitution through ordinary procedures and to *abolish* the Senate (so that each state would have the equal representation of zero senators) or simply reduce greatly the powers of the Senate, as happened with the British House of Lords? Perhaps the Senate's role could be confined to confirming those selected to serve as ambassadors to foreign countries. If one does believe that there are benefits to bicameralism, perhaps the amendment could also create a new "third house" elected along more defensible principles than the present Senate. Would that not be perfectly faithful to the letter of the Constitution, as well as the democratic spirit of the twenty-first century, even those who brokered the Compromise in 1787 would be mightily offended? But why should we care?

In any event, when contemplating amendment procedures, we're caught once more in Goldilocks's dilemma of figuring out the "just right" position between the "too hot" of a too easily changeable constitution and the 'too cold" of one that is impervious to change, especially if the imperviousness is across the board instead of with regard to only one or two value commitments of the very highest order. There may be something to be said for requiring extraordinary procedures to alter the most fundamental of our national commitments—or even preventing change altogether. But why should the procedures for changing Inauguration Day or the number of votes required to override a presidential veto be the same as those for altering the Bill of Rights?

II. THE SPECIFICS OF CONSTITUTIONAL AMENDMENT IN THE UNITED STATES

So, with regard to the Goldilocks question, it is easy to determine where the U.S. Constitution stands. Since the demise of the Yugoslav Constitution, the U.S. Constitution is, as Lutz demonstrated, the hardest constitution in the world to change through formal amendment. But Lutz and John Dinan also demonstrate that it is truly fallacious to say that the U.S. Constitution is typical of the U.S. constitutional order(s) as a whole, which requires paying some attention to the other fifty constitutions within the United States. The most banal reality, as noted above, is that state constitutions not only have been formally amended far more frequently than the national one but have also, with some frequency, been supplanted by new ones; the average number of constitutions per state in the United States is almost three.

Lutz notes that the average duration of state constitutions in the United States is seventy-seven years, and the median age, as of 1994, appears to have been ninety-six years. Since no new constitutions have been written since 1994, we can say that the median age of U.S. state constitutions is now over 110 years. Interestingly enough, a recently published book by Tom Ginsburg and Zach Elkins, titled *The Endurance of Constitutions*, studied all national constitutions over the past two centuries and concluded that the average endurance of a national constitution is only eighteen years. As with amendment rates, it is hard to know whether to be elated or depressed by such data unless one knows about specific constitutions and also has some sort of general notion of the desirable frequency of change. Thomas Jefferson, for example, notably defended the principle of revolution every generation, about nineteen years, which is astonishingly close to the typical endurance found by Ginsburg and Elkins. It is safe to say, though, that even most self-styled "Jeffersonians" find this one of Jefferson's more dubious ideas.

Still, under any measurement, there are multiple "traditions" within the United States of either constitutional amendment or full-scale replacement, as noted above, of an existing constitution by another. State constitutions evidence far more change than does the U.S. Constitution.

What explains this? The most obvious answer is that state constitutions are far easier to amend than the U.S. Constitution. Lutz has put together fascinating tables setting forth the amazing array of possibilities found in American states and foreign countries regarding the procedures of constitutional amendment. (By now, though, one should be used to such array of possibilities, since we've seen them earlier with regard to various forms of bicameralism and selection of judges.) Some states allow their citizens to take control of the amendment process away from legislators via the initiative and referendum; interestingly enough, Lutz concludes that legislatively initiated proposals fare better than do citizen-initiated ones. Some popular initiatives, such as the requirement that the California budget get the support of two-thirds of the legislators in both houses,[3] are especially important in their consequences. Still, Lutz finds the main variable in explaining different amendment rates to be the difficulty of getting a proposal through the legislature. Not surprisingly, the larger the majority that is required, the less likely are successful proposals. One should certainly not underrate the importance of formal rules (which is a major point of this book).

III. WHAT ABOUT "VENERATION"?

But is the formal difficulty of amending the U.S. Constitution the only, or even the best, explanation for the infrequency of formal change? To what extent do we refuse even to think about amending the Constitution, let alone actually do so, because of the success of James Madison's arguments in *Federalist* 49? Madison directly confronted arguments made by his close friend and colleague, Thomas Jefferson, who had pronounced himself in favor of frequent conventions.

In what became a recurrent theme of his writings, Madison expressed great doubts about the capacity of ordinary citizens to engage in self-governance. The period 1787–1788 was like an astrological convergence, and we should never expect it to happen again. And one way to help assure that there will never be another convention is to generate among the populace a "veneration" for the Constitution. To use again the analytical terminology developed by Filippov and his colleagues, if Article V itself serves as a level-two reinforcement of the existing Constitution, given the difficulty it imposes on anyone who supports constitutional change, "veneration" is a level-three cultural reinforcement.

Veneration is presumably reinforced by the way we teach the Constitution to the young, whether in grade-school civics courses or in college and law school courses. But there is the broader culture to consider as well. Almost all colleges and universities now celebrate Constitution Day—on or close to September 17, the anniversary of the signing of the final draft of the Constitution in Philadelphia—which is most often an occasion for celebrating our good fortune in having the Constitution. The explanation for these programs, incidentally, is a congressional statute passed at the behest of the late Senator Robert Byrd of West Virginia in 2004 that basically requires all educational institutions that accept federal funds to put on an appropriate program acknowledging Constitution Day.

Recent events in the wider culture have also reinforced veneration. Thus Dick Armey, the former majority leader of the House Republicans and now a major organizer of the Tea Party, has been described in a *New York Times* article as elevating the Constitution to "something like a sacred religious text, written by Christian believers, possibly divinely inspired and intended to be read in the most literal way. It contains solutions to any civic problem faced by modern Americans…To Armey, the Constitution is not a 'living document'—a phrase he mocks at rallies, to laughs and great applause." Thus, at one of the speeches covered in the article, Armey "emphasized that everyone must stay focused on the polestar, the nation's essential document. 'What should be your guide?' he said, pausing for a beat before shouting out the answer. 'The Constitution. This ain't no thinkin' thing.'"[4]

Paradoxically or not, some Tea Party adherents or sympathizers have suggested some constitutional amendments, but they scarcely exhibit any discontent with the 1787 Constitution itself. One proposal, adopted by the Idaho Republican Party in 2010, suggests repealing the Seventeenth Amendment and returning to selection of senators by state legislatures. Another, drafted by Georgetown Law Center Professor Randy Barnett and supported by a number of Republicans under the rubric of the "Reform Amendment" would give the state legislatures of two-thirds of the states the legal right to nullify any federal legislation deemed unacceptable. The impetus for this proposal is the perception that the original Constitution, ostensibly designed to create only a limited national government and to protect residual state autonomy, has gotten dangerously out of kilter. One can well doubt that either proposal stands any chance of passage, not least because the "Reform Amendment" further entrenches the power of small states by giving a remarkable new potential power to two-thirds of the states that contain less than a third of the total American population.

IV. DOES IT MAKE A PRACTICAL DIFFERENCE?

In any event, to the extent that the general public venerates the 1787 Constitution—not only its Framers—it may be almost irrelevant that Article V makes it functionally impossible to amend the Constitution with regard to anything truly important. There would be no impulse to do so in the first place. It is like telling someone in what is felt to be a wonderful marriage that he or she could get a divorce. So what? Why should that be of any interest at all?

But maybe it isn't so important that formal amendment is so difficult, or even that we purport to venerate the Constitution. If one teaches about the Constitution of Conversation instead of the Constitution of Settlement, one is thereby teaching a course about a multitude of important changes—many without the benefit of formal constitutional amendment—in the way we have interpreted the Constitution over our history. Indeed,

David Strauss has argued that our constitutional system has proved supple enough that what might even be described as "amendatory change" has frequently occurred without any formal amendment at all. All one needs, according to Strauss, is a legislature willing to propose new laws, a governor or president who backs them, a Supreme Court that legitimizes them, and a public that believes that this is an overall good thing. And that, he says, describes the most important aspects of our constitutional tradition.

Bruce Ackerman presents a more complex version of what is essentially a similar argument. American constitutional development, as he portrays it, consists of a series of "constitutional moments"; during such moments, visionary leaders, ultimately backed by "We the People," more or less violate existing constitutional norms in favor of responding to what is thought to serve our deepest national interests. The first constitutional moment, for Ackerman, was the Constitutional Convention itself, which he views as clearly breaking the legal bounds set by the Congress that authorized the Convention and, more to the point, the Articles of Confederation that set out the process of legal amendment. We will examine this aspect of Philadelphia at length in the next chapter. His second great moment is immediate aftermath of the Civil War, when the Thirteenth, Fourteenth, and Fifteenth Amendments were added to the Constitution. For Ackerman, the Fourteenth Amendment is especially important precisely because it is basically impossible to defend as an orthodox Article V amendment. Given the fundamental importance of the Fourteenth Amendment in what has become our standard conception of the Constitution, it is worth looking closely at Ackerman's argument.

Begin with the fact that the three-quarters of the states ratifying the Thirteenth Amendment included the former Confederate states that had been recognized as once again part of the Union by President Andrew Johnson. Twenty-seven (of thirty-six) states were required for ratification, and among the twenty-seven who had ratified it by December 6, 1865 (when it was declared part of the Constitution) were Arkansas, Tennessee, Louisiana, Alabama, North Carolina, South Carolina, and Georgia. (Mississippi, Delaware, Kentucky, and New Jersey had rejected it.) But, and here is where things get very interesting, the senators elected by the state governments who had ratified the Thirteenth Amendment and the representatives chosen in elections run by these states were not allowed in December 1865 to take their seats in the Congress, presumably under Article I, Section 5, which gives "Each House" the power to "be the Judge of the Elections, Returns, and Qualifications of its own Members." The Republican majority in the House and the Senate simply refused to seat the Democrats sent to Washington by the former Confederate states.

Why? The answer is remarkably simple: if they had been seated, they would have been able to uphold any and all vetoes being issued by Andrew Johnson, for whom the war was *only* about the principles of "no secession" and "no chattel slavery." Lee's surrender secured the first goal, and the ratification of the Thirteenth Amendment by the new post-Appomattox governments guaranteed the second. The defeated states, save for Mississippi, were willing to acknowledge that slavery had been eliminated as a legal possibility in part because the war had eliminated it as a practical one. (And Johnson had made it clear that acceptance of the amendment was the *quid pro quo* for re-entry to the Union.) But Johnson's vision included no place for racial justice beyond the elimination of the formal institution of the ownership of one human being by another. He thus had no real complaint at the spate of "black codes," designed to preserve white supremacy, being passed by the governments whose legitimacy he recognized. Johnson vetoed twenty-one laws passed by Congress during his term that were subject to congressional override; eight others were so-called pocket vetoes consisting of bills that Johnson refused to sign after Congress had already adjourned. Fifteen of the twenty-one were overridden, but almost 30 percent were sustained. Had the Southern members of Congress been seated, one can easily predict that none of the bills would have been overridden, including such fundamental legislation as the Civil Rights Bill of 1866. Nor would the Fourteenth Amendment ever have received the necessary two-thirds support in each house of Congress to be proposed to the states.

Things were bad in 1866; they would have been even worse after 1870, the time of the next census, had Johnson's generosity toward the defeated Confederacy been tolerated. For, following the new constitutionally required enumeration of population, the former Confederate states would return to the Congress with *enhanced* power: former slaves would now be counted as *whole*, instead of three-fifths of, persons, but they would still have no right to vote or otherwise participate in government. Many Republicans had a far more robust vision of what was implied by the slaughter of 600,000 Americans, including the "new birth of freedom" spoken of by Lincoln at Gettysburg. They were not about to tolerate the effective erasure of their vision because of the standard-form operations of the political system as established by the Constitution. This also, incidentally, explains the decision of the Republican House to impeach Johnson, even if the Senate, by one vote, refused to convict him. If one was at all serious about achieving "regime change" in the South, it was necessary not only to exclude the purported representatives and senators, but also to militarily occupy most of the defeated states and reorganize their governments.

The most important change was to require that the former slaves be allowed to vote, even before the Fifteenth Amendment. This new electorate is what explains the fact that Mississippi sent Hiram Revels to serve as the first African American senator in 1870. But, as added incentive to accept the new order, the former Confederate states were told in no uncertain terms that none of their representatives or senators would be seated until they ratified the Fourteenth Amendment. This, for Ackerman, was our second great constitutional moment, whose momentous changes can by no means be viewed simply through the lens of the existing Constitution and the amendment process set out in Article V.

For Ackerman, the third great constitutional moment was the New Deal, when the national government seized, or was acknowledged as having, far more power to control the economy than was ever imagined before. Unlike Reconstruction, there was not even the pretense of formal changes in the constitutional text. Instead, Congress and the president acted, and by 1942, a Supreme Court basically appointed by Roosevelt (with two exceptions) ruled unanimously in favor of New Deal measures similar to those that had been struck down by the conservative Supreme Court in 1935–1936.

To the extent that one accepts the Strauss and Ackerman arguments (though they differ in important respects), one will be less concerned about Article V as an impediment to change, though one may still find it disquieting to observe so much playing fast and loose with what one might have thought were constitutional requirements for amendatory change. Donald Lutz argues that there is an inverse relationship between the difficulty of formal change and the amount of change procured through inventive judicial interpretations and the like.

The fatal flaw in both Strauss's and Ackerman's arguments is that they tend to ignore the structural features that are the focus of this book. That is, I do not disagree with Ackerman that the vision of national power is transformed during the 1930s without the presence of a formal constitutional amendment. But what are not transformed are such institutional practices as the formalities of passing legislation in a bicameral system, the existence of the presidential veto, and so on. And the central point of this book is that these features are at least as important as the clauses that are part of the Constitution of Conversation. The latter is tightly interwoven with what I have elsewhere called the Narrative of Change[5] regarding our understanding of what the Constitution, properly interpreted, means. But just as the Constitution of Settlement complements the Constitution of Conversation, so should we be aware of the importance of attending to a complementary—and, I would argue, less happy—Narrative of Stasis, concentrating on the basically *unchanging* aspects of the Constitution.

V. SO HOW MIGHT FORMAL CHANGE OCCUR?

The answer to this question would be very different if we were discussing particular states instead of the United States. Delaware, for example, requires only that two-thirds of its house and senate agree to an amendment in two consecutive sessions to amend the constitution. Many other states require ratification by the electorate. California, notably but not uniquely, allows popular proposal of amendments and then popular ratification of these proposals. Quite obviously, the process is very different at the national level, and there is no reason to rehearse the differences again.

But note that Article V *does* contemplate an alternative to Congressional proposal of amendments: the calling of a new constitutional convention to consider any necessary changes. John Dinan's book is based on the more than two hundred state conventions that have occurred over the past two centuries and the rich history of debates they have left in the public record. Only nine of the fifty states have had just one constitutional convention. What one usually thinks of as the sober state of New Hampshire has had seventeen such conventions, no doubt because Article 100 in the state constitution requires that the electorate be able to vote at least once every ten years as to whether they wish a convention to be called. Thirteen other states, as Dinan notes, have similar provisions in their constitutions. So an obvious question is this: is it a source of pride or lament that the U.S. Constitution includes no such provision?

An unduly strict reading of the Constitution's text would tie a new constitutional convention to the collective decision of at least two-thirds of the state legislatures to petition Congress to call such a convention. That is, it would make satisfaction of this supermajority requirement a *necessary* condition for convening a new convention. It seems far more plausible, however, to treat it as establishing only a *sufficient* condition, as a safeguard against congressional recalcitrance. But why should we choose to read the Constitution to deprive Congress of that power? This question may demonstrate that it is not always easy to distinguish between the Constitutions of Settlement and Conversation. As is shown in the next chapter, we are most inclined to "unsettle" what some view as unambiguous texts if we are persuaded that the consequences of accepting the settled version would be unfortunate, if not calamitous.

But the next question is whether it would be a good idea to have a convention. Not the least problem of the text of Article V is that it provides no clue as to how a convention would be organized, including the all-important question of allocation of voting power within a convention. Would it emulate the Philadelphia Convention and assign each state equal voting power, or would it follow the principal of one delegate, one vote? But how would the delegates be chosen? Recall the earlier discussion of lottery selection as an alternative form of "representative government" that does not require elections. Might that be a good way of selecting delegates?

One might well wonder how any proposals emanating from the convention would in fact be ratified. Akhil Amar argues quite strongly and, I think, persuasively for the validity of a national referendum that would bypass the state legislatures and the requirement of approval by three-quarters of the states. This would mimic the decision of the Philadelphia Convention to disregard the stringency of the Thirteenth Article of Confederation and its requirement of unanimous approval by state legislatures. No doubt many readers will disagree with me and Amar in believing that Article V could in effect be side-stepped if a new convention generated the same degree of popular legitimacy as was achieved by the Philadelphia Convention. Suffice it to say that such side-stepping could occur if and only if the convention established itself as truly legitimate and sagacious in the eyes of most Americans—who might well be watching it on C-Span, given the impossibility of replicating the secrecy of the original Philadelphia Convention.

VI. A FINAL POINT ABOUT TIME, AND A SEGUE TO OUR NEXT TOPIC

Donald Lutz has sketched out an almost amazing array of possibilities in his invaluable work on constitutional amendment. Each has its particular strengths and weaknesses. Consider only the role of time. The U.S. Constitution allows for the possibility of relatively rapid amendment, assuming that one can surmount the supermajority problem. The Twentieth Amendment, one of my own favorites inasmuch as it reduced the period between election and inauguration *and* sped up the pace by which newly elected representatives and senators would take office and begin doing their jobs, was proposed in March 1932 and declared ratified in January 1933. The Twenty-first Amendment repealing the Eighteenth Amendment that prohibited the sale of alcohol throughout the land was even quicker: it was proposed on February 20, 1933 and declared ratified on December 5, 1933. Compare this with states that, like Delaware or Massachusetts, require agreement by two separate legislatures (i.e., an intervening election) before an amendment can take effect, with or without popular ratification. This kind of procedural limitation has become of recent significance in Iowa, which doesn't allow initiative and referendum and requires two legislatures to agree on a proposed amendment. This means that a 2009 decision by the Iowa Supreme Court invalidating the prohibition of same-sex marriage on state constitutional grounds could not be overturned until 2014 at the earliest. Compare this with California, where a March decision 2008 on the same issue was overturned the following November.

One might want such a delay with regard to "fundamental" rights and when time is not thought to be of the essence. (Indeed, as already suggested, one might even want to bar amendment completely) But what if one believed that it was really important to amend a constitution quickly? Is it possible that timely change would be thought to be absolutely necessary? Assume, for example, that the U.S. Constitution correctly understood requires that there be congressional approval before the president can suspend habeas corpus, perhaps the most fundamental of all civil rights inasmuch as it forces the government to justify the detention of its citizens (and all other persons, for that matter). But maybe Congress is not in session. Or, more ominously, perhaps Congress has been the victim of a major attack and it is impossible to reach the constitutionally required quorum of a majority of its members in order to legislate. Then what? Perhaps most people wouldn't be thinking of constitutional amendment at all. But, if they did, they might discover the practical impossibility of achieving that goal. For starters, Congress, because of its inability to achieve a quorum, couldn't meet in order to propose an amendment in the first place. Do we want to provide for a "fast track" procedure for constitutional amendments in at least some situations? Or is it preferable for presidents and other officials to do what is necessary and to count on popular approval of their actions, whatever their presumptive "constitutionality"?

Needless to say, this is most likely to be a decidedly non-hypothetical issue in times of perceived "crisis" or "emergency," the subject of the next chapter.

16

"Exigencies," "Emergencies," and Adherence to Constitutional Norms (and Settlements)

A central theme of this book is the important (and sometimes unfortunate) role played by constitutional "settlements," rules clearly laid down in the text of the documents that structure the political process and about which litigation is basically unthinkable. The difficulties of amendment, particularly at the national level, provide their own imperviousness to change. But one should be under no illusions that even the most rule-like norms will necessarily prevail. The acid test for any constitutional order arises during perceived "emergencies," when the costs of adhering to such rules may seem to be extremely high and the tensions posed by potential "ungovernability" especially great. Any readers of this book are certainly familiar with the reality of exceptional circumstances, whether the September 11, 2001, attack on the World Trade Center, Hurricane Katrina, the near collapse of the American (and world) economy in 2008, or fears of a swine flu pandemic in 2009—not to mention the 2011 nuclear catastrophe in Japan (as a result of an exceptional earthquake that in turn triggered an exceptional tsunami). But the Constitution itself was drafted under the perception of what eighteenth-century writers described as political "exigencies," and it is well worth looking at some of their justifications for seeming indifference to legal norms before turning to the more contemporary debates.

I. DID THE FRAMERS ADHERE TO THE "RULES SET DOWN" (AND DO WE CARE WHAT THE ANSWER IS)?

Few Americans are aware of the deep uncertainties surrounding the conduct of those who framed and adopted our Constitution. The Constitution was conceived and given life in a process that required a self-conscious decision to go well beyond both the congressional mandate given to delegates at the Philadelphia Convention and the explicit rules set down in the Articles of Confederation—which was America's first, albeit now forgotten, constitution. So what?

Proponents of the 1787 Constitutional Convention, at least in private letters with one another, freely conceded its "questionable" legality.[1] Madison confronts these problems head-on in *Federalist* 40, and the nature of his response is also useful with regard to one of the basic analytic concepts of this book, the difference between the Constitution of Conversation and the Constitution of Settlement. After all, among the most important things that should be settled, one might believe, is the mechanism for changing the text of the Constitution, the topic of the previous chapter. With rare exceptions, those who draft new constitutions often elicit guarantees *against* change, at least without going through procedures considerably more difficult than those required to pass ordinary legislation. A danger is that a given constitution might require a too-arduous process for change. What then?

Madison and his colleagues in Philadelphia offer illuminating, though perhaps troublesome, answers. These answers also relate to the ability of constitutions to be *self-enforcing* documents through their ability to create incentives (or loyalties) that will lead members of the polity to adhere to the rules set down, whether this means simply not engaging in acrimonious litigation or resorting to violence. Recall that there is nothing automatic about such self-enforcement, even when the language is absolutely clear, if enough persons view acquiescence as presenting far more risks than disobedience. No one, for example, will feel obligated to obey speed limits or to stop at all red lights when rushing someone to a hospital. Indeed, we would probably regard someone who would be meticulously "law-abiding" in such a situation as something of a fanatic. It is one thing to say "Let justice be done though the heavens fall"; it is quite different to say "Let every law be followed though the heavens fall." Only a truly crazed "legalist" would find this remotely plausible, even if the law in question is found in a constitution itself.

If an existing constitution seems significantly out of synch with the values and desires of those with significant power within a polity, radical transformation may appear far preferable to meek submission. So we must ask about the degree to which Madison and his associates played by the rules that presumably faced them as they arrived in Philadelphia in May 1787. Any conclusions that they did play fast and loose with regard to the rules triggers an accompanying normative question. Did Madison really care about what might be termed legal fidelity; more to the point, should we? So let us look more deeply at the two central criticisms that were leveled at Madison and his colleagues and his responses thereto.

A. What kind of convention did Congress authorize?

The first criticism involves the specifics of the mandate given the members of the Philadelphia Convention by Congress, which invited all thirteen states to send delegates to Philadelphia in May 1787 "for the *sole and express purposes of revising the Articles of Confederation* and provisions therein, as shall, when agreed to in Congress, and confirmed by the States [presumably under the procedures set down in the Articles, but more on that later] render the federal Constitution *adequate to the exigencies of government and the preservation of the Union*" (emphasis added).

Did the Convention adhere to these instructions? One state, Rhode Island, sent no delegates at all, because it correctly feared that the gathering would turn into a "runaway convention" that would basically do away with the Articles and replace them with something far worse, at least from the perspective of Rhode Islanders. Moreover, two of the three New York delegates walked out of the Convention when they—again accurately—perceived that their colleagues were going well beyond the given instructions.

How does Madison respond to such criticisms? To some extent, he engages in the rhetorical maneuvering associated with constitutions of conversation. That is, although Madison was not a lawyer himself, he does exactly what one expects lawyers to do, which is to argue that what might appear relatively clear on the surface is in fact open to legitimate differences of interpretation and therefore varied meanings. It thus turns out that "revision," under careful examination, means tearing the governmental house down and starting all over again. It is as if you hire a contractor to repair a house and discover, on your return home from a vacation, that the contractor has instead leveled it to the ground because of deep foundational problems that made "repair" impossible. Moreover, you're told that it would simply be impossible to replace the colonial-style home you had; instead, you are offered the plans for an ultramodern home designed by Frank Gehry. So, here at least, "repair" means "demolition and replacement" by a significantly different design that will presumably avoid the problems that doomed the original home. Is it relevant that your expectations have been violated—that you assumed a more modest outcome when you left for vacation? Or is the point that the contractor was correct in believing both that repair was impossible and that a truly radical substitution for the initial house was necessary to meet the basic need for secure shelter?

Madison suggested in *Federalist* 37 that "the existing Confederation is founded on principles which are fallacious; we must consequently change this first foundation, and with it the superstructure resting upon it." The purpose of the convention was to create a truly functioning government adequate to the needs of the country created by the American Revolution, and the system created by the Articles of Confederation simply could not do that. Interestingly enough, Madison and other adherents of a convention had scarcely used such language, at least in public, *before* Congress issued its call for a convention? But so what? Note also that Madison never says in so many words that he and his colleagues "defied" Congress; instead, he offers a capacious "interpretation" of Congress's mandate that legitimizes what the Convention did, even if some of those who voted for the initial authorization might be shocked at what then took place. Without tracing the particularities of his argument, let us assume agreement with Madison, that "revision" can be made to cover what the Convention did to the Articles.

B. When "settlements" become too costly: what is there to say about Article XIII?

For better or worse, the congressional mandate and the meaning we attach to "revision" pose only one problem. The heart of the matter, in terms of legal fidelity, is the thirteenth Article of Confederation, which very clearly sets out a procedure by which amendments to the Articles take place: the procedure requires that *all* of the *legislatures* of the thirteen existing states agree to any proposals for change. The veto of even one state is therefore enough to doom any proposed amendment. That's just what the text says; it really doesn't lend itself to fancy arguments about interpretation or meaning. Madison doesn't deny that this is the meaning of Article XIII. He seems to recognize that one purpose of the Articles was to "settle" how changes would take place, with no ambiguities. If any part of the Articles illustrated the Constitution of Settlement, one might think it was Article XIII.

Moreover, consider in this context the closing paragraph of the Articles of Confederation, which came into force in 1781 upon ratification by the last state, Maryland (and which was signed by no fewer than six of the Philadelphia delegates)[2]:

> And Whereas it hath pleased the Great Governor of the World to incline the hearts of the legislatures we respectively represent in Congress, to approve of, and to authorize us to ratify the said articles of confederation and perpetual union. Know Ye that we the undersigned delegates, by virtue of the power and authority to us given for that purpose, do by these presents, in the name and in behalf of our respective constituents, fully and entirely ratify and confirm each and every of the said *articles of confederation and perpetual union*, and all and singular the matters and things therein contained: And we do further solemnly plight and engage the faith of our respective constituents, that they shall abide by the determinations of the united States in congress assembled, on all questions, which by the said confederation are submitted to them. *And that the articles thereof shall be inviolably observed by the States we respectively represent*, and that the union shall be perpetual. (emphasis added)

In addition to the six signatories of the Articles, a full forty-one of the fifty-five delegates were or had been members of the Continental Congress. So the question for (at least) these delegates was whether they—or the states they represented, whether in Congress or at the Convention—had a duty of "inviolabl[e]" observance. Or did they indeed have a higher loyalty that justifiably took precedence over whatever commitments had been made when signing and ratifying the Articles?

So what does Madison say in response to such questions, since, as a pragmatic matter, he certainly cannot initiate a conversation about the "true meaning" of Article XIII? *Federalist* 37 offers us a key clue, for Madison has already announced that there are "fallacious" principles, and the principle of unanimity is one such fallacy. He makes an unabashedly normative argument that even if it is a rule (which can scarcely be denied), it is one of those rules made to be broken when the costs of adherence are simply too high. To adhere to it would be disastrous; therefore, the right thing to do is basically to ignore it. This is exactly what the Framers did in what is perhaps the most important single article of the 1787 Constitution, Article VII. That article specifies that the Constitution comes into being when ratified by the *conventions* (*not* the state legislatures) of *nine* (not *all*) of the states. This is why there were only eleven states in the Union when George Washington was inaugurated on April 30, 1789. It did not matter, under the terms of the new Constitution, that North Carolina and Rhode Island had not ratified. If, on the other hand, one had taken the Articles of Confederation seriously, the failure of even one of those states to ratify would have doomed the entire enterprise (which would almost certainly have delighted Rhode Islanders).

Was Madison correct in describing the unanimity principle as fallacious? Although some political theorists can be read as suggesting that the best political principles deserve unanimous consent—at least if we define these as principles that any rational person would agree to, since it is untenable to require agreement from those who are irrational—no serious political theorist has ever defended the *actuality* of unanimous agreement in order to legitimize political activity. There is a very good reason for this. A requirement of actual unanimity will place veto power in the most extreme member of any given group, even if one stops short of regarding such a member as irrational. They may, after all, simply be more zealously committed to one particular principle that you yourself recognize as "rea sonable," but they are far less willing to "balance" against other equally compelling principles. This obviously returns us to the political logic of compromise, the subject of chapter 2.

Unanimity requirements mean, by definition, that one will be forced either to submit to the extortionate demands of the recalcitrant holdout or to accept the defeat of the desired proposal. These are not merely abstract observations. We saw this played out when the framers of what many termed a draft "constitution" for the European Union decided to require the unanimous assent of all twenty-six member states in order to declare it ratified. More recently, as the European Union faced the potential default by Greece and other member states, the fate of entire world economy may have been in the hands of Slovakia. European Union rules require that all seventeen members using the Euro as their currency consent to measures needed to stabilize its economy. The Slovakian Parliament, after initially rejecting the "euro-rescue" and bringing down the country's existing government,[3] changed its collective mind two days later and decided to support the rescue. The *New York Times* described the final vote as bringing "to a close a nearly three-month process that underscored the complexity and difficulty of decision making in the 17-nation bloc."[4] There may be a defense for placing such power in the parliament of a country of 5.5 million persons, but, as with the earlier decision to require unanimous approval of even more countries to effectuate the draft constitution, any such defense has nothing to do with smoothing the actual decision making. Indeed, the initial draft constitution was defeated when it failed to receive approval in referenda held in France and the Netherlands, and a modified text written in light of the defeats, the subsequent "Lisbon draft" still required unanimous approval. So countries like Ireland (population 4.6 million) continued to exercise an exaggerated role in determining the fate of the entire union, similar to the role that Rhode Island might have played had the Philadelphians honored the rule set down in the thirteenth Article of Confederation.

In theory, the new U.S. Constitution was given life when New Hampshire became the ninth state to ratify on June 21, 1788. Virginia ratified four days later, followed by New York's ratification, by a vote of 32–29, on July 26. North Carolina did not ratify the Constitution until well over a year later, on November 21, 1789, and Rhode Island submitted to the new order only on March 28, 1790. It really didn't matter that North Carolina and Rhode

Island were absent from early meetings of the new Congress. Would we have said the same, though, if it had been the extremely important states of Virginia or New York that adopted the posture of the militant holdout? It would be illusory to believe that Article VII was truly "self-enforcing," independent of the identity of the states that acquiesced to the new Constitution. Had two New York anti-Federalists stuck to their original principles—or had the New York convention met and voted earlier, well before New Hampshire's ratification made the new Constitution a fait accompli—one can easily imagine a dramatically different rendering of American history (assuming that we even thought of ourselves as Americans had, for example, the failure of the constitutional project led to three independent countries in the newly independent region of North America).[5]

So what does this show? One lesson is that constitutions of settlement do not necessarily settle, once and for all, the issue under examination. They cannot, in fact, foreclose all conversation. But Madison demonstrates that ensuing conversation will go directly to considerations of principle, wisdom, or empirical consequences, because clever legal arguments as to "meaning" or "interpretation" are unavailable. Thus, in *Federalist* 40, he invites us to join him in recognizing "the absurdity of subjecting the fate of twelve States to the perverseness or corruption of a thirteenth." The possibility that the option to exercise such a veto was part of the original bargain by which Rhode Island (and perhaps other states) agreed to accept the Articles of Confederation in the first place is totally irrelevant to Madison.

C. The centrality of "crisis"

Key to understanding Madison's all-important argument for ignoring the limits posed by Article XIII is his invocation in *Federalist* 40 of the presence of crisis and exigency. The fate of the country was at stake, and one should hardly feel obliged to conform to a provision of the existing constitution that if followed in its clear, unequivocal, and semantically undebatable meaning would doom the enterprise of what Madison and others viewed as absolutely necessary constitutional revision.

It is well worth considering parts of at least three speeches made at the Philadelphia Convention about the limits of fidelity to the rules laid down.

Virginia's governor, Edmund Randolph, who became the first attorney general under George Washington, told his colleagues that "there are great seasons when persons with limited powers are justified in exceeding them, and a person would be contemptible not to risk it." His fellow Virginian, George Mason, who ultimately refused to sign the Constitution because it didn't include a Bill of Rights, told the Convention that "in certain seasons of public danger it is commendable to exceed power." And then there was New York's Alexander Hamilton, who would become not only the chief co-author, with Madison, of *The Federalist* but also George Washington's secretary of the treasury, a position from which he helped to shape the American state. On June 18, 1787, Hamilton insisted that "to rely on & propose any plan not adequate to these exigencies, *merely because it was not clearly within our powers*, would be to sacrifice the means to the end." Consider especially the meaning of *merely* in this sentence.

But this is not all. Madison in *Federalist* 40 also hearkens back to the lessons taught a decade earlier during the American Revolution, which obviously involved a "great change[] of established government[]."According to Madison, what justified the Revolution and made it a useful precedent for those gathered in Philadelphia and then for those called upon to ratify what happened there was the fundamental liberty of "the people" to "abolish or alter their governments as to them shall seem most likely to effect their safety and happiness." Constitutions, then, are *never* "settled" in the face of plausible argument that they rest on fundamentally "fallacious" premises and generate seriously adverse consequences. (Would one really recommend otherwise?) Their "unsettlement," however, necessarily takes the form of what may well be called defiance rather than clever interpretations that are ostensibly part of ordinary legal conversation.

As Professor Christian Fritz notes in an important article on American constitutional theory in the eighteenth and nineteenth centuries, Madison was *not* simply evoking the Declaration of Independence and its justification of revolution in light of the "long train of abuses" visited upon the hapless colonists by King George III and his minions. There was no serious argument, for example, that the government of the United States of America established by the Articles of Confederation was oppressing the citizenry. Rather, the argument was that it was grievously *ineffectual,* in large part because the Articles created too weak a central government. As Fritz notes, several early American state constitutions drafted in the years prior to the 1787 Convention included "alter or abolish" clauses that evoked the theory of "sovereignty of the people" presumably announced by the very first words of the Preamble to the new Constitution. One can find the most notable articulation of such a theory in what for some Americans of the time was the truly primary source of John Locke's *Second Treatise of Government*. As Madison told his colleagues in Philadelphia, "The people were in fact, the fountain of all power, and resorting to them, all difficulties" relating to the legitimacy of Convention's decisions would be resolved.[6] One need not demonstrate that doom was threatening; it might well be enough to persuade people that change might better enable them to "pursue their own happiness," a powerful notion from the Declaration. The Massachusetts Constitution of 1780, drafted in large measure by John Adams, had specified the right of the people "to reform, alter, or totally change" their government whenever their "happiness require[d] it," perhaps with regard to their legitimate wishes for "protection, safety, [or] prosperity."[7] Such a right to "alter or abolish" existing forms of government meant the ability to ignore existing procedural rules that if followed would make such alteration or abolition impossible. Lest one think, incidentally, that such views are entirely limited to our long-past history, it is worth noting that the Kentucky Constitution of 1966, whose provenance was challenged by some lawyers, was declared legitimate by that state's supreme court on the basis of the people's sovereignty, which was demonstrated by the popular ratification of the proposals made by a "Constitutional Revision Assembly."[8]

Akhil Reed Amar has asked us to imagine the possibility of Congress creating such an assembly, which then submits its own proposals, however radical, to the general national electorate for ratification—not, as seemingly required by Article V, to the legislatures of the various states or to conventions elected by each state. Amar suggests that such popular approval would render the new Constitution perfectly legitimate. This is, he argues, just what it means to base our system of government on "We the People." Others disagree, but it is not clear how one can defeat Amar's argument if one is genuinely committed to "popular sovereignty." To be sure, one might be frightened by this vision of decisionmaking by a genuinely active "We the People," but that is just to suggest that close analysis of the Constitution—or at least the political theory underlying the opening words and justifying actions taken in Philadelphia—might generate deep challenges to our complacent understandings.

So return to Madison's argument in *Federalist* 40, where he discusses the Revolution and its awesome reality of joining together to overthrow by violence the governments established by Great Britain. He almost contemptuously refers to those with "ill-timed scruples" or "zeal for adhering to ordinary form"; they were likely to become "unpatriotic" Loyalists instead of joining in the revolutionary venture. Article XIII is precisely such an "ordinary form," and only someone with "ill-timed scruples" would really feel bound by it. So what, beyond the force of argument that Article XIII was "fallacious," justifies the actions taken in Philadelphia?

Madison offers three justifications, the first being the sheer importance of the crisis facing the new nation and the need to act accordingly. So maybe it does not suffice to say that we could be "happier" under a new system of government; rather, one has to argue that we are faced with a certain degree of misery if we stick with the status quo. But he goes on to emphasize the *trustworthiness* of those proposing such radical transformation. Madison describes them (and himself) as "patriotic and respectable citizens" devoted to the public good. We have seen throughout this book the reliance that Madison and others of his generation placed on civic virtue for the effective operation of our political system. But, finally, the handiwork of these worthies "was to be submitted *to the people themselves*" (emphasis Madison's).[9] Had it been rejected, as it almost was in several of the ratifying states, then the work in Philadelphia would have been for naught, as appeared to be the case with the Brussels draft of the European Constitution. However—and this is the more important point—popular approbation would serve to "blot out antecedent errors and irregularities." Indeed, we would even build monuments to the heroes who knew when to ignore "forms" or legalistic "scruples" and instead to do what was necessary to serve (or save) the country.

D. Can/should constitutions ever be treated as once-and-for-all settlements?

There is nothing "innocent" about any of these arguments. What Madison is suggesting, at bottom, is that constitutions can never truly "settle" basic issues forever and ever. And Professor Fritz argues powerfully that the history of American *state* constitutions offers powerful evidence that these arguments are not merely "theoretical" in a pejorative sense. "The exercise of the people's right to bring about constitutional change," he writes, "even if contrary to established constitutional procedures—is one of the hallmarks of American constitutionalism."[10] Before 1851, constitutional conventions took place in no fewer than eleven states without clear warrant for them in the existing state constitutions.[11] Some were successful in achieving basic changes; others were not, but that is almost beside the point. Rather, the question involves what might be called "constitutional imagination" and the working out of the relationship between sovereignty of "the people" and an existing constitutional order that is perceived, by significant elements of the public, to no longer serve their needs.

The basic problem is that changing the Constitution of Settlement requires a different politics than changing those parts of the Constitution that are recognized as falling within the Constitution of Conversation. The latter can be addressed, usually, by innovative legislation and consequent interpretations. But the Constitution of Settlement is almost always thought to require formal amendment, which may, as with the Articles of Confederation, be impossible as a practical matter. This may be the case today with regard to amending the U.S. Constitution through Article V, though *not* with regard to changing those *state* constitutions that allow for popular initiative and referendum.

If we conclude that the presuppositions underlying any given "settlement" are so fallacious as to threaten the basic foundations of our common political enterprise, then is the proper path to emulate the Madison of *Federalist* 40—and many citizens of many states—and do whatever we can to rectify the situation regardless of what the Constitution itself might say about the "ordinary forms" to be followed? Or does legal fidelity, especially if based on an oath required by the Constitution itself (at least of all public officials), require scrupulous adherence to all of its forms?

II. MACHIAVELLI AND LOCKE

Madison and his contemporaries were speaking and writing against a background of works by well-known political theorists who addressed similar questions. They could write with greater candor, and sometimes use more pointed language, than Madison felt free to do. After all, he was most concerned, when writing his contributions to *The Federalist*, with appearing sufficiently unthreatening to garner support for the new Constitution from potential opponents. It is illuminating, therefore, to look briefly at both Niccolo Machiavelli and John Locke, who spoke to the concerns raised by Madison. Locke is often regarded as a seminal figure in the tradition of Anglo-American political thought, whereas Machiavelli is probably more of an "underground" figure because of the accusations by his adversaries that he was "unchristian" and "immoral," even "Satanic." But both of these philosophers help us to understand what is at stake, not only in Madison's arguments, but also in those of his successors up to our own time.

A. Machiavelli

Although Machiavelli is undoubtedly best known for his brief book *The Prince*, far more important for our purposes is his discourse on ancient Rome as described by the historian Livy. These *Discourses on Livy* are devoted to articulating the bases for a truly republican political order. Indeed, in his recent book *Machiavellian Democracy*, John McCormick argues that Machiavelli was actually a progenitor of a truly democratic vision of government going well beyond the forms of minimally democratic representative government that Madison defended. One need not confront these fine points of how best to interpret Machiavelli. For the purposes of this chapter, what is crucial is his praise of the Romans for including the institution of "dictator" as part of their basic constitutional structure for hundreds of years before the procedures undergirding the Roman dictatorship degenerated and were supplanted by Julius Caesar, the last of the (initially) constitutional dictators.

Perhaps the most succinct presentation of what is at stake in the debate about including the role of a "dictator" within one's conception of constitutionalism was a conversation in *The Dark Knight* between Harvey Dent, the crusading district attorney of Gotham City in the struggle against the truly nihilistic Joker, and his girlfriend Rachel (who is, unbeknown to him, also involved with Bruce Wayne/Batman).[12] "When their enemies were at the gates," Dent tells Rachel, "the Romans would suspend democracy and appoint one man to protect the city. It wasn't considered an honor; it was considered a public service." Rachel responds: "Harvey, the last man they appointed to protect the republic was [Julius] Caesar...and he never gave up his power." Does Rachel deliver a knockout blow to Harvey's argument, or does she simply remind us, yet again, that there are no perfect constitutional designs and that we must always be attendant to strengths and weaknesses, costs and benefits, risks and opportunities? As already suggested, Harvey Dent could well have cited Machiavelli as the most eloquent defender of his position.

"Among all the other Roman institutions," Machiavelli argued, the dictatorship "truly deserves to be considered and numbered among those which were the source of the greatness of such an empire, because without a similar system cities survive extraordinary circumstances only with difficulty."[13] Dictatorship was central to Rome's success because "the usual institutions in republics are slow to move...and, since time is wasted in coming to an agreement, the remedies for republics are very dangerous when they must find one for a problem that cannot wait."[14] When emergency—or the appearance of emergency—strikes, there must be political leadership to recognize the situation and make immediate decisions, without fear of bureaucratic hindrances, time-consuming attempts at consensus building, and all the various veto points characteristic of representative government. In an important essay in the *Weekly Standard* defending some of the actions of the Bush Administration, Harvey Mansfield cites Machiavelli.[15] One of Mansfield's most important books is *Taming the Prince*, significantly subtitled *The Ambivalence of Modern Executive Power*, which reflects on the nature of executive power even in a presumptively constitutional system. "No law or system can actually ensure the behavior it summons," he concludes, "without depending on an executive who is at least in part outside the law and not explained by the system."[16] There is, therefore, a crucial difference between what might be termed a "Machiavellian Republic" and what Mansfield calls, somewhat dismissively, a "little r-republic" that fails to recognize Machiavelli's insights.

Returning to Machiavelli, we read that "republics must therefore have among their laws a procedure...[that] reserve[s] to a small number of citizens the authority to deliberate on matters of urgent need without consulting anyone else, if they are in complete agreement. When a republic lacks such a procedure, it must necessarily come to ruin." Like Hamilton in *Federalist* 70, Machiavelli emphasizes the desirability, at least under some circumstances, of what is basically one-person rule.

What is the cause of this "ruin" in the absence of adequate procedures to establish such rule? Machiavelli identifies two possibilities. First, republics can come to ruin by stubbornly "obeying their own laws" even when these laws prevent measures necessary to save the country. Isn't this the "ill-timed zeal" to obey the law that Madison criticizes in *Federalist* 40? Such excess fidelity to the law means that political leaders will choose to follow the law (as they understand it) strictly, even if it involves driving the political order over a cliff. And, as suggested earlier, this would be justified not in the name of "justice," but, rather "Let the law be followed though the heavens fall."

Political leaders, faced with exigent circumstances, might well publicly announce that they must break the law in order to save the republic. But Machiavelli identifies this as the second cause of ruin: "break[ing] laws" in order to avoid" disastrous consequences. The problem is that if one is willing to break laws in urgent circumstances, one creates a precedent for breaking them again where the urgency is more controversial (or nonexistent); moreover, it encourages political leaders to retain unconstitutional powers even after the emergency has passed. What start as emergency measures may become normalized, and that might well spell the death of a vision of constitutional government that includes due respect for its own limits. Ultimately, recourse to suspending the laws eats away at the foundations of republican government. That is why Machiavelli argues, "In a republic, it is not good for anything to happen which requires governing by extraordinary measures." We must, Machiavelli teaches, be aware of the possibility of crises and exigent circumstances when we design a constitution and include ways of responding to emergencies that do not require political leaders to choose between Scylla and Charybdis: the disaster caused by hyperfidelity to legal constraints or the destruction of republican government by recourse to out-and-out illegality. Once again we are presented with the Goldilocks problem of the "too hot" form of government, in which leaders feel free to engage in illegal conduct in the name of defending vital public interests, and the "too cold" form, in which an unimaginative leader takes pride in his devotion to legal norms even if that is leading to all-too-predictable disaster.

B. Locke

John Locke was far better known to most eighteenth-century Americans than Machiavelli. His *Second Treatise on Government* was widely read and discussed (even if, as a matter of fact, Montesquieu's *The Spirit of the Laws* was more frequently cited by the Framers). Although Locke developed the basic theories of limited government based on popular consent (in the form of the "social contract" metaphor), he also included an extremely important discussion of what he called "prerogative" power within a monarchical system. Like Machiavelli (and later Hamilton), Locke recognizes the problem presented by a "too numerous" group of decisionmakers: it may, among other things, generate a structure of governance that is "too slow for the dispatch requisite to execution."[17] Thus, according to Locke, the king always retained the power to suspend the law more or less by fiat whenever he thought it in the public interest. "This power to act according to discretion, for the public good, without the prescription of the law, and *sometimes even against it*, is that which is called prerogative." To be sure, one can offer a relatively moderate reading of Locke's argument, for he seems to emphasize the practical contingency that "in some governments the lawmaking power is not always in being." That is, parliament may be in recess or, in America, Congress may be dispersed and re-convening—before the age of modern transportation—would be time consuming indeed. This, from Lincoln's perspective, was the situation he faced upon his inauguration on March 4, 1861 and especially after the attack on Fort Sumter a month later. Even the "moderate" argument gives executives great power to act, legally or otherwise, before the legislature reconvenes.

But Locke presents no truly institutional theory or what might be called "constitutional design," perhaps because he was handcuffed, as a political theorist, by the reality that England *did* have a monarch. It would have been tactless, if not dangerous, to suggest that someone other than the presumptively "sovereign" monarch should exercise the kinds of extraordinary powers linked with prerogative. Machiavelli is a far more sophisticated analyst of institutions. What concerned Machiavelli, the republican theorist, was the rise of an extraconstitutional dictatorship in cases where the constitution lacked a procedure for appointing a dictator and ending the dictator's reign. The Roman dictatorship was institutionalized, requiring a particular process in order to name the dictator and ending the dictatorship at a specified time, usually after no longer than six months. Naming a dictator might signal an emergency, but it did not entail a "constitutional crisis," precisely because the Roman constitution provided for the institution of a dictator. Moreover, it wisely separated the institution with the power to identify an emergency and call for emergency powers from the person who executed those powers, the better to prevent the dictator from trying to extend his rule by recharacterizing the situation to his advantage.

If the last time "exigency" raised its head was the Philadelphia Convention, one could treat these discussions, like those of Madison, as simple historical relics. But that is clearly not the case, and the issues raised by these political philosophers and those who devised the Constitution have presented themselves throughout American history.

III. A CONSTITUTION INTENDED TO ENDURE

One of the most important passages in the history of the American Supreme Court, which can be found in *McCulloch v. Maryland* (1819), is John Marshall's declaration, "We must never forget that it is a constitution we are expounding." You might well ask what is so amazing about this sentence, which seems glaringly tautological. What makes the sentence worthy of comment is what follows, when Marshall sets out what is most important about the legal documents we call constitutions. He emphasizes that the U.S. Constitution is "intended to endure for ages to come, and consequently, to be adapted to the various *crises* of human affairs." Interestingly enough, he italicizes "crises," though one might believe that the phrase "to be adapted" is equally worthy of emphasis. An analogous quotation, perhaps, can be found in a famous opinion by Justice Oliver Wendell Holmes that upheld the conviction in a federal court of someone viewed as advocating draft resistance during World War I, over objections that the clear language of the First Amendment prevented any such punishment. "When a nation is at war," Holmes wrote for a unanimous Supreme Court, "many things that might be said in time of peace are such a hindrance to its effort that their utterance will not be endured so long as men fight, and that no Court could regard them as protected by any constitutional right."[18]

We return, then, to the topic of Chapter 15. To what extent do we want a truly "unchanging"—or at least a very hard to change—Constitution? Or, on the contrary, do we wish a more "flexible" Constitution that can easily be adapted to the exigencies of the day, especially when we describe those exigencies as "crises" or "emergencies," as wars almost always are? James Boyd White has described Marshall's opinion in *McCulloch* as basically "amendatory" in its sweep, and it is clear that White does not mean to be critical.[19] Many such opinions—especially, it is important to add, those *upholding* actions taken by Congress or by presidents—have been described that way. Marshall also suggests what may even seem to be a paradox: it is *only* through adaptation that the Constitution—or, perhaps more to the point, the United States as a political entity—will in fact endure. Rigidity is fatal to the constitutional enterprise, precisely because it will prevent constitutions from changing as times change.

But one might argue with equal confidence that too much flexibility destroys what is thought to be the strongest promise of constitutionalism. After all, Marshall had written in another famous decision, *Marbury v. Madison*, that "all those who have framed written constitutions contemplate them as forming the fundamental and paramount law of the nation." "The powers of the legislature are defined, and limited: and that those limits may not be mistaken, or forgotten, the constitution is written. To what purposes are powers limited, and to what purpose is that limitation committed to writing, if the limits may, at any time, be passed by those intended to be restrained?"[20] This serves as Marshall's foundational argument for judicial review, but it should be clear that his basic premise can as easily be adopted by institutional "protestants" like Andrew Jackson or Lincoln. Even if they rejected *judicial supremacy*, the premise that the Supreme Court is the "ultimate interpreter" of the Constitution, they most certainly did not reject *constitutional supremacy*.

Anyone committed to such supremacy might well be tempted to quote a key sentence from a dissenting opinion written by Justice George Sutherland in an important 1934 case in which the majority upheld the power of the Minnesota legislature to suspend the operation of mortgage contracts, lest too many people lose their homes in the midst of the Great Depression. The "problem" is the Contracts Clause of the Constitution, which forbids states from "impairing" the obligations of contract. The majority decision emphasized the dire emergency facing the people of Minnesota and, therefore, the reasonableness of the legislature's de facto impairment. It turned out that the words "no law" in the Contracts Clause of Article I, Section 10 did not settle the issue of Minnesota's powers to pass debtor-relief legislation. One might say the same thing about the inability of the words "no law" in the First Amendment to protect from the Wilson Administration during World War I political dissidents, including Eugene V. Debs, the most important Socialist political figure in our history and a candidate for the presidency in 1912 and then again (from jail) in 1920. Whatever the language might have suggested, it did *not* figure in the Constitution of Settlement, as do the clauses emphasized in this book. These words turn out to be part of the Constitution of Conversation, which means that they are subject to necessarily conflicting interpretations. Justice Sutherland, writing for a minority of four, protested against interpretive flexibility and instead emphasized what he thought was the clear text plus the original understanding of the Framers that the Constitution would prevent states from emulating Rhode Island by passing such debtor-relief laws. "If the provisions of the Constitution be not upheld when they pinch as well as when they comfort," Sutherland wrote, "they may as well be abandoned."[21] Similarly, the greatest defender of civil liberties in the mid-twentieth century, Justice Hugo Black, always carried a copy of the Constitution in his pocket. He asked his colleagues to explain what part of "no law" they did not understand when offering what he considered indefensibly malleable readings of the First Amendment by which, for example, leaders of the American Communist Party were jailed basically for their political heresies.

One might ask if the two visions of the Constitution originally enunciated by Marshall are truly consistent. One could offer a confident yes if one believes that the written Constitution, even prior to any given amendment, *does* authorize our leaders, whether Congress or the president, to take effective measures to counter perceived emergencies and resolve any given "crisis." Perhaps this is what Hamilton is arguing in *Federalist* 23, where he states that the powers "essential to the care of the common defense…ought to exist without limitation." And then he adds his own italicized gloss: "*because it is impossible to foresee or define the extent and variety of national exigencies, or the correspondent extent and variety of the means which may be necessary to satisfy them.*" If one accepts Hamilton's rather dour reminder that "the circumstances that endanger the safety of nations are infinite," then it is easy enough to agree with him that "no constitutional shackles can wisely be imposed on the power to which the care of it is committed." An obvious question is whether this counts as the best understanding of the Constitution. To explore this at sufficient length would take us deep into the Constitution of Conversation.

But our current task is somewhat different. We should ask ourselves what we would want the Constitution to say about such exigencies. We might well believe that the extent of governmental power during times of crisis is precisely the sort of issue that should be *settled* and not open to acrimonious controversy, which might only inflame a given crisis (and perhaps generate ever-diminishing capacity to govern). But can any settled notion of "limited government" co-exist with Hamilton's argument? The same question can easily be asked with regard to Madison's chilling statement in *Federalist* 41 that "*It is in vain to oppose Constitutional barriers to the impulse of self-preservation. It is worse than in vain; because it plants in the Constitution itself necessary usurpations of power, every precedent of which is a germ of unnecessary and multiplied repetitions.*" (emphasis added) Are *all* supposed limitations mere "parchment barriers" that will inevitably be broken through if a given "crisis of human affairs" is perceived to be threatening enough?

One of the most famous discussions of the problem of legal fidelity occurred in an 1810 letter by Thomas Jefferson. It is famous in part because of Jefferson's almost ostentatious commitment to limited government also reflected in his *Notes on Virginia*, a well-known denunciation of those who suggested that the situation in Virginia during the Revolutionary War, when he was serving as a not very successful governor, called for a dictatorship. The experience of having been president and doubling the size of the

United States through what he himself believed was the constitutionally dubious Louisiana Purchase seems to have changed his mind in important respects. "On great occasion," he wrote in 1807, "every good officer must be ready to risk himself in going beyond the strict line of the law, when the public preservation requires it." These constituted what he called the "extreme cases where the laws become inadequate to their own preservations, and where the universal recourse is a dictator, or martial law."[22]

The fullest explication of his mature view occurred in an 1810 letter to one John Colvin, in which he rejected a "scrupulous adherence to written law" when such fidelity "would be to lose the law itself, with life, liberty, property and all those who are enjoying them with us; thus absurdly sacrificing the end to the means." It's worth reading his entire argument with great care:[23]

> The question you propose, whether circumstances do not sometimes occur, which make it a duty in officers of high trust, to assume authorities beyond the law, is easy of solution in principle, but sometimes embarrassing in practice. A strict observance of the written laws is doubtless *one* of the high duties of a good citizen, but it is not *the highest*. The laws of necessity, of self-preservation, of saving our country when in danger, are of higher obligation. To lose our country by a scrupulous adherence to written law, would be to lose the law itself, with life, liberty, property and all those who are enjoying them with us; thus absurdly sacrificing the end to the means. When, in the battle of Germantown, General Washington's army was annoyed from Chew's house, he did not hesitate to plant his cannon against it, although the property of a citizen...In [this and other] cases, the unwritten laws of necessity, of self-preservation, and of the public safety, control the written laws of [private property].
>
> Further to exemplify the principle, I will state an hypothetical case. Suppose it had been made known to the Executive of the Union in the autumn of 1805, that we might have the Floridas for a reasonable sum, that that sum had not indeed been so appropriated by law, but that Congress were to meet within three weeks, and might appropriate it on the first or second day of their session. Ought he, for so great an advantage to his country, to have risked himself by transcending the law and making the purchase? The public advantage offered, in this supposed case, was indeed immense; but a reverence for law, and the probability that the advantage might still be *legally* accomplished by a delay of

only three weeks, were powerful reasons against hazarding the act. But suppose it foreseen that a [political enemy] would find means to protract the proceeding on it by Congress, until the ensuing spring, by which time new circumstances would change the mind of the other party. Ought the Executive, in that case, and with that foreknowledge, to have secured the good to his country, and to have trusted to their justice for the transgression of the law? I think he ought, and that the act would have been approved....

From these examples and principles you may see what I think on the question proposed. They do not go to the case of persons charged with petty duties, where consequences are trifling, and time allowed for a legal course, nor to authorize them to take such cases out of the written law. In these, the example of overleaping the law is of greater evil than a strict adherence to its imperfect provisions. It is incumbent on those only who accept of great charges, to risk themselves on great occasions, when the safety of the nation, or some of its very high interests are at stake....

Whatever else may be said about Jefferson's argument, it should be clear that he, like Madison in *Fedealist* 40, ultimately seems to rely on the good faith and integrity of high-level decisionmakers, particularly presidents, to know when to go beyond the law. He might have regretted that the Constitution, in his view, did not really allow him to authorize the purchase of Louisiana from Napoleon. But that was not the end of the matter for him. What he perceived as the national interest took precedence over what Madison dismissed at the Convention as "ill-timed scruples" or undue "zeal for adhering to ordinary form." It is easy to believe that Jefferson was grateful for Locke's argument on prerogative even if, perhaps for reasons of prudence, he chose not to mention it.

It is worth noting that the Constitution itself is largely silent on the possibilities that justify the kind of actions that might be termed dictatorial. There is, to be sure, a "war power" given to Congress, and some awful invasions of individual rights have been upheld under that power. And there is the explicit authority, in Article I, Section 9, to suspend the right of habeas corpus, which in many ways is the most important of all rights inasmuch as it requires the state to justify its detention of persons before a court. The most controversial of the very few actual suspensions of habeas corpus was Abraham Lincoln's suspension in 1861, on his own authority as president. John Merryman, a Marylander suspected of sympathy with the secessionists who were trying to take control of the state and thus isolate our nation's capital, was seized by the army. Chief Justice Roger Taney, acting in one of his other capacities, issued a writ of habeas corpus, which Lincoln ordered the relevant military officials to ignore. Taney denounced Lincoln as claiming more authority than King George III.[24]

Lincoln famously defended his actions in a message to Congress on its return on July 4, 1861, the date that Lincoln chose for it to reconvene:

> Of course some consideration was given to the questions of power, and pro-priety, before this matter was acted upon. The whole of the laws which were required to be faithfully executed, were being resisted, and failing of execution, in nearly one-third of the States. Must they be allowed to finally fail of execu-tion, even had it been perfectly clear, that by the use of the means necessary to their execution, some single law, made in such extreme tenderness of the citizen's liberty, that practically, it relieves more of the guilty, than of the inno-cent, should, to a very limited extent, be violated? To state the question more directly, are all the laws, but one, to go unexecuted, and the government itself go to pieces, lest that one be violated? Even in such a case, would not the official oath be broken, if the government should be overthrown, when it was believed that disregarding the single law, would tend to preserve it?[25]

As it happens, Lincoln denied that he had in fact "disregarded" the Constitution, for he claimed that the proper interpretation of the Constitution was that he did indeed have the power to suspend habeas corpus, that it was not a power assigned exclusively to Congress. Many, if not most, consti-tutional lawyers tend to disagree with Lincoln, but the central question is whether anyone really cares whether Lincoln was "faithful" to the text of the Constitution or not. One may ask the same questions, incidentally, about the Emancipation Proclamation, which is also constitutionally controversial as an exercise of a basically unlimited and unilateral presidential "war power." Does one really care about its constitutionality, though, given its purpose of ending slavery?[26]

Both Jefferson and Lincoln might well have been grateful for Locke's arguments on prerogative. But is it clear that Locke should prevail over Machiavelli, or should we think more deeply about what form we might want our constitutional dictatorship to take on occasions when it seems appropriate (or do you believe that it is *never* appropriate, so there is really nothing to think about)?[27]

IV. WHAT IS A CONSTITUTIONAL DICTATORSHIP?

With this in mind, we might define a constitutional dictatorship as a system (or subsystem) of constitutional government that bestows on a certain individual or institution the right to make binding rules, directives, and decisions at will and apply them to concrete circumstances unhindered by timely legal checks to authority. When the institution or individual acts according to this right, it acts clothed with all of the authority of the state. This person or institution, however, is subject to various procedural and substantive limitations that are set forth in advance. These may include the time and or circumstances in which authority may be exercised, the subjects over which authority may be exercised, and specific means for implementing rules.

The constitutional dictatorship is a dictatorship because the power conferred on the dictator combines elements of judicial, legislative, and executive power. This combination is a dangerous brew: indeed, in *Federalist* 47 Madison argued that "the accumulation of all powers legislative, executive and judiciary in the same hands, whether of one, a few or many, and whether hereditary, self appointed, or elective, may justly be pronounced the very definition of tyranny." It is worth noting that Madison hedges his definition by speaking of the accumulation of *all* powers. If the accumulation is only temporary, only over certain subject matters, or may only be exercised using certain specified means, it becomes something less than tyranny.

For example, if we assumed that the president has the power to initiate war, commandeer funds and resources for war, and conduct it at any time for any reason in any manner he pleases, he would be a constitutional dictator with respect to war and all matters related to war. That is because he would combine the right to assess the need for military action with the power to carry it out and the sole right to judge whether what he did was lawful. To the extent that the president may create rules, apply them, and execute them on his own without anyone else in the system having the ability to check him, the president is a law unto him or herself.

A constitutional dictatorship is constitutional because it comes with various limits prescribed by law and institutional structures. The dictator exercises power according to constitutional procedures that bring the dictatorship into being, structure its scope and reach, and end it when its purpose is no longer justified. For example, the president might have complete discretion to gather foreign intelligence through surveillance of persons outside the United States, but not within. (The difficulty arises when, as in the digital world, the distinction between foreign and domestic surveillance threatens to evaporate.)

Whether paradoxically or not, many elements of republican government could be seen as "dictatorial" to the extent that they endow government actors with essentially unreviewable discretion to set policy and execute it immediately with the force of law. Again, it is this *endowment* or *delegation* of power that is essential to the notion of *constitutional* dictatorship, for it differentiates it from the sheer *usurpation* of power (often by way of a military coup) that we tend to associate with contemporary dictatorships.

Moreover, a full analysis of the concept should lead us to realize that those who exercise prerogative or dictatorial powers need not be the president alone (or, some instances, at all). Consider the joint decision made by Federal Reserve Chairman Ben Bernanke and Secretary of the Treasury Henry Paulson to bail out troubled financial institutions, or the authority of the Centers for Disease Control to institute a quarantine. It may be a fundamental mistake to presume that constitutional dictators are always synonymous with presidents or prime ministers. One of the important realities of the Federal Reserve, for example, is that it is, in some very important ways, "independent" of the administration even though its members are appointed by the president and confirmed by the Senate. But this is the case, too, of the judiciary. What is crucial for both judges and Federal Reserve officials is that they cannot be fired in the way that cabinet officials can be fired. Their tenure in office is not derived from the Constitution, as is the case with federal judges, but, rather, from congressional statutes establishing independent agencies. As noted earlier, some lawyers believe that such independence in the case of executive branch agencies, including the Federal Reserve, violates the Constitution, but they are in a minority. Most lawyers and political elites accept the desirability of cordoning

off at least some executive agencies, including the one responsible for setting basic monetary policy, from presidential influence. The reason is very
simple: presidents might find it irresistible to adopt economic policies that
would have predictable short-run advantages (i.e., help in winning the next
election), but just as likely lead to long-term disaster.

The *New York Times* published a story on March 16, 2008, tellingly
headlined "Fed Chief Shifts Path, Inventing Policy in Crisis."[28] It led off
as follows:

> As chairman of the Federal Reserve, Ben S. Bernanke has long argued that a
> central bank should base its policies as much as possible on consistent prin-
> ciples rather than seat-of-the-pants judgment.
>
> But now, as the meltdown in credit markets threatens major institutions
> on Wall Street and a recession appears inevitable, Mr. Bernanke is inventing
> policy on the fly.
>
> "Modern monetary policy-making puts a lot of weight on rules, but there
> is no rule book for an economic crisis," said Douglas W. Elmendorf, a senior
> fellow at the Brookings Institution and a former Fed economist.

Is it true, then, that all rules are made to be broken, and that at some
level we trust those in high positions of leadership to know when those
occasions arise? After all, one could imagine similar articles about response
to the next great pandemic, where the focus would be not on Mr. Bernanke
but instead on the head of the Centers for Disease Control or the secretary
of health and human services. Section 361 of the Public Health Service Act,
for example, gives the secretary of health and human services the authority
"to make and enforce such regulations as in his judgment are necessary to
prevent the introduction, transmission, or spread of communicable diseases
from foreign countries into the States or possessions, or from one State
or possession into any other State or possession." These regulations may
include, "inspection, fumigation, disinfection, sanitation, pest extermination,
destruction of animals or articles found to be so infected or contaminated
as to be sources of dangerous infection to human beings, and other measures, as in his judgment may be necessary." They may even include "appre-
hension, detention, or conditional release of individuals" if necessary "for
the purpose of preventing the introduction, transmission, or spread of such

communicable diseases as may be specified from time to time in Executive orders of the President upon the recommendation of the Secretary, in consultation with the Surgeon General." To be sure, it would be the president issuing the order, but can one seriously imagine the president rejecting the advice of the surgeon general of the United States, presumably backed by the head of the Centers for Disease Control, that draconian measures were necessary to prevent a pandemic from sweeping the nation?

And the president would not have to claim extraordinary authority precisely because Congress has delegated to the executive the powers to require such measures. Many opponents of the New Deal denounced Congress for engaging in what even the liberal justice Benjamin N. Cardozo called "delegation running riot."[29] He had stated in an earlier opinion that the Constitution does not "grant to the Executive of any roving commission to inquire into evils and then, upon discovering them, do anything he pleases."[30] Yet one cannot possibly understand contemporary American government without recognizing the vast amount of authority that Congress has delegated to the executive branch and its administrative agencies.[31] The judiciary has long since given up on any attempt to control such delegations, and there are many good reasons to support that judicial withdrawal. But we should not kid ourselves about some of its implications, including the possibility that "governability" is purchased only by giving multiple "blank checks" to the president and other executive branch officials that can be filled in whenever they deem it necessary. And, all the while, they can quote Douglas Elmendorf's observation that "there is no rule book for an economic crisis" or perhaps any other kind of crisis.

Does this mean that there is no difference, at the end of the day, between the U.S. President, the head of the Federal Reserve Board, or the head of the Centers for Disease Control and iconic twentieth-century dictators like Adolf Hitler and Josef Stalin? Perhaps some more paranoid elements of the public might think it so. But this confuses the diminishing sunlight of four o'clock on a winter afternoon with the pitch darkness of four o'clock in the morning. No system of government, no matter how well prepared in advance, can do without discretion. This is particularly true of a modern administrative state, which from its formation has been in tension with traditional rule-of-law notions. With respect to thousands of minute individual decisions, ranging from the allocation of resources in a public hospital to a police officer's decision to stop a motorist or pedestrian, this discretion may be effectively unreviewable. However, the hallmark of a constitutional system is that it reins in discretion in various ways without ever fully eliminating it. In most cases a constitutional system binds discretion through statutory restrictions on the exercise of power, through reporting and oversight mechanisms, and through judicial review. We can nevertheless imagine a continuum of possibilities running from the relatively minimal discretion that always exists in the interstices of an administrative state to very broad and effectively unreviewable delegations of discretionary power over fundamental issues of life and death. The existence of substantial patches of practically unreviewable discretion on issues of far-reaching importance becomes a criterion of constitutional dictatorship.

There is an important relationship between constitutional dictatorship and declarations of emergency. Emergency is the standard justification for dictatorship. Nevertheless, dictatorial powers may not be connected to any real crisis or emergency. Even if dictatorship is initially justified by emergency, it may continue after the emergency is over. In this way dictatorial powers may become normalized. Executive officials, noting the ability of emergency to focus the public's attention, may find themselves in quest of new emergencies to justify its continuation. This can lead to a policy of government through emergency, which normalizes dictatorial powers in a different way. Moreover, dictatorial powers may be granted because of the fear of an emergency, even if it has not yet materialized. This gives incentives to magnify both the probability and the dangers of possible scenarios. Finally, by declaring an emergency and bestowing dictatorial powers, a government may create a self-fulfilling prophecy. The executive judges the situation as an emergency deserving of dictatorial powers, makes rules that frame the situation in this way; if he acts on the basis of that framing, perhaps by engaging in a so-called preventive military attack on an identified "enemy," the emergency is thus confirmed. In this way, dictatorship constructs reality according to its own vision and perpetuates society's need for such dictatorship. Consider in this context the famous paragraph from Ron Suskind's portrait of the presidency of George W. Bush in 2004, in which an aide to Bush

said that guys like me were "in what we call the reality-based community," which
he defined as people who "believe that solutions emerge from your judicious

study of discernible reality." I nodded and murmured something about enlight-
enment principles and empiricism. He cut me off. "That's not the way the world
really works anymore," he continued. "We're an empire now, and when we act,
we create our own reality. And while you're studying that reality—judiciously, as
you will—we'll act again, creating other new realities, which you can study too,
and that's how things will sort out. We're history's actors...and you, all of you,
will be left to just study what we do."[31]

A vital question is how best to design a system of emergency powers
and, if you wish, constitutional dictatorship. Again, the central question is
a comparative one, and in this instance other national constitutions rather
than the constitutions of the American states will provide the most valuable comparisons.[33] But this requires us to return to the question raised
particularly by Machiavelli, which is how we might best design a constitution that includes a self-conscious recognition that it might be necessary
at times to suspend ordinary constitutional norms and even accept a temporary dictatorship as desirable.

V. DESIGNING A CONSTITUTIONAL
DICTATORSHIP

The central question is whether there might be helpful rules for *planning*
for inevitable crises, even if one concedes that when the moment comes
one might have to place great discretion in the person or persons confronting the particularities of the crisis. So *is* there a way of combining
what might be thought to be the advantages of de facto dictatorial decisionmaking in crisis situations while minimizing, even if not completely
eliminating, the risks that those granted dictatorial authority will indeed
become tyrants?

Clinton Rossiter concludes his fascinating—and troublesome—1948
book *Constitutional Dictatorship* by asserting that it is "hardly a matter
for discussion" that "constitutional dictatorship does have a future in the
United States."[34] What *must* be discussed, he suggested, was our structuring of such future moments—he was writing in 1948, and his primary
examples at that point were Abraham Lincoln, Woodrow Wilson, and

Franklin Delano Roosevelt, our three notable "war presidents"—in a way that would guard the United States as much as possible from emulating distinctly less-happy examples of dictatorship that could be found in Europe in the early twentieth century.

He offered eleven suggestions, some of them fairly obvious, including the belief that a dictatorship is truly necessary, "indispensable to the preservation of the state and its constitutional order." Though this seems almost banal, this suggestion is more difficult to implement than it first appears: everything depends on how many forms of executive discretion in the modern administrative and national security state we wish to label as examples of constitutional dictatorship. Many different agencies and individuals, ranging from the head of the Federal Reserve to that of the Centers for Disease Control, may have basically unreviewable discretion. Jack Balkin and I use the term "distributed dictatorships" to refer to this modern phenomenon, where it is a mistake to believe that one person has an unlimited domain to exercise dictatorial authority. No rational system would allow for such a possibility, precisely because we would want someone with specific skills and expertise appropriate to the occasion. Our presidents are at best gifted amateurs, and we would often want skilled professionals to lead the response to a given crisis, whether it be military, economic, or public health.

Rossiter's second suggestion for a well-designed institution of constitutional dictatorship is adopted from ancient Rome: "The decision to institute a constitutional dictatorship should never be in the hands of the man or men who will constitute the dictator." As we have seen, the American system flunks this essential test. To the extent that the American Constitution seemingly allows a president to both declare the existence of an emergency and engage in extraordinary action that may well skirt the boundaries of the law, is the extent to which we move far closer to the possibility of tyrannical dictatorship. And, recall, it may not really matter if the president can claim constitutional or statutory authority. Such authority does establish the *constitutional* nature of the dictatorship, but a badly designed constitution may place insufficient limits even on what we are willing to call "dictatorship."

One possibility, suggested by the South African Constitution, is to require the legislature to vote to activate the executive's emergency powers for each particular emergency rather than to write blank checks to be cashed later at the president's sole discretion. Indeed, it is worth quoting the Article 37 of the South African Constitution at length in order to get a sense of how those concerned with writing a new constitution to overcome a discredited South African past confronted the issue of "states of emergency." The first thing one notices is that only parliament is given the authority to declare a state of emergency and "only when (a) the life of the nation is threatened by war, invasion, general insurrection, disorder, natural disaster, or other public emergency; *and* (b) the declaration is necessary to restore peace and order" (emphasis added).

Any such declaration initially takes effect "for no more than 21 days from the date of the declaration, unless the National Assembly resolves to extend the declaration." Extensions are limited to three months at a time. What is especially interesting, though, is the adoption of a special supermajority procedure for any extensions beyond the first one. Any further extensions must be "supported by at least 60 per cent of the members of the Assembly…following a public debate in the Assembly." Such a procedure could be especially important if the dominant political party or party coalition has fewer than 60 percent of the seats in parliament, as it assures that the "opposition" parties must acquiesce to the extension.

Even more striking is the assignment to the judiciary of a role in determining the "validity" of a state of emergency and any "action taken in consequence of a declaration of a state of emergency." This seemingly authorizes a court to state that the circumstances do not justify the extraordinary declaration of a state of emergency, in spite of a parliamentary declaration to the contrary. Finally, the constitution includes a "Table of Non-Derogable Rights" limiting the powers of parliament even in times of acknowledged emergencies with regard to basic protections of human dignity or life or the norms of racial and gender equality. In the nature of the case, one cannot know for sure whether these constitute mere "parchment barriers" or, on the contrary, will serve as genuine limitations even when political elites—perhaps backed by public opinion—believe that the country faces an "existential crisis" that requires doing "whatever is necessary." What one can say, though, is that the South African Constitution does a better job than U.S. counterpart in at least addressing the possibilities of emergency governance. Indeed, one might say this of most constitutions drafted after World War II.

One could spend an entire chapter—indeed, book—analyzing all of these various sections. Return to the implications that a court may be given authority to assess the validity of a declaration of a state of emergency. The Columbian Supreme Court's has invalidated such declarations by the Columbian authorities on the grounds that the objective situation did not warrant the extreme response attached to declarations of emergency and the suspension of ordinary constitutional rights. An American analogue would be the Supreme Court's refusing to countenance the suspension of habeas corpus on the grounds that the Constitution allows suspension only in cases of "insurrection" and "invasion" and that the "war on terror" simply doesn't fulfill these constitutional prerequisites. At the American state level, a number of governors and legislatures claim special authority upon the enunciation of an "emergency." In Texas, for example, ordinary legislative rules can be suspended if the governor describes legislation as linked to an emergency. One might well doubt the accuracy of such proclamations by Governor Rick Perry in 2011 as to the "emergency" status of bills requiring enhanced identification from would-be voters or that women seeking an abortion first watch a sonogram—both bills were passed—but it was presumably unthinkable that a Texas court would subject gubernatorial descriptions to further analysis.

The protections offered by the South African Constitution against the suspension of certain rights even in dire circumstances can be analogized to Article 2 of the United Nations Convention on Torture, which explicitly makes the prohibition of torture absolute: "No exceptional circumstances whatsoever, whether a state of war or a threat or war, internal political instability or any other public emergency, may be invoked as a justification of torture." Nor might one claim that a superior authority, including even the president, has ordered one to ignore the prohibition: "An order from a superior officer or a public authority may not be invoked as a justification of torture." Given that the United States clearly did engage in torture during what the Bush Administration labeled the "Global War on Terror" with the encouragement and approval of the president and vice president, one can wonder whether the Convention, which was ratified by the United States, is just another example of a "parchment barrier."

In any event, Congress has created a series of framework statutes that bestow emergency powers, including the power to declare an emergency in the first place, on the president or some other executive official. So, although Congress has technically authorized these powers, it may be a Congress that sat long ago. The Militia Act of 1792 and the Insurrection Act of 1807 are both exemplary in this regard. Moreover, an obscure 1932 banking act, passed over President Hoover's veto, was viewed as empowering Ben Bernanke in 2008, seventy-five years later. There is no contemporaneous congressional vote on whether an emergency exists; instead, the framework statute leaves that question to the executive, thus doing an end run around the South African (and Roman) model. The closest that the American system comes to this model is the declaration of war, which activates the president's war powers or, following World War II (the last declared war), authorizations for the use of military force, which never seem to be repealed.

There are two problems with the South African and Roman models, which require the legislature or consuls to declare emergencies and activate special powers each time. The first arises when we are indeed faced with a crisis that demands *immediate* decisionmaking, when there simply isn't enough time to gain legislative authorization. Although the most obvious examples may involve military attack, certain kinds of economic emergencies or health emergencies may also occur suddenly and call for the political equivalent of instantaneous decisionmaking.

The second problem may be even more basic. It operates even when time is not of the essence. In his classic book on the American presidency, Clinton Rossiter emphasized that one of the six "hats" worn by the president is that of "party leader." Richard Pildes and Daryl Levinson have argued that legislative oversight of an aggressive president, even in a presidential system, may not operate adequately when the legislature is dominated by the political party of which the president is the leader. To the contrary, it may be in the electoral interest of the president's party to join in suggesting that the country faces a particularly fearful situation, which demands the kind of radical action that can be provided only by the president and members of his party. For many people, the Bush Administration's war on terror is a recent example.

Pildes and Levinson call for emulating the German practice and guaranteeing that certain important committees in the legislature are in the hands of the opposition party, precisely to assure some measure of significant oversight. Similarly, Professor David Fontana has also addressed how to constitutionalize the role of the "party in opposition" in a modern party system. But even these proposals may not respond adequately to the possibility that a legislature controlled by the executive's own party will be more than happy to delegate to the chief executive all sorts of discretionary powers associated with constitutional dictatorship. Bruce Ackerman has endorsed taking a leaf from the South African book by requiring supermajorities for the declaration of emergencies and/or the delegation of emergency powers. His particular twist is to require ever larger majorities to keep emergency powers in place after specified time limits. This, he argues, will make dictatorial powers increasingly difficult to obtain and to keep.

Finally, one might imagine taking the decision out of the ordinary political process completely. The model might be the Federal Reserve Board, which is relatively independent from the president and Congress and uses its expertise to manage the money supply in what it views as the public interest. Imagine the creation of a "Council of Elders" who would be required to declare the existence of a state of emergency that would presumably trigger the exercise of extraordinarily powers. In the United States, such a council might consist of all former presidents, vice presidents, retired secretaries of state, former heads of the Joint Chiefs of Staff, former heads of the Federal Reserve Board, and the like, including significant leaders from the private sector who have demonstrated good judgment in times of stress and challenge. Some members of the council, like former presidents, might serve ex officio, while others might be nominated by the president and confirmed by the Senate (perhaps by a two-thirds vote).

Moreover, we might doubt that a given president, however attractive he or she might be in many respects, would be just the right person to serve as the constitutional dictator for a particular kind of emergency. If the problem is staving off a threatened military invasion, one might prefer someone with demonstrated military experience. If, on the other hand, the threat is imminent economic collapse, military experience would presumably be irrelevant, and a senior economist with wide-ranging government experience might be just the person desired. Rossiter and other admirers of ancient Rome have noted that the Roman consuls could not select themselves for the office of dictator; hence they had incentives to ensure that the person they chose for the office had the character, skills, and judgment needed for the particular task Just as in the Roman context, the term of emergency power would be limited.

The U.S. Constitution seems to recognize only two possible emergencies, "insurrection" and "invasion," and it provides for one particular response, which is the suspension of habeas corpus (though it does not clearly specify who can suspend habeas, or for how long). But it should be glaringly obvious that there are many other possible emergencies, which most modern constitutions recognize, including natural disasters, economic crises, and public health threats. Suspending habeas corpus is literally irrelevant with regard to a mortgage crisis, though it might be very useful to suspend for a limited time the contractual duty to meet the monthly payments in spite of the Contract Clause of Article I, Section 10, which seems explicitly to invalidate such "impairments of contracts." As with so many other issues, the question is whether we in the United States have anything to learn from the rich body of materials provided by the dozens of constitutions drafted in the past sixty years that take account of the multitude of threats that might be presented to constitutional orders and attempt to provide modes of response.

VI. EMERGENCY AND THE PROBLEM OF CONTINUITY IN GOVERNMENT

Understandably, the events of September 11, 2001, triggered many reflections on emergency powers and even constitutional dictatorship, and we have been living with the consequences ever since. But consider that an apparent purpose of Flight 93, which went down in Pennsylvania, was to destroy either the Capitol or the White House and generate additional havoc for our political system precisely by calling its basic continuity into question. Who would, after all, take the reins of government if the president and vice president were both killed or otherwise incapacitated? And what would be the consequences of the multiple deaths or incapacitations of representatives and senators, not only as a matter of public psychology and confidence, but even *legally* in terms of the ability of Congress to meet the quorum rules set out in the Constitution itself as necessary conditions for passing legislation?

I addressed this subject in *Our Undemocratic Constitution*, but there has been (at least) one important development since then, which is worth examining as a model of how even intelligent people can be remarkably obtuse when they do not take a sufficiently broad view of what one should think about when designing a constitution. The very smart person I am referring to is Rhodes Scholar and former senator Russell Feingold. He was so furious in 2009 at the baseness of Illinois politics—which manifested itself in the soon-to-be-impeached governor Rod Blagojevich's appointment of the undistinguished Roland Burris to the Senate to succeed former senator Barack Obama—that he proposed a new amendment to the Constitution. It would amend the Seventeenth Amendment by eliminating the ability of governors to fill vacancies in the Senate. It would make the Senate like the House of Representatives—*all* members would be *elected* and none would be appointed. The amendment has been endorsed by the editorial board of the *New York Times*.

It is difficult indeed to defend the procedures by which Senator Burris was appointed. But remedies for such actions that might make sense at the "retail level," when one is thinking of only one or two vacancies in the Senate or the House, may make little sense at the "wholesale level," when there might be multiple vacancies in either body. So consider now the problems posed by "wholesale" vacancies, of the type that might follow an attack on Washington. Would we necessarily have the same preferences concerning elected versus appointed members of Congress in that instance as in the "retail" situation? Or would we want the House and the Senate to be replenished as soon as humanly possible, which would almost certainly mean some version of gubernatorial appointment? To be sure, one can imagine a number of ways of limiting gubernatorial power. Wyoming, for example, requires that if the governor is not of the same political party as the senator whose death or resignation created the vacancy, then he or she must fill the vacancy from a list of three possibilities selected by the state committee of that particular party. Other suggestions have included voting for an "alternate" at the time of the general election who could automatically succeed the elected representative or senator should a vacancy occur. This would prevent having to wait for an election.

A proposed Twenty-eighth Amendment to the Constitution, based on the findings of a study group organized by the conservative American Enterprise

Institute and the liberal Brookings Institution, would establish procedures for such filling vacancies in case of dire national emergencies, defined as the demise or disability of 25 percent of either chamber. Note, incidentally, that dead senators do not present the same problem that dead representatives do, since the former can be replaced immediately, assuming that states have exercised the Seventeenth-Amendment authority to empower their governors to name new senators. But a multitude of only disabled senators could present their own threat to governability, which is why it would be desirable to provide a method for at least temporary replacement.

So what explains the fact that Congress has made no serious move toward proposing such an amendment in the decade since 2001? Perhaps one believes that it is a bad idea, deservedly assigned to the scrap heap. But if that's not the case, then Congress's failure to address it—or to propose a presumptively even better amendment—might tell us something more ominous about the (in)ability of Congress to respond even to the most basic kind of foreseeable (though relatively improbable) threat to our constitutional order.

VII. "DECONSTRUCTING" THE CONSTITUTION OF SETTLEMENT?

This book has emphasized the critical difference between the Constitution of Conversation, which encourages expansive debate about the *meaning* of constitutional terms, and the Constitution of Settlement, which rests on the notion of stable—even rigid—meaning, so that any debate can be only about *wisdom*. Moreover, as suggested especially in the previous chapter, formal amendment is far more important with regard to the Constitution of Settlement, and the absence of such amendment requires us to stick with the status quo, however unattractive it may be. But this chapter, which has focused on "exigencies" and "emergencies," suggests that the reality is more complicated. Perhaps the Constitution of Settlement can itself become unsettled when it is viewed as leading to what Machiavelli so tellingly described as the "ruin" of the republic.

What establishes the Constitution of Settlement, then, is not the presence of particular linguistic properties, even if it is certainly the case that one can hardly ignore the texts in question. Yet we must ask ourselves why "what part of 'no law' do you not understand" has not prevailed with regard to either the First Amendment or the Contract Clause, whereas the text seems dispositive with regard to Inauguration Day, the length of the presidential term, and the other foci of this book. Imagine, for example, that we are in the midst of war, with a president who possesses truly unusual talents as both commander-in-chief and "diplomat-in-chief" when conferring with both allies and even enemies with whom negotiating some kind of acceptable peace is the goal. But the president is deep into her second term, and the Twenty-second Amendment explicitly bars her from serving a third term. Might we not wish to "suspend" the amendment, either by allowing her to run again or even by suspending the election itself and, as sometimes occurs in legislative sessions, symbolically "stopping the clock" and allowing a given "legislative day" to last considerably longer than twenty-four hours?

To be sure, as Charles de Gaulle once remarked, graveyards are filled with purportedly indispensable men, and it would be quite frightening to believe that any given individual is truly "indispensable," so that the consequence of losing his or her talents would be a descent into chaos. Still, it seems easy enough to believe that some individuals are particularly gifted and that we would be taking a genuine risk in depriving them of a public office they were filling with special skills. So we must still ask whether insistence on fidelity to the Twenty-second Amendment—or the fixed four-year term—in certain circumstances is admirable or simply fetishistic. Given what we have learned about the Philadelphia Convention, not to mention subsequent American history, we can scarcely be confident that we know exactly how committed even the Framers would have been to the Constitution of Settlement in times of emergency.

17

Conclusion: America the Ungovernable?

The overarching topic of this book has been the importance of the political structures that are established by constitutions. Well-designed structures contribute to the welfare, however defined, of communities—the various "we the people of..."—that are the proclaimed subject of most contemporary constitutions. Concomitantly, poorly designed constitutions may ill serve their communities, leading to various dysfunctionalities or, at the worst, out-and-out "ungovernability." Thus this book has emphasized such "civics course" issues as offices that constitutions establish; their clear powers or, in some cases, lack of power; how people are chosen to fill those offices; when they take their respective offices; and for how long they will serve. It is a perverse feature of American education that such topics, if taught at all, are usually regarded as "boring," mere way stations on the road to what most people find interesting about constitutions, which are the rights they ostensibly protect. This book has downplayed such rights provisions.

If a constitution does not provide clear answers with regard to the examples set out above, then one might well pronounce it to be a failure without knowing much more about it. However, one must consider those few—but obviously interesting and important—countries such as the United Kingdom, Israel, and New Zealand that to this day have not adopted what might be termed a "standard-form" written constitution that specifies the answers to such questions and makes it formally difficult to change these structures. There are strong "conventions" in Great Britain, for example, and an act of Parliament specifies that elections shall be held no later than every five years. But these conventions and parliamentary acts are presumably capable of being repealed or otherwise overridden by any subsequent ordinary act of Parliament. Unlike the United States, which held its regularly scheduled elections in 1942 and 1944, Parliament simply chose to suspend the requirement for elections once World War II broke out in 1939. Thus, the Parliament elected in 1935 governed until the conclusion of the war in 1945 (when Winston Churchill was thrown out of office by the electorate). Still, almost no one has described Great Britain as "ungovernable," and the same is certainly true of New Zealand.

Israel, on the other hand, may present a closer case. As Hanna Lerner has argued, one reason that Israel did not adopt a constitution after its declaration of independence in 1948 was because of serious cleavages within the Jewish community. Although the Declaration spoke of Israel as a "Jewish state," most supporters also assumed it would be a democratic one. It has been a source of deep and often bitter contention whether this joinder is the equivalent of being assigned to square the circle.[1] Moreover, any contemporary Israeli constitution would have to come to terms with the fact that 20 percent of the population is not only non-Jewish but has also received systematically unequal treatment over the life of the state of Israel.

But Israel also necessarily forces us to return, albeit briefly, to a point made much earlier, which hovers over this entire book. Even if we can agree that country (or state) A is "well-governed," while another country (or state) B is badly governed or even "ungovernable," does the explanation lie in the strengths and weaknesses of formal institutions or rather in other factors, especially what has come to be called "political culture"? "I do worry about the populist idea that there is nothing wrong with the American people," one friend responded to an earlier draft of this book, "but [that it is] our institutions [that] need fixing... Truth of the matter is that I think we presently have the sort of population that is incapable of operating the machinery of a constitutional democracy." James Madison might be quite sympathetic to such an observation inasmuch as he was obsessed with trying to assure the presence of leaders, including those elected by the people, who had the capacity to operate "the machinery of a constitutional democracy." Those capacities included not only knowledge of a kind that could presumably be gained by formal education or certain kinds of experience, but also possession of traits of personal character that would place the public interest ahead of selfish "factional" concerns. On many occasions, politically virtuous leaders might need to possess a willingness to make hard compromises that, in an ideal (and non-existent) world, they (and their followers) would never have to make.

Moreover, as one looks around the world, one scarcely find examples of contented populations whose political systems we might want to emulate. So it would be naïve in the extreme to argue that the solution to our problems is, for example, to adopt the parliamentary system because it is less conducive to gridlock than our separation-of-powers model.[2] One need only look at the political systems of Italy and Greece—or of Israel—to be wary that parliamentarianism is any kind of cure for deep problems within a social order. But it seems equally naïve to deny that formal structures at both the state and national levels within the United States can explain at least *some* important things about ongoing political systems and their capacity to surmount basic challenges. This is especially true if we subject constitutions to the equivalent of "stress tests" at different points in time. An undoubtedly tremendous achievement of those who framed and ratified the Constitution in 1787–1788 was helping to put into place a "governable America" between 1789, when George Washington was inaugurated, and 1801, when Thomas Jefferson took office. New political systems may in their own way be comparable to start-up businesses, most of which fail, but that was not the case in the United States. One might wonder how much credit should go to the almost singular figure of George Washington, but some surely has to go to the Constitution as well. But I picked 1801 for a reason, which is that the country was at the brink of civil war because of the imbroglio generated by the tie vote in the electoral college between Jefferson and Aaron Burr.[3] Nonetheless, we survived, and one might point to the almost incredible flourishing, by many measures, of at least whites within the United States in the decades thereafter. But sixty years later, Abraham Lincoln took office after seven states had already proclaimed their withdrawal from the Union.

Can one really describe the United States as "governable" during a decade in which, for starters, 2 percent of its population lost their lives over a dispute about the degree to which the Constitution protected slavery? Perhaps more to the point, as Mark Graber has demonstrated, it was the

Constitution itself that, in a variety of ways, contributed to the inability of the Constitution to forestall dissolution and war. Think only of the fact that Lincoln, whose election precipitated secession, received the votes of only 39.8 percent of the voting public. Had we not had the electoral college foisted on us in 1787 (and reaffirmed in the Twelfth Amendment in 1803 that solved only the particular problem posed by the Jefferson–Burr tie vote), it is altogether possible that someone else would have been elected and the Union saved. However, given the centrality of slavery to secession and to Lincoln's monumental achievements as president, perhaps we should praise the electoral college for giving us a minority president whose election triggered a cleansing bath of blood. That is a normative judgment, and it is, to say the least, a peculiar sort of praise for the electoral college. What seems impossible to disagree with is the empirical claim that the electoral college and the fact that every member of Congress was elected locally rather than by a national constituency each made their own contributions to the onset of war.

There has been nothing close to civil war since 1865, but we ought not forget repeated episodes of violence that tested the meaning of "government" (let alone "democracy") in America.[4] Civil war may be a too easy—even misleading—example of "ungovernability." It is too easy inasmuch as almost no one would deny the relevance to "governability" of civil war, whether in the United States or elsewhere. This is true even if we can distinguish between a country whose institutions continue to operate in important respects, as was the case with the United States, and total breakdown into "anarchy." But what is misleading is to believe that anything less than a civil war demonstrates a very useful notion of "governability." At the very least, adopting that notion requires that we define governability by the sole criteria of providing security and stability.

Thomas Hobbes, the most dour (and perhaps most brilliant) of all English-language political philosophers, would have been sympathetic to this minimalist notion of governability. But one of the implications of such minimalism is that it dispenses with any concern about democracy or the provision of other important goods—we might even call them "rights"—beyond security and stability. Many highly unattractive countries can be said to provide their citizens (or subjects) with stability and at least a certain kind of security against foreign enemies, but little else. One meaning of the Arab Spring is a rejection of such limited notions of "good government," even if the immediate aftermath includes the transformation of countries like Egypt, Tunisia, or Libya from the category of "governable" to "ungovernable," at least with reference to the long-established "leaders" who were forced to leave their office and, in some cases, to flee their countries or lose their lives. By the time this book is published, readers may know whether Syria or Yemen has entered their company.

This book is in many ways a successor to a book published in 2006, *Our Undemocratic Constitution: Where Our Constitution Goes Wrong (and How We the People Can Correct It)*. That book, as suggested by the title, focused on the extent to which the United States Constitution deviated from an acceptable twenty-first-century notion of democracy. To be sure, that remains a subject of this book as well. I hope it has become clear that the U.S. Constitution is, by a far measure, the most undemocratic constitution among the fifty-one constitutions that exemplify constitutionalism in America. We often speak of "American exceptionalism" vis-à-vis the rest of the world, and devotees of that dubious notion are often hesitant to believe that we have anything to learn from the rest of the world. I disagree, which is why there have been frequent references to the provisions of some foreign constitutions, such as South Africa's "emergency powers" schema. But even if one ignores every other country and discounts any lessons they might provide, we should regard as an intellectual scandal the systematic disregard of the rich array of American state constitutions and the lessons they might teach us, for good or for ill. And we should wrestle more than we do with the fact that the U.S. Constitution is "exceptional" within the United States itself.

Still, one could simply respond that even if the U.S. Constitution is "undemocratic" or otherwise significantly different from most of the fifty state constitutions, that is a subject largely of interest only to academics or political zealots. The real test of a constitution or political system, many would argue, is not its conformance to some abstract theory of democracy, but, instead, whether it produces a *contented* populace. A truly "benevolent despot," concerned to maximize the welfare of his or her subject population, would be preferable to a democratic political system that with some frequency would put into office leaders with objectionable, perhaps even horrendous, views.

Moreover, an advantage of membership in a political system that asks little other than loyalty is that these members—should one even call them "citizens"?—do not have to spend much time on politics. Life as a democratic (or "republican") citizen, on the other hand, inevitably takes lots of time. There is much discussion these days of the conflicts between career and family. Both of those are private goods, however. What time is left for one's tasks of citizenship? The "problem with socialism," Oscar Wilde reportedly said, "is that it will take up too many evenings." But, if truth be known, that's the problem with any serious political engagement. It explains why many people ask only about the payoffs of a particular political system rather than about its democratic bona fides. This book, for all of its remaining interest in democratic bona fides, is also vitally interested in the payoffs and the relationship between what governments actually do and the formal political structures within which they operate. This is why there has been recurrent mention of polling data about American dissatisfaction with their governmental institutions and fears that the country is going in the wrong direction.

Indeed, almost literally as this book was going to press, the *New York Times* announced that a "New Poll Finds a Deep Distrust of Government."[5] "Not only do 89 percent of Americans say they distrust government to do the right thing, but 74 percent say the country is on the wrong track and 84 percent disapprove of Congress." No doubt the disaffection will grow because of the failure in November 2011 of the so-called congressional "super committee" to reach any accord regarding the reduction of the federal deficit in a responsible manner.[6]

The Gallup organization found in mid-December 2011 that an astounding 86 percent disapproved of Congress. The first poll taken in 2012, by CBS, showed that 80 percent of those polled disapproved of Congress and only 12 percent approved.

Anyone who has gotten this far has already vindicated Oscar Wilde's maxim; after all, reading this book has taken a decent amount of time. Given that this book is scarcely happy in its message, I assume that many other uses of this time would have given greater private pleasure. Perhaps I should have begun it, as did Tom Paine many years ago writing about an earlier "American crisis," by suggesting that "these are the times that try men's souls." This book *is* a call, if not to revolution, than at least to active citizenship. We really need not quibble about what social scientists might call the "operational" meaning of "ungovernability." It is enough that you find yourself worrying—perhaps even staying up at night—that your children and grandchildren will grow up in a far less attractive world (including, most importantly, that part of the world defined as the United States or the state you happen to live in) in part because of dysfunctionalities in our political systems that could at least be addressed, even if not wholly corrected. (To require complete correction would be utopian and signify the truth of the maxim that insistence on the best works as an enemy of the good.) Even if we are blasé about the consequences for ourselves, don't we owe our loved ones—and our fellow members of the American political community, if we take seriously the notion of being part of "We the People"—at least some reflection about what those dysfunctionalities are and what in turn might be possible? One might even offer a more cosmopolitan perspective and ask if we might not also think of persons around the world who inevitably pay costs for the dysfunctionalities of American government, given the domain of influence of the United States and even many individual states.

So what *is* to be done? Here, I reiterate the conclusion to *Our Undemocratic Constitution:* We need a new constitutional convention, one that could engage in a comprehensive overview of the U.S. Constitution and the utility of many of its provisions to twenty-first century Americans. I also hope that the electorate in states that allow voters to call new state conventions exercise that option and provide a classic modern "laboratory" that might convince their fellow Americans of the possibility of new constitutional conventions, even in America, in the new millennium. How would the delegates be selected? As suggested by the earlier discussion of lotteries as alternatives to elections or appointment, I would advocate that delegates from each state, proportionate to overall population, be selected by lottery, with very limited restrictions on selection (the most obvious one being age). I would give these delegates the salary for two years of a Supreme Court justice or senator, given the public importance of their job, and also to make possible service by the less well off. They would also collectively operate with a budget sufficient to allow hearings all over the United States and the world that would allow them to make the most informed choices possible regarding the kinds of issues examined throughout this book.

I know all too well from discussions with friends and family that many, probably most, readers will reject this call out of hand. Only rarely, I suspect, will rejection simply reflect high support for the constitution(s) we now have. If one believes it isn't broken, then there is no reason to think it needs a convention (or anything else) to "fix" it. But I have found that many of my interlocutors agree with many, whether or not all, of my criticisms. However, they are basically terrified of what might happen if their fellow citizens, however selected, actually embarked on serious reflection about the Constitution with the possibility of changing it should they find it inadequate. Their terror derives from a basic mistrust of their fellow Americans. No doubt these readers resonated with many of the unflattering descriptions of "lower orders" offered by Madison and Hamilton, among other architects of our Constitution who were less than enamored with the capacities of ordinary people to engage in the tasks of governance. This is why there is not an iota of direct democracy in the U.S. Constitution; yet we live in a country where forty-nine of the fifty state constitutions express, in their basic structures, a higher regard for ordinary Americans.

I believe that lottery selection would protect us against takeovers of a constitutional convention by single-issue zealots who might, with the support of generous financing, prevail in elections. I earlier rejected the analogy between legal interpretation and "rocket science." This is also true with regard to "constitutional design." Many of the issues raised in the book involve basic value choices that ordinary Americans are capable of making. Take presidential vetoes based only on policy grounds. One might like them if one agrees with Hamilton that we should be fearful of basically impetuous (or corrupt) legislatures; one would reject them, or at least make it easier for legislatures to override vetoes, if one had greater faith in the "wisdom of crowds" instantiated in legislatures. And so on.

Gordon Wood, whom I have quoted in several places, concludes his recent book, *The Idea of America*, with a chapter tellingly titled "The American Revolutionary Tradition, or Why America Wants to Spread Democracy Around the World."[7] He ends his essay by writing of a very meaningful encounter back in 1976 with a young student in Warsaw, where he had given what he describes as a "very ordinary lecture on the American Revolution." (It was, after all, the Bicentennial of the Declaration of Independence.) The "young Polish intellectual rose to tell me that I had left out the most important part…She said that I had not mentioned the Bill of Rights—the constitutional protection of individual liberties against the government."[8] I do not want to deny the importance of the Bill of Rights, or of similar provisions in state constitutions, including those that go beyond the U.S. Constitution by, for example, guaranteeing a right to an education[9] or environmental protection.[10] But perhaps Polish students, as well as the rest of us, should become more aware of less inspiring features of our constitutional order—our Constitution of Settlement—and ask how worthy *they* are of admiration and emulation. We can ask such questions whether we view ourselves as instantiating the American revolutionary heritage or whether we are simply concerned about the capacities of our institutions to govern effectively in response to the challenges of the twenty-first century. These are not abstract questions, any more than was the case in 1776. As was true then, the quality of our future is at stake.

Acknowledgments

By far the most enjoyable part of writing any book is acknowledging those who helped make it possible. There are self-starting authors who write alone, but I am not one of them. For me the "community of scholars (and friends)" is no cliché but, rather, an important reality that explains much of what I have been able to write over the years. I begin, appropriately, with the specific dedicatees of this volume. Jack Balkin is a beloved friend and sometime colleague, first at the University of Texas and then intermittently at the Yale Law School. And he is not only the co-author of (so far) nineteen articles we have written together, the co-editor of a casebook on constitutional law and the co-author of a future book on the U.S. Constitution in times of crisis. He is also someone who reads everything I write, even if not formally as co-author, and with whom I have extensive conversations about everything and anything I happen to be interested in. Moreover, it is primarily because of Jack that I developed an institutional connection with the Yale Law School, which has been extremely important to me both personally and professionally. Finally, as the creator of the blog site *Balkinization*, he has given me a platform from which to opine (and occasionally rant) on various issues of the day involving American constitutionalism, broadly defined.

Mark Graber, another old friend who has remained a close colleague, even since leaving the University of Texas, is also someone I regularly turn to for comment and critique (which he offers with alacrity) and, even more, for unfailing illumination on the complex history of American constitutional development. We disagree on some quite basic issues, and much of this book is "my turn" in an ongoing argument both about how broken the United States Constitution is and, more to the point, what constitutes a proper response if one agrees that it is defective in important respects. He has turned out to be a latter-day Madisonian, whereas I have discovered, in part because of Mark, my "inner Jefferson." Mark is also the current major domo of an important institution, the annual Baltimore "schmooze" (founded by Mark Tushnet when he was at Georgetown) that brings together a wonderful array of law professors and political scientists, of all ages and methodological dispositions, to discuss important issues, including, on occasion, my own work. He is indispensable not only to me, but to a nationwide community of scholars.

I have also benefitted inestimably from the opportunity over the past decade to be part of the Harvard Law School community and to teach "reading courses" and an occasional seminar basically on whatever interests me. And, of course, I benefitted as well from the opportunity to discuss topics of mutual interest with many members of its exceptional faculty, whom I refrain from naming individually only because of my fear that I would inevitably leave someone out. All of this happened because of the solicitude and kindness of Elena Kagan, who inquired at lunch one day in 2002 why I was visiting at Yale instead of Harvard. My answer—that one must be asked to dinner before showing up with plate in hand—led to her paving the way, when she became Dean, for my visiting Harvard, an act of grace on her part that immeasurably enhanced my life. My delight in her becoming a member of the United States Supreme Court, to which she is already contributing her distinctive and illuminating voice, is tempered by the reality that opportunities to further deepen our friendship, which my visits to Harvard made possible, will now be infrequent. I am also grateful that her successor, Martha Minow, has been equally solicitous.

Although there are clear connections between this book and my previous book, *Our Undemocratic Constitution*, this is very much a new book, I hope both wider and deeper than the earlier volume. Many of these chapters began as lectures prepared for undergraduate courses, first at the University of Texas and then Harvard College. The first was the result of my friend Paul Woodruff, who has taken on the sometimes thankless task of developing a "signature course" program for UT first-year undergraduates that is designed to assure them at least one relatively small course with a full professor. I could not resist his entreaties to join the program; it is also the case, for reasons explained in this book, that it is enormously important to convey the realities of "the Constitution of Settlement" to undergraduates (and even younger students) on their way to becoming informed members of the American political community (or, more properly, communities). Similarly, another friend, Nancy Rosenblum, as Chair of Harvard's Department of Government, asked me if I would be interested in "filling in" as a visitor to teach the basic undergraduate course on American constitutionalism. This was, in effect, like being offered a guaranteed winning ticket in the lottery, though I am afraid that some of the undergraduates were disappointed that the course—like this book—dealt so much with structures and so little with rights.

Several chapters of this book were prepared for presentation as formal lectures or as parts of symposia over the years. I am therefore grateful to Dean Loren Robel at the Indiana Law School for inviting me to deliver the Jerome Hall Lecture in 2008; Prof. Robert George for asking me to present the Walter Murphy Lecture at Princeton in 2009; Professor Robert Cochran and Dean Kenneth Starr for the opportunity to give the Louis Brandeis Lecture at Pepperdine Law School in 2010; Professor Scott Gerber for arranging an invitation to deliver the Kormendy Lecture at the Ohio Northern Law School, also in 2010; and Professor Stephen Griffin for inviting me to deliver the McGlinchey Lecture at Tulane in February of 2011. I benefitted greatly from the invitation by Ellen Frankel Paul and Jeffrey Paul, directors of the Social Philosophy and Policy Center at Bowling Green State University, to participate in a wonderful conference on constitutionalism co-sponsored by the Liberty Fund. I am similarly grateful to David Fontana for giving me the opportunity to present some of my work to a conference on comparative constitutional law at the George Washington School of Law. All these events not only forced me to organize my ideas, but also provided me with valuable feedback from the faculty and students in attendance, as was true in less-formal colloquia at the Columbia, Harvard, Michigan, University of Minnesota, and St. Thomas law schools.

This is also the proper context to mention what has been my cherished home institution since 1980, the University of Texas. I have been granted the ability to flourish by its providing me, always and not only on special occasions, wonderful colleagues, students, and financial support, including, crucially, the ability to organize many conferences over the years about topics that I thought were important and, often, under-examined. The opportunity to co-teach seminars with my Department of Government colleagues Jeff Tulis (on emergency powers) and Zach Elkins (on constitutional design) left obvious traces in this book, as have conversations over the years with a true master of comparative constitutionalism, Gary Jacobsohn. I have been blessed by unusually supportive Deans, most recently Bill Powers (currently President of the University of Texas) and Larry Sager.

Then there are the family members, friends, and colleagues—not that these are mutually exclusive categories—who read, sometimes several times, one or another version of the manuscripts that ultimately became this book. Primary thanks should certainly go to my wife Cynthia, who properly took me to task for a number of writing tics in addition to offering many valuable suggestions for clarifying various arguments. Others who read the entire manuscript include my colleague and friend Scot Powe at the University of Texas Law School; my government department colleague and friend Bat Sparrow; my friend, sometime colleague, confidante, and book-club associate Betty Sue Flowers (unfortunately now departed from Austin); Linda Greenhouse, an always supportive friend who now graces the Yale Law School after her remarkable career at the *New York Times*; Booth Fowler, who has remained a valued (and contrarian) friend since we met as graduate students at Harvard almost fifty years ago; Bruce Ackerman, a friend and sometime colleague at Yale who has led me and many others to re-conceive the very subject matter of "constitutional law"; and two non-academic friends who put to shame many members of the academy in the breadth of their reading and intellectual interests, Steve Jackobs and Kerry Grumbacher. Daniel Halberstam provided very helpful reactions to my chapter on federalism, a subject on which he is a master. Liav Orgad provided similar help with regard to thinking through the importance of constitutional preambles.

I must also mention in this regard one truly superogatory act of friendship: Stanford historian Jack Rakove was asked to read a version of this manuscript submitted to the Harvard University Press. In responding, he provided the Press (and, ultimately, me) with what can only be called a line edit of the entire manuscript (perhaps because, like my wife, he was perturbed by some of my writing tics). Given his remarkable skills as a writer, I gladly accepted approximately at least 90 percent of his suggestions—and I am open to the possibility that I should have accepted the rest. Elizabeth Knoll, justifiably famous as a gifted editor for the Harvard Press, also sent me a set of comprehensive suggestions, most of which I gladly adopted. In the best of all worlds, this book would have been jointly published by the

Oxford, Harvard, and Princeton university presses. The only bad thing about bringing this book to publication was ultimately having to choose among a group of people (including Chuck Myers at Princeton) all of whom I value as editors and friends. It was certainly not irrelevant to the final decision that I have known Niko Pfund, now the president of the Oxford Press, for two decades and have forged a friendship with my current Oxford editor, David McBride. (Nor will I ever forget Niko's over-the-top gesture of sending me a link, just before the final anguished decision, to Peaches and Herb singing "Together Again." That, plus the promise of dining at the Second Avenue Deli in New York City, clinched the deal!) I am grateful to Oxford as well for hiring an excellent copyeditor, Heather Hambleton.

I am, as my friends know all too well, a sometimes incessant talker about whatever ideas compel me at a given moment, and I must therefore also single out for their patience frequent companions on walks around Lake Austin—Scot Powe, Gerald Torres, and Philip Bobbitt—and, around the Brookline Reservoir, Morton Horwitz. I should also single out yet another old friend, Akhil Reed Amar, with Jack a co-editor of our constitutional law casebook, with whom I have been conducting intense conversations about the U.S. Constitution for over a quarter century. Although Akhil's book *America's Constitution: A Biography* is frequently cited, those citations do not adequately measure the stimulation he has provided. Friendship and stimulation do not always result in agreement, and I expect that Akhil, like Philip Bobbitt, will be quite dismayed by much of this book. He is, I think it is safe to say, far more admiring of the present United States Constitution than I have come to be. That simply means that we will continue our conversations and arguments for, I hope, a long time to come.

I want to mention two other persons (and friends) who have served as important inspirations. I begin with Alan Wolfe, whom I have known now for more than forty years. He is, I believe, the pre-eminent public intellectual in the United States, not least because he tackles the most important subjects—his latest book is *Political Evil: What It Is and How to Combat It*—with candor and relentless intellectual independence. Larry Lessig, a much younger friend whom I've known only for fifteen years, joins a remarkable intellect with a literally extraordinary passion about preserving the United States as a constitutional republic that lives up to the magnificent aspirations set out in the Preamble. I take great comfort in knowing that he has found some of my past ideas useful, just as I draw on both his insights and his passion as I enter ever further (and invite my readers to join me) into a project of constitutional critique and, one hopes, potential ways out of some of our crises of governance. His new book, *Republic, Lost: How Money Corrupts Congress—and a Plan to Stop It*, is essential reading for anyone concerned with the fate of the American republic. The subtitles of both books are evidence that neither Alan nor Larry is willing to stop at detached political diagnosis. They are, instead, engaged citizens and, dare one say it, genuine patriots.

I have also be benefitted from the helpful insights provided by three teaching assistants: Jacqueline Hunsicker for my courses at UT and Prithviraj Datta and Evan Schnidman at Harvard. My thoughts about the limitations of election-based "representative government" have also been deeply affected by the work of Joel Parker, who prepared a fine dissertation on "lottery selection" of public officials under my supervision.

I have, since my first book in 1988, always recognized the status of my two then-teenage daughters, Meira and Rachel, as absolutely "splendid people." That certainly continues to be true. But they have also become colleagues in their own ways over the years. A fundamental theme of this book involves what Americans should know about their constitutions in order to be informed—and, ultimately, effective—citizens. That is the central concern of Meira, who now teaches at the Harvard Graduate School of Education and who is publishing in 2012 her own important and illuminating book on civic education, *No Citizen Left Behind*. Rachel has become a gifted lawyer whose work on the future of institutions of higher education is consistently illuminating, particularly at a time when they are not only under great financial pressures but are also subjected to criticism from those resentful of attacks on sometimes cherished ideas. Splendidness and a capacity to illuminate are also attributes of Meira's and Rachel's respective husbands, Marc Lipsitch and Ariel Levinson-Waldman. Meira's and Marc's daughters, Rebecca and Ella, and Rachel's and Ariel's recent arrival, Sarah, now take over the slot reserved for those who made no contribution at all to this book but who deserve recognition, nonetheless, as splendid people. Moreover, they are truly the source of my passion concerning what I call in the title the "crisis of governance" in contemporary America and the role played, if only marginally, by the fifty-one constitutions within the United States in making it more difficult to resolve the problems that will dominate their futures. They deserve better.

Notes

Chapter 1

1 · http://www.nytimes.com/2011/07/11/us/11shutdown.html?_r=1&scp=1&sq=minn esota%20shutdown&st=cse. Interestingly enough, Minnesota's budget is not the subject of any provisions in the state constitution. See http://www.leg.state.mn.us/lrl/issues/issues.aspx?issue=budget. The process of budget formation and passage is structured only by legislatively passed statutes. Thirty-two of the fifty states do have provisions in their state constitutions requiring "balanced budgets." However, as spelled out by the National Conference of State Legislatures, it is no easy matter to determine the consequences of such requirements, constitutional or statutory. See *NCSL Fiscal Brief 3: State Balanced Budget Provisions*, Table I (Balanced Budget Requirements), available at http://www.ncsl. org/documents/fiscal/StateBalancedBudgetProvisions2010.pdf. There are "on-budget" and "off-budget" expenditures, for example, which are only the tip of the iceberg. The experience of states that require balanced budgets might suggest some caution on the part of those who call for adoption of a similar amendment to the national Constitution.

Moreover, as *Washington Post* economics columnist Robert Samuelson notes in a discussion of the federal "balanced-budget amendment" unsuccessfully proposed by congressional Republicans in the summer of 2011, states have, at least since the New Deal, been able to rely somewhat on "countercyclical" deficit spending by the national government during times of national economic downturns. Were the national government required to balance its budget, such countercyclical spending would be impossible, as reductions in national tax revenues provoked by recessions would automatically require cuts in federal spending as well. The alternative of raising taxes, even if politically palatable, would be counterproductive with regard to returning to economic growth. See Robert J. Samuelson, "A Balanced-budget Amendment: A Bad Idea for Many Reasons," *Washington Post*, July 18, 2011, available at http://www.washingtonpost.com/blogs/post-partisan/post/a-balanced-budget-amendment-bad-idea-for-many-reasons/2011/07/18/gIQAZ8nNMI blog.html?hpid=z2.

2 · See Adam Nagourney, "Political Shift in California Trips Brown," New York Times, September 20, 2011, available at http://www.nytimes.com/2011/09/21/us/politics/brown-says-california-gop-is-harder-to-work-with-decades-later.html?_r=1&scp=1&sq=Jerry%20 Brown%20on%20California%20politics&st=cse.

3 · See, e.g., Bob Egelko, "S.F. Courts Warn of Budget Disaster, Huge Delays," *San Francicso Chronicle*, July 19, 2011, available at http://www.sfgate.com/cgi-bin/article.

cgi?f=/c/a/2011/07/19/MN351KBV0G.DTL. "It will soon take hours," the article begins, "to pay a traffic ticket in San Francisco, months to get court records and at least a year and a half to get a divorce. With a few exceptions, only criminal cases will go to trial."

4 · See, e.g., Michael D. Shear, "White House Paints Doomsday Default Scenario," *New York Times,* July 7, 2011, available at http://thecaucus.blogs.nytimes.com/2011/07/07/white-house-paints-doomsday-default-scenario/?scp=8&sq=Timothy%20Geithner%20on%20consequences%20of%20a%20default&st=cse.

5 · http://blogs.wsj.com/marketbeat/2011/08/05/sp-downgrades-u-s-debt-rating-press-release/.

6 · http://www.guardian.co.uk/commentisfree/2011/aug/03/gridlock-the-us-may-be-reformed.

7 · http://thecaucus.blogs.nytimes.com/2011/09/16/approval-of-congress-matches-record-low/?scp=1&sq=NYTimes%20poll%20on%20Congress&st=cse.

8 · According to an NBC/Wall Street Journal poll, available at http://www.pollingreport.com/CongJob.htm.

9 · http://www.gallup.com/poll/149678/Americans-Express-Historic-Negativity-Toward-Government.aspx. There are, to be sure, partisan differences. Ninety-two percent of Republicans are "dissatisfied," whereas "only" 65 percent of Democrats are similarly disaffected.

10 · http://www.rasmussenreports.com/public_content/politics/general_politics/august_2011/new_low_17_say_u_s_government_has_consent_of_the_governed. Even if one has quibbles about the methodology of the poll, it nevertheless remains an astounding result, even if one doubles the number affirming the legitimacy of the government to 34 percent.

11 · http://www.gallup.com/poll/148163/Americans-Confident-Military-Least-Congress.aspx.

12 · It is worth noting that recent studies of the American Revolution have emphasized the significant numbers of "loyalists" who wanted no part of the Revolution. See, notably, Maya Jasanoff, *Liberty's Exiles: American Loyalists in the Revolutionary World* (New York: Alfred A. Knopf, 2011).

13 · E.J.Dionne,"WhattheDeclarationReallySaid,"availableathttp://www.washingtonpost.com/opinions/what-our-declaration-really-said/2011/07/02/AGugyvwH_story.html.

14 · Anjeanette Damon and David Schwartz, "Nevada Senate Hopeful Sharon Angle Talks of Armed Revolt," *Las Vegas Sun,* June 17, 2010, available at http://www.scrippsnews.com/content/nev-senate-hopeful-sharron-angle-talks-armed-revolt.

15 · http://www.neontommy.com/news/2010/09/approval-rating-california-legislature-record-low; http://www.sacbee.com/2010/09/28/3061369/field-poll-california-legislature.html.

16 · http://maristpoll.marist.edu/1123-voters-want-change-in-albany/.

17 · "Viewpoint: America the Ungovernable," *Newsweek,* January 24, 2010, available at http://www.newsweek.com/2010/01/24/america-the-ungovernable.html.

18 · "California: The Ungovernable State," *The Economist* 33, May 16–22, 2009, available at http://www.economist.com/world/unitedstates/PrinterFriendly.cfm?story_id=13649050. As a matter of fact, the California electorate amended its state constitution in 2010 by passing Proposition 25, which eliminated the supermajority requirement in favor of a simple majority. In addition, the amendment requires that legislators receive no salary for every day past June 15 that they are unable to pass a budget. See http://ballotpedia.org/wiki/

index.php/California_Proposition_25,_Majority_Vote_for_Legislature_to_Pass_the_ Budget_(2010). There is no reason to believe that this fix resolves California's dysfunctionality inasmuch as tax increases, which still require a two-thirds majority, are necessary to finance California's needs. For a thoroughly depressing overview, see Michael Lewis, "California and Bust," *Vanity Fair*, November 2011, pp. 173ff.

19 ∙ See Bruce E. Cain et al., "Constitutional Change: Is it Too Easy to Amend Our State Constitution," in Bruce E. Cain and Roger Noll, *Constitutional Reform in California: Making State Government More Effective and Responsive* (Berkeley: Institute of Governmental Studies Press, 1995), 288–289. California's Chief Justice, Ronald George, has been especially critical of the California Constitution's endorsement of "initiative and referendum" procedures to pass laws and even change the state constitution itself. See "Chief Justice: Initiative Process Has Led to Dysfunctional State," California Bar Journal (November 2009), available at http://archive.calbar.ca.gov/Archive.aspx?articleId=96727&categoryId= 96665&month=11&year=2009.

20 ∙ And this doesn't even take into account the threat of earthquakes or the potential inundation of Sacramento, the state capital, should its two rivers break through aging levees disrupted by an earthquake. See Alex Prudhomme, "California's Next Nightmare," *New York Times Magazine*, July 3, 2011, available at http://www.nytimes.com/2011/07/03/ magazine/sacramento-levees-pose-risk-to-california-and-the-country.html?_r=1&scp= 1&sq=Sacramento%20and%20river%20levees&st=cse.

21 ∙ Thomas L. Friedman and Michael Mandelbaum, *That Used To Be Us: How America Fell behind in the World It Invented and How We Can Come Back* (New York: Farrar, Straus and Giroux, 2011), 33.

22 ∙ David R. Mayhew, *Partisan Balance: Why Political Parties Don't Kill the U.S. Constitutional System* (Princeton: Princeton University Press, 2011), 82.

23 ∙ Thomas Friedman, "An X-Ray of Dysfunction," *New York Times*, October 9, 2010, available at http://www.nytimes.com/2010/10/10/opinion/10friedman.html?ref= thomaslfriedman.

24 ∙ *That Used To Be Us*, 242 (emphasis in original).

25 ∙ Ibid., 243.

26 ∙ See ibid., 243ff.

27 ∙ Ibid., 232.

28 ∙ Ibid., 274.

29 ∙ Ibid., 331.

30 ∙ Ibid., 334–337.

31 ∙ I offer an extended description and critique of the electoral college in *Our Undemocratic Constitution: Where the Constitution Goes Wrong (and How We the People Can Correct It)* (New York: Oxford University Press, 2006), 81–97.

32 ∙ David Brooks, "Britain is Working," *New York Times*, May 23, 2011, available at http:// www.nytimes.com/2011/05/24/opinion/24brooks.html?ref=davidbrooks.

33 ∙ Brooks, "The Road Not Taken," *New York Times*, July 18, 2011, available at http://www. nytimes.com/2011/07/19/opinion/19brooks.html?ref=opinion.

34 ∙ Bill Schneider, " The Deepening Partisan Divide," *National Journal*, January 8, 2010, available at http://perspectives.thirdway.org/?p=624.

35 ∙ Dionne, "Chris Dodd, the Senate's Happy Warrior," *Washington Post*, August 29, 2010, available at http://www.washingtonpost.com/wp-dyn/content/article/2010/08/08/ AR2010080802395.html.

36 · Hendrik Hertzberg, "Framed Up: What the Constitution Gets Wrong," *The New Yorker,* July 29, 2002, available at http://www.newyorker.com/archive/2002/07/29/020729crbo_books.

37 · Hertzberg, "Oh, Shut Up," *The New Yorker,* January 10, 2011, available at http://www.newyorker.com/talk/comment/2011/01/10/110110taco_talk_hertzberg.

38 · See, e.g., Hertzberg, "Count 'Em," *The New Yorker,* March 6, 2006, available at http://www.newyorker.com/archive/2006/03/06/060306ta_talk_hertzberg.

39 · Fareed Zakaria, "Are America's Best Days Behind Us?" *Time,* March 3, 2011, available at http://www.time.com/time/nation/article/0,8599,2056610,00.html.

40 · There will be many references to *The Federalist* in the pages that follow. I will not offer specific citations, given the literally dozens of printed editions of those essays as well as the multiple sites on the Internet that can be easily consulted. For the latter, see, e.g., http://thomas.loc.gov/home/histdox/fedpapers.html (prepared by the Library of Congress) or http://avalon.law.yale.edu/subject_menus/fed.asp (prepared by the Yale Law School).

41 · Dustin Hurst, "Idaho GOP Accepts Platform with Loyalty Oath," *Idaho Reporter,* June 27, 2010, http://www.idahoreporter.com/2010/idaho-gop-accepts-platform-with-loyalty-oath-call-for-repeal-of-17th-amendment/.

42 · See Chris Moody, "Seven Ways That Rick Perry Wants to Change the Constitution," available at http://news.yahoo.com/blogs/ticket/seven-ways-rick-perry-wants-change-constitution-131634517.html.

43 · See, e.g., http://3ago.com/2011/03/04/on-the-tea-party%E2%80%99s-challenge-to-the-u-s-senate/.

44 · See, e.g., Sanford Levinson, "If We Have an Imperfect Constitution, Should We Settle for Remarkably Timid Reform? Reflections Generated by the General Phenomenon of Tea Party Constitutionalism and Randy Barnett's Particular Proposal for a Repeal Amendment Designed to Rein in an Overreaching Congress," *Northwestern University Law Review Colloquy* 271 (March, 2011), available at http://www.law.northwestern.edu/lawreview/colloquy/2011/9/.

45 · Kathleen M. Sullivan, "Constitutional Amendmentitis," *The American Prospect,* September 21, 1995, available at http://prospect.org/cs/articles?article=constitutional_amendmentitis.

46 · Fay v. New York, 332 U.S. 261, 282 (1947).

47 · Ibid.

48 · A recent addition to the list is Jack M. Balkin, *Living Originalism* (Cambridge, MA: Harvard University Press, 2011), which I consider the best book on interpreting the U.S. Constitution I've ever read. Still, there can be no doubt that many readers will be unconvinced and will proclaim the priority of their own favorite approaches. The best overview of the various approaches to interpretation that contend with one another is Philip Bobbitt, *Constitutional Interpretation* (Cambridge, MA: Blackwell, 1991).

49 · Douglas Rae, *Equalities* (Boston: Harvard University Press, 1981).

50 · A fine book making this point is Hanna Lerner, *Making Constitutions in Deeply Divided Societies* (Cambridge: Cambridge University Press, 2011), focusing on the constitutional histories of Israel, India, and Ireland. In all cases, it appeared prudent to engage in "can-kicking" with regard to certain vital questions, especially involving language and religion, rather than risk collapse of the entire enterprise by trying to force through "solutions" that would only exacerbate the existing deep divisions within the respective societies.

51 · The most important articulation of this view is Frederick Schauer, *Playing by the Rules: A Philosophical Examination of Rule-Based Decisionmaking in Law and in Life* (New York: Oxford University Press, 1991).

52 ∘ Or, a third possibility, when the new Congress actually mustered a constitutionally required quorum to count the electoral votes that had been received from the eleven states then in the Union (since neither North Carolina nor Rhode Island had ratified the Constitution). I owe this point to Jack Rakove.

53 ∘ "And if the House of Representatives shall not choose a President whenever the right of choice shall devolve upon them, before the fourth day of March next following, then the Vice-President shall act as President, as in the case of the death or other constitutional disability of the President." This assumes that the Senate will have successfully elected a vice president, which is made far easier by the fact that senators vote as individuals, rather than as state delegations of two, and they select their choice only from the top two persons awarded electoral votes.

54 ∘ A helpful list of inauguration dates is provided by the National Governors Association at http://www.nga.org/files/live/sites/NGA/files/pdf/GOVLIST.PDF.

55 ∘ I have greatly benefited from an unpublished paper by Rivka Weill, "War and Peace and Other Sundry Matters," which focused on the limitations imposed by the Israeli Supreme Court on the scope of decisionmaking by "caretaker governments" in that country.

56 ∘ In *Too Young to Run: A Proposal for an Age Amendment to the U.S. Constitution* (University Park, PA: Penn State University Press, 2011), political theorist John Seery offers an interesting argument that the American political system would benefit from allowing persons under twenty-five or thirty to run for, and serve in, the House and Senate.

57 ∘ This obviously requires the perhaps questionable assumption that information about Schwarzenegger's "love child" with his and Maria Schriver's housekeeper would have remained secret.

58 ∘ Laura Scalia, *America's Jeffersonian Experiment: Remaking State Constitutions 1820–1850* (DeKalb: Northern Illinois University Press, 1999), 157.

59 ∘ John Dinan, *The American State Constitutional Tradition* (Lawrence: University of Kansas Press, 2006.)

60 ∘ James A. Gardner, *Interpreting State Constitutions: A Jurisprudence of Function in a Federal System* (Chicago: University of Chicago Press, 2005), 23. Even worse, as former Oregon state justice Hans Linde—also a distinguished legal academic—has observed, "General constitutional law courses, which everyone takes, create the impression that contemporary majority opinions and dissents in the United States Supreme Court exhaust the terms as well as the agenda of constitutional litigation." Hans A. Linde, "State Constitutions Are Not Common Law: Comments on Gardner's Failed Discourse," 24 *Rutgers Law Journal* 927 (1993): 933.

61 ∘ The most important exception is the residents of the District of Columbia.

62 ∘ Robert F. Williams, *The Law of American State Constitutions* (New York: Oxford University Press, 2009), 1.

63 ∘ Ibid., 1–2.

64 ∘ Daniel B. Rodriguez, "State Constitutionalism and the Scope of Judicial Review," in *New Frontiers in State Constitutional Law: Dual Enforcement of Norms*, ed. James A. Gardner and Jim Rossi (New York: Oxford University Press, 2011). Consider, for starters, only the issues of zoning (and general land-use planning) and property taxes, two issues guaranteed to roil any state or local polity. Similarly, an "op-ed" in the *New York Times* by former Justice Sandra Day O'Connor—who had been both an elected official and a state judge within Arizona—states that "[s]tate courts resolve the most important legal matters in our lives, including child custody cases, settlement of estates, business-contract disputes, traffic offenses, drunken-driving charges, most criminal offenses, and most foreclosures." She presents this in the context of a column condemning the way that most states currently elect their judges. Sandra Day O'Connor, *Take Justice Off the Ballot*, New York Times D9, May 23, 2010. Obviously, most of the examples chosen by O'Connor rarely involve constitutional issues as such, though states often have constitutionally mandated norms of criminal procedure that differ in important ways from national norms as interpreted by the Supreme Court. For example, eleven states extend "constitutional protection to privacy, which has been interpreted as affording a broader substantive right than the Fourth Amendment's search-and-seizure claims." See Helen Hershkoff, "State Common Law and the Dual Enforcement of Constitutional Norms," in *New Frontiers in State Constitutional Law: Dual Enforcement of Norms*, 151. The issue of immediate concern to Justice O'Connor, elected judiciaries, is considered at length in Chapter 12.

Chapter 2

1 · James Madison, letter to Edward Everett, August 28, 1830, in Anthony J. Bella Jr., ed., *Federalism* (New York: Wolters Kluwer, 2011), 104.

2 · This remarkable fact was brought home to many New Yorkers (and other Americans) in an exhibit at the New York Historical Society in 2005, https://www.nyhistory.org/web/default.php?section=exhibits_collections&page=exhibit_detail&id=1643453. See also Ira Berlin and Leslie M. Harris, eds., *Slavery in New York* (New York: New Press, 2005).

3 · Edmund Burke, "Speech on Conciliation with the Colonies," March 22, 1775, quoted in Avishai Margalit, *On Compromise and Rotten Compromises* (Princeton, NJ: Princeton University Press, 2009), 12.

4 · Clinton Rossiter, *Parties and Politics in America* (Ithaca: Cornell University Press, 1967). Rossiter is probably best known to readers as the editor of the most widely used version of *The Federalist*.

5 · Mickey Edwards, "How to Turn Republicans and Democrats into Americans," *The Atlantic*, July/August 2011, p. 103 (emphasis in original).

6 · Arye Carmon, Introduction, in Arye Carmon and Meir Shamgar, eds., *Constitution by Consensus* (Jerusalem: Israel Democracy Institute, 2007), 17.

7 · Ibid., 104.

8 · Jefferson's notes, available at http://pasleybrothers.com/mocourses/texts/anas.htm.

9 · http://www.whitehouse.gov/blog/2010/12/07/president-obama-middle-class-tax-cuts-and-unemployment-insurance-agreement-a-good-dc.

10 · Hanna Lerner, *Making Constitutions in Highly Divided Societies* (Cambridge: Cambridge University Press, 2011), 64, quoting Meir-David Levonstein, *Knesset Record* 4 (1950): 744.

11 · Ibid., 63, quoting Minister of Welfare Rabbi Yitzhak Meir Levi, *Knesset Record* 4 (1950): 812.

12 · Margalit, *On Compromise and Rotten Compromises*.

13 · Ibid.

14 · William Freehling, *The Road to Disunion: Secessionists at Bay 1776–1854* (New York: Oxford University Press, 1990), 487.

15 · Ibid., 56.

16 · Pauline Maier, *Ratification: The People Debate the Constitution, 1787–1788* (New York: Simon & Schuster, 2010), 284.

17 ∘ Andrew Cayton, "To Save the Union," *New York Times Book Review*, July 4, 2010, p. BR17, available at http://www.nytimes.com/2010/07/04/books/review/Cayton-t.html? scp=3&sq=Book%20reviews%20by%20Andrew%20Cayton&st=cse.

18 ∘ http://paul.senate.gov/record.cfm?id=330804.

19 ∘ There was a reason, after all, that Muhammed Ali's original name was Cassius and not Henry Clay.

20 ∘ http://www.washingtonpost.com/wp-dyn/content/article/2011/02/02/ AR2011020204773.html?referrer=emailarticle.

21 ∘ Paul Finkelman, "The Cost of Compromise and the Covenant With Death," *Pepperdine Law Review* 38 (2011): 845, 851–855.

22 ∘ Jack N. Rakove, *Revolutionaries: A New History of the Invention of America* (New York: Houghton Mifflin, 2010), 372.

23 ∘ See Jon Elster, "Constitutional Bootstrapping in Philadelphia and Paris," *Cardozo Law Review* 14 (1992–1993): 549.

24 ∘ Consider in this context the possible political costs of the disclosure of leaked information indicating that the Palestinian leadership bargaining with Israel was willing to make substantially greater concessions than had previously been acknowledged (or defended to the Palestinian people by their ostensible leaders).

25 ∘ Carrie Menkel-Meadow, "The Ethics of Compromise," in Andrea Kupfer Schneider and Christopher Honeyman, eds., *The Negotiator's Fieldbook* (Chicago: American Bar Association, 2006),159, citing Dana Lansky, "Proceeding to a Constitution: A Multi-Party Negotiation Analysis of the Constitutional Convention of 1787," *Harvard Negotiation Law Review* 5 (2000): 279 and Jack Rakove, "The Great Compromise: Ideas, Interests and Politics of Constitution Making," *William & Mary Law Review* 44 (1987): 424. See also Carrie Menkel-Meadow, "Compromise and Constitutionalism: The Variable Morality of Constitutional (and Other) Compromises: A Comment on Sanford Levinson's Compromise and Constitutionalism," *Pepperdine Law Journal* 38 (2011): 903.

26 ∘ Peter Orszag, "Too Much of a Good Thing: Why We Need Less Democracy," *The New Republic*, October 6, 1011, pp. 11–12.

27 ∘ Margalit, p. 3.

28 ∘ And, one might well believe, on *everyone* who had to adjust to a social order founded on the racialized ownership and subordination of other human beings.

Chapter 3

1 ∘ Available at http://press-pubs.uchicago.edu/founders/print_documents/v1ch16.html.

2 ∘ Chisholm v. Georgia, 2 Dall. (2 U.S.) 419, 465 (1793), available at http://supreme.justia. com/us/2/419/case.html.

3 ∘ McCulloch v. Maryland, 17 U.S. 316 (1819).

4 ∘ Jacobson v. Massachusetts, 197 U.S. 11 (1905).

5 ∘ Relevant excerpts of the three memoranda can be found in Paul Brest et al., *Processes of Constitutional Decisionmaking* (New York: Aspen Publishers, 5th ed. 2006), 32–37.

6 ∘ Thomas Jefferson, letter to Samuel Kercheval, July 12, 1816, available at http://etext. virginia.edu/etcbin/toccer-new2?id=JefLett.sgm&images=images/modeng&data=/ texts/english/modeng/parsed&tag=public&part=244&division=div1, quoted in Sanford

Levinson, *Our Undemocratic Constitution: Where the Constitution Goes Wrong (And How We the People Can Correct It)* IX (New York: Oxford University Press, 2006).

7 · See, e.g., Oliver Wendell Holmes, "The Common Law," in Sheldon Novick, ed., *The Collected Works of Oliver Wendell Holmes, Vol. 3* (Chicago: University of Chicago Press, 1995), 115.

8 · See Decision of the Constitutional Council No. 44–71 (1971). As Israeli author Liav Orgad has written, "In later decisions, the council held that the Preamble to the 1946 Constitution enjoys legal force and constitutes an independent source of rights." The Preamble to the 1958 French Constitution begins as follows: "The French people hereby solemnly proclaim their dedication to the Rights of Man and the principle of national sovereignty as defined by the Declaration of 1789, reaffirmed and complemented by the Preamble to the 1946 Constitution." http://www.servat.unibe.ch/icl/fr00000_.html. The 1946 preamble itself is considerably longer and more detailed. See http://www.conseil-constitutionnel.fr/conseil-constitutionnel/root/bank_mm/anglais/cst3.pdf. "Interestingly," Orgad notes, "at the time it was drafted, the 1946 Preamble did not enjoy any legal status. Thus, the constitutional Council, through a reference to the 1946 Preamble in the 1958 Preamble, effectively granted the 1946 Preamble a higher status than it had previously enjoyed." Orgad, "The Preamble in Constitutional Interpretation," *International Journal of Constitutional Law* 8 no. 4, (2010):714, 726–27. Ibid., 14, n. 95, citing Alec Stone, *The Birth of Judicial Politics in France: The Constitutional Council in Comparative Perspective* (New York: Oxford University Press, 1992), 40–45, 66–78. Stone notes that seven out of the sixteen annulments made by the Council between 1971 and 1981 were based on interpretations of the 1958 preamble.

9 · Ibid., 13, n. 53, citing Alec Stone, *The Birth of Judicial Politics in France*.

10 · An especially interesting example is provided by South Africa, which possesses one of the most inspiring constitutions in all the world. Its new 1996 constitution was, by all accounts, intended to serve as a radical break with the past and a harbinger of a trans-formed future. Anyone who doubts this must merely read its preamble:

> We, the people of South Africa,
> Recognise the injustices of our past;
> Honour those who suffered for justice and freedom in our land;
> Respect those who have worked to build and develop our country; and
> Believe that South Africa belongs to all who live in it, united in our diversity.

The preamble, moreover, is immediately followed by "founding provisions," specifying that "the Republic of South Africa is one, sovereign, democratic state founded on the following values":

a. Human dignity, the achievement of equality and the advancement of human rights and freedoms.
b. Non-racialism and non-sexism.
c. Supremacy of the constitution and the rule of law.
d. Universal adult suffrage, a national common voters roll, regular elections and a multi-party system of democratic government, to ensure accountability, responsiveness and openness.

Yet, whatever the "foundational" qualities of both the preamble and Article I, these passages apparently are treated as what lawyers call *nonjusticiable*, that is, unsuitable for judicial enforcement. This means, practically speaking, that professional lawyers (and most legal academics) will simply tend to ignore such passages inasmuch as they presumptively provide no "added value" to explicitly legal arguments that focus on clauses that courts *will* enforce. Thus, in an interesting case dealing with the voting rights of imprisoned felons, the chief justice of the South African Constitutional Court, though acknowledging that "[t]he values enunciated in section 1 of the Constitution are of fundamental importance," went on to proclaim that "they do not, however, give rise to discrete and enforceable rights in themselves," even if, on occasion, the South African Court has cited the preamble in one of its decisions. See *Minister of Home Affairs v Nicro and Others* 2005 (3) SA 280 (CC) at para [21], available at http://www.saflii.org/za/cases/ZACC/2004/10.html.

11 · Constitution of Switzerland, available at http://www.servat.unibe.ch/icl/sz00000_.html.

12 · Constitution of South Africa, preamble, available at http://www.info.gov.za/documents/constitution/1996/96preamble.htm.

13 · http://www.un.org/en/documents/charter/preamble.shtml.

14 · http://www.efc.ca/pages/law/charter/charter.text.html.

15 · http://www.servat.unibe.ch/icl/gm00000_.html.

16 · http://www.hri.org/docs/syntagma/.

17 · http://www.taoiseach.gov.ie/attached_files/Pdf%20files/Constitution%20of%20Ireland.pdf.

18 · http://www.pakistani.org/pakistan/constitution/preamble.html.

19 · Constitution of Poland, available at http://www.servat.unibe.ch/icl/pl00000_.html.

20 · See http://european-convention.eu.int/bienvenue.asp?lang=en.

21 · See http://www.anayasa.gov.tr/images/loaded/pdf_dosyalari/THE_CONSTITUTION_OF_THE_REPUBLIC_OF_TURKEY.pdf.

22 · It is worth noting, though, that John Jay, in *Federalist* 2, wrote that he had "often taken notice that Providence has been pleased to give this one connected country to one united people—a people descended from the same ancestors, speaking the same language, [and] professing the same religion." This, frankly, seems to require a highly tendentious notion of "sameness," even if it might illustrate a yearning for homogeneity that Jay, whose own ancestors were Huguenots persecuted by French Catholics, might well have had.

23 · The collected preambles can be found at http://www.usconstitution.net/states_god.html.

24 · Preambles to state constitutions, http://ballotpedia.org/wiki/index.php/Preambles_to_state_constitutions.

25 · David Wilkins, *Documents of Native American Political Development 1500s to 1933* (New York: Oxford University Press, 2009), 439.

26 · Constitution of the Oglala Sioux Tribe, available at http://www.narf.org/nill/Constitutions/oglalaconst/oglalaconst.pdf.

27 · Zorach v. Clausen, 343 U.S. 306 (1952).

28 · Gordon Wood, *The Empire of Liberty: A History of the Early Republic* (New York: Oxford University Press, 2009), 583.

29 · Which is itself basically a creation of post–World War II theologians attempting to make amends for the extent to which traditionally "exclusivist" versions of Christianity played their own part in demonizing Jews and making the Holocaust at least somewhat more thinkable. See, e.g., Arthur A. Cohen, *The Myth of the Judeo-Christian Tradition* (New York: Harper & Row, 1970). Not all American public officials, particularly at the state level, have signed on to this new "tradition." Thus Alabama Governor Robert Bentley told a church gathering—ironically or not, celebrating Martin Luther King Day—immediately after his inauguration on January 17, 2011, "Anybody here today who has not accepted Jesus Christ as their savior, I'm telling you, you're not my brother and you're not my sister, and I want to be your brother." Interestingly enough, he apologized the next day, saying, "If anyone from other religions felt disenfranchised by the language, I want to say I am sorry." He also pledged to work for people of all faiths. Needless to say, he did not say that he considers anyone who does not share his particular Christian beliefs to be his "brothers or sisters," only that, as a public official, he would ignore the fact that, from his perspective, they are condemned to eternal damnation for having rejected the "good news" of salvation through accepting Jesus as the Messiah. See http://www.nytimes.com/2011/01/20/us/20brfs-GOV-ERNORAPOL_BRF.html?scp=1&sq=Alabama%20governor%20on%20%22brothers%20and%20sisters%22&st=Search.

30 • Part of the reason involves the Court's use of so-called standing doctrine to hold that no particular person has the right to challenge a law unless that person can point to some specified harm not similar to the populace in general. The Court used standing as the reason (or, some would say, excuse) for dismissing a case challenging the presence of "under God" in the national pledge of allegiance. See Elk Grove Unified School District, 542 U.S. 1 (2004).

31 • http://www.constitution.org/cons/croatia.htm.

32 • Constitution of Vietnam, available at http://www.servat.unibe.ch/icl/vm00000_.html.

33 • Sujit Choudhry, *Constitutional Design for Divided Societies* (New York: Oxford University Press, 2008).

34 • Lochner v. New York, 198 U.S. 45, 76 (1905).

Chapter 4

1 • John Adams, *The Works of John Adams, Second President of the United States*, ed. Charles Francis Adams, vol. 6 (Boston: Charles C. Little and James Brown, 1850), 484, letter to John Taylor of April 15, 1814.

2 • See Luther v. Borden, 48 U.S. 1 (1849).

3 • Given that the clause is not part of the Constitution of Settlement, we should perhaps refer to it, like the Preamble, as part of the Constitution of Silence.

4 • Gordon S. Wood, *The Idea of America* (New York: Penguin, 2011), 133.

5 • Ibid., 134.

6 • John Quincy Adams, "The Jubilee of the Constitution. A Discourse Delivered at the Request of the New York Historical Society, in the City of New York on Tuesday, the 30th of April 1839; Being the Fiftieth Anniversary of the Inauguration of George Washington as President of the United States, on Thursday, the 30th of April, 1789" (New York: Samuel Colman, 1839), 53.

7 • Thus he wrote to Baron F. H. Alexander Von Humboldt in 1817 that "to consider the will of the society to be enounced by the majority of a single vote, as sacred as if unanimous, is the first of all lessons of importance." *The Writings of Thomas Jefferson*, vol. 10, pp. 88, 89, quoted in Michael Kang, "Voting as Veto," *Michigan Law Review* 108 (2010): 1221, 1228, n. 11. See also Wood's essay on Jefferson and Thomas Paine in *The Idea of America*, which emphasizes their devotion to popular democracy.

8 · See Henry Sidgewick, "Aristotle's Classification of Forms of Government, *The Classical Review* 6 (April 1892): 141–144. See also *Stanford Encyclopedia of Philosophy*, "Aristotle's Political Theory," available at http://plato.stanford.edu/entries/aristotle-politics/.

9 · Nor is it clear that Smith, who also famously wrote about "moral sentiments," would have agreed with later proponents of unmitigated self-interest.

10 · Wood goes so far as to suggest that the anti-Federalist opponents of the Constitution were in some ways the harbingers of a more "modern" approach to politics, while Madison and other Framers were still ensconced in what was a "passing" mode of consciousness. See *The Idea of America*, 130. Readers should also be aware of the importance placed on certain insights connected with Machiavelli regarding the best ways to organize and maintain a "republican" political order. See, e.g., J. A. G. Pocock, *The Machiavellian Moment: Florentine Political Thought and the Atlantic Republican Tradition* (Princeton, NJ: Princeton University Press, 1975).

11 · Gordon S. Wood, *Empire of Liberty: A History of the Early Republic* (New York: Oxford University Press, 2009), 276.

12 · One of his favorite authors, after all, was the former Russian dissident then–Israeli politician Natan Sharansky, the author of a best-selling book (in part because of President Bush's enthusiastic endorsement), *The Case for Democracy*.

13 · "Transcript: Obama's Strasbourg Remarks," April 3, 2009, available at http://www.cbsnews.com/stories/2009/04/03/politics/100days/worldaffairs/main4918137.shtml. Interestingly enough, Obama went on to say:

> But democracy, a well-functioning society that promotes liberty and equality and fraternity…does not just depend on going to the ballot box. It also means that you're not going to be shaken down by police because the police aren't getting properly paid. It also means that if you want to start a business, you don't have to pay a bribe. I mean, there are a whole host of other factors that people need to—need to recognize in building a civil society that allows a country to be successful.

As I write this, in November 2011, the extent of this commitment is being tested in Egypt, Tunisia, Libya, and, by the time this book is published, possibly in other countries as well. Not only will the people of those countries have to decide what compromises may be "necessary" to generate a stable polity, but the United States will also have to make its own choices about the relative importance of stable oil supplies or staving off Islamic radicalism as against promoting "democracy."

14 · "Obama's Mideast Speech," May 19, 2011, available at http://www.nytimes.com/2011/05/20/world/middleeast/20prexy-text.html?pagewanted=all. An earlier speech justifying American intervention in Libya referred to "the democratic impulses that are dawning across the region" that would, without such intervention, "be eclipsed by the darkest form of dictatorship." See http://www.npr.org/2011/03/28/134935452/obamas-speech-on-libya-a-responsibility-to-act.

15 · Laura J.. Scalia, *America's Jeffersonian Experiment: Remaking State Constitutions 1820–1850* (De Kalb: Northern Illinois University Press, 1999), 156.

16 · Proposition 8 was declared unconstitutional in August 2010 by a federal district judge in San Francisco, but that decision is currently (January 2012) on appeal to the Ninth Circuit Court of Appeals and, whatever its decision, will undoubtedly be appealed to the Supreme Court.

17 · As Jack Rakove has noted, "Andover, MA, for example, has no foreign policy," which was obviously not true of Athens.

18 · Pauline Maier, *Ratification* (New York: Simon and Schuster, 2011), 271.

19 · Wood, *Empire of Liberty*, 53.

20 · https://www.cia.gov/library/publications/the-world-factbook/geos/us.html.

21 · See Hans A. Linde, "When Is Initiative Lawmaking Not 'Republican Government'"? *Hastings Constitutional Law Quarterly* 17 (1989): 159. Linde is critical of initiative and referendum for violating notions of deliberation key to representative government.

Chapter 5

1 · Though, as we shall see, there is a legitimate controversy about exactly where to place vice presidents.

2 · See generally Alexander Keyssar, *The Right to Vote: The Contested History of Democracy in the United States*, revised ed. (New York: Basic Books, 2009).

3 · See Jeff Manza and Christopher Uggen, *Locked Out: Felon Disenfranchisement and American Democracy* (New York: Oxford University Press, 2006). A full list of state felony disenfranchisement laws can be found at http://www.brennancenter.org/page/-/d/download_file_48642.pdf.

4 · Consider that the original California Constitution of 1879 explicitly barred the vote to Chinese immigrants.

5 · Pauline Maier, *Ratification: The People Debate the Constitution, 1787–1788* (New York: Simon and Schuster, 2010), 225.

6 · Although a 1962 case, Baker v. Carr, placed reapportionment on the judicial agenda, it was the 1963 case of Wesberry v. Sanders, arising in Georgia, that first articulated the one person, one vote slogan.

7 · See, e.g., "Rough Justice," *The Economist*, July 22, 2010. "America is different from the rest of the world in lots of ways, many of them good. One of the bad ones is its willingness to lock up its citizens. One American adult in 100 festers behind bars (with the rate rising to one in nine for young black men). Its imprisoned population, at 2.3 million, exceeds that of 15 of its states. No other rich country is nearly as punitive as the Land of the Free. The rate of incarceration is a fifth of America's level in Britain, a ninth in Germany and a twelfth in Japan. http://www.economist.com/node/16640389. See also Adam Liptak, "Inmate Count in U.S. Dwarfs Other Nations'," *New York Times*, April 23, 2008, available at http://www.nytimes.com/2008/04/23/us/23prison.html?pagewanted=all. "The only other major industrialized nation that even comes close [to the incarceration rate of the United States"] is Russia, with 627 prisoners for every 100,000 people…The median among all nations is about 125, roughly a sixth of the American rate."

8 · See John Allen Paulos, "Tsongker clintkinbro Wins," *New York Times*, March 2, 1992, available at http://www.nytimes.com|1992|03|02|opinion|tsongkerclintkinbro-wins.html. James Glanz, "A Lesson from Hamas: Read the Voting Law's Fine Print," *New York Times*, February 19, 2006, available at http://www.nytimes.com/2006/02/19/weekinreview/19glanz.html?scp=1&sq=A%20Lesson%20From%20Hamas:%20Read%20the%20Voting%20Law's%20Fine%20Print%20&st=cse.

9 · See Anthony Gottlieb's illuminating review in the *New Yorker*, July 26, 2010, available at http://www.newyorker.com/arts/critics/books/2010/07/26/100726crbo_books_gottlieb.

10 · See Michael Cooper, "New State Rules Raising Hurdles at Voting Booth," New York Times, October 3, 2011, A1, available at http://www.nytimes.com/2011/10/03/us/

new-state-laws-are-limiting-access-for-voters.html?_r=1&scp=1&sq=state%20voting%20
rules%20&st=cse.

11 · Alexander Aleinikoff and Samuel Issacharoff, "Race and Redistricting: Drawing Constitutional Lines after Shaw v. Reno, Michigan Law Review" and 92 (1993): 588, 601.

12 · See Glantz, n. 8.

13 · Jonathan W. Still, "Political Equality and Election Systems," *Ethics* 91 (1981): 375.

14 · Norman Ornstein, "Vote—or Else," *New York Times*, August 10, 2006, available at http://www.nytimes.com/2006/08/10/opinion/10ornstein.html. Ornstein repeated these arguments in an August 2010 symposium in *The Nation* magazine discussing the current American political scene.

15 · http://socialcapital.wordpress.com/2010/11/04/the-youth-democratic-surge-that-wasnt/.

16 · Article II, Section 1: "No person except a natural born Citizen…shall be eligible to the Office of President; neither shall any Person be eligible to that Office who shall not have attained to the Age of thirty-five Years, and been fourteen Years a Resident within the United States." The meaning of "natural born" is not itself without some difficulties, as illustrated by the debate, at least among some law professors, about John McCain's eligibility for the presidency given his own birth in the Panama Canal Zone several months before Congress had passed a statute stating that anyone born there would be treated as an automatic citizen. See Gabriel Chin, "Why Senator John McCain Cannot Be President: Eleven Months and a Hundred Yards Short of Citizenship," *Michigan Law Review First Impressions* 107 (Sept. 2008), available at http://www.michiganlawreview.org/firstimpressions/vol107/mccain.htm; Adam Liptak, "A Hint of New Life to McCain Birth Issue," *New York Times*, July 11, 2008, available at http://www.nytimes.com/2008/07/11/us/politics/11mccain.html.

17 · See "Age of Candidacy Legislation in United States,"http://en.wikipedia.org/wiki/Age_of_candidacy_legislation_in_the_United_States, which canvasses such legislation in twenty states.

18 · See Thomas E. Cronin, *Direct Democracy: The Politics of Initiative, Referendum, and Recall* (Cambridge, MA: Harvard University Press, 1989); David Butler and Austin Ranney, eds., *Referendums around the World* (Washington, AEI Press, 1994).

19 · John J. Dinan, *The American State Constitutional Tradition* (Lawrence: University of Kansas Press, 2006), 87. See, e.g., Michael Cooper, "A Failure Is Absorbed With Disgust and Fear, but Little Surprise," New York Times, November 21, 2011, p. 430 n. 6, available at http://www.nytimes.com/2011/11/22/us/politics/disgust-but-no-surprise-at-supercommittee-failure.html?_r=1&hp, the first sentence of which, based on interviews with a variety of Americans, is "Does the American political system even work anymore?"

20 · http://www.ballotpedia.org/wiki/index.php/Forms_of_direct_democracy_in_the_American_states.

21 · See Clara O'Rourke, "Budget-balancing Remark True in Spirit, if not Letter of Laws," *Austin American Statesman*, December 25, 2010, B1, B3.

22 · Stephen Griffin, "California Constitutionalism, Trust in Government and Direct Democracy," Tulane University School of Law, Public Law and Legal Theory Research Paper Series No. 08–04, March 2008.

23 · In addition to the sources cited, I have been much influenced by the PhD dissertion of Joel Parker, "Randomness and Legitimacy in Selecting Democratic Representatives," University of Texas Department of Government, 2011.

24 · For a basically laudatory presentation of ancient Athens, see Paul Woodruff, *First Democracy: The Challenge of an Ancient Idea* (New York: Oxford University Press, 2005).

25 · See Anthony Gottlieb, "Win or Lose," *New Yorker*, July 26, 2010, available at http://www.newyorker.com/magazine/bios/anthony_gottlieb/search?contributorName=anthony%20gottlieb.

26 · See Jeffrey Abramson, *We, the Jury: The Jury System and the Idea of Democracy* (Cambridge, MA: Harvard University Press, 1994).

27 · See Akhil R. Amar, "Choosing Representatives by Lottery Voting," *Yale Law Journal* 93 no. 7 (1984): 1283.

28 · See James F. Fishkin, *When the People Speak: Deliberative Democracy and Public Consultation* (New York: Oxford, 2009).

29 · Fishkin, 179.

30 · I do not know if he ever put his dictum in writing, but I vividly recall his presenting it at an American Political Science Association convention in the tumultuous 1960s.

31 · A full analysis, beyond the scope of this book, would have to address the implications of the Internet for our political system. A relatively modest example is that some states are beginning to replace standard-form elections, with ballots or voting machines, in favor of online voting. Anyone aware of the "Arab Spring" of 2011 is aware of the roles played by new "social networks" in mobilizing disenfranchised movements. No doubt anyone writing in 2030 on "democratic" or "republican" forms of government will address many concrete realities that can only dimly be imagined by anyone not deeply ensconced within Silicon Valley, let alone undergraduate successors to Mark Zuckerberg. Can anyone designing a constitution for the twenty-first century entirely ignore contemporary social technology?

Chapter 6

1 · 377 U.S. 533, 576 (1964).

2 · See George Tsebelis and Jeannette Money, *Bicameralism* (Cambridge: Cambridge University Press, 1997), 56–62, Table 2.2A (Institutional features of the navette [nonfinancial]).

3 · Ibid., 55.

4 · Ibid., 1.

5 · See, generally, Alexander Keyssar, *The Right to Vote: The Contested History of Democracy in the United States* (New York: Basic Books, 2000).

6 · Akhil Reed Amar, *America's Constitution: A Biography* (New York: Random House, 2005), 66.

7 · Ibid., 412–413.

8 · The two richest senators were incumbent Democrats John Kerry (estimated net worth of $750 million) and Herb Kohl ($243 million).

9 · "Your Senator Is (Probably) a Millionaire," *New York Times*, November 25, 2009, available at http://economix.blogs.nytimes.com/2009/11/25/your-senator-is-probably-a-millionaire/.

10 · http://www.opensecrets.org/news/2011/03/as-a-class-congressional-freshmen-e.html. Connecticut Democrat Richard Blumental actually headed the list of newcomers, with an estimated net worth of close to $95 million, though the next seven persons on the list were

Republican representatives with a net worth between $22 and $49 million. At least two new Republican senators, however, declared decidedly limited net worth. "Sen. Marco Rubio (R-Fla.)…has a minimum net worth of -$210,989, but a maximum net worth of $135,999. Likewise, Sen. Mike Lee (R-Utah) reports assets that range from a minimum of -$32,995 to $193,998."

11 · "The 50 Richest Members of Congress," available at http://www.rollcall.com/50richest/the-50-richest-members-of-congress-112th.html?gclid=CM_oyo6n8KsCFYSK4AoduR8JGw.

12 · Mark A. Graber, *Dred Scott and the Problem of Constitutional Evil* (Cambridge: Cambridge University Press, 2006).

13 · To be sure, if each house passes legislation on the same subject, the varying bills are sent to a "conference committee," which is charged to resolve the disputes between the houses and agree on a bill that will indeed be passed, with no further changes, by each house. Conference committees themselves raise a host of interesting questions; final decisions are made by a relatively small number of members of the House and Senate, who may well add provisions to bills that never received support in either body or strip from bills provisions that indeed enjoyed majority support from both houses. Still, they are somewhat tangential to this particular book insofar as the Constitution does not meaningfully speak to their organization. Should a committee, for example, vote as a single collective body or as a de facto bicameral body insofar as a majority of the conferees from each house must agree on the final version? There may be "settled practices," but their source is not the specific language of the Constitution. If sufficiently settled, they may be treated as examples of what Ernest Young calls "the Constitution outside the Constitution." Ernest Young, "The Constitution Outside the Constitution," *Yale Law Journal* 117 (2007): 408–473.

14 · David Mayhew discusses this literature in *Partisan Balance: Why Political Parties Don't Kill the U.S. Constitutional System* (Princeton, NJ: Princeton University Press, 2011), 115–120.

15 · Ibid., 2, quoting Phillips, *Cosmopolitan* 40, essay #5 (March 1906): 6.

16 · Ibid., 155–156. I should emphasize that Mayhew himself is relatively unsympathetic to such critiques.

17 · Norman Ornstein, "Our Broken Senate," *The American*, March/April 2008, available at http://www.american.com/archive/2008/march-april-magazine-contents/our-broken-senate.

18 · George Packer, "The Empty Chamber," *The New Yorker*, August 9, 2010, available at http://www.newyorker.com/reporting/2010/08/09/100809fa_fact_packer.

19 · See Richard Primus, "The Riddle of Hiram Revels," *Harvard Law Review* 119 (2006): 1680.

20 · The Supreme Court has invalidated durational residency voting requirements extending beyond roughly fifty days. The Court in the 1970s rejected opportunities to review lower-court cases that had upheld five- and seven-year residential requirements for candidates for elective office.

21 · Larry J. Sabato, *A More Perfect Constitution: 23 Proposals to Revitalize our Constitution and Make America a Fairer Country* (New York: Walker & Co., 2007), 26–27.

22 · Or, more accurately, Congress thought about these matters only in the course of rejecting presidential initiatives—by Presidents Truman, Eisenhower, and Kennedy—to adopt national health insurance or, with Kennedy, to adopt federal aid to education. See Table 2.1, "Presidential Requests" for legislation, in Mayhew, *Partisan Balance*, 42–43.

23 · Congressional Research Service, Jennifer Manning, "Membership of the 111th Congress: A Profile," February 2010.

24 • Michael Lewis, "California and Bust," *Vanity Fair,* November 2011, p. 183. Lewis quotes Mark Paul, the co-author the book *California Crackup: How Reform Broke the Golden State and How We Can Fix It* (Berkeley: University of California Press, 2010), in which he describes "the vicious cycle of contempt."

25 • Mayhew, *Partisan Balance.*

Chapter 7

1 • See Kenneth Shepsle, "Congress Is a 'They,' Not an 'It': Legislative Intent as Oxymoron," *International Review of Law and Economics* 12 (1992): 239.

2 • This was demonstrated in 2011 by the mixed judicial response to challenges to President Obama's health care legislation. Though there have been literally a couple of important exceptions, judges holding the law unconstitutional have been predominantly conservative Republicans, while judges upholding it have primarily been Democrats appointed by President Clinton.

3 • Though, interestingly enough, the North Carolina governor was not given veto power until 1996.

4 • *The Founders' Constitution,* vol. 2, Article 1, Section 7, Clauses 2 and 3. Document 7 (Chicago: University of Chicago Press), available at http://press-pubs.uchicago.edu/founders/documents/a1_7_2-3s7.html.

5 • Max Farrand, *Records of the Federal Convention,* vol. 2 (New Haven: Yale University Pres, 1927), 73.

6 • See http://www.fjc.gov/history/home.nsf/page/talking_co_hd.html.

7 • Michael Grynbaume, "A Veto of a Cabby Bill, and Countdown Walk Signals," *New York Times,* September 20, 2010, available at http://cityroom.blogs.nytimes.com/2010/09/20/a-veto-of-a-cabby-bill-and-countdown-walk-signals/.

8 • NBC, "Paterson Begins a Veto Marathon," July 2, 2010, available at http://www.nbcnewyork.com/news/local-beat/Paterson-Veto-Marathon-Session-97609144.html.

9 • This point would surely apply as well to Gerald Ford, who had a long career in the House of Representatives before being chosen by Richard Nixon to succeed the disgraced Spiro Agnew as vice president. Ford, of course, also presents the unique example of a president who was never voted on by the electorate prior to his taking office. Under the Twenty-fifth Amendment (which applies to the filling of vice-presidential vacancies), he needed only to be confirmed by both the House and the Senate following his nomination by the president.

10 • Quoted in B. Dan Wood, *The Myth of Presidential Representation* (Cambridge: Cambridge University Press, 2009), 13.

11 • Ibid., 15.

Chapter 8

1 • Jose Antonio Cheibub, *Presidentialism, Parliamentarism, and Democracy* (Cambridge: Cambridge University Press, 2006).

2 • See, e.g., Juan Linz, ed., *The Failure of Presidential Democracy: Comparative Perspectives* (Baltimore: Johns Hopkins University Press, 1997).

3 · Jack Rakove, "The Political Presidency: Discovery and Invention," in James Horn, Jan Lewis, and Peter S. Onuf, eds., *The Revolution of 1800: Democracy, Race and the New Republic* (Charlottesville: University of Virginia Press, 2002), 31.

4 · Ibid., 33.

5 · Ibid., 34.

6 · See Akhil Reed Amar, *America's Constitution: A Biography* (New York: Random House, 2005), 148–159.

7 · Jack Rakove, "Presidential Selection: Electoral Fallacies," *Political Science Quarterly* 119 (2004): 21, 28.

8 · Ibid., 31.

9 · Ibid., 32.

10 · No legislature has exercised this option since South Carolina in 1876, and electors are popularly elected, but there was actually a suggestion in the heated days after the November 2000 election in Florida that the Florida legislature, controlled by Republicans, appoint the electors should the Florida courts order a recount that would have resulted in an apparent victory by Al Gore.

11 · See Table Aa5607–5707, "South Carolina's Population by Race, Sex, Age, Nativity, and Urban-rural Residence: 1790–1990," in *Historical Statistics of the United States*, vol. 1 (Cambridge: Cambridge University Press, 2006), 1–337.

12 · See, generally, Bruce Ackerman, *The Failure of the Founding Fathers* (Cambridge, MA: Harvard University Press, 2005).

13 · A debate among the three of us can be found at http://www.pennumbra.com/debates/debate.php?did=8.

14 · A list of all "faithless electors" can be found at http://archive.fairvote.org/e_college/faithless.htm. In 1796, a Federalist elector, Samuel Miles, presumably committed to John Adams, unexpectedly cast his ballot for Thomas Jefferson and John Adams's Federalist running mate, Charles Pinckney. The last such episode occurred in 2000, when one of the three District of Columbia electors, Barbara Lett-Simmons, though elected as part of the slate pledged to the Gore-Lieberman ticket, simply left her ballot blank. She was apparently the first elector to abstain since 1832. She saw this as a useful way of protesting the fact that the District of Columbia, though represented in the electoral college, otherwise has no representation in Congress and has only an attenuated form of home rule, ultimately subject to congressional power. See http://mdarchives.us/megafile/msa/speccol/sc2200/sc2221/000031/000008/html/lett_simmons.html. She had, however, earlier indicated that she would cast her vote for Gore if he in fact needed it. "I would never do anything that would cause George Bush to have the presidency," she declared. See http://www.slate.com/id/1006533/. It is not clear, therefore, that Lett-Simmons, a longtime party activist like most electors, truly counts as a "faithless elector."

Chapter 9

1 · Incidentally, no one reads this as denying the president authority over the Air Force, however much it is absent from the Constitution's text. Thus even the most determined "textualist"—that is, someone who believes that we must above all be faithful to the raw language of the Constitution—is happy to infer power over the Air Force by treating "the Army and Navy" as meaning "any and all the armed forces, including any that might be created in the future because of changes in technology."

2 · See Schlesinger v. Reservists to Stop the War, 418 U.S. 208 (1974). A good discussion of this general issue can be found in Michael C. Dorf, "The Nation's Top Military Court Rules That a Senator Cannot Wear Two Hats: Does the Ruling Call into Question Reserve Duty by Members of Congress?" available at http://writ.news.findlaw.com/dorf/20060925.html.

3 · See John Leubsdorf, "Deconstructing the Constitution," *Stanford Law Review* 40 (1987): 181.

4 · John Dinan, "The Pardon Power and the American State Constitutional Tradition," *Polity* XXXV (2003): 389, 403.

5 · See http://www.msnbc.msn.com/id/19586943/.

6 · U.S. v. Wilson, 150, 160 (1833).

7 · See Dinan, 411.

8 · See, e.g., Brian Kalt, *Constitutional Cliffhangers* (New Haven, CT: Yale University Press, 2011).

9 · Charlie Savage, "In a First for Obama, Nine Pardons are Granted," *New York Times*, December 3, 2010, available at http://www.nytimes.com/2010/12/04/us/politics/04pardon.html?_r=1&scp=1&sq=pardons%20by%20President%20Obama&st=cse.

10 · http://www.pardonpower.com/search/label/Obama.

11 · Campbell Robertson, "Despite Uproar Over Clemency, Barbour Finds Lucrative Nest," *New York Times*, Jan. 15, 2012, available at http://www.nytimes.com/2012/01/15/us/despite-clemency-uproar-haley-barbour-finds-lucrative-nest.html?_r=1&scp=2&sq=haley%20barbour&st=cse.

12 · Bernadette Meyler, "Updating the Executive, or, the Character of the Pardoning President," *Tulsa Law Review* 45 (2011): 605, 616.

13 · http://www.law.yale.edu/news/11487.htm. They feared that there would be insufficient Republican support to reach the magic number of sixty-seven senators, instead of treating it as an executive agreement that could in effect be ratified by a majority vote in both the House and the Senate, which, at least before the Republican takeover of the former in January 2011, would have been no problem. As it happens, sufficient Republican senators supported the treaty to ratify it in the waning days of the outgoing Congress in December 2010.

14 · http://www.senate.gov/reference/resources/pdf/RS21308.pdf.

15 · http://www.answers.com/topic/special-sessions-of-congress.

16 · Giorgio Agamben, *State of Exception* (Stanford, CA: Stanford University Press, 2005), 20.

17 · Clinton Rossiter, *Constitutional Dictatorship* (Princeton, NJ: Princeton University Press, 1948), 224.

18 · Abraham Lincoln, Message to Congress, July 4, 1861, available at (among many other sites) http://www.fordham.edu/halsall/mod/1861lincoln-special.asp.

Chapter 10

1 · Akhil Reed Amar, *America's Constitution: A Biography* (New York: Random House, 2005), 437–438.

2 · See, e.g., Frederick Schauer, *Playing by the Rules: A Philosophical Examination of Rule-Based Decision-Making in Law and in Life* (Clarendon/Oxford: Oxford University Press, 1991).

3 · Philip B. Kurland and Ralph Lerner, eds., *The Founders' Constitution*, vol. 2 (Indianapolis, IN: Liberty Fund, 2000), 154 .

4 · Ibid., 165.

5 · See, e.g., Bruce Ackerman, *The Decline and Fall of the American Republic* (Cambridge, MA: Harvard University Press, 2010).

6 · See, e.g., Barton Gellman, *Angler: The Cheney Vice Presidency* (New York: Penguin Books, 2008).

7 · http://topics.nytimes.com/top/reference/timestopics/people/c/hugo_chavez/index. html?scp=3&sq=recall%20elections&st=cse.

8 · See Anthony King, *The Founding Fathers v. the People: The Paradox of American Democracy* (Cambridge, MA: Harvard University Press, 2012) pp. 122-124.

9 · Michael Cooper, "Recall Campaigns Become a Hazard for Mayors," *New York Times*, September 22, 2010, available at http://www.nytimes.com/2010/09/23/us/23recall.html?_ r=1&scp=1&sq=recall%20elections&st=cse?

10 · King, *The Founding Fathers.*

11 · Section 4: "Whenever the Vice President and a majority of either the principal officers of the executive departments or of such other body as Congress may by law provide, transmit to the President pro tempore of the Senate and the Speaker of the House of Representatives their written declaration that the President is unable to discharge the powers and duties of his office, the Vice President shall immediately assume the powers and duties of the office as Acting President."

"Thereafter, when the President transmits to the President pro tempore of the Senate and the Speaker of the House of Representatives his written declaration that no inability exists, he shall resume the powers and duties of his office unless the Vice President and a majority of either the principal officers of the executive department or of such other body as Congress may by law provide, transmit within four days to the President pro tempore of the Senate and the Speaker of the House of Representatives their written declaration that the President is unable to discharge the powers and duties of his office. Thereupon Congress shall decide the issue, assembling within forty-eight hours for that purpose if not in session. If the Congress, within twenty-one days after receipt of the latter written declaration, or, if Congress is not in session, within twenty-one days after Congress is required to assemble, determines by two-thirds vote of both Houses that the President is unable to discharge the powers and duties of his office, the Vice President shall continue to discharge the same as Acting President; otherwise, the President shall resume the powers and duties of his office."

12 · See Brian Kalt, *Constitutional Cliffhangers: A Legal Guide for Presidents and Their Enemies* (New Haven: Yale University Press, 2012), 64–82.

13 · See David J. Garrow, "Mental Decrepitude on the U.S. Supreme Court: The Historical Case for a 28th Amendment, *University of Chicago Law Review* 67 (2000): 995.

14 · Philip B. Kurland and Ralph Lerner, eds. *The Founders' Constitution,* vol. 5 (Indianapolis, IN: Liberty Fund, 2000), 458.

15 · Ibid., 459.

16 · Ibid., 462.

17 · Ibid., 466.

18 · See, for example, Seth Barrett Tillman, "Why Our Next President May Keep His or Her Senate Seat: A Conjecture on the Constitution's Incompatibility Clause," *Duke Journal of Constitutional Law and Public Policy* 4 (2009): 107; *Duke Journal of Constitutional Law and Public Policy Sidebar* 4 (2008): 1, *available at* http://tinyurl.com/2bjzkc8. He argues that the historical record tells a more complicated tale that legitimizes placing succession in the Speaker and the president pro tempore.

19 · Again, see Kalt, *Constitutional Cliffhangers.*

Chapter 11

1 · Winston Churchill, *The Gathering Storm*, quoted in Lloyd N. Cutler, "To Form a Government," *Foreign Affairs* 59 (Fall 1980): 126.

2 · See David C. Kimball, "A Decline in Ticket Splitting and the Increasing Salience of Party Labels," in Herbert F. Weisberg and Clyde Wilcox, eds., *Models of Voting in Presidential Elections: The 2000 U.S. Election* (Palo Alto, CA: Stanford University Press, 2003), available at http://www.umsl.edu/~kimballd/chapter.pdf.

3 · Jonathan Rauch, "Divided We Thrive," *New York Times*, November 6, 2010, available at http://www.nytimes.com/2010/11/07/opinion/07rauch.html?scp=1&sq=Jonathan%20Rauch&st=cse.

4 · William P. Marshall, "Break Up the Presidency?: Governors, State Attorneys General, and Lessons from the Divided Executive," *Yale Law Journal* 115 (2006): 2446.

5 · I owe this point to Richard Danzig.

6 · Jacob Gerson, "Unbundled Powers," *Virginia Law Review* 96 (2010): 301.

Chapter 12

1 · "Brutus," incidentally, is widely thought to have been the pen name for Robert Yates, one of New York's delegates to the Philadelphia convention, who, together with John Lansing, left Philadelphia in mid-summer when they concluded that it had been taken over by people determined to scrap the Articles of Confederation.

2 · See Brutus, No. 15, March 20, 1788, in Philip B. Kurland and Ralph Lerner, eds., *The Founders' Constitution*, Vol. 4 (Indianapolis: Liberty Fund, 2000), 141, available at http://press-pubs.uchicago.edu/founders/documents/a3_1s10.html.

3 · Stephen B. Burbank and Barry Friedman, eds., *Judicial Independence at the Crossroads: An Interdisciplinary Approach* (Thousand Oaks, CA: Sage Publications, 2002).

4 · Ibid., 54.

5 · See Terri Jennings Peretti, "Does Judicial Independence Exist? The Lessons of Social Science Research," in *Judicial Independence at the Crossroads*, ed. Burbank and Friedman, 103–133; Charles M. Cameron, "Judicial Independence: How Can You Tell It When You See It? And, Who Cares?" in *Judicial Independence at the Crossroads*, 134–147. See also G. Alan Tarr, "Without Fear or Favor: Judicial Independence and Judicial Accountability in the American States," (unpublished mansuscript).

6 · Peter H. Russell, "Toward a General Theory of Judicial Independence," in Peter H. Russell and David M. O'Brien, eds., *Judicial Independence in the Age of Democracy: Critical Perspectives from around the World* (Charlottesville: University Press of Virginia, 2001), 12. Russell immediately goes on to describe as "quite unreal" the call by the 1983 World Conference on the Independence of Justice that all judges "shall be free ... to decide matters before them impartially, in accordance with their assessment of the facts and their understanding of the law without any restriction, influence, direct or indirect, from any quarter and for any reason."

7 · See, e.g., William Eskridge and Philip Frickey, "The Supreme Court, 1993 Term—Foreword: Law as Equilibrium," *Harvard Law Review* 108 (1994): 26.

8 · See http://supremecourtofindia.nic.in/history.htm.

9 · Akhil Reed Amar, *America's Constitution: A Biography* (New York: Random House, 2005), 215. As Amar notes, this even number generated the possibility of tie votes among the justices (and the de facto requirement that four of the six justices agree on a particular outcome). A similar requirement today would make the agreement of six of the nine justices a prerequisite to holding a law unconstitutional.

10 · See Jeff Shesol, *Supreme Power: Franklin Roosevelt vs. the Supreme Court* (New York: Norton, 2010).

11 · See Rebecca Gill, "A Framework for Comparative Judicial Selection Research," available at ssrn.com/author=792278.

12 · http://www.religioustolerance.org/chr_prac2b.htm.

13 · See Supreme Court Act of Canada, Article 6, available at http://laws-lois.justice. gc.ca/eng/acts/S-26/page-2.html#h-3.

14 · http://www.theglobeandmail.com/news/politics/tories-axing-bilingual-requirement-for-supreme-court-judges/article1830762/.

15 · Jed Handelsman Shugerman, "Economic Crises and the Rise of Judicial Elections and Judicial Review," *Harvard Law Review* 123 (2010): 1061. See also Shugerman, *The People's Courts: The Rise of Judicial Elections and Judicial Power in America* (Cambridge, MA: Harvard University Press, 2012).

16 · See, e.g., Chris W. Bonneau and Melinda Gann Hall, *In Defense of Judicial Elections* (New York: Routledge, 2009),

17 · She offered this description at an Aspen Institute panel on judicial selection on which I served as moderator in June 2009.

18 · Indeed, the last "cross-party" appointee to the Supreme Court was William J. Brennan, appointed by Dwight Eisenhower shortly before the 1956 presidential election because Eisenhower wanted to shore up his political appeal to northeastern Catholics, and Brennan was thought to be just right for that purpose. Eisenhower later publicly regretted his decision.

19 · See the extremely helpful table in Neal Devins, "How State Supreme Courts Take Consequences into Account: Toward a State-Centered Understanding of State Constitutionalism," *Stanford Law Review* 62 (2010): 1629, 1645–1647. Devins lists New Hampshire as requiring retirement at age seventy, but I do not find such a requirement in the New Hampshire constitution. See http://www.nh.gov/constitution/judicial.html. The New Hampshire legislature will apparently consider in 2012 a proposed amendment to the state constitution to replace tenure during "good behavior" with five-year terms. See http://www.gavelgrab.org/?p=23398.

20 · However, as Kim Lane Scheppele has informed me, although the new supreme court created in the United Kingdom continues the now centuries-old practice of *seriatim* opinions by each judge, "most cases feature a 'lead opinion' that summarizes the questions raised and report the facts and procedural posture of the case. It also reports the shared reasoning of a majority of the court, if there is such agreement." She suggests that this practice was developing even before the creation of the new supreme court. The most obvious break between the old Law Lords and the new supreme court justices is that the latter do not wear wigs!

21 · See Paul M. Angle, *The Complete Lincoln-Douglas Debates of 1858* (Chicago: University of Chicago Press, 1991), 58, also available at http://www.bartleby.com/251/1005.html .

Chapter 13

1 · See Scott D. Gerber, *A Distinct Judicial Power: The Origins of an Independent Judiciary, 1606–1787* (New York: Oxford University Press, 2011).

2 · This is emphasized in Stephen B. Burbank and Barry Friedman, "Reconsidering Judicial Independence," *in Judicial Independence at the Crossroads* (Thousand Oaks, CA: Sage Publications, 2002), 16–22.

3 · See *Annual Report of the Director for Judicial Business of the US Courts 2010*, pp. 16, 20, available at http://www.uscourts.gov/uscourts/Statistics/JudicialBusiness/2010/judicial-businespdfversion.pdf.

4 · http://www.democraticunderground.com/discuss/duboard.php?az=view_all& address=132x8102330.

5 · http://en.wikipedia.org/wiki/List_of_federal_judges_appointed_by_Barack_Obama.

6 · See Paul A. Brest et al., *Processes of Constitutional Decisionmaking*, 5th ed. (New York: Aspen Publishers, 2006), 73, also available at http://avalon.law.yale.edu/19th_century/ajveto01.asp.

7 · Quoted in Brest et al., 258.

8 · Ibid.

9 · http://press-pubs.uchicago.edu/founders/documents/a3_1s10.html.

10 · Planned Parenthood of Southeastern Pa. v. Casey, 505 U.S. 833, 867 (1992).

11 · See Barry Friedman, *The Will of the People: How Public Opinion Has Influenced the Supreme Court and Shaped the Meaning of the Constitution* (New York: Farrar, Straus and Giroux, 2009); Lucas A. Powe, Jr., *The Supreme Court and the American Elite, 1789–2008* (Cambridge, MA: Harvard University Press, 2009).

12 · Fay v. New York, 332 U.S. 261, 282 (1947).

13 · William H. Rehnquist, "Remarks on the Process of Judging," *Washington and Lee Law Review* 49 (1992): 263–264.

14 · Felix Frankfurter, "Supreme Court, United States," *Encyclopedia of Social Science* (New York: Macmillan Co., 1930), 480, quoted in Sanford Levinson, "The Democratic Faith of Felix Frankfurter," *Stanford Law Review* 25 (1973): 430.

15 · This almost certainly explains why it takes years for most cases actually to be decided by that court.

16 · Ressler v. Minister of Defence, HCJ 910/86 [1988] at para. 22, quoted in Eileen Kaufman, "Deference or Abdication: A Comparison of the Supreme Courts of Israel and the United States in Cases Involving Real or Perceived Threats to National Security" (unpublished manuscript).

17 · Alexander Bickel, "The Supreme Court, 1960 Term. Foreword: The Passive Virtues," *Harvard Law Review* 75 (1961): 40.

18 · See Steven H. Steinglass and Gino J. Scarselli, *The Ohio State Constitution: A Reference Guide* (2004), 46–47, available at https://www.law.csuohio.edu/sites/default/files/lawlibrary/ohiocon-law/ohioconstitutionessay.pdf. All of the quotations in this paragraph come from this article.

Chapter 14

1 · Jenna Bednar, *The Robust Federation: Principles of Design* (Cambridge: Cambridge University Press, 2009).

2 · Mikhail Filippov, Peter C. Ordershook, and Olga Shvestsova, *Designing Federalism: A Theory of Self-Sustainable Federal Institutions* (New York: Cambridge University Press, 2004), 5.

3 · See, e.g., Kamel S. Abu Jaber. "The Millet System in the Nineteenth-Century Ottoman Empire," *The Moslem World* 57 (1967): 212–223. "The millet system of the Ottomans," Jaber writes, "may be defined as a political organization which granted to the non-Muslims the right to organize into communities possessing certain delegated powers, under their own ecclesiastical heads" (id. at 212). See also Filippov et al., p. 8, ft. 5 and the works cited there.

4 · Bednar, 18.

5 · Malcolm Feeley and Edward Rubin, *Federalism: Political Identity and Tragic Compromise* (Ann Arbor: University of Michigan Press, 2008), 69.

6 · Ibid., 19.

7 · Filippov et al., 9.

8 · This was the conclusion of the U.S. Supreme Court in Hunter v. Pittsburgh, 207 U.S. 161 (1907).

9 · See Lynn Baker and Daniel Rodriguez, "Constitutional Home Rule and Judicial Scrutiny," *Denver University Law Review* 86 (2009): 1337. This was part of a symposium on the general subject of "home rule."

10 · A good discussion of this point can be found in Ferran Requejo, "Politial Liberalism in Multinational States: The Legitimacy of Plural and Asymmetrical Federalism," in *Multinational Democracies*, ed. Alain-G. Gagnon and James Tully (Cambridge: Cambridge University Press, 2001), 115–116. This entire collection of essays is an invaluable resource for anyone interested in federalism in multinational states, which, in today's world, might well be said to be almost all states other than Iceland or "microstates" like Andorra.

11 · I am grateful to Daniel Halberstam for emphasizing this point.

12 · See Alfred Stepan, "Federalism and Democracy: Beyond the U.S. Model," *Journal of Democracy* 10 (October 1999): 19–34, reprinted in Dimitrios Karmis and Wayne Norman, eds., *Theories of Federalism: A Reader* (New York: Palgrave Macmillan, 2005), 255. Belgium, Canada, and Great Britain are the focus of *Multinational Democracies*, cited in ft. 3, One might also add the old Soviet Union, which did, of course, break apart once Mikhail Gorbachev and then Boris Yeltsin decided that they would not try to maintain the USSR by force.

13 · This distinction is important to the work of the Canadian political theorist Will Kymlicka, perhaps the most systematic theorist of "multinational" and "multicultural" societies. See, e.g., Will Kymlicka, *Multicultural Citizenship: A Liberal Theory of Minority Rights* (New York: Oxford University Press, 1996).

14 · See, e.g., Sujit Choudhry, ed., *Constitutional Design for Divided Societies: Integration or Accommodation?* (New York: Oxford University Press, 2008).

15 · For such an argument, see Ilya Somin, "Foot Voting, Political Ignorance, and Constitutional Design," *Social Philosophy and Policy* 28 (2010): 202, reprinted in *What Should Constitutions Do?* ed. Ellen Frankel Paul, Fred D. Miller, Jr., and Jeffrey Paul (Cambridge: Cambridge University Press, 2010).

16 · Probably the New York anti-Federalist Melancton Smith. See Gordon Wood, "The Great American Argument" (book review of Pauline Maier, *Ratification: The People Debate the Constitution, 1787–1788*), *The New Republic*, December 30, 2010, p. 36.

17 · Philip B. Kurland and Ralph Lerner, eds., *The Founders' Constitution*, vol. 1 (Indianapolis: Liberty Fund, 2000), 256.

18 · This is a central theme of Michae S. Greve, *The Upside-Down Constitution* (Cambridge: Harvard University Press, 2012). Greve, a conservative associated with the American Enterprise Institute, lauds what might be termed "classical" American federalism for the disciplining role it provided with regard to states that might be tempted to adopt policies deemed "unfriendly" to business. He thus bewails "modern," post–New Deal federalism inasmuch as it allows "cartels" of pro-regulation states to seek federal legislation as a way of clamping down on outlying states that would be protected under a stronger notion of state autonomy. Full analysis of Greve's important book would take us too far into the Constitution of Conversation for our purposes here.

19 · See, e.g., Campbell Robertson, "After Ruling [by a court upholding Alabama's law], Hispanics Flee an Alabama Town," *New York Times,* October 4, 2011, A1, available at http://www.nytimes.com/2011/10/04/us/after-ruling-hispanics-flee-an-alabama-town.html?_r=1&scp=1&sq=exodus%20from%20Alabama%20schools%20by%20Hispanics&st.=cse. These laws are under challenge as violations of the national Constitution, but it very much remains to be seen how much, if at all, states imposing restrictive regulations will be clipped by the judiciary.

20 · Stanley Fish, "Boutique Multiculturalism, or Why Liberals Are Incapable of Thinking about Hate Speech," *Critical Inquiry* 23 (Winter, 1997): 378–395.

21 · See Sanford Levinson and Rachel Levinson, "'Culture,' 'Religion,' and the Law," in Sanford Levinson, *Wrestling with Diversity* (Durham, NC: Duke University Press: 2003), 285–293 (detailing cases particularly involving Christian Scientist parents).

22 · On the origins of Mormon polygamy theologically, see Richard Bushman, *Joseph Smith: Rough Stone Rolling* (New York: Knopf Doubleday Publishing Group, 2005).

23 · See Dimitrios Karmis and Alain-G. Gagnon, "Federalism, Federation and Collective Identities in Canada and Belgium: Different Routes, Similar Fragmentation," in *Multinational Democracies,* 137.

24 · Sujit Choudhry, "Managing Linguistic Nationalism through Constitutional Design. Lessons from South Asia," *International Journal of Constitutional Law* 7 (2009): 577.

25 · Thomas Benedikter, *Language Policy and Linguistic Minorities in India: An Apprasial of the Linguistic Rights of Minorities in India* (Berlin: Lit Verlag, 2011), 43.

26 · Benjamin Franklin, "Observations Concerning the Increase of Mankind, Peopling of Countries, etc.," available at http://bc.barnard.columbia.edu/~lgordis/earlyAC/documents/observations.html.

27 · See, e.g., Michael Keating, "So Many Nations, So Few States: Territory and Nationalism in the Global Era," in *Multinational Democracies,* 39. Keating seemingly agrees with Burke in writing that "compromise and bargaining [are] the essence of politics." As Chapter 2 noted at length, the question is whether there are limits on what can be compromised, or whether the acknowledged good of political stability justifies overriding the demands of abstract "justice." On this see the excellent essay by Wayne Norman, "Justice and Stability in Multinational Societies," in *Multinational Democracies,* 90.

28 · See Paul Finkelman, "Prelude to the Fourteenth Amendment: Black Legal Rights in the Antebellum North," *Rutgers Law Journal* 17 (1985–1986): 415, 425 (Table II, "Rights of Free Blacks in North in 1860"). These three states were outliers; the rest of the northern states had no color lines regarding settlement.

29 · See Edwards v. California, 314 U.S. 160 (1941). It should be obvious that such loss of control of borders is scarcely part of our Constitution of Settlement, given contemporary developments in states ranging from Arizona to Georgia regarding so-called illegal aliens.

30 · See, e.g., Suzanne Daley, "Denmark Leads Nationalist Challenge to Europe's Open Borders," *New York Times*, June 24, 2011, available at http://www.nytimes.com/2011/06/25/world/europe/25denmark.html?scp=1&sq=Denmark%20and%20immigration&st=cse.

31 · Daniel Halberstam, "Federalism: Theory, Policy, Law," forthcoming in Michel Rosenfeld and András Sajó, eds., *Handbook on Comparative Constitutional Law* (New York: Oxford University Press, 2012).

32 · See, e.g., Yongnian Zheng, *De Facto Federalism in China: Reforms and Dynamics of Central-Local Relations* (Hackensack, NJ: World Scientific Publishing Company, Incorporated, 008): cf. Gabriella Montinola, Yngyi Qian, and Barry R. Weingast, "Federalism, Chinese Style: The Political Basis for Economic Success in China," *World Politics* 48 (1995): 50.

33 · Gary Marks, Liesbet Hoogh, and Arjan H. Schakel, *The Rise of Regional Authority: A Comparative Study of 42 Democracies* (New York: Routledge, 2010), 52.

34 · Quoted in Pauline Maier, *Ratification* (New York: Simon and Schuster, 2010), 36.

35 · See David Schleicher, "The City as a Law and Economic Subject," *Illinois Law Review* 2010 (2010): 1507.

36 · This point is made very forcefully in Naomi Schoenbaum, "Mobility Measures," *Brigham Young University Law Review* 2012 (forthcoming).

37 · New State Ice Co. v. Liebmann, 285 U.S. 262 311 (1932) (Justice Brandeis, dissenting).

38 · The realities of German federalism are interestingly complicated. See, for an excellent short overview, Daniel Halberstam and Roderick M. Hills, Jr., "State Autonomy in Germany and the United States," *Annals of the American Academy of Political and Social Sciences* 574 (2001): 173–184.

39 · Calvin Johnson, *Righteous Anger at the Wicked States, The Meaning of the Founders Constitution* (Cambridge: Cambridge University Press, 2005), 1.

40 · Bednar. p. 64, Table 3.1 State Compliance with Requisitions for Troops (1777–1783) and Money (1784–1789).

41 · See, e.g., T. H. Breen, *American Insurgents, American Patriots: The Revolution of the People* (New York: Macmillan, 2010).

42 · A contemporary example of nullificationist argument is Thomas E. Woods, *Nullification: How to Resist Federal Tyranny in the 21st Century* (Chicago: Regnery Publishing Co., 2010).

43 · The quoted language can be found in the excerpts from "The Virginia Report" in Paul Brest et al., *Processes of Constitutional Decisionmaking*, 5th ed. (New York: Aspen Publishers, 2006), 92–93.

44 · http://www.scrippsnews.com/content/nev-senate-hopeful-sharron-angle-talks-armed-revolt.

45 · A July 2011 Gallup poll indicated that only 16 percent of their sample was satisfied with "the way things were going in the United States." http://www.christianpost.com/news/americans-satisfaction-with-countrys-direction-at-2-year-low-52316/.

46 · See Brest et al., 264.

47 · Franz L. Neumann, "Federalism and Freedom: A Critique," reprinted in Karmis and Norman, *Theories of Federalism: A Reader* (New York: Palgrave Macmillan, 2005), 212, 217.

48 · William Riker, Federalism: Origin, Operation, Significance (New York: Little Brown, 1964), 4, quoted in Halberstam, "*Federalism: Theory, Policy, Law.*"

49 · Even if it is important to realize that most contemporary issues of federalism are far more part of the Constitution of Conversation than the Constitution of Settlement. But "most" does not mean "all."

Chapter 15

1 · See Lutz, "Toward a Theory of Constitutional Amendment," in Sanford Levinson, ed., *Responding to Imperfection: The Theory and Practice of Constitutional Amendment* (Princeton, NJ: Princeton University Press, 1995).
2 · http://sos.ri.gov/library/history/constitution/.
3 · Which was in turn repealed by popular initiative in 2010.
4 · http://www.nytimes.com/2009/11/08/magazine/08Armey-t.html?ref=magazine&page wanted=print.
5 · Sanford Levinson, "Our Schizoid Approach to the United States Constitution: Competing Narratives of Constitutional Dynamism and Stasis," *Indiana Law Review* 84 (2009): 1337–1356.

Chapter 16

1 · See Christian Fritz, "Recovering the Lost World of America's Written Constitutions," *Albany Law Review* 68 (2005): 261, 290.
2 · http://www.archives.gov/exhibits/charters/constitution_founding_fathers_overview.html.
3 · Nicholas Kulish and Stephen Castle, "Slovakia Rejects Euro Bailout," *New York Times,* October 12, 2011, A4, available at http://www.nytimes.com/2011/10/12/world/europe/slovak-leader-vows-to-resign-if-bailout-vote-fails.html?_r=1&scp=3&sq=Slovakia&st=cse.
4 · Nicholas Kulish, "Slovakia Approves European Rescue Fund," *New York Times,* October 14, 2011, A8k, available at http://www.nytimes.com/2011/10/14/world/europe/slovakia-approves-european-rescue-fund.html?scp=2&sq=Slovakia&st=cse.
5 · See, generally, Pauline Maier, *Ratification: The People Debate the Constitution, 1787–1788* (New York: Simon & Schuster, 2010).
6 · Fritz, 290, quoting Madison's speech of August 31, 1787.
7 · Ibid., 276. Similarly, the Pennsylvania Constitution of 1790, itself the product of irregular procedures, thus spoke of the inherent right of the people "at all times [to] alter, form, or abolish their government, in such manner as they may think proper." And the Connecticut Constitution of 1818, which replaced its colonial charter, spoke of the people's inherent right "at all times…to alter their form of government in such a manner as they may think expedient."
8 · Ibid., 290–291.
9 · It is worth digressing for an additional moment to note the perhaps obvious fact that "the people" is scarcely a self-evident term. We might refer to the fact that many, almost certainly most, individuals living in the new country had no right to participate in the deliberations over the Constitution. The most important examples are all slaves, almost all "free blacks," almost all women, and all American Indians. But even if we confine ourselves to those who were given participatory rights—and Akhil Amar correctly argues that the electorate was the broadest that had in fact been allowed in any country in the world up to that time—we note that the Constitution was not ratified by a popular referendum, but,

rather, by conventions of delegates chosen in popular elections. One can well wonder—and doubt—whether the Constitution would have been ratified had it been submitted to such referenda rather than to the state conventions. So what? Is it relevant that almost all new constitutions today—whether in Iraq, Kyrgystan, or Kenya—require popular ratification, as is true of the adoption of new constitutions by states within the United States.

10 · Fritz, 262.

11 · Ibid., 281, n. 84.

12 · http://www.joblo.com/scripts/The_Dark_Knight.pdf.

13 · Niccolo Machiavelli, *Discourses on Livy*, trans. Julia Conaway Bondanella and Peter Mondanella (New York: Oxford University Press, 1997), 95 (originally published in 1517), available (in a different translation) at http://www.constitution.org/mac/disclivy.pdf., see pp. 51–52.

14 · Ibid. For additional discussions of the Roman dictatorship in the context of contemporary debates over emergency powers, see Clinton Rossiter, *Constitutional Dictatorship: Crisis Government in the Modern Democracies* (Princeton, NJ: Princeton University Press, 1948), 3–32; Nomi Claire Lazar, "Making Emergencies Safe for Democracy: The Roman Dictatorship and the Rule of Law in the Study of Crisis Government, *Constellations* 13 (2006): 506–521; John Ferejohn and Pasquale Pasquino, "The Law of the Exception: A Typology of Emergency Powers, *International Journal of Constitutional Law* (I.CON) 2 (2004): 210–239.

15 · See Harvey Mansfield, "The Law and the President: In a national emergency, who you gonna call?" *Weekly Standard,* January 16, 2006, available at http://www.weeklystandard. com/print/Content/Public/Articles/000/000/006/563mevpm.asp?page=3.

16 · Harvey C. Mansfield, Jr., *Taming the Prince: The Ambivalence of Modern Executive Power* (Baltimore, MD: Johns Hopkins University Press, 1993), 297.

17 · John Locke, *Second Treatise on Government* (1690), ch. 14, available at http://constitution. org/jl/2ndtr14.htm.

18 · Schenck v. U.S., 249 U.S. 47 (1919). Holmes seemingly had no trouble writing a similar opinion a week later upholding the ten-year prison sentence of Eugene V. Debs, the most important socialist leader of the age, who had received almost a million votes for the presidency, for advocating similar resistance to the war.

19 · James Boyd White, *When Words Lose Their Meaning* (Chicago: University of Chicago Press, 1984), 265.

20 · *Marbury v. Madison,* 5 U.S. 137, 176–177 (1803).

21 · Blaisdell v. Home Savings and Loan Corp., 290 U.S. 398, 483 (1934).

22 · Quoted in Arthur M. Schlesinger, Jr., *The Imperial Presidency*, Mariner ed. (Boston: Houghton Mifflin, 2004), 24.

23 · See, e.g., Merrill D. Peterson, ed., *The Political Writings of Thomas Jefferson* (Chapel Hill: University of North Carolina Press, 2002).

24 · See Ex parte *Merryman, 17* F.Cases 144 (1861).

25 · See, among many available sources, http://www.classic-literature.co.uk/american-authors/19th-century/abraham-lincoln/the-writings-of-abraham-lincoln-05/ebook-page-117.asp.

26 · See Sanford Levinson, "Was the Emancipation Proclamation Constitutional? Do We/Should We Care What the Answer Is?" *University of Illinois Law Review* 2001 (2001): 1135–1158.

27 · For a much longer discussion, see Jack Balkin and Sanford Levinson, "Constitutional Dictatorship: Its Dangers and Its Design," *Minnesota Law Review* 94 (2010): 1789–1866.

28 · Available at http://www.nytimes.com/2008/03/16/business/16bernanke.html?scp=1&sq=%22Fed%20Chief%20Shifts%20Path,%20Inventing%20Policy%20in%20Crisis.%22%20%20&st=cse.

29 · Schecter Poultry Corp. v. United States, 295 U.S. 495, 553 (1935) (Justice Cardozo, concurring.)

30 · Panama Oil Refining Co. v. Ryan, 293 U.S. 388, 435 (1935).

31 · See Eric A. Posner and Adrian Vermeule, *The Executive Unbound: After the Madisonian Republic* (New York: Oxford University Press, 2011) for a full-throated presentation of such an argument.

32 · Ron Suskind, "Faith, Certainty and the Presidency of George W. Bush," *New York Times Magazine*, October 14, 2004, available at http://www.nytimes.com/2004/10/17/magazine/17BUSH.html.

33 · See, generally. Oren Gross and Fionnuala Ni Aolain, *Law in Times of Crisis: Emergency Powers in Theory and Practice* (New York: Cambridge University Press, 2006).

34 · Rossiter, *Constitutional Dictatorship*, 306.

Chapter 17

1 · See Gary Jacobsohn, *Apple of Gold: Constitutionalism in Israel and the United States* (Princeton: Princeton University Press, 1994).

2 · See, for such an argument from the political right, F. H. Buckley, "Going North," *The American Spectator,* October 2011, available at http://spectator.org/archives/2011/10/13/going-north

3 · See Bruce Ackerman, *The Failure of the Founding Fathers: Jefferson, Marshall, and the Rise of Presidential Democracy* (Cambridge, MA: Harvard University Press, 2007).

4 · See, e.g., Ted Robert Gurr, ed., *Violence In America: Protest, Rebellion, Reform*, vol. 2 (Thousand Oaks, California: Sage Publications, 1989). Gurr had earlier been part of the staff of the National Commission on the Causes and Prevention of Violence, established in the wake of the 1968 assassinations of Martin Luther King and Robert Kennedy by President Lyndon B. Johnson. With Hugh Davis Graham, he prepared the widely discussed report *Violence in America: Historical and Comparative Perspectives*, which became a best seller at the time.

5 · Jeff Zeleny and Megan Thee-Brenan, "New Poll Finds a Deep Distrust of Government," *New York Times,* October 26, 2011, available at http://www.nytimes.com/2011/10/26/us/politics/poll-finds-anxiety-on-the-economy-fuels-volatility-in-the-2012-race.html?_r=1&emc=eta1 .

6 · See, e.g., Michael Cooper, "A Failure is Absorbed with Disgust and Fear, but Little Surprise," New York Times, November 21, 2011, p. A19, available at http://www.nytimes.com/2011/11/22/us/politics/disgust-but-no-surprise-at-supercommittee-failure.html?_r=1&hp, the first sentence of which, based on interviews with a variety of Americans, is "Does the American political system even work anymore?"

7 · Gordon S. Wood, *The Idea of America: Reflections on the Birth of the United States* (New York: Penguin, 2011), 321.

8 · Ibid., 334–335.

9 · As is true in all fifty state constitutions.

10 · See, e.g., the constitutions of Massachusetts or Montana.

Index